I0820093

Gardening
FOR ALL SEASONS

Gardening

FOR ALL SEASONS

CREATIVE HOMEOWNER®, Upper Saddle River, New Jersey

GARDENING FOR ALL SEASONS

WRITERS Anne Halpin, Roger Holmes, Eleanore Lewis
MANAGING EDITOR Fran Donegan
EDITOR Lisa Kahn
GRAPHIC DESIGNER Maureen Mulligan
PHOTO RESEARCHER Amla Sanghvi
EDITORIAL ASSISTANTS Jennifer Calvert, Nora Grace
COPY & TECHNICAL EDITORS Miranda Smith, Elizabeth P. Stell
EDITORIAL CONSULTANT Barbara Pleasant
INDEXER Schroeder Indexing Services
COVER DESIGN Maureen Mulligan, David Geer
FRONT COVER PHOTOGRAPHY (main) Derek Fell (top to bottom left) David Cavagnaro; Derek Fell; Christel Rosenfeld/ Garden Picture Library; Walter Chandoha
INSIDE FRONT COVER PHOTOGRAPHY Michael S. Thompson
BACK COVER PHOTOGRAPHY (top) John Glover (bottom left to right) Gardens Alive; Derek Fell; Neil Soderstrom
INSIDE BACK COVER PHOTOGRAPHY David Cavagnaro
ILLUSTRATORS Mavis Torke, Vincent Alessi, Todd Ferris, and Michele Angle Farrar

Printed in China
First Printing

Gardening for All Seasons, First Edition
Previously Published as *Year-Round Flower Gardener* and *Creating Good Gardens* Library of Congress Control Number: 2007922561
ISBN: 978-1-58011-627-5

Creative Homeowner®, *www.creativehomeowner.com*, is an imprint of New Design Originals Corporation and distributed by Fox Chapel Publishing Company, Inc., 800-457-9112, 903 Square Street, Mount Joy, PA 17552.

Health & Safety Considerations

All projects and procedures in this book have been reviewed for health and safety; still, it is not possible to overstate the importance of working carefully and with common sense when addressing the procedures described in this book. The following are related reminders and rationale.

Determine locations of utility lines underground before you dig, and then avoid them by a safe distance. Buried lines may be for natural gas, electricity, communications, or water. Start research by contacting your local building officials. Also contact local utility companies; they will often send a representative free of charge to help you map their lines. In addition, private utility locator firms may be listed in your Yellow Pages. *Note:* Previous owners may have installed underground drainage, sprinkler, and lighting lines without mapping them.

Follow manufacturer instructions for use of tools, chemicals, solvents, and other products. Provide ventilation if advised, and never work with power tools when you are tired or under the influence of alcohol or drugs.

Ensure a safe electrical setup. Be sure that no circuit is overloaded and that all power tools and electrical outlets are properly grounded and protected by a ground-fault circuit interrupter (GFCI). Do not use power tools in wet locations.

Wear eye protection when using chemicals, sawing wood, pruning trees and shrubs, using power tools, and striking metal onto metal or concrete.

Consider nontoxic and least-toxic methods of addressing unwanted plants, plant pests, and plant diseases before resorting to toxic methods. When selecting among toxic substances, consider short-lived toxins, those that break down quickly into harmless substances.

Never use herbicides, pesticides, or other toxic chemicals unless you have determined with certainty that they were developed for the specific problem you hope to remedy.

Wear protective clothing, including a face mask and gloves, when working with toxic materials.

Wear appropriate gloves when working with rough and thorny materials. Because soil dries the skin, use lightweight gloves for prolonged exposure to soil. *Tip:* Prior to exposuring your hands to soil, apply moisturizing lotion and claw into a bar of soap to embed soap under your fingernails, thereby blocking "dirt" out; wash after gardening and reapply lotion.

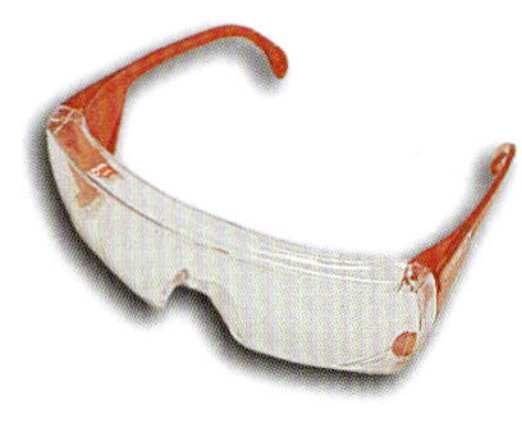

Substitute rock phosphate for bonemeal when amending soil. Authorities suggest there's hazard in using bovine-based products such as bonemeal, blood meal, and cow manure because they could harbor the virus that causes Mad Cow disease in cattle and humans.

Contents

Introduction

People have always found plants a source of joy and inspiration. For true plant lovers, the greatest joy is to grow flowers and plants for themselves. Spring and summer, when the whole world is in bloom, are the gardener's happiest seasons. Yet it's possible to extend the bloom period into autumn and winter. During the bleak and gray days of January, nothing is so welcome as a fragrant jasmine or a vivid magenta cyclamen on a windowsill.

Many gardeners outside the Sunbelt assume that they can't have flowers in bloom year-round without access to a greenhouse or without frequent purchases of cut flowers. Not so. With some planning and careful plant selection, anyone can grow flowers throughout the year. All you need is enough growing space, a sunny window or fluorescent light fixture, and a few hours a week.

This book shows you how to grow flowers in every season and how to combine their colors in gardens, both outdoors and indoors. No matter where you live or how severe your winter weather, you can have flowers blooming constantly the year-round.

Spring tulips and other early bulbs, such as daffodils and narcissus, grape hyacinths, and crocuses, are the very essence of the season.

Summer perennials and annuals provide lush color, from the violet salvias in this foreground to the tall blue delphiniums and yellow heliopsis in back.

Seasonal Organization

This book is organized in three sections. The first discusses the information you need to buy, start, grow, and care for plants of all kinds. The middle section divides the year into seasons and concentrates on the growing of flowers. There are two reasons for this: (1) to avoid tying blooming schedules and growing instructions to specific calendar dates, thereby making the information useful to gardeners throughout the continental United States and southern Canada, and (2) to make it possible for you to start growing flowers any time of the year.

- **In spring,** you can plant perennials to bloom in late spring, summer, or autumn, and you can start seeds of annuals that will bloom lavishly in summer.
- **In summer,** you can buy annuals as young plants at your local garden center and have masses of flowers in your garden in a matter of weeks. Summer is also the time to order and plant bulbs that will bloom in autumn. When frost danger is past, you can also plant tender bulbs to bloom in summer.
- **In fall,** you can plant bulbs for outdoor bloom in late winter and early spring, as well as spring-blooming perennials. You can also plant bulbs in pots to force an indoor bloom in winter. And you can take cuttings from some garden annuals to pot up and grow as winter-flowering houseplants.
- **In winter,** you can enjoy African violets and other houseplants, as well as bulbs of paperwhite narcissus and amaryllis that produce flowers in a few weeks.

Use the information in this book to create a colorful garden within a matter of weeks. Also use this book to plan for seasons to come. A well-planned garden is far more rewarding than a hastily assembled hodgepodge of plants. If you take the time to think carefully about what you want from your garden, and the colors and kinds of flowers you like best, your efforts will give you greater rewards. In time, your garden will become an expression of your creativity and personal tastes and a source of pride, fulfillment, and great pleasure. Each seasonal part of the book contains sections devoted to design ideas, plants, and activities for that season.

Gardens Section. Each seasonal section begins with information on the blooms and the predominant colors and plant types that are associated with that time of year.

Flowers Section. The Flowers section for each season tells you how to grow some of the season's most beautiful plants—especially focusing on plant species and cultivars that are readily available.

Activities Sections. This includes suggestions for the activities you would normally perform in each season, including planning and planting. The information is divided into climate zones. (See the map on page 10.)

Autumn gardens can still be rich with color, including 'Ruby Glow' sedum (seen here), asters, and other late bloomers.

Winter flowers bloom mostly indoors. Here (top to bottom) are amaryllis, cyclamen, and kalanchoe.

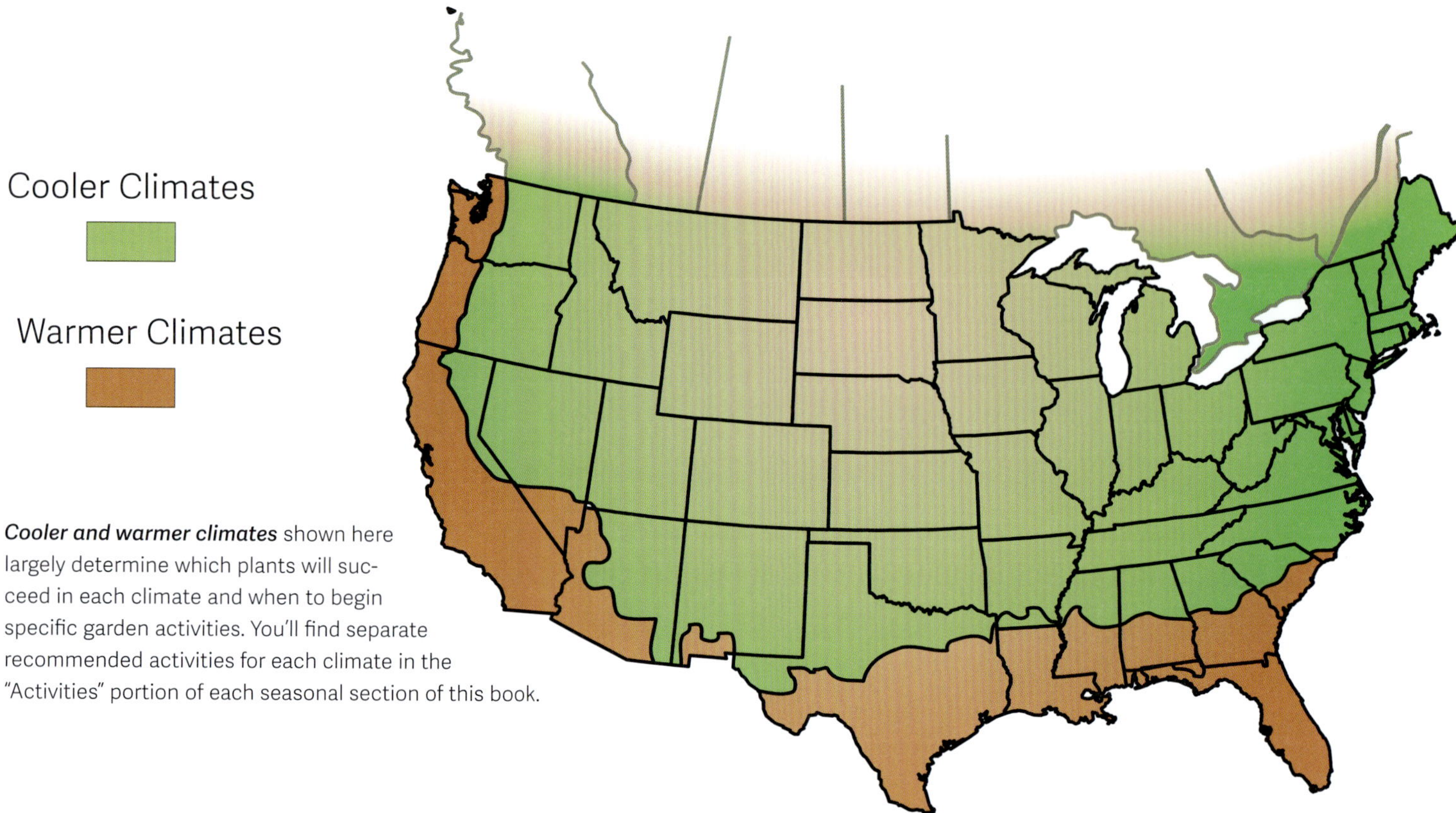

Cooler and warmer climates shown here largely determine which plants will succeed in each climate and when to begin specific garden activities. You'll find separate recommended activities for each climate in the "Activities" portion of each seasonal section of this book.

Other Gardening Pursuits

As every gardener know, flowers are only part of the home landscape. To that end, chapters on herb gardens, ground covers, and trees and shrubs are also included. These chapters provide suggestions on which plants to choose for your property, garden design, and how to care for the plants. You will also find information on planting difficult locations, such as on slopes or in heavily shaded areas. Each of these chapters contains a Gallery of Plants that provides information on the most popular plants for the home gardener.

About the Seasons

The seasons in this book aren't based on the solstices and equinoxes. Instead, they correlate closely to three-month periods and the gardening weather in each. According to the standard calendar, spring begins on March 21. But by then many spring bulbs may already have bloomed. So it makes more sense to place the gardener's start of spring close to March 1. The seasonal breaks are simplified so spring includes March, April, and May; summer June, July, and August; autumn September, October, and November; and winter December, January, and February.

Mar Apr May	Jun Jul Aug	Sep Oct Nov	Dec Jan Feb
Spring	**Summer**	**Autumn**	**Winter**

Blooming Schedules. The blooming schedules in the Appendix (beginning on page 284) list and describe plants in bloom, both indoors and out, in each season. Use these schedules as a general guide; plants in southern gardens may bloom earlier, and plants farther north may bloom later. Then too, you'll find that the bloom schedules in your locality will vary somewhat from year to year, just as local weather conditions differ from year to year. For example, a cold winter and a late spring will delay flowering times, and mild weather will advance them. In addition, the microclimate of your garden (which may differ from microclimates in other parts of your own property) will also influence flowering times. In this case, plants in a sheltered location will bloom earlier, and plants in an exposed site will bloom later.

Plant Names

In this book, all plants are listed by common name and scientific (botanical) name. Although most gardeners rely on common names, common names differ from region to region. Because many plants have several common names, using only the common name can be confusing. Scientific names provide a more reliable way to find the plant you want.

The Naming System. The scientific name for any given plant is based on its position in a family tree that is recognized throughout the world. Within this family tree, each plant is assigned a name that shows its relationship to other closely related plants. For this, scientists use a two-word (binomial) system. The first word identifies the *genus* (a grouping of plants with closely related reproductive structures); the second word names the *species*. The words that describe a plant characteristic are usually Latin; however, sometimes one of the words may simply be a Latinized version of its discoverer's name.

Although taxonomists (the botanists who name plants) change botanical names when scientific evidence suggests a plant should be reclassified, they sometimes disagree. Botanists have reclassified and changed the names of some plants that are still more often sold in nurseries and catalogs by their "old" botanical names. In these cases plant descriptions in this book either use the old name, or both the old and the new name. But it is important to remember that plans names are often reclassified.

This book employs the scientific names used by the Royal Horticultural Society's ***Index of Garden Plants***, the most recent general reference work available (although even some of these names are now out of date). However, because many suppliers of plants still use the older scientific names, you may see "formerly" in this book followed by a second scientific name if the older name is still widely used. If plant names in this book cause you any confusion about identity, consult the book's Index, which should lead you to the name for which you are looking.

If you are new to gardening, you may not realize that you already use some scientific names. When a plant has no common name, the scientific name is coined as the common name, as with aster, begonia, and cosmos. (When used as a common name, the scientific name isn't capitalized or italicized.)

Again, scientific names contain at least two words. But because variants can exist within species, in special cases an additional name may be required as discussed below.

Genus. The first part of a plant's scientific name indicates its genus, a subdivision of a plant family based on broad similarities of reproductive structures. The genus name is written with an initial capital letter and is italicized. (The plural for genus is *genera.*) In *Coreopsis auriculata* 'Nana' for instance, the genus name is *Coreopsis*.

Species. The second word in the name indicates the species, which is a group of related plants that are alike except for small variations. The species name is also italicized but is not capitalized. In the example just given, *auriculata* is the species name.

Coreopsis auriculata 'Nana'

Variety vs. Cultivar. Scientists take nomenclature further by assigning a name if the plant is a ***variety*** (a variant of a species that occurs as a result of natural mutation) or a ***cultivar*** (meaning a **culti**vated **var**iety, resulting from human intervention).

The terms variety and cultivar are often used interchangeably, even though there is a technical difference. A variety is indicated by the abbreviation "var." (as in *Coreopsis tinctoria* var. *atkinsoniana*). A cultivar is listed with single quote marks (as in *Coreopsis auriculata* 'Nana'). When a cultivar is used as part of the common name, as in the example 'Nana' coreopsis, single quotes may or may not be used, and the words aren't italicized.

Hybrid. A hybrid is a plant that results from the breeding of two genetically different parents (usually two different species). Often written with a multiplication sign, a hybrid may differ in significant ways from its parents and even from its siblings. A hybrid species is listed like this: *Begonia* × *tuberhybrida*.

Begonia tuberhybrida hybrid

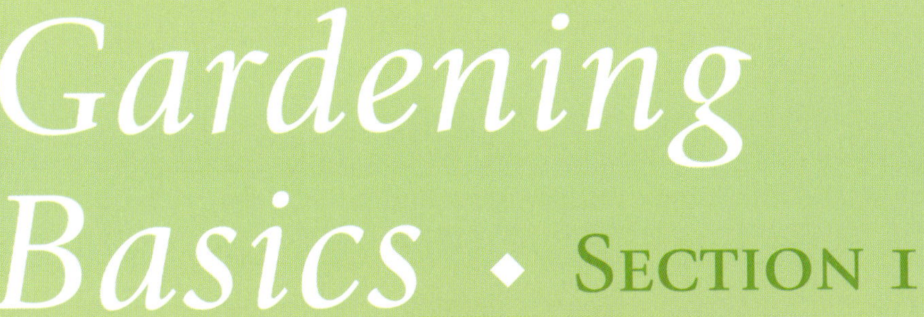

Gardening Basics ◆ Section 1

Chapter 1 Designing Your Garden

It's an understatement to say there's plenty to do, indoors and out, as the spring season gets under way.

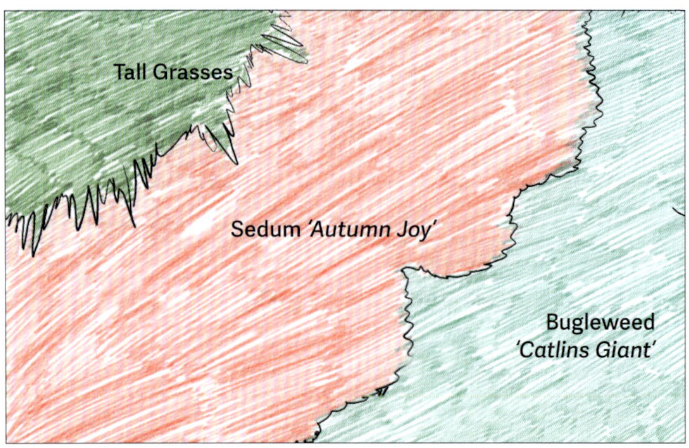

Planning the design of your garden before you rush out to buy plants will save you money, time, and aggravation. At left is a top view (called a **site plan**) of the garden shown in the photo above.

Designing a Flower Garden

Try to design your flower garden a season or two before you begin planting, rather than trying to accomplish all tasks hastily in the spring. To spread out the work, start preparing the soil in enough time to let it mellow and settle a bit before planting. Unplanted soil gives you an opportunity to spot and remove weeds that sprout after working the soil exposes their seeds to light.

It's also smart to decide what you'll be planting in time to order hard-to-find seeds and plants from mail-order suppliers, and to create your shopping list for local garden centers before they sell out of popular or unusual plants. However, if you're a new gardener with spring upon you, don't let the lack of a detailed plan keep you from planting at least a few flowers. You can always grow flowers in containers for transplanting into the garden later on.

Starting on designs well before planting gives you time to play with the design and modify it until you feel satisfied. Otherwise, if in a fit of spring fever you rush to buy a bunch of plants and stick them hastily into the ground, you probably won't be happy with the results. So take the time to work out a good plan. Use a photo or two of a beautiful garden and a simulated pencil sketch of its plan.

Garden design can be a somewhat complex or even tricky process. In addition to knowing which plants bloom in which colors, you'll need to know when plants bloom; how tall they grow; and what kind of soil, moisture, light, and nutrients they need. You'll also need to decide which colors and shades of colors you want to see together.

Professional garden designers develop their skills over a lifetime of study and hands-on experience. Still, there are several basic principles that every flower gardener—from beginner to expert—can learn and apply in creating a garden that is pleasing in terms of color, form, and style.

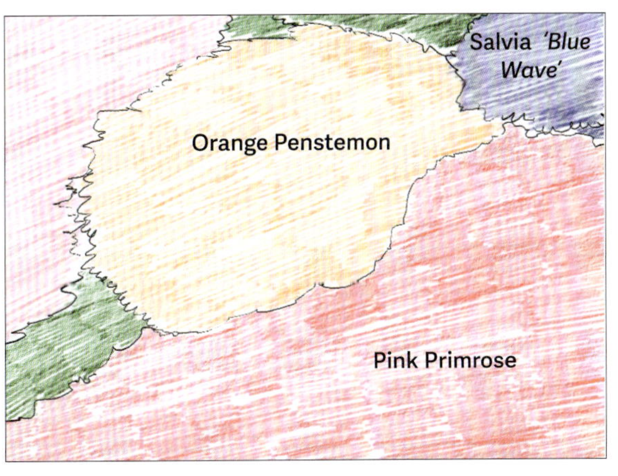

Design your flower garden so it pleases you. This gardener's mix of pink primrose, 'Blue Wave' salvia, and orange penstemon is delightful.

Choosing the Site

If you're starting a new bed or border, the first decision is where to place it. The best location for a flower garden is not necessarily the most obvious one. Consider these vital environmental factors:

Light. A location that receives full sun—unobstructed sunlight for at least five or six hours a day—will afford you the broadest choice of plants. However, there are quite a few flowers that prefer (or at least tolerate) light, dappled shade throughout most of the day. Other plants, particularly early spring bulbs, like plenty of sun when they are in bloom but prefer shade when the sun is hotter.

Air. If your location is subject to strong prevailing winds, you'll need to install a windbreak to protect your plantings. The windbreak can take the form of plants—such as a row of evergreen shrubs—or it can be a wall or fence. Walls and fences used as windbreaks are most effective when they are of open construction that allows some air to pass through. A solid wall can create damaging airflow patterns that may be as bad for plants as unobstructed winds.

Moisture. The amount of moisture available to plants is largely determined by regional climate, but local factors can also be important. If your soil is generally moist, you'll do best with plants that prefer wet conditions, such as irises and astilbe. If your soil is almost continuously wet, you can either install drainage pipes or build raised beds. If you create raised beds, make them 6 to 12 inches high and ensure that the soil is porous and drains well. A mixture of topsoil, compost, and peat moss, leaf mold, or builder's sand should help drainage.

Light for a garden depends on the sun's path, as well as features that cast shade. To gauge how much sun and shade plants will receive in different locations, sketch your property in relation to compass directions and the sun's path.

Strong winds can dry out plants excessively and break their stems. Solid windbreaks, such as brick walls, tend to create strong turbulence over plants. Hedges or fences with open construction help reduce the damaging effects of wind.

Drainage aids include raised beds, left, and 4-inch flexible tubing. To test soil drainage in an area, fill an 18-inch-deep hole with water twice and let it drain. If the water drains completely the second time in less than 15 minutes, drainage is excellent.

Selecting Plants by Climate

Heat-Zone Map. This map, created by the American Horticultural Society (AHS), divides the United States into 12 color-coded heat zones based on the average number of days per year that maximum temperatures exceed 86°F. Increasingly, commercial growers are rating their seeds and plants according to these heat zones. All warm-climate gardeners, especially, should check heat-zone labeling.

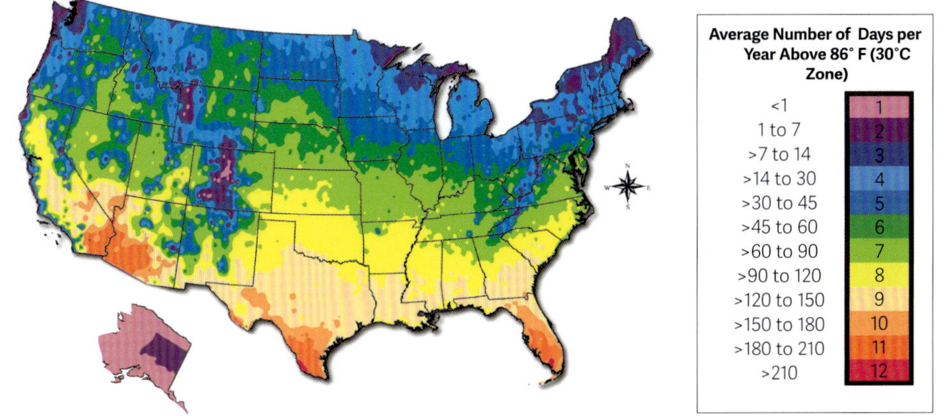

Cold Hardiness Zone Map. This U.S. Department of Agriculture (USDA) map divides North America into zones according to average minimum winter temperatures. The lower the number, the colder the zone. Commercial growers rate their seeds and plants by hardiness zones, helping you determine if a plant is likely to survive your winters or be on the risky borderline.

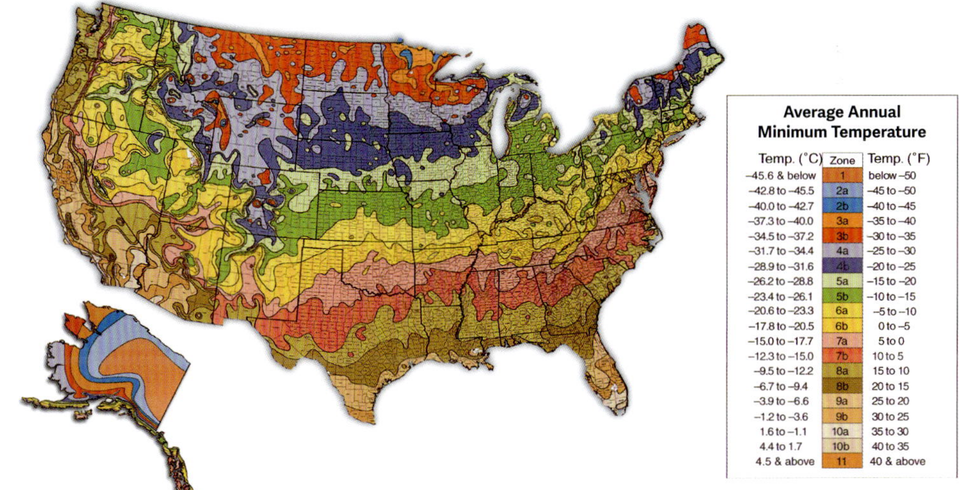

Canada's Plant Hardiness Zone Map outlines the different zones in Canada where various types of trees, shrubs, and flowers will most likely survive. It is based on the average climatic conditions of each area. The hardiness map is divided into nine major zones: the harshest is 0 and the mildest is 8. Relatively few plants are suited to zone 0. Subzones (e.g., 4a or 4b, 5a or 5b) are also noted in the map legend. These subzones are most familiar to Canadian gardeners. Some significant local factors, such as micro-topography, amount of shelter, and subtle local variations in snow cover, are too small to be captured on the map. Year-to-year variations in weather and gardening techniques can also have a significant impact on plant survival in any particular location.

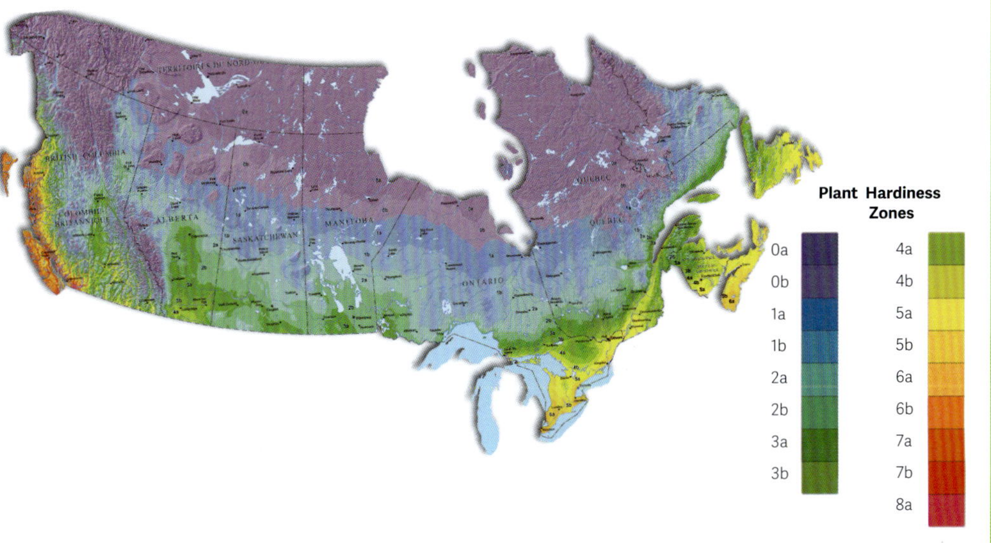

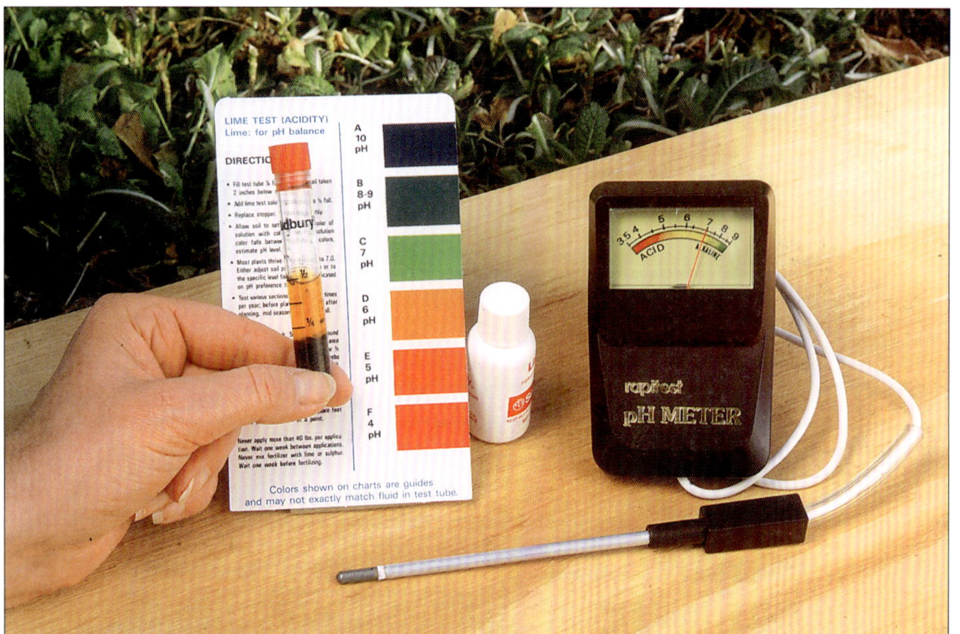

Soil acidity or alkalinity (pH levels) can be measured either with an electronic gauge and soil probe or with an inexpensive kit that lets you mix soil with a solution and compare the resulting color to colors on a chart. In the soil test shown, a lime solution was added to a soil sample, with the resulting orange color suggesting a pH of 6, an acidity level that is good for most plants.

Soil texture can be checked by placing a 6-in. deep slice of soil in a jar. Shake jar thoroughly. Rough debris will be on the surface, followed by layers of clay, organic matter, silt, and, at the bottom, sand.

Soil. The ideal soil for most plants is porous and crumbly. It contains plenty of organic matter and drains well, while still retaining moisture. Light, sandy soils drain too quickly and don't hold moisture and nutrients long enough for plant roots to absorb much. Heavy clay soils pose the opposite problem—they are sticky, dense, and difficult for plant roots to penetrate, and they drain so slowly that roots can become waterlogged. Few properties are blessed with ideal soil initially, but any soil can be improved.

One way to gain clues to the character of your land is to study what grows wild there. The weeds that come up in your garden can tell you a great deal about the moisture content, acidity (measured in pH numbers), texture, and overall fertility of your soil. (See "Plants that Indicate Soil Characteristics" on page 19.) If you've never conducted a soil test or never had one performed by a laboratory, have your soil analyzed for nutrient content and pH. A number of home soil test kits are available, and some United States Department of Agriculture (USDA) County Extension offices provide a soil-testing service or can direct you to commercial testing laboratories. You should be able to locate a nearby Cooperative Extension Service in your local telephone directory or by searching the internet using the keyword "Soil Testing."

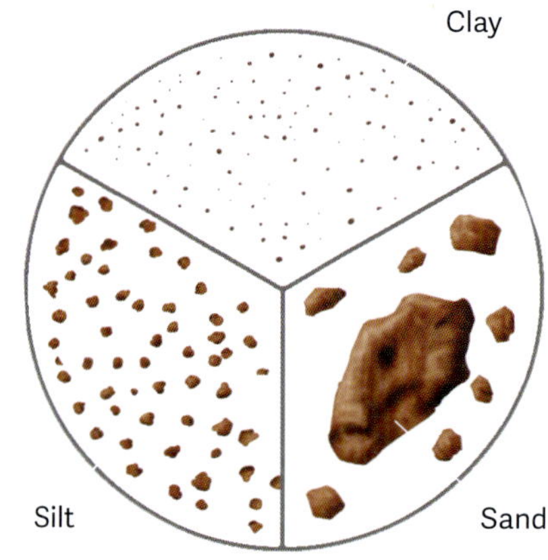

Soil particle sizes of sand, silt, and clay, as shown, suggest why water drains faster through the larger air spaces created by sand. A roughly equal mix of sand, clay, and organic matter provides a nearly ideal texture for most plants.

After testing your soil, you will be able to correct any deficiencies with the materials recommended in the test kit or lab report. If your soil is too acidic or too alkaline, plants won't be able to absorb fertilizer to the fullest extent.

Once you've chosen your site and tested the soil, you can begin designing the garden as explained in upcoming sections. As for the physical labor of creating the garden, you can prepare the soil at any time of the year that the ground isn't frozen or soggy. Fall is a great time because it gives you a head start on spring planting. Or you can dig in the spring for later plantings. (See "Digging a New Garden Bed" on page 93 for details.)

Plants That Indicate Soil Characteristics

Here are some common wild plants that offer clues to soil type. One of these plants alone is not necessarily an indicator of soil characteristics, but if you spot several of these plants in an area, they suggest the soil type indicated below.

Heavy Soil
Plantago major (plantain)
Rumex obtusifolius (broadleaved dock)
Taraxacum officinale (dandelion)

Plantain

Sandy Soil
Lactuca pulchella (arrowleaved wild lettuce)
Linaria vulgaris (yellow toadflax)
Silene latifolia, formerly *Lychnis alba* (white campion)

Wet, Poorly Drained Soil
Acer rubrum (red maple)
Carex species (sedges)
Eupatorium purpureum (Joe-Pye weed)
Mosses
Podophyllum peltatum (mayapple)
Rumex crispus (curly dock)

Mayapple

Acid Soil
Lepidium species (cresses)
Fragaria vesca and *F. virginiana* (wild strawberry)
Kalmia latifolia (mountain laurel)
Leucanthemum vulgare (ox-eye daisy)
Mosses
Vaccinium species (wild blueberry)
Capsella bursa-pastoris (shepherd's purse)
Rumex acetosella (sheep sorrel)

Ox-eye daisy

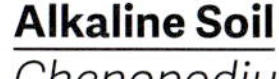

Alkaline Soil
Chenopodium species (goosefoot)
Lepidium virginicum (field peppergrass)
Silene vulgaris (bladder campion)

Lamb's quarters

Humusy, Well-Drained Soil
Amaranthus retroflexus (pigweed)
Arctium lappa (burdock)
Chenopodium album (lamb's quarters)
Portulaca oleracea (purslane)
Stellaria media (chickweed)

Great burdock

Fitting Your Garden into Its Setting

In addition to growing conditions, you should also consider visual aspects to determine the best place for a flower bed or border. Flower gardens should relate in terms of scale and style to the rest of the landscape and fit comfortably into their setting. They should also accommodate your lifestyle and, of course, please your aesthetic sense.

To design a garden that "works" on your property, consider carefully the architectural style of your house and its surroundings. If the other elements of your property are very formal, the layout of your garden should echo that feeling. For example, how will the garden relate to architectural features on the property (the house, garage, sidewalks, fences, walls)? From what vantage points will the flowers most often be viewed (from inside the house, from the yard, from the street)? Do you want to use the garden as a place for entertaining and dining, or just for reading and relaxation?

Design your garden to fit the setting. This formal home is beautifully complemented by a neatly edged, formal garden.

Laying Out the Garden

Flower gardens come in various shapes and sizes. You can grow flowers in borders composed of long, narrow plantings that serve as edgings or as dividers between different areas. You can also plant in beds of just about any size and shape. Then too, you can simply grow plants in containers grouped on a patio, deck, or rooftop. Except for cottage gardens, flower gardens traditionally were formally structured, with straight edges, plants lined up in rows, and walkways and planting beds laid out in regular geometric patterns. The enormous, manicured flower borders of the estate gardens in Great Britain and Europe required armies of gardeners to tend them.

This informal border includes large rocks that provide a strong visual link to the dramatic rocky shoreline beyond.

Modern Shapes. The old, rigidly formal styles have given way to looser, more free-flowing designs. The grandiose scale of estate gardens has shrunk to fit today's smaller properties, and they are more manageable for a single gardener for whom gardening is a hobby rather than a full-time job. Borders today tend to curve gracefully, and flowers are planted in flowing drifts instead of straight lines. Island beds carved out of lawns usually take a circular, elliptical, or even irregular shape.

Starting Small. Size is the next factor to consider in laying out your garden. It's easy to succumb to wanting more flowers than you can realistically manage. But

Gracefully curving borders suit the informal design of many homes (and lifestyles).

Tips for Good Garden Design

- Start small and simple.
- Keep the plantings in scale with the site.
- Plan a succession of bloom times.
- Plan the flower garden to have some flowers blooming when trees and shrubs in the surrounding landscape are flowering.
- Plant drifts of color, not single plants, and let the colors melt into one another.
- Have a gradation of heights, front to back, but let a few plants float in and out of their groups for a softer, more integrated look.
- Use a variety of plant forms and flower shapes: round, clustered flowers, flat daisylike flowers, trumpet-shaped flowers, tall spires and spikes, and branching flowers.

nothing is sadder or more frustrating than finding yourself completely overwhelmed in June or July by a garden overrun with weeds, the spent plants with their dead flowers still clinging to the stems and any blooms all but hidden in the wreckage.

If this is your first garden, it's better to start small. Pick out just a few different kinds of plants to grow in a modest bed in a simple scheme of one or two colors. It's more effective to have several specimens of a few plants than one or two specimens of a lot of different plants. It's also easier to coordinate colors and blooming schedules when you're working with fewer kinds of plants. Building your garden on an uncomplicated plant grouping that is repeated two or three times will give even a small garden a sense of continuity and a finished, well-planned look. This approach also makes garden care far simpler.

Siting for access requires a narrow flower bed. If a bed is more than 2 feet deep, provide a mulched path in back for easy reach. The curved, brick edging here allows for efficient mowing.

Siting for Access. In laying out your garden, consider the practicalities of tending the plants. Remember that you'll need easy access to all the plants in the garden in order to weed, fertilize, deadhead, and divide. If your garden is more than 2 feet deep, you'll need to be able to reach it from both front and back in order to get to all the plants. If you plan to install your border along a wall or hedge, allow for a little walkway along the back of the garden so you can reach all of your plantings.

- Be willing to change next year what you don't like this year.
- Follow your instincts.
- Remember to include a bench or chairs in your garden to sit and enjoy your flowers.

Making the Most of Limited Space. If your available space is small, such as a courtyard or small backyard, consider designing the garden in a series of multilevel raised beds. Instead of making one flat garden bed, you can make a raised bed that has two or three different levels forgrowing flowers. This sort of terracing creates an illusion of more space and also allows you to fit in more plants than you could in a single flat bed. Terracing is also a good solution to the problems posed by a steep hillside.

If you have no ground space at all for your garden and will be growing your flowers in containers on a patio or rooftop, it's still important to plan the layout carefully. You can group containers in various configurations and on different levels to create both height and depth, or even serve as a screen. A well-planned container garden can be as lush and colorful as an in-ground garden bed or border.

A limited space, such as these steps, can yield a delightful multilevel garden.

The Color Wheel

Working with Color

Figuring out your color scheme can be the most challenging part of planning, because color theory can be complex. Still, it's enjoyable because you can work with your favorite colors and color combinations. Although there's no substitute for experience when combining garden colors, your own tastes should be your guide. This section offers basic guidelines for working with color. However, don't be afraid to bend the rules. Let yourself play with colors on paper and experiment in your garden.

Also consider the color of your house and other elements in the landscape when choosing a color scheme for your garden. Try to have everything work together.

Harmonious colors can look surprisingly dramatic as these red nicotiana and orange celosia attest.

Types of Color Schemes

Here are some color-scheme issues. First, do you tend to prefer harmonious, subtle combinations of colors, or do you like contrast? What is the color scheme in your home? You may choose to repeat it in the garden, especially if you will be growing flowers for cutting. Do you want a single color to dominate the garden all season, or would you rather have several colors working together?

Harmonious Color Schemes. Gardens planted in related, or analogous, colors are quite harmonious, but they can also be surprisingly dramatic. (Analogous colors are those that lie near each other on the artist's color wheel; see illustration, above left.) Consider a bed of sunny yellow, yellow-orange, and orange flowers, or an autumn garden of orange, bronze, red, and russet chry-

Contrasting color schemes in both photos at left achieve maximum effect from close placement of complementary colors. At far left are golden rudbeckia and purple heliotrope. On the steps are purple hyacinths and yellow narcissus.

santhemums, accented with a little purple. A beautifully soft mixture of related colors is blue, violet, red, and warm pink—colors found in asters and petunias.

One way to achieve a harmonious mix of colors is to grow several varieties of one type of flower—delphiniums, for example, or phlox, or Oriental poppies. The colors among varieties may differ in intensity and in hue, but they will harmonize with one another. Another way to create harmony is to grow different kinds of flowers in the same color. For example, a spring perennial garden might combine the rosy pink of rock cress *(Aubrieta deltoides)* with the brighter, clearer pink of moss pinks *(Phlox subulata)*.

Contrasting Color Schemes. There are any number of ways to create contrast in the flower garden. Complementary colors, those that lie opposite one another on the color wheel, create the sharpest contrast. Orange and blue are complementary, as are yellow and purple, and red and green. Also be aware that contrasting colors modify one another when planted together. Blue flowers tend to cast a yellowish shadow on neighboring blossoms; whereas red flowers look orangey when they're next to white.

Contrasting color schemes can be unpleasantly jarring or lively and jazzy. Results will be more pleasing if you avoid combining pure contrasting colors. For example, pure purple and clear yellow look harsh next to each other. But when the purple is deepened toward violet-blue and the yellow is soft and light, the combination is exquisite.

To make a contrasting color scheme work, choose a paler version of one of the two colors. Use the brighter color sparingly as an accent, and use the less intense color over a larger area to balance the brighter color. For example, if you want to combine red tulips with blue forget-me-nots, you'll get the best results by planting lots of forget-me-nots among and surrounding the tulips.

Flower Selection Guide

Some important questions to consider when choosing plants for your garden:

- When do you want flowers to bloom? Do you want some color from spring to fall? Do you have a favorite time of year when a lavish display will be especially gratifying? Do you use the garden during a particular season, such as summer at a weekend home?
- Why do you want flowers? If bringing cut flowers indoors is most important to you, concentrate on growing the long-stemmed annuals and perennials best suited for cutting. If you like dried flowers, grow everlastings and other flowers that dry well. (See "Cutting Gardens," page 124, and "Flowers for Drying," page 132.)
- How big is the garden? If your garden is small, rely on just a few different plants with long blooming periods, such as coreopsis, summer phlox, achillea, veroncia, and fringed bleeding heart (Dicentra eximia).
- How much time can you devote to maintaining the garden? If your time is limited, concentrate on sturdy, low-maintenance flowers such as annuals and daylilies, butterfly weed, rudbeckias, impatiens, and salvias.
- What colors do you want, and how flexible is your color scheme? If you'd like to experiment with different colors for a few seasons, or if you want a lot of color quickly, grow annuals (flowers that grow and bloom for just one growing season).

You can also tone down contrasting colors by introducing neutral tones—some white-flowered or silver-leaved plants—into the garden or by planting blending colors such as green foliage plants to absorb some of the color. Many gardeners prefer not to put strong colors next to each other if the garden is meant to be viewed at close range rather than from across a lawn. A small garden combining magenta, orange, and purple located right next to a deck or patio will look brighter and fresher with some touches of silver or white.

Monochromatic Color Schemes. Relying on one color to dominate the garden all season is probably the least complicated approach and the most successful one for new gardeners. If you choose yellow, for instance, you might have daffodils and basket-of-gold in spring, yellow irises and cinquefoils or potentillas in late spring and early summer, rudbeckia and yellow daylilies in summer, and buttery or gold dahlias or chrysanthemums in fall. Against the succession of yellow flowers that form the backbone of the garden, other color choices can come and go. The other colors will serve to accentuate—not compete with—the yellow flowers.

Monochromatic schemes generally work best in small gardens, where they give a sense of added space and openness. Schemes based on a light color, or pastel versions of a strong color, can brighten a partially shaded garden. Single-color gardens need not be boring either. You can vary flower sizes, shapes, and tones of color (pale, bright, or dark), as well as plant heights, shapes, and textures.

Monochromatic colors, such as white tulips and deutzia, make small gardens look larger.

Polychromatic Color Schemes. Some gardeners like a polychromatic, or multicolored, scheme. Cottage gardens, with their cheerful riot of colors, are a good example of the polychromatic style. In a mixed-color garden, the variety of colors included depends entirely on the gardener's taste. Sometimes they work, and sometimes they don't.

Polychromatic color schemes can be lively and interesting if colors are repeated in several plants to unify the garden.

Warm and cool colors can mix beautifully when used in soft shades, as in this blend of pale pinks, lavender, and soft yellow enriched with deep golden roses.

Warm colors—reds, oranges, and golden yellows—harmonize, as seen in this combination above of gold achillea and red dahlias and crocosmias.

Blender Colors

A useful trick for integrating a garden and harmonizing colors that might otherwise be unsettling is to include blender colors. Groups of white or pale yellow flowers make effective harmonizers for groups of stronger colors. Deep green foliage can be used to harmonize bright colors such as red and orange. Gray or silvery-white foliage pulls together soft blues, lavenders, and pinks. And distance also blends colors that otherwise contrast when viewed close up.

Warmth & Coolness in Colors

Warm colors (pink, red, orange, yellow) project themselves toward you, appearing closer. On the other hand, cool colors (blue, violet, green) recede, appear to be farther away. To create an illusion of depth and space in a small garden, try planting warm shades in the front and cool shades behind them.

Warm colors are also stimulating and active—even aggressive if they are strong, while cool colors are restful and quiet. For a peaceful, subtle effect, plant your garden in blues and purples. The cool colors will also create a feeling of distance. For a cheerful but not aggressive feeling, plant warm shades of apricot, salmon, and pink accented with touches of red and purple. Shades on the borderline between warm and cool—yellow-green, for instance, or rosy-purple—may convey the cheerfulness of the warm colors and the calmness of the cool colors.

Cool shades of these salvias, hardy geraniums, and lupines (front to back) create a serene harmony.

Using Color Effectively

Here are more guidelines for working with color:

- Use simple colors that relate to the landscape and site.
- Plant in generous groups of color for the best effect; single plants here and there get lost in the design. Even flowers that are used for accent color should be planted in groups of at least three.
- In all but the smallest gardens, plant in drifts instead of straight rows (as in a vegetable garden). Also plant a few flowers of each color over the boundary between adjoining drifts, so the drifts melt into each other.
- Avoid bicolored flowers in multicolored gardens, unless you really know what you're doing. Flowers in solid colors will usually produce a more sophisticated look, and they are far easier to design with.
- Dark colors are best seen close up. From a distance or in the shade, they tend to disappear.
- Pastels and white flowers can light up shady areas, where they gleam against the dark background. Pastels are also effective in front of stone walls, gray rocks, and hedges. They are especially wonderful in gardens viewed at night or seen as the sun goes down. At dusk, light-colored flowers take on a special glow.
- Strong, bright colors are especially effective in very sunny gardens. Hot colors are subdued by strong sunlight, but they aren't overpowered the way pastels and dark colors are. Brilliantly colored flowers can also be quite striking against dark foliage, a point to keep in mind if you have foundation plantings of evergreens.

Finally be aware that warm colors harmonize with one another (yellow-orange, orange, red-orange, scarlet), and cool colors harmonize (blue, blue-green, green). This can be important in multicolor gardens because the warmth or coolness of a particular tint can make or break the color scheme. For example, if you're using pink with violet (which can be quite beautiful), choose a cool shade of pink. On the other hand, a warm shade of pink will be more effective with yellow or red.

Drifts and Gradations of Color

Whatever color scheme you choose, it will be most effective if you plant substantial drifts or clumps of color. Don't just sprinkle your plants in ones and twos through the garden unless you are deliberately aiming for a pointillist effect.

Another useful technique is to plant more than one shade of your chosen colors, which creates a softer effect.

Plant masses of flowers for visual impact.

Plant in drifts in informal gardens to use colors most effectively.

Keeping a Journal

In addition to this book, perhaps the most useful gardening book you will ever own is the one that you will write yourself in the form of a garden journal. A journal gives you a place to keep track of seeds and plants you purchase each year, record when you sow seeds and set out plants, and catalog which flowers perform well or poorly for you.

It's a good idea to sketch your garden plans in your journal, updating them as you make changes in your beds and borders. The journal also gives you a central place to keep track of weather conditions from year to year; eventually this can help you develop a good understanding of the microclimates in your garden. You may find that two different locations on your property yield very different sets of results.

Then too, a journal will give you a place to keep your thoughts and dreams, "want" lists of plants, and inspirations that would otherwise end up on stray bits of paper floating around the house. Take a look at the illustration to the right to see some of the information you might record in your garden journal.

Worth Noting in Your Journal

Seeds

Cultivar, color, source
Dates of start, germination, transplanting
Where planted
Dates of first and last bloom
Size of plant
Overall performance
Maintenance (watering, fertilizing, pinching, deadheading)
Pest or disease problems

Garden plans

What's planted where
Changes, expansions, renovations
Fine-tuning of color scheme
Plants added to fill holes in bloom sequence

Plants

Cultivar, color, source
Dates of planting out, and first and last bloom
Size of plant
Overall performance
Maintenance (watering, fertilizing, propagation of perennials)
Pest or disease problems

Bulbs

Cultivar, color, source
Date of planting and bloom
Propagation
For tender bulbs, dates of indoor starting, and lifting and storing in fall

Weather

Weather conditions week to week
Precipitation patterns
First and last frost dates
Dates of phenological indicators (see the accompanying sidebar)

Sketches of Planting Plans

Phenological Indicators: Natural Timekeepers

Phenology is the study of events that occur in predictable time relationships in the lives of plants and animals. Gardeners can use phenology to relate different stages in the growth of garden plants to the growth of other plants in the landscape, the yearly migration or hibernation patterns of animals, and the emergence of insect pests.

As an example, the development of local trees and shrubs can serve as indicators of weather conditions that are favorable for the planting of various garden flowers. One of the most widely used "indicator" plants is the common lilac. Because weather conditions vary from year to year, timing some of your plantings by the development of lilacs in your neighborhood can be a more reliable guide than mere calendar dates.

When the lilacs begin to leaf out (that is, when the widest part of the leaves grows out past the bud scales that had enclosed the leaf), it's safe to plant hardy annuals such as sweet alyssum, pansies, and calendulas. And when the lilacs are in full bloom, it's time to plant tender annuals, such as impatiens and marigolds, as well as summer bulbs, such as dahlias, gladiolus, and tuberous begonias.

Common lilac is a good phenological indicator.

Chapter 2 Gardening Essentials

A well-designed garden, started with healthy plants and fertile, well-prepared soil, is on its way to being successful. You'll find that all aspects of getting started, from browsing in nurseries to digging and amending your garden beds, are truly enjoyable.

Buying Healthy Plants

While many annuals and some perennials are easy to start from seed, the majority of the plants most gardeners want are only sold as plants.

Look for a nursery or garden center that supplies quality plants and sound advice about selecting and growing them. At a good local supplier, you can inspect the plants before purchase and learn from knowledgeable staff how specific plants perform in your area.

Seek recommendations about suppliers from veteran gardeners in your area. When you're deciding where to shop, look for suppliers that offer plants and gardening supplies year-round, or at least for the entire growing season, rather than those that sell plants only seasonally. Also, inquire about the store's policy on replacements. Some suppliers provide a replacement or give a credit if a plant dies within the first year, depending on the plants and the circumstances. If you're buying large, expensive plants such as shrubs and trees, a performance guarantee is prudent as well as reassuring.

Getting started on creating a garden like this, opposite, involves tasks as diverse as choosing plants appropriate to the site, laying out and designing garden beds, and improving the soil by adjusting the pH and adding organic matter and nutrients.

Selecting Size. Plants may be sold in containers ranging from an inch to a foot or more across. In general, large plants are older and more expensive than the same types of plants at a smaller size. However, a perennial purchased in a quart pot and the same kind of perennial in a gallon pot will often be the same size after each has been in the ground for a year. The size gap usually closes more slowly for shrubs and trees.

When buying annuals, beginners are often tempted to pick the biggest plants or those already in flower. Resist the urge. Younger plants without blooms are likely to have more well-developed roots, and will perform better once they are planted.

Choose plants carefully. Smaller plants, left, that have not yet bloomed usually outperform those in flower, especially those with small rootballs. Larger rootballs can offset the stress that early blooms create.

Match the Plant to the Site. Lastly, as you select plants, remember to match their preferences for growing conditions to the places where you'll plant them. The grower's label or tag sometimes tells how much sun and what type of soil and moisture the plant needs. If you're not sure what conditions a plant requires, ask for advice at the nursery or garden center. Many gardeners like to try growing new plants, and some enjoy the challenge of growing plants in adverse conditions. If you decide to place a plant in a potentially unfriendly situation, be sure your yen for gambling suits your wallet. It's disappointing to spend several years tending an expensive shrub or tree only to have it die because it wasn't hardy enough or received too little sun.

Water-Wise Gardening

Communities throughout North America have become increasingly conscious of the need to conserve water. From the arid Southwest to lush New England, no region has been spared water shortages during the last 20 years, and droughts have become more commonplace. Prodded by regulation, the increasing cost of water, or environmental concerns, gardeners have become more sensitive to water use in their yards and gardens. The suggestions on page 32 can help reduce the amount of water your landscape requires. For more extensive and detailed information, contact your Cooperative Extension Service or your city, county, or state water board.

Plant-Buying Know-How

Whether you're buying annuals, perennials, or a tree, examine each plant carefully according to the following criteria:

- Foliage should have consistent color. Avoid plants with discolored or missing leaves and those with limp or wilted foliage.
- The plant's overall shape should be well-branched and bushy, uniform and symmetrical. Avoid plants with a few long, sprawling shoots or shoots that appear stunted; also avoid plants with broken or bent shoots, stems, or branches.
- The size of the container should be in proportion to the plant. Big plants in small pots are likely to be rootbound, as shown to the right.
- A few small roots protruding from the drainage holes in the bottom of the container are acceptable. Avoid plants with long, thick, protruding roots. Also avoid plants with roots coiling on or near the soil surface.
- Soil should fill the pot to within 1 inch of the rim. Avoid plants in dry soil that has pulled away from the sides of the container.
- Avoid plants showing symptoms of insect or disease damage, including misshapen flowers and contorted steams or branches.
- Look for an identification tag securely attached to the plant or inserted into the pot. Plants are sometimes mislabeled, but those with no label at all are too risky.

***Rootbound plants** often have a mass of roots protruding from the drainage holes at the bottom.*

***Tease circling roots apart** with your fingers before you transplant to keep them from strangling the plant.*

What's in a Name? Common vs. Botanical

Botanical names often come as a surprise when you are beginning to garden. Many people are put off when they learn that the black-eyed Susan they admired in grandmother's garden is more properly called Rudbeckia fulgida 'Goldsturm.' This discovery can make the pleasant flower bed they were planning seem more like a botany field trip.

Don't let plant names flummox you. First, be assured that common names like black-eyed Susan are perfectly acceptable means of identifying and discussing plants. As long as you and the person with whom you're talking are using the same names for the same plants, common names serve just as well as botanical ones. But distinctly different plants can share a common name, and one plant can be known by several different common names. For example, at least three familiar plants share the name black-eyed Susan: one is a vine, one is a short-lived perennial often grown as an annual, and one is a hardy perennial. If you want to be certain when discussing and ordering plants, it's a good idea to use the botanical name.

Fortunately, gardeners need not master the intricacies of botanical nomenclature. For the black-eyed Susan mentioned earlier, Rudbeckia is the plant's genus; fulgida is its species; and 'Goldsturm' is the name of the particular cultivar. The genus and species are classifications scientists have devised to distinguish and group plants with similar botanically significant features. Cultivars (short for cultivated varieties) are names plant breeders have given to unique versions of a plant that were created by breeders, researchers, or even gardeners. Many garden plants are not cultivars and so are identified just by their genus and species name, as for the flowering dogwood, Cornus florida. Some plants may be identified by a genus and cultivar name only, as in Sedum 'Autumn Joy.' You'll encounter other variations in botanical nomenclature. Remember that you needn't know what the botanical names mean in order to use them when identifying or ordering plants, just as you needn't know what people's names "mean" when using them.

In this book, you'll find common names used in general discussion. In profiles of specific plants, you'll also see the botanical names so you can be certain when you go shopping for them. Many gardeners find that they use common names at some times and botanical names at other times, de-pending on which is most helpful in the particular situation.

Rudbeckia fulgida 'Goldsturm' is the botanical name for these black-eyed Susans.

'Autumn Joy' sedum is one of the plants more widely known by its cultivar name than by its botanical name.

Plant Hardiness

When choosing plants, select those that will be able to withstand the rigors of your climate. The most common measure of this ability is the minimum temperature at which a plant can survive. The U.S. Department of Agriculture has divided North America into 11 "hardiness zones" based on average minimum winter temperatures. Horticulturists and expert gardeners have rated many plants according to the zone in which they will dependably survive the coldest temperature. The hardiness zone rating is frequently given on plant labels, in catalogs, and in books. Annuals aren't rated, unless they are actually perennials grown as annuals in the north and are hardy only in warm zones.

Recently, more attention has been paid to the effects of heat on plants. The American Horticultural Society (AHS) has developed a heat zone map, and increasingly, plant labels also indicate ratings for heat zones. Opposite, you'll find maps showing the North American cold-hardiness zones and the United States heat zones. If you're uncertain at which zones your area is rated, ask at a local nursery or at the Cooperative Extension Service.

Cooperative Extension Services

The Cooperative Extension Service is one of the best sources of information about all aspects of gardening in your area. Drawing on the resources of state-funded universities, extension service offices in more than 3,500 cities and counties include or have access to horticulturists, entomologists, and soil scientists. Extension agents are excellent sources of local information—which plants perform best, which pests are most problematic, and which controls are most effective.

For information on the Cooperative Extension Service in your area, look in the phone book under County Government or visit the U.S. Department of Agriculture website, www.csrees.usda.gov/Extension.

If plants at local nurseries and garden centers aren't labeled for cold hardiness or are rated for a different zone than yours, check with staff to determine what conditions they might require.

Water-Wise Tips

- Seek out plants native to your region. These plants thrive on the moisture nature usually provides.
- With non-native plants, look for those that are well-adapted to your region's conditions. However, even drought-tolerant plants require regular moisture during their first year or two in the garden.
- Group plants with similar water needs in the same bed.
- Plant perennials and woody plants in fall in warm-winter regions and in early spring in cold-winter regions to take advantage of natural rainfall.
- Mulch garden beds to conserve moisture.
- Monitor soil moisture so you can water when necessary, not according to a schedule.
- Water with soaker hoses or install a drip irrigation system to minimize waste and evaporation loss.
- In container plantings, use plastic instead of porous clay pots, which dry out faster. You may also put a plastic pot inside a clay one or a clay pot inside another clay pot. Fill the space between the pots with peat moss, and water this "stuffing" to help keep roots cool and moist.

Moderate to heavy water needs link the gloriously diverse plants in this garden bed.

Areas on a particular property often have slightly different environments, called microclimates, as a result of their exposure or position on a slope. South-facing areas tend to heat up more quickly than north-facing ones; wind may be more severe at the top of a hill than at the bottom; and low-lying areas may be wetter or experience frost slightly earlier in the fall and later in the spring than other places on your property.

Careful design and good plant selection will help ensure a successful garden that will thrive in your area, below. Discuss any problems with a local garden center or the local Cooperative Extension Service.

How to Store Plants

Mail-order plants often arrive before weather conditions are favorable for planting. Pop small plants into the vegetable drawer of the refrigerator, where they will keep for a week or more. Larger plants can be stored in an unheated garage, garden shed, or protected porch. Wrap the roots in old blankets if the temperature plunges below freezing. They will keep for several weeks as long as you check every few days to make sure the roots are moist.

Building Good Gardens

Successful gardening doesn't start with picking the loveliest or even the most robust plants. Instead, it starts with narrowing your plant choices to those that are right for each of your sites. The quality of the soil, as well as exposure to wind, sun, or shade, may vary from place to place on your property. Sun-loving plants such as yarrow will hardly grow or flower in a shady spot. And a dry, sunny site can cause shade-lovers such as impatiens to wither and die. Other conditions, such as winter cold and summer heat, affect whole regions. Before you start digging a garden bed, learn about all the possible bed sites on your property and the kinds of plants that will grow well in each of them.

Soil Preparation

Few gardening tasks are as beneficial to plants as good soil preparation. Healthy soil creates healthy plants. It is firm enough to anchor roots but loose enough to allow them to spread; retains enough water to supply plant needs but not so much that roots rot or are starved of oxygen; supplies adequate plant nutrients without requiring large doses of supplemental fertilizer; and supports a large and diverse population of earthworms, soil fungi, insects, and microorganisms that help keep it healthy.

In general, soils with a high clay content drain slowly but are nutrient-rich. Sandy soils drain rapidly and are often nutrient-poor. Loam—consisting of balanced amounts of clay, silt, and sand liberally mixed with organic matter—is the ideal garden soil. It drains neither too quickly nor too slowly, has plenty of air spaces for oxygen and root penetration, and retains sufficient nutrients to support healthy growth.

Soil texture is determined by the percentage of sand, silt, and clay. It's difficult to change the texture, but you can improve soil structure with compost and organic mulches.

Approaches to Preparation. All new garden beds benefit from some form of soil preparation. If your native, unimproved soil is largely loam, you can do as little as remove the existing vegetation and loosen the underlying soil. But most soils require additional work to improve their structure, fertility, and drainage. Fortunately, these qualities can all be improved simply by adding organic matter and minerals in sufficient quantities. Many gardeners produce good soil by working grass clippings, rotted manure, or compost into the top few inches of garden beds. In vegetable gardens, yearly additions of organic matter can transform poor soil in a few seasons. Soil in beds of perennial plants can't be extensively reworked each year, but supplements of mulch, compost, and necessary fertilizer can maintain and even improve soil quality.

Testing the Soil

Gardeners can test their soil and amend it according to the test results. Although easy-to-use kits are available at garden centers, their results will usually be less extensive and less accurate than those from a professional laboratory. Soil tests are offered through some Cooperative Extension Services, as well as through university and private laboratories. Cooperative extension tests usually fall within the price range of simple home test kits. Private labs usually do more extensive testing and charge more for it. A few home test kits are quite elaborate and approach or exceed the costs of having a test performed by a commercial lab.

Soil tests vary in the factors they evaluate. Those conducted by labs and some of the more extensive home tests measure nutrients, and some labs recommend amendments or fertilizers to rectify deficiencies for the plants you're growing. All soil tests measure the soil's pH, or its degree of acidity or alkalinity as expressed on a scale of 1 to 14. Of all the tests provided by home test kits, the most useful and accurate are those for pH. Generally speaking, the soil's pH affects the ease with which plants can use nutrients in the soil. A pH of 7 is neutral, neither acid nor alkaline. Numbers lower than 7.0 indicate increasingly acidic soil, while those above 7.0 indicate soils that are increasingly alkaline.

Testing the soil with a home kit is fast and easy. Using the same type of kit every year gives you a good indication of changes in your soil.

Collecting Soil Samples

To collect a soil sample for testing, brush any debris off the soil surface, and use a clean trowel (plastic if possible) to dig a hole 4 to 6 inches deep. Then take a ½-inch slice of soil from the side of the hole, and put that soil into a clean plastic container. (Because the samples are so small, a metal container or trowel can affect the results of the test.) Take a number of samples like this from different spots around the planting area; from a large bed, you might take as many as a dozen samples. Thoroughly mix the samples in the container, and send at least a cup of this mixture to the lab. To compare soil from different parts of your property, prepare separate samples for separate tests. Label samples with the intended use (vegetables, perennials, etc.).

Dealing with pH. Garden plants will tolerate soil with a pH between 4.5 or 5 and 8.0, though most perform best at 6.0 to 6.5. Because most garden plants tolerate a fairly wide range of soil pH, some gardeners never need to adjust the pH. Occasionally, gardeners need to balance naturally acidic or alkaline soil, increase acidity for plants such as rhododendrons and camillias, or increase alkalinity for those that prefer a pH closer to neutral.

To adjust soil pH, follow the recommendations of the soil-testing lab or consult with your Cooperative Extension Service. The materials generally used to adjust soil pH—lime to decrease acidity and sulfur, peat moss, or woody organic amendments to increase acidity—are inexpensive and widely available. But the types, quantities, and frequency of application will vary according to your soil and circumstances.

Drainage

Soil drainage is as important to plants as soil fertility. Roots rot and are deprived of needed oxygen in soggy soil and wither if it's too dry.

When you're planning a bed, test the site's drainage. Dig one or more holes 1 to 2 feet deep, fill them with water, let them drain, and fill them a second time.

- If the water is gone after 24 hours, the drainage should be adequate for most plants.

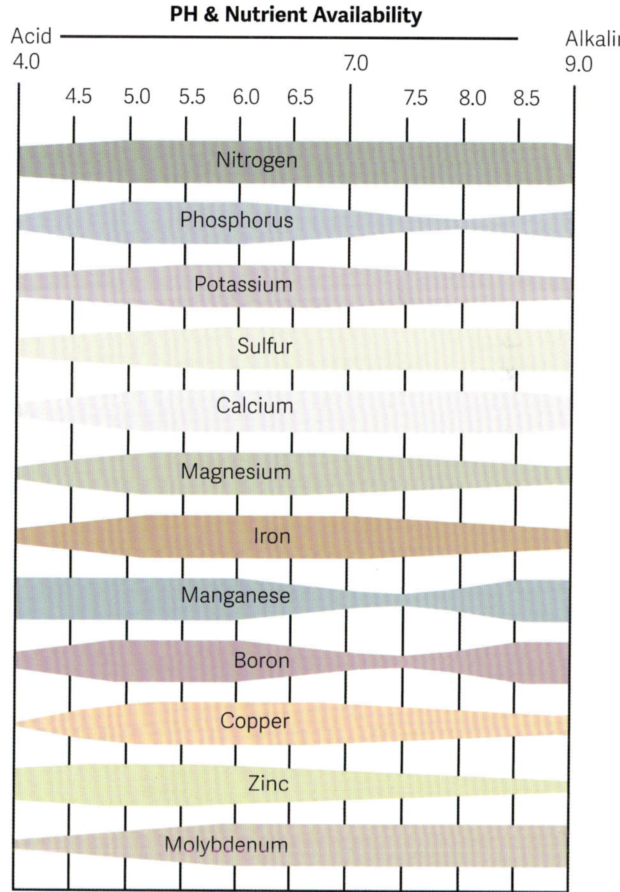

Nutrient availability as a result of soil pH is indicated by the width of the various bars on this chart. The wider the bar, the more nutrient is available. It's easy to see why most plants grow best at a soil pH of 6.0–6.5.

- If a few inches of water remain, plants described as preferring "very well-drained soil" may find this soil too wet. In this case, you can improve drainage by double-digging and adding large amounts of organic matter. (See "Digging a Garden Bed," page 43.) Both soil type and conditions influence the quantities and materials you should add, so your best bet is to consult with a knowledgeable person at your nursery or garden center.
- If more than a few inches of water remains in the test hole after 24 hours, relocate the bed. If you have no alternative site, construct a raised bed, as discussed on page 40.

Note: When you test for drainage, you may discover a hard, impervious layer of soil at the bottom of your hole. Called hardpan, this layer is often created by heavy equipment that has compacted the soil or by tillers used repeatedly when the soil was too wet. In the Southwest, hardpan occurs naturally and is called caliche. If you discover hardpan, consult with a landscape contractor.

Amendments vs. Fertilizers

The terms amendment and fertilizer are often used interchangeably. But there are differences. For the purposes of this book, amendments are materials that improve soil structure, drainage, and nutrient-holding capacity. Some add nutrients. All fertilizers supply nutrients. Peat moss is strictly an amendment, and a bag of 5-5-5 granular fertilizer is strictly a fertilizer. Some materials, such as compost, act as both a fertilizer and an amendment.

Many woodland species thrive in soils that are exceptionally wet in spring and fall.

Drainage is easy to check with test holes. If water remains in the hole a day after the second filling, correct the drainage before planting.

Organic Soil Amendments. Soil amendments include both organic and inorganic materials. Organic amendments are the decomposing remains of once-living organisms. Finding organic amendments can be as easy as collecting grass clippings and leaves from your own yard or buying compost in bags. Some useful amendments, such as oyster and crab shells, or buckwheat and rice hulls, are available on a regional basis. Many of these materials are excellent additions to your soil, but some, such as cotton gin waste or leather meal, can contain potentially harmful residues of pesticides or heavy metals.

Organic materials improve aeration and drainage in both clay and sandy soils and increase nutrient retention in sandy soils. As they decompose, organic materials also provide plant nutrients. You can add organic amendments liberally to any soil with beneficial results. For example, if you're digging

12 inches deep, you can add up to 6 inches of organic amendments. Use only well-decomposed materials, such as compost that is dark and crumbly, or peat moss, which is partially decomposed sphagnum peat. Materials with high concentrations of chemical salts, such as raw manure, or those with high concentrations of carbon, such as fresh sawdust, can damage or stunt the growth of plants. Mulching an existing bed with a few inches of dried grass clippings or chopped-up leaves, on the other hand, is a good way to incorporate these organic materials.

You can make your own compost, as described on page 49. If you need large quantities, buy it from a nursery. An increasing number of towns and cities compost organic waste. Leaf and yard waste composts are generally safe. But be cautious about municipal waste composts; avoid those of mixed municipal wastes unless they don't contain plastic and have been tested and shown to be free of harmful levels of heavy metals.

Inorganic Soil Amendments. Inorganic materials include greensand, which supplies potassium, and rock phosphate, which supplies phosphorus, in addition to lime, sulfur, and gypsum. Green-sand and rock phosphate are becoming more widely available at nurseries, and almost all outlets sell lime, sulfur, and gypsum.

Using Inorganic Materials. While it's almost impossible to add too much decomposed organic material to soil, be careful to add only the correct amounts of inorganic amendments. To adjust pH, apply lime, sulfur, or gypsum in the precise quantities recommended by a soil lab or extension service.

Many fertilizers are made of inorganic materials that provide the mineral nutrients required by plants. A new bed amended with a lot of well-rotted organic compost should grow healthy plants without additional fertilizers. However, if you're uncertain about the fertility of the soil, you can add a balanced fertilizer blend made of rock powders and organic materials, or up to 2 pounds per 100 square feet of a 5-5-5 synthetic granular fertilizer without fear of overdoing it. But remember that too much fertilizer can damage plants. Applying fertilizers according to a soil test is the best course of action.

Fertilizers containing organic materials are becoming more widely available. Before buying, check to see if they are approved for organic growers.

Figuring Out Fertilizers

The wide range of fertilizers can be baffling. They're usually distinguished from each other by the nutrients they provide, the materials that make them up, and the form in which they come. There are fertilizers for specific plants and situations as well as general-purpose fertilizers. Some are made from organic materials, others from inorganic; some come from "natural" sources (plants, rocks, and animals), others are synthesized in chemical factories. Many are granular, but liquids and powders are also common. Additionally, certain fertilizers, usually made from minimally-treated natural products, are approved for use by organic gardeners, while others (usually synthetic) are not.

All fertilizers provide nutrients in the form of inorganic ions. Organic fertilizers tend to take effect more slowly than synthetic ones but can improve the soil structure and contribute to the long-term health of the soil. Plants require nitrogen (N), phosphate (P), and potassium (K) in larger amounts than other nutrients (called micronutrients), so fertilizers are labeled according to the relative concentrations of these macronutrients, or primary nutrients. The ratio of N to P to K (always in that order) is usually displayed prominently on the label: 10-10-10, for example. A 10-10-10 fertilizer will have twice as much of each of the three primary elements as a 5-5-5. When preparing a planting bed and for ordinary care, a fertilizer with roughly the same amounts of these three elements usually fills the bill. Such fertilizers are sometimes called balanced. If a soil test shows a nutrient deficiency, ask the staff at the nursery which fertilizers will meet the recommendations of the test and how much to apply. If you want to avoid synthetics, ask for an organically acceptable fertilizer.

Garden Tools

Gardening can be a low-tech activity. You can garden for years with just the tools shown here. Better tools may cost more initially but are less expensive in the long run because they don't break and need replacement. Look for garden spades and forks with blades, tines, and ferrules (the part that houses the handle) forged from a single piece of thick steel.

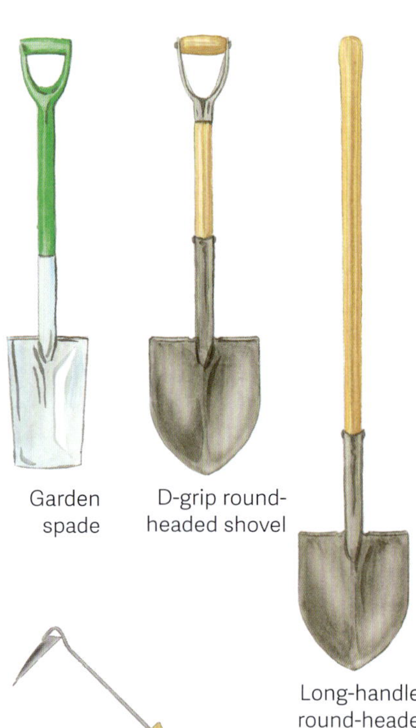

Garden spade

D-grip round-headed shovel

Long-handled round-headed shovel

Garden Spade & Shovels. The most important digging tool for many gardeners is the versatile flat-bottomed garden spade. It is used for initial bed preparation, transplanting, and maintaining bed edges. The blade of a round-headed shovel has a greater curve across its width than the garden spade, making it more useful for very sandy soils and for scooping and moving piles of gravel or rock. Tools with short D-grip handles are convenient and provide more than enough leverage, but taller people may find a long-handled tool easier on the back.

Garden (Spading) Fork. This tool loosens compacted earth that a spade won't budge and is ideal for mixing amendments into the soil or reworking the loose soil of a vegetable garden in the spring or fall. Thick square-section tines resist bending better than flat tines, though a thick-tined tool is heavier.

Hand Weeder. Use weeders to work wherever plants are close together.

Hand Sprayer. Buy two sprayers, one for liquid fertilizers and the other for pesticides. Wash them well after every use to keep the nozzles clear.

Tiller. A small tiller is ideal for working fertilizers into the soil and making a smooth seedbed.

Garden rake

Lawn rake

Garden & Lawn Rakes. Garden rakes can smooth the soil surface in preparation for setting out plants or sowing seeds. They are also invaluable for spreading surface amendments. For removing leaves and twigs and for general tidying up, use a lawn rake with a wide fan of long tines.

Hoes. Choose a garden or standard hoe for routine work, a stirrup hoe for small weeds, and a collinear hoe for very fine, tight work. Sharp blades make work more efficient; sharpen your hoes before every use.

Pruning Shears. A pair of bypass pruning shears will handle almost all the pruning chores you'll encounter. Bypass shears (above, left) have two curved blades that cut like scissors; a good pair will cut through living stems and branches up to about ½ inch thick. Anvil-pattern shears (above, right), in which one straight blade cuts against the soft metal surface of the other blade, tend to crush stems and leave wounds that aren't as clean.

Garden Cart. A sturdy cart is the best choice for hauling heavy loads. Some have removable front panels for easy dumping.

Wheelbarrow. Use wheelbarrows for hills and easy maneuvering. Buy the strongest available model for durability.

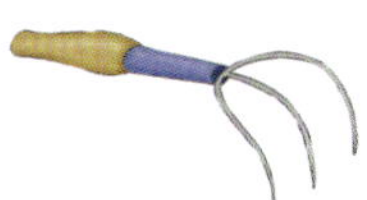

Hand Cultivator. The strong tines on this tool loosen and aerate soil and are invaluable for removing weed roots and rhizomes.

Trowel. You can dig small planting holes using a sturdy trowel with a fairly narrow blade. Trowels are also handy for removing tenacious tap-rooted weeds.

Laying Out & Clearing the Site

The first steps in starting a new garden bed are laying it out and clearing it of vegetation. Begin by outlining its perimeter. For beds with straight sides, you can tie string to stakes. For beds with curved or undulating outlines, use a garden hose or powdered horticultural lime.

Remove whatever vegetation is currently growing inside the bed's perimeter (usually lawn grasses and weeds). Don't be tempted to dig or till the sod or weeds into the bed because many grasses and weeds spread by creeping roots that can sprout new plants. Instead, cut plants as close to the ground as possible, and skim off the sod with a spade. Bury the pieces of sod upside down at the bottom of the new bed or in a compost pile. If you're removing pernicious weeds such as quack grass or Bermudagrass, it's safest to get rid of them in the trash.

If the bed is large or especially weedy, you may want to kill the vegetation first. You can smother plant roots by spreading sheets of black plastic over the site for five to six weeks in the heat of the summer.

Using Herbicides. If your site is infested with intractable weeds such as poison ivy, digging or smothering may be too difficult or ineffective. Another option is a nonspecific herbicide. Products based on the chemical glyphosate can kill persistent weeds that are difficult to remove by other means. These herbicides kill by moving through the entire plant from leaves to roots. Caution: Use herbicides exactly as the label specifies, including wearing protective clothing.

It may take a week or more for herbicide-sprayed plants to die, and it may take several applications to kill all the vegetation. Once all vegetation is dead, you can till the remains into the soil. While the manufacturers' tests show that glyphosate quickly breaks down into nontoxic substances, others cite research disputing this claim. Organic gardeners often avoid glyphosate because of damage it may do to soil organisms.

Leaves of nearby plants must be protected from herbicide oversprays. If possible, apply the herbicide on a windless day. You can use a large sheet of cardboard to shield nearby plants. If you're applying it to weeds in an existing bed, apply the herbicide with a sponge or brush.

Making a Raised Bed

If your soil is less than ideal, you can still make a garden with raised beds. Consider this solution if your soil is shot through with heavy clay, exceedingly sandy, poorly drained and boggy, underlain by tough hardpan, laced with greedy tree roots, or packed with rocks.

By building up good garden soil on top of the problem soil, you can avoid the problems these conditions create. Raised beds are also an effective way to meet the special soil conditions required by acid-loving plants without trying to amend large areas of native soil.

To create a raised bed, use soil from your property, or buy topsoil. Regardless of its source, test and amend the soil to make it suitable for the plants you want to grow. You can build raised beds by mounding soil up to 8 inches above the surrounding area and firming the edges with the back of a rake. If the plants you want to

Clearing a Site Using a Spade

Tools & Materials: Spade, tarp (optional) **Difficulty:** Easy

1 Remove the sod by cutting blocks about the same size as your spade. Push the spade under the sod layer and lift.

2 Pile sod pieces, grass sides together, in a compost pile or place them face down at the bottom of the bed.

Tilling to Clear a Site & Plant a Garden Bed

Tools & Materials: Tiller, trowel, plants, fertilizer, water, mulch **Difficulty:** Moderate

1 Till the sod only if you are certain that it contains no grasses, such as quack grass or Bermudagrass, that spread by rhizomes. When you till these grasses, you increase their populations and your weed problems.

2 Wait a week or so before transplanting. During this time, root fragments and weed seeds will sprout. Disturb the soil as little as possible when you remove these weeds; place transplants according to your plan.

3 Mulch to eliminate weed problems through the season; fertilize and water as needed; and stand back to watch the show. Before long, your new garden bed will be brimming with attractive flowers and foliage.

grow require deeper soil or if you'd like a tidier look, enclose the bed with stones, bricks, or landscape timbers.

Outsmarting the Weeds

A newly dug garden bed is a satisfying sight. Unfortunately, the digging and raking that produced that lovely manicured surface also dredged up millions of weed seeds. All it takes is a little warmth and moisture to make them germinate. If you can bear to postpone planting, you can get rid of this unwanted crop by using a farmer's technique called a stale seedbed. Since you won't spend so much time weeding later in the season, this method is well worth the wait. Let the soil sit undisturbed for a week or two, until the little weed seedlings are about an inch high. Then dislodge them with a rake or hoe, and rake them off the surface of the bed. Take care not to stir the soil any more than you have to, or you'll bring more weed seeds close to the surface. Unless your soil is unusually weed-free, you'll need to repeat this process a few times to eradicate a significant portion of the annual weeds. This weed-control method works best in spring and summer. In fall, seeds don't germinate, even though they may be present.

Raised beds are popular for vegetable gardens because plants in these beds tend to be healthy and yield well.

Testing Soil Before Digging

With the site cleared, you're ready to dig—but only if the soil is also ready. You can destroy a soil's structure by working it when it is too wet or too dry. Test the soil by squeezing a handful. If it crumbles into powder when you open your hand, it's too dry (A). Water the area thoroughly, and try the squeeze test again in a day or so. If the soil forms a tight wet ball, it's too wet to dig and you'll have to wait a day or more to let the soil dry (B). If the soil forms a ball that breaks apart easily when you tap it gently with your fingers, it's ready to dig and amend (C).

For most soils, single digging to a depth of 8 to 10 inches (the length of the spade) is sufficient. This kind of digging aerates the soil, gives you a chance to remove rocks and roots, and lets you add several inches of organic amendments. Double digging refers to the process of aerating the soil at the trench bottom as shown opposite. It is the best method for improving poorer soils and those with inadequate drainage.

The best tools for digging a new bed are a garden spade and fork. In compacted soil, using a gas-powered tiller can be more work than digging by hand. Because single and double digging involve many of the same steps, they can be described together, as shown on page 43.

Begin by taking a handful of soil and squeezing it.

Soil that won't hold together is too dry to work.

Soil that holds together when squeezed . . .

. . . and compresses when tapped is too wet to work.

Soil that holds together when squeezed . . .

. . . but crumbles apart when tapped is just right to work.

Digging a Garden Bed

Tools & Materials: Spade or shovel, tarp, fertilizer, soil amendments **Difficulty:** Easy

1 Remove the sod by cutting through the roots in blocks that are about the same size as your spade. Push the spade under the sod layer and lift.

2 Single- and double-digging both start by digging a 2-foot-wide trench, one spade deep, across one end of the bed. Move soil from this first trench to the other end of the bed.

3 Spread a layer of amendments on the trench bottom. If double-digging, use a spading fork to loosen the soil at the trench bottom to another spade's depth.

4 Dig a second trench, filling the first with soil from the second. Repeat this, using the soil from the first trench to fill the last one.

Chapter 3 *Gardening Care*

After giving your garden a good start, you'll want to ensure that the plants stay healthy and attractive as the garden matures. Keeping plants well watered, well fed, and well groomed can be, part of the fun of gardening. Tending your plants gives you a good excuse for being outdoors, and observing plants at close range deepens your appreciation and understanding of them.

Observation, in fact, is one of the most important aspects of plant care. Problems seen early are much easier to remedy than those that have progressed far enough to be visible from across the lawn. Try to take a slow stroll around your plantings every day or so—morning and evening if possible. As you grow more familiar with your plants, you'll be able to anticipate things that need doing and spot problems in the making.

Routine Care

Gardens require routine maintenance to stay healthy, beautiful, and productive. As a garden becomes established, you'll find that it requires less and less care, but only if you've done a thorough job in the beginning.

Mulching

Mulch is the garden's miracle material. Organic mulches a few inches deep help soil retain moisture, keep plant roots from getting too cool or too hot, hold weeds in check, provide nutrients as they decompose, and contribute organic matter to feed soil organisms and improve soil structure. As a bonus, mulches give the garden a neat, tidy appearance.

Many loose organic materials can be used as mulch—chopped leaves, straw, grass clippings, newspaper, shredded or chipped wood or bark, and seed or nut hulls and shells. You can collect leaves and grass clippings from your own property and buy other mulching materials in bags or bulk from a nursery or garden center. Shredded wood (and bark) is an ideal mulch because it's unobtrusive, easy to spread, heavy enough to stay put when the wind blows, and noncompacting (unlike grass clippings). Shredded wood also decomposes relatively slowly and needs renewing only every year or so.

Garden care becomes less time consuming and more enjoyable as the season and the years progress, opposite.

Good mulches include such materials as newspapers, straw, cardboard, compost, autumn leaves, and shredded wood.

Organic mulches, such as the straw used in this garden, add beauty, increase soil health, and cut your work time.

Gravel is effective at keeping plant roots cool and helping to retain soil moisture, but it doesn't supply organic matter or appreciable nutrients. Water-permeable landscape fabrics are useful for mulching shrub borders and other low-maintenance landscape plantings, but they're difficult to cut through and impractical in plantings where you're occasionally adding or moving plants around. Plastic sheeting isn't a good mulch material for ordinary gardens for numerous reasons. It doesn't allow water to penetrate, can overheat plant roots, and is difficult to work with and remove. It also deteriorates after a few seasons into shreds that blow around.

Pull mulches back a few inches from plant stems to avoid rotting problems.

Beds started with young plants, rather than by direct seeding, should be mulched at the time of planting. Layer the mulch no more than 3 inches deep, and leave a few inches around the stem of each plant mulch-free. You can mulch direct-seeded plants once the seedlings have been thinned and are at least a few inches tall. Depending on climate and materials, organic mulches may last for several years or mere months. Hot, humid conditions tend to speed decomposition, and fresh, moist materials such as grass clippings decompose more quickly than dry ones.

Watering

Although mulch helps hold existing water in the soil, it doesn't add moisture. Most gardeners have to supplement natural rainfall to keep plants healthy. In some regions, irrigation is a regular requirement; in others, an infrequent one. In any region, young plants in new beds need regular watering to get established. (See "Water-wise Tips," Chapter 2, page 32.)

Watering needs are easy to determine by using an unfinished wooden stick as a gauge of soil moisture.

Frequent Inspection. Check on water needs during your daily garden stroll. Wilted leaves often indicate water stress, and dull or curling leaves are pre-wilting symptoms. But the condition of leaves can be misleading, even for experienced gardeners. Symptoms common to water stress may be due to disease or insect damage instead. The best way to determine when to water is to check the soil regularly. If the soil beneath the mulch feels dry to the touch, dig down and see if it is moist 2 or 3 inches below the surface. If you don't want to disturb roots, shove a thin stick of light-colored, unfinished wood 2 or 3 inches into the soil. (The wooden stirrers given out by paint stores make fine moisture-testing sticks). Pull up the stick after an hour. If the bottom few inches are not discolored by moisture, you need to water.

Water Thoroughly. When you water, water deeply. Garden plant roots can grow from 1 foot to more than 5 feet deep. Wetting just the top few inches of soil encourages shallow root growth, making it necessary to water more frequently. You can water small plants or widely separated plants adequately with a hand-held hose. But hand-watering an entire bed for even as long as an hour can provide less water than ½ inch of rainfall. Providing enough water to soak down a foot or more into the soil requires a sprinkler or irrigation system.

Drip Irrigation Systems

Drip irrigation systems deliver water at low pressure to plants through a network of plastic pipes, hoses, tubing, and a variety of emitters. In addition to ground-level emitters that drip water in controlled amounts, systems can include porous soaker tubing and sprayers or sprinklers positioned at ground level or up to several feet above the soil surface. Simple drip systems can be attached to regular garden hoses and controlled manually from an outdoor faucet, just like a sprinkler. The most sophisticated systems include their own attachment to your main water supply, a system of valves that allows you to divide your property into zones, and an electronic control system that can automatically water each zone at preset times for preset durations.

A person with modest mechanical skills and basic tools can plan and install a simple drip irrigation system. Unless you're mechanically inclined, leave complex systems to professional installers. You can buy kits or individual system components from garden centers, nurseries, or specialty suppliers. The main components are outlined below. Good criteria for choosing among different suppliers are their knowledge of system design and installation and their willingness to help you with both. They may charge for this service, but good advice is worth the money.

- A drip system connected to a domestic water supply needs a backflow prevention device (also called an antisiphon device) at the point of connection to the water supply to protect drinking water from contamination. Backflow devices are often specified in city building codes, so check with local health or government officials to determine whether a specific type of backflow prevention device is required.
- Install a filter to prevent minerals and flakes from coming off metal water pipes and clogging the emitters. You'll need to clean the filter regularly. Between the filter and emitters, all hoses and tubing should be plastic because metal can flake off and clog the system.
- A pressure regulator reduces the water pressure supplied by the household pipes to the low pressure required by the emitters.
- Install a timer or electronic controller for convenience. Unlike you, it won't forget and leave the water on too long. It irrigates during the day or while you're away. However, without resetting, it may also water in a rainstorm.
- To automate your gardening further, consider installing fertilizer injectors to deliver nutrients to your plants along with timed watering.
- Water is delivered from the pipes to the emitters by flexible plastic tubing, sold specifically for drip systems. Systems installed just under the soil surface often have an air/vacuum relief valve placed at the high point in the line (as shown below).
- A range of emitters and mini-sprinklers is available for different kinds of plants and garden situations. Consult with your supplier about which best meet the needs of various gardens.

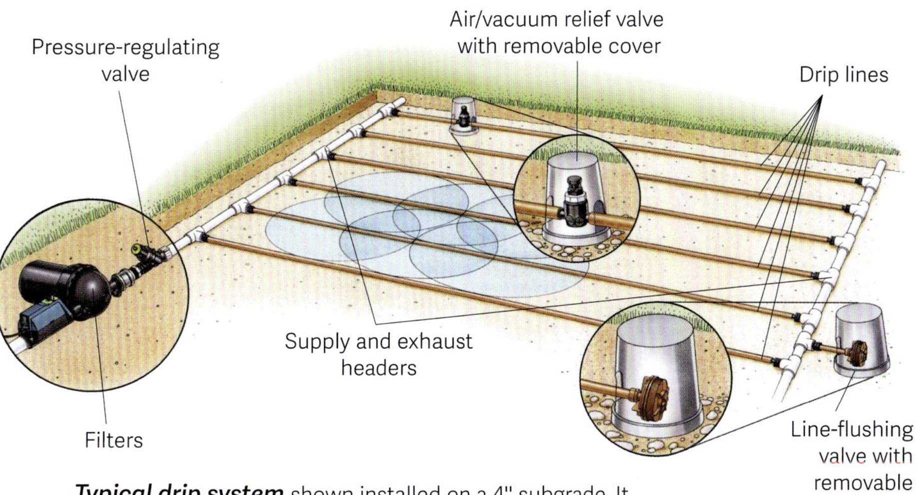

Typical drip system shown installed on a 4" subgrade. It can also be installed on the surface or under mulch.

Sprinklers as Watering Tools. Sprinklers are inefficient tools because water is blown away by wind, runs off sloped or paved areas, or falls too far away from individual plants to be of use to them. The water soaks leaves as well as the soil, and damp foliage can be a breeding ground for disease. But sprinklers are inexpensive and easy to use, so many people find them convenient when they are just getting started.

To make best use of your sprinkler, determine the rate at which it delivers water and the rate at which your soil absorbs water. To determine the sprinkler's delivery rate, set a number of empty cans (empty tuna cans work well) in a line from the sprinkler to its farthest reach. Note how long it takes to deposit an inch of water in any one of the cans. You'll see that water accumulates in the cans at different rates; few sprinklers deliver water evenly.

Efficient Watering Systems. Soaker hoses and drip irrigation systems both apply water directly to the roots. Very little water is lost, and the risk of water-borne foliage problems is reduced. Drip irrigation systems are the more expensive and involved option, but most people can install a simple system. For an overview of drip systems, see page 47.

Soaker hoses are inexpensive, easy to install, and easy to use. Made of perforated plastic or water-permeable canvas, soaker hoses seep or drip water along their length. They deliver water much more slowly than sprinklers, so you'll have to check the manufacturer's information for delivery rates. Soaker hoses are well suited for watering plants grown in rows, as in vegetable or cutting gardens. In ornamental plantings, you can encircle large shrubs or trees and snake the hose beside smaller plants. Because water doesn't spread very far sideways as it soaks into soil, plants that are not next to the hose will not get watered. Soaker hoses are best on level sites; the flow will be inconsistent if the hose rises and falls over uneven terrain.

After threading the soaker hose through the bed, attach it to the faucet with a length of standard hose. Once positioned, soaker hoses can be covered with mulch and left in the garden for an entire season; in ornamental plantings they can be left in place longer, adjusted as necessary when you add new plants or renew the mulch. After a number of years, ultraviolet light, hard winters, or salt accumulation will degrade the hoses. Covering them with mulch can prolong their life.

How Much Water Do You Need?

You can determine your soil's absorption rate by watering an area and digging to determine penetration, but this is messy and imprecise. As a general rule of thumb, 1 inch of slow, steady rainfall soaks about 4 to 5 inches deep in clay soil, 7 inches deep in loam, and 12 inches in sandy soil. So if you want to water 12 inches deep in loam, you'll need to provide a little less than 2 inches of water.

Soaker hoses allow water to seep out into the soil, while sprinklers spray droplets into the air and onto the leaves.

Maintenance Fertilizing

Most ornamental plants get a good start if their beds are prepared and amended as discussed in Chapter 2. (See information beginning on page 36.) In subsequent years, you can maintain healthy soils and provide nutrients by spreading a couple of inches of well-rotted compost on the surface of the soil. The decomposition of regularly renewed organic mulch also builds and maintains soils.

Many gardeners augment these good soil-husbandry practices during the season by fertilizing their entire gardens or only a few selected plants such as bulbs, annuals, roses, and rhododendrons. Applied at the right time and in the correct amounts, additional fertilizer can help to establish sturdy stems and foliage, boost bloom, and build up reserves for dormancy and reemergence in the spring. balanced, or complete, fertilizers generally suit these purposes. (See Chapter 2, page 37, for an overview of fertilizers.) Sub-par performance is sometimes remedied by additional nutrients, though it is often difficult to pin a problem on a single cause, and fertilizing a plant that doesn't need it can do more harm than good. Excess nitrogen, for example, can promote foliage growth at the expense of flowers and fruit. Whether you're seeking to boost healthy plants or rejuvenate ailing ones, it's best to seek advice at a good local nursery or from your Cooperative Extension Service on what type of fertilizer, if any, is most appropriate for your plants. Follow package instructions precisely for application and dosage.

Fertilizing Vegetable Gardens. Many gardeners rework the soil in their vegetable gardens every spring. During this process, nutrients can be augmented and adjusted, either with specific nutrient sources or by the addition of liberal amounts of well-rot-

Compost for Maintenance Fertilizing

Well-rotted organic matter, or compost, is an excellent soil amendment and mulch. It's easy to compost plant waste collected from your yard, garden, and kitchen. The simplest method is to pile plant wastes together in a homemade wire bin. Make one from sturdy wire mesh; chicken wire is too flimsy to stand on its own. A piece 4 feet wide by 14 feet long will make a bin 4 feet in diameter, the smallest volume that works well. A grid up to 1½ inches by 3 inches or so will hold material inside. The smaller the grid, the tidier the composting area will be.

Toss in grass clippings, plant material from the garden, and plant wastes from the kitchen. If you add fallen leaves, first shred them by running over the pile a few times with a lawn mower. Farm-animal manure and straw are excellent compost materials, if you can get them. Don't add animal bones or flesh from the kitchen, because they attract carnivorous rodents and other unwanted animals. Dog and cat waste may contain parasites or disease organisms that can affect humans; don't add them to your compost piles. Don't compost diseased plant parts or weeds with seeds either. Some disease organisms survive the composting process, so burn them or toss them in the trash.

Within six months to a year, depending on the ingredients and your climate, much of the material in the bin will have decayed into a crumbly, rich brown substance. To harvest the compost, just remove the wire bin and set it up nearby. Transfer the uncomposted material on top of the pile into the bin to start the next batch, and dig out the composted material from the center of the old pile. You can increase the speed of composting by turning the pile regularly with a garden fork. If the art of composting intrigues you, ask your Cooperative Extension Service for information on more-sophisticated methods.

Composting transforms ordinary kitchen and yard waste into a valuable soil amendment and fertilizer. Pile a 6-inch layer of dry material on the bottom of the bin. Add 4 inches of fresh materials, as shown in the top photo, add a sprinkling of garden soil, and repeat the layers. In a month or so, materials will have started composting, as shown in the second photo from the top. The third photo shows fully finished compost, which takes 6 months to a year to develop in ordinary conditions.

Compost bins made from wire or plastic mesh (as shown here) are easy to set up. They prevent compost ingredients from blowing around, keep animals out, and allow moisture and air movement.

Fertilize plants according to their needs. Here, a gardener is applying wood ash, which supplies potassium, to asparagus beds in early spring.

ted manure or compost. Gardeners seeking to boost yields often apply supplementary fertilizers to all or some of the plants. The principles are the same as those described for ornamentals, as is the caution to avoid overfertilization.

Granular fertilizers, whether organically derived or synthetic, are easy to measure out and apply to ornamental and vegetable garden beds. Sprinkle granules around the base of the plants, taking care to keep them away from stems and off leaves. Work the granules into the soil with your fingers or a *hand cultivator,* and apply water to begin dissolving them. *Slow-release* fertilizers can be spread as little as once a year, in the spring. They're especially valuable for plants that become increasingly difficult to get to or to work around as the season progresses. In general, slow-release fertilizers are more expensive to use than ordinary formulations. Most organically derived fertilizers release their nutrients slowly, although their labels don't usually advertise them as slow-release fertilizers. While these fertilizers may also cost more, many contribute to the long-term health of the soil and supply important trace elements missing from synthetic fertilizers.

Fertilizing Other Plants. Potted plants need regular doses of fertilizer. The nutrients in potting soil are quickly taken up by the plant or leached out by watering. Liquid fertilizers are easy to apply to container plants. Although these fertilizers are expensive, potted plants require relatively small amounts. Slow-release granules are also handy and can reduce the number of applications considerably.

Young trees and shrubs can benefit from fertilization until they're nearly full size. But many do well with no fertilizer at all. Trees and shrubs grown in garden beds or in the lawn will benefit from fertilizer you apply to annuals and perennials in the beds or to the turf around the trees. To boost bloom in flowering shrubs, apply additional balanced fertilizer or spread one inch of compost every spring.

Add fertilizers carefully. Learn plants' nutrient requirements before fertilizing with materials other than compost.

Garden Hygiene

In addition to watering, fertilizing, and mulching, there are a variety of garden maintenance tasks that need to be done from time to time during the course of the year.

Seasonal Care

Spring and fall are busy gardening times, particularly in cold winter climates. In fall, you prepare plants for winter. Cut old leaves and stems of most deciduous perennials back to the ground, and remove the debris from the garden. To protect roses from the cold and drying winds of winter, mulch the plants loosely or set up protective covers and barriers around them.

In spring, you clear away winter's detritus and prepare the plantings for a new growing season. Remove or pull back protective coverings from emerging plants, renew mulches, and give the beds a general tidying up. Inspect the shrubs and perennials whose stems and foliage have overwintered, and prune out dead, diseased, or weak stems and foliage.

If you live in a warm-winter climate, you'll perform many of the same seasonal tasks, but you'll have to work around plants that grow year-round.

During seasons of active growth, some plants need to be cut back to control their size or to promote bushy growth. Removing spent flowers, called "deadheading," encourages reblooming in annuals and a number of perennials. The plant descriptions in the following chapters will note if these practices are recommended.

Weed Patrol

No matter how carefully you prepare the bed and mulch the soil, your garden will still harbor at least a few weeds. Keep an eagle eye out for weeds on your regular inspection tours. Weeds are far easier to control if you pull them when they're just a few inches high and their roots haven't spread far and wide.

Detected early enough, most weeds can be easily hand pulled. Tap-rooted weeds, such as dandelions, may require assistance from a garden knife or trowel. Try to get the entire root, or you'll be pulling the same weed in a few days. Weeds that spread by their roots, such as bindweed, can grow quickly, so you may need to remove them from an area using a scuffle hoe. Then smother the soil with mulch. Even well-mulched weeds may resprout from root fragments. Check the area frequently, and keep pulling new plants out. Eventually you'll get rid of them.

Some weeds, such as Bermudagrass, are so tenacious that chemical controls (discussed in Chapter 2, page 40) are just about the only line of defense. If this is the case, use them exactly as the label specifies, and wear protective clothing.

Good garden hygiene discourages pests and diseases that live in debris both during the season and over the winter months.

Pest & Disease Control

Pest and disease control starts with prevention. Select plants that are adapted to the conditions of your region, and whenever possible, resistant to pests and diseases common in your area. Prepare the soil well, keep plants well watered and fed, and keep the garden tidy. Healthy plants have greater recuperative powers, and well-tended gardens provide fewer areas for insects to breed and congregate. Be vigilant. During your daily garden strolls, be on the lookout for insect damage. Similar to weed control, it's easiest to correct insect problems at the beginning. When you see a little damage, don't mount a war. Monitor the problem. The forces of nature may resolve it for you or keep the damage to an acceptable level. If the problem gets worse, identify the culprit before taking action. A chewed leaf, for example, may be obvious, but unless you actually catch the culprit in the act, it can be difficult to determine which insect is to blame. If you're uncertain, catch the insect you feel is causing the damage and take it to a nursery or the Cooperative Extension Service for identification and help in determining the extent of the problem and the best treatments.

Insect Pests

Increased concern about the effects of toxic chemicals has shifted the emphasis on garden pests from eradication to control. Today, we're encouraged to view the garden as a natural system, where a balance of good, bad, and benign insects is maintained by natural processes with assistance from the gardener.

Gardens abound in insect life. Some insects, such as aphids, grubs, grasshoppers, and spider mites, can damage and some-

Encourage beneficial insects by growing plants with small flowers, such as this bee balm, or mint, yarrow, or salvia.

times kill plants. Others, such as lady beetles and certain wasps, are beneficial; they destroy or disable plant-damaging insects. Still others, such as caterpillars and the butterflies they become, cause some damage as well as provide beauty and enjoyment.

Controlling insect pests involves determining which pests are unacceptably harmful to the plants (most plants being able to withstand some damage) and which methods of control are least harmful to the benign, beneficial, or beautiful insects and other creatures in the garden. Common pests are shown on pages 56-59.

Control Methods. When you've determined that something needs to be done about an insect pest, consider the least-toxic methods of control first. Some insects are easy to pick off plants with your fingers. Squash them or drop them in a jar of soapy water. Other insects, such as aphids, can sometimes be kept under control by knocking them off leaves with a blast of water from the garden hose. You can protect plants in vegetable or cutting gardens by using barriers such as floating row covers, which are made of a thin fabric permeable to light, rain, and air but not to bugs.

Least-toxic insect controls include diatomaceous earth, household detergents or specially formulated insecticidal soaps, and horticultural oils. Biological controls, including certain insects and insect diseases that destroy garden pests, can be purchased and released in the garden. (See the box at right for common biological controls.)

If these methods prove impractical or ineffective, you can turn to a wide range of insecticides. Some, such as sabadilla, ryania, neem, and pyrethrin, are made from substances produced by plants. Organic gardeners prefer these pesticides because of their plant origins and because they break down quickly into nontoxic materials. Other pesticides are synthetic. Many of the newer synthetic pesticides are safer for the environment than older synthetic products. To use an insecticide, identify the pest you're after. Pesticides are formulated and registered for use only on specific plants. It is illegal and inappropriate to use them on plants other than those listed on the label. Whether organic or synthesized, *all insecticides are toxic and should be handled and applied exactly as described on the product label, including wearing protective clothing and a mask.* (See "Taking Cover," page 55.)

Prevent insect damage with row covers. Drape the material over hoops, as shown here, or simply lay it over plant rows. Use soil, rocks, or ground staples to hold it in place.

Biological Pest Controls

Lace wing: Both larvae and adults feed on aphids, mites, and other small, soft-bodied pests. Adults require nectar and pollen in order to reproduce.

Lady beetle (ladybug): Both larvae and adults eat a wide range of soft-bodied insects. Provide a pesticide-free environment to grow your own because purchased beetles tend to fly away when released.

Trichogramma wasps: Larvae feed inside caterpillars before emerging and pupating on them, as shown here.

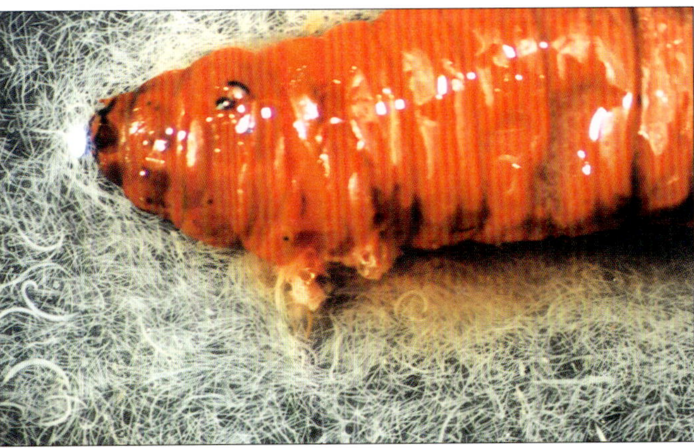

Parasitic nematodes: These microscopic worm-like creatures eat grubs, webworms, and hundreds more soil-dwelling pests.

Predatory mites: These tiny arachnids feed on other mites and thrips that wreak havoc with some plants.

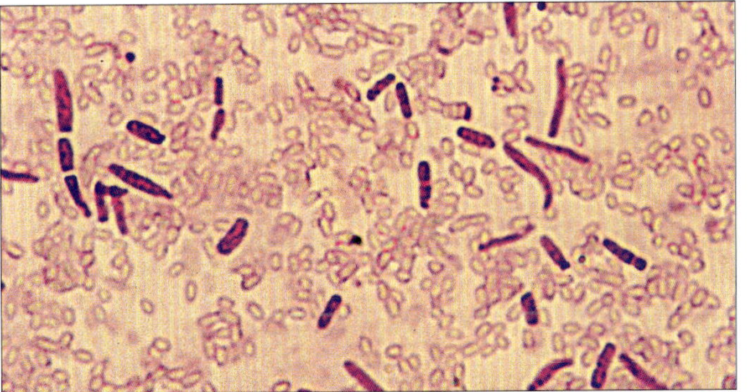

BT (Bacillus thuringiensis): This bacterium kills caterpillars and is harmless to humans (can be used on all food crops).

Animal Pests

Some gardeners make a special effort to attract animals to their plantings. Others work equally hard trying to keep them out. Whether welcomed or repulsed, deer, woodchucks, rabbits, squirrels, chipmunks, voles, and moles can do considerable damage to garden plants, both above- and below-ground. Few of the products that claim to repel these animals are effective, and then usually only if the animals aren't really hungry. The most effective controls are fences and traps. Electric fences up to 18 inches high, with strands placed at 4- to 6-inch intervals, can discourage small aboveground animals. Deer can jump tall fences but are held at bay by wide ones. One excellent design consists of poles set at about a 30- to 40-degree angle and strung with electric wires at 1-foot intervals, with the top wire being about 5 feet off the ground.

To stop burrowing animals, dig a 1-foot-deep (2-foot-deep for gophers), ½-foot-wide trench, and erect a chicken-wire fence that extends from the bottom of the trench to 2 to 3 feet above the ground. Fill in the trench with soil. At the top of the fence, leave an additional foot of fencing material unattached to the posts so that it will flop out and discourage small climbing animals. Traps are available that kill animals or capture them for release somewhere else. In some areas, local animal-control authorities may provide such traps. In other areas, it's illegal to trap and relocate wildlife.

Plant Diseases

Bacteria, fungi, and viruses disfigure or discolor leaves or flowers, produce powdery or moldy films or spots, and rot stems and roots. Knowing whether a disease is fungal, viral, or bacte-

Fool-Proof Animal Fencing

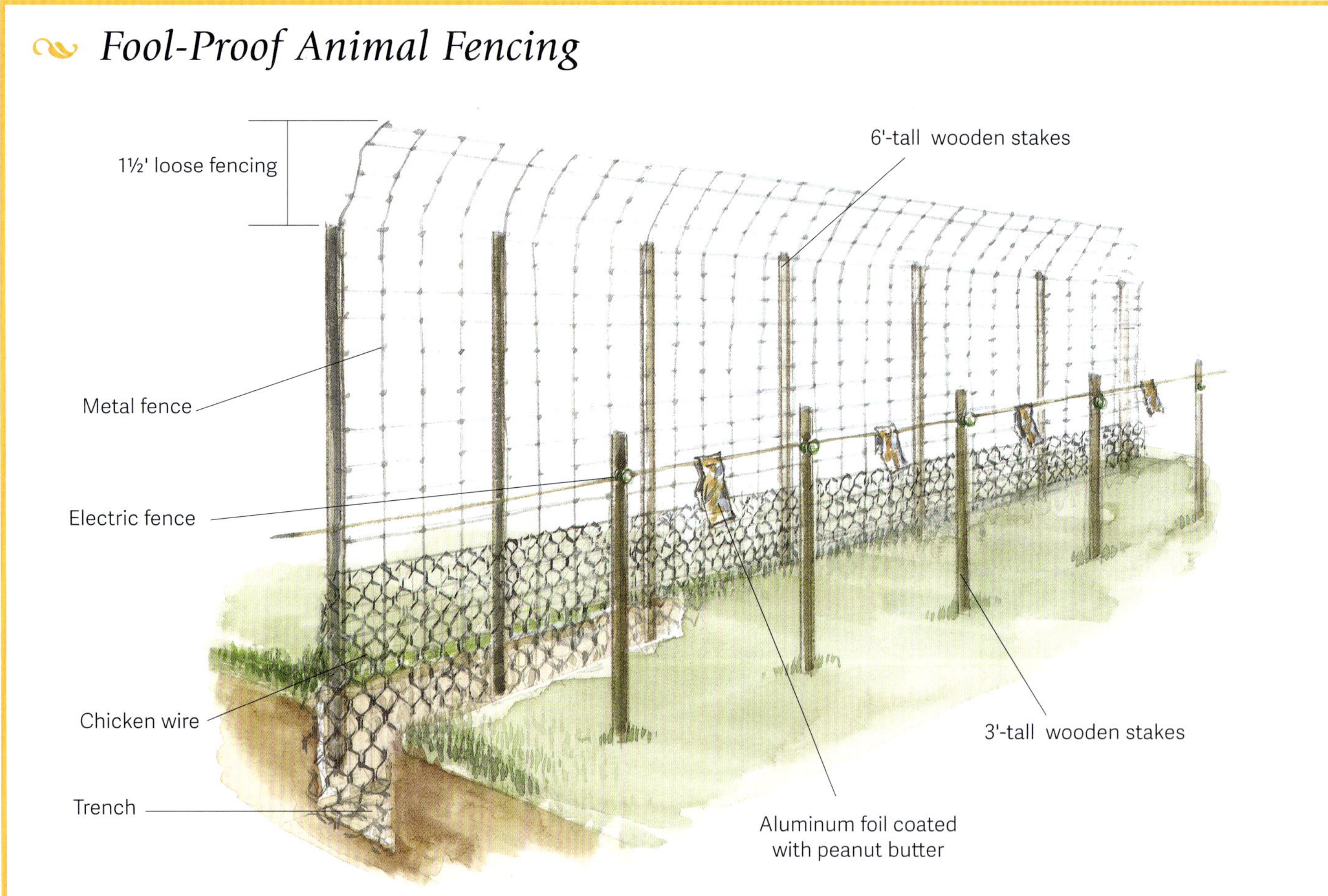

Fences that extend belowground will keep digging animals out of a garden and loose fencing on top discourages climbers. Use chicken wire on the underground portion and for about 2 feet above the soil surface. For deer, add a second, electric, fence five feet from the first. Attach aluminum foil covered with peanut butter to the electric fence; deer get a jolt they don't soon forget.

Taking Cover

Using insecticides and herbicides derived from botanical, biological, mineral, or synthetic materials requires basic precautions. Read product labels thoroughly, and apply these products with great care. If your clothing becomes wet with pesticides, remove it immediately and shower before changing into uncontaminated clothes. Following is a list of basic protective clothing and gear that you may need.

- Long-sleeved shirt, pants, and socks made of tightly woven material (all cotton). Do not leave skin exposed!
- Waterproof, unlined gloves
- Waterproof footwear
- Hat, scarf, or hood to completely cover scalp and to overhang face
- Goggles
- Disposable dust mask designed for pesticide dusts
- Tight-fitting respirator when using liquid sprays. Respirators contain activated-charcoal cartridges that filter pesticide vapors from the air. Make sure the respirator is approved by the National Institute of Occupational Safety and Health (NIOSH).

Note: Be sure to rinse off your waterproof gear and pesticide applicator with plenty of clean water before removing your protective apparel. Avoid handling the outside of the contaminated clothing—use gloves if necessary—and if it will not be laundered immediately, place the clothing in a sealable plastic bag. Wash these garments separately from your regular laundry. Pre-soak them in a pre-soaking product; then wash them on the highest temperature setting for a full cycle with detergent. If the clothing has any residual pesticide odor after the rinse cycle, repeat the washing procedure until the odor is gone. Air-dry the wet clothes on a line. Clean the washing machine by running it through the wash cycle with deter- gent but without clothes. Or simply throw the clothes away.

rial helps you treat it. But a variety of problems besides diseases can cause symptoms of ill health—including insect pests, water stress, air pollution, nutrient problems, and too much or too little sunlight. Additionally, while diseases such as powdery mildew have characteristic signs or symptoms, many others cause similar-looking damage, making them difficult to identify. (See pages 57–59 for photos of some of the most common plant diseases.) In cases when you can't be certain of the identity of a disease, take samples of the diseased tissue to a nursery or Cooperative Extension Service.

Plant diseases can be difficult to treat, so it's best to do everything you can to avoid them in the first place. Rotate annual plants so that their diseases don't have a chance to build up in the soil. Seek out resistant cultivars. Take good care of your plants; well-watered, well-fed plants grown in good soil are less susceptible to and better able to tolerate many diseases. Poor air circulation breeds fungal diseases; plant at recommended spacings and thin out dense growth. Monitor plants regularly for disease. When you spot a disease, cut away the affected plant parts, or remove entire plants. Remove and discard the diseased material, but put it in the trash; don't compost it. After cutting diseased tissue, disinfect pruning shears with alcohol to avoid spreading the infection.

Common Pests and Diseases

Japanese beetles are an eastern and midwestern pest. Beginning in midsummer, adults quickly skeletonize leaves of many ornamental plants and vegetables. Control by handpicking the adults into a can of soapy water. Japanese beetle pheromone traps may or may not be effective.

Japanese beetle larvae eat many types of roots but prefer those of lawn grasses. After a year or sometimes two, they pupate. Adults emerge in midsummer. Control larvae by treating the lawn with beneficial nematodes or, south of Zone 5, milky spore disease (both available from garden centers).

Caterpillars, the larvae of moths and butterflies, feed on many plants, from cabbages to roses. Because they grow into butterflies and moths, you may not want to kill them. For pest species such as gypsy moth larvae, use BT (Bacillus thuringiensis) while the caterpillars are small.

Leafhoppers spread diseases as they suck cell sap. Affected plants are often distorted. Avoid problems with floating row covers or, in small areas, aluminum foil mulches. Dust foliage with diatomaceous earth (available from garden centers or feed stores). Renew the dust after every rain.

Imported cabbage moth larvae eat cabbage crops from Canada to Florida. Protect plants with floating row covers. Handpick the caterpillars into a jar of soapy water. If the infestation is severe, spray plants with BT when the cabbage worms are small.

Mexican bean beetles and their larvae, inset, skeletonize the leaves of bean plants in most regions of North America. Adults lay clusters of yellow eggs on leaf undersides. Larvae and adults also eat from leaf undersides, but populations build so fast that you will see them. Use floating row covers, but monitor them daily. If the bugs appear, handpick adults, and squash larvae and eggs, wearing gloves if you're squeamish. Dust leaves with diatomaceous earth. In serious infestations, spray with neem or ryania.

Thrips are too small to see with the naked eye, but you can sometimes see their small dark droppings. They suck cell sap from leaves, fruit, and flowers, making the affected leaves look silvery or bleached and wilted and the fruit look scabby or russeted. Some species spread spotted wilt virus. Spray dormant oil on fruit trees in late winter. Dust plants with diatomaceous earth when you first see damage. Predatory mites control them and are worth the trouble on fruit trees. Spray insecticidal soap or, as a last resort, neem or pyrethrins.

Crown gall bacteria live in all regions of the continent and attack many different plants. Roots or stems near the soil line develop abnormal growths, usually covered by roughened tissue. Remove whole plants, including the roots, and throw in the trash. Inspect all planting stock carefully.

Slugs and snails live in moist regions and under organic matter. They eat ragged holes in plant leaves and flowers and leave slimy trails. Set boards in the garden, and capture resting pests each morning. They won't cross copper. You can trap them in shallow pans of beer set flush with the soil surface.

Common Pests and Diseases (continued)

Bacterial leaf spot diseases attack plants all over North America and are difficult to diagnose because so many diseases cause spotted leaves. Prevent outbreaks with good cultural practices. Excess nitrogen levels make plants susceptible. Pick off affected leaves at the first sign of attack and discard them. Use copper spray on fruit trees when buds open and until temperatures reach 85°F. Rake up and destroy dropped leaves.

Spider mites are pests all across North America. Although they are difficult to see, their webs are quite visible. Other pest mites do not make webs, but all species suck cell sap, giving plants a papery appearance. If you suspect mites, use a hand lens to inspect leaf undersides and new growth. If the mites are present, mist plants with water every morning. Release predatory mites. Use insecticidal soap spray or ryania as a last resort.

Powdery mildew produces white patches on leaf surfaces. It requires less moisture than most fungi to germinate and grow. It thrives in all parts of North America and tends to attack older leaves or stressed plants after midseason. It rarely kills plants but weakens them and looks unattractive. Good soil nutrition helps to prevent attack as does proper spacing. Use baking powder spray from midseason on or horticultural oil spray when infection first strikes. Repeat sprays every 7 to 10 days until fall.

Mosaic viruses are common in all regions and attack everything from vegetables to roses. Leaves develop light green, yellow, or white areas, giving them a mottled "mosaic" look. Plants are often stunted. Tomato fruit may have yellow patches or may ripen unevenly. Different types of viruses cross easily, and some crosses produce thin, shoestring leaves or leaf curling. There is no control. Prevent viruses by controlling insects (aphids and leafhoppers) that spread them. Choose resistant cultivars when possible. Remove diseased plants from the garden.

Fusarium wilt fungus is most common in Zone 6 and southward. Symptoms include general wilting, yellowing, and eventual death of the plant. Choose resistant cultivars. Remove plant tissue from the garden in fall. Rotate crops, and plant only in well-drained soil.

Corn earworms (tomato fruitworms) live in every region. Choose corn cultivars with tight husks to prevent earworms from entering them. Apply 10 drops of mineral oil on ear tips when silks begin to dry. Dig out larvae at husk tips when they are small.

Botrytis blight attacks plants in humid conditions in every region. Prevent it with good spacing and high air circulation. Plant only in well-drained soils, and water carefully. Prune off infected plant tissue at the first sign of attack, and put in the trash.

Cedar-apple rust lives in the east but at least one rust disease lives in every region. Many rusts have two alternate plant hosts. Rusts can form galls on plants or show as rust-colored spots on leaves or fruit. Separate hosts by at least 4 miles. Choose resistant cultivars. Remove and burn galls; rake up and destroy all infected leaves.

Aphids live in all parts of North America. They suck cell sap, spread diseases, and often distort plant growth. Many beneficial insects prey on them, including ladybugs, lacewings, and beneficial wasps. Plant small flowers for the beneficials. Squash insects; for severe infestations, spray with insecticidal soap. Use pyrethrins as a last resort.

Blackspot fungi attack only roses, primarily in moist regions in eastern North America. Pick off affected leaves, and put them in the trash. At the end of the season, rake up old mulch and leaves, spread compost, and remulch with new material. Baking soda often controls this fungus. Use sulfur sprays as a last resort. Select resistant roses.

CHAPTER 4 Annuals & Perennials

Most people picture flower gardens when they think of annual and perennial plants. These two vast groups provide colorful flowers and handsome foliage in almost unlimited variety. Whether your gardening aspirations involve a simple window box or backyard acreage, basic understanding of annuals and perennials is vital.

What Are Annuals & Perennials?

Technically speaking, an annual is a plant that lives for only a single growing season, during which time it flowers, sets seed, and dies. Perennials are plants that don't die after setting seed; they keep growing year after year unless killed by drought, temperatures beyond their tolerance, or other adversity. Some perennials stay green all year, especially where winters are mild. Others go dormant; that is, their tops turn brown or die down to the ground, but the roots live on and send up new shoots the next year.

The distinction between annuals and perennials isn't clear-cut, because many plants that are used as annuals are actually perennials in frost-free environments. These plants, called tender perennials, are often grouped with annuals or bedding plants. Gardeners in warm-winter climates can grow them outdoors year-round. In cold-winter climates, tender perennials can survive from year to year by bringing them indoors for the winter.

A few garden plants are biennials, meaning that they form leaves but no flowers or seeds the first season. The following year, they make flowers and seeds before dying. Foxgloves and many hollyhocks are common garden biennials.

Annuals produce an abundance of flowers, typically for long periods during the growing season. Perennials also produce beautiful flowers but often for a shorter season, giving them time to store energy to fuel their yearly rejuvenation. Annuals give quick results in the garden, but you need to start from scratch every year.

Annuals and perennials, opposite, combine to make a season-long display in this lovely garden.

Annual flowers at the front of this bed bloom for the season, providing color no matter which of the perennials is in flower.

Although some perennials produce flowers in their first growing season, many take two or three years to become established and bloom well. After that, they commonly live for years. A good way to start a garden is by growing annuals interspersed among a few perennials, adding more perennials as your garden and gardening interests grow.

Choosing Plants

Annuals and perennials are most often prized for their flowers. But despite this, the prevailing colors in a garden are the various greens, grays, and other hues of the foliage. For perennials that flower only a short time, foliage is a crucial consideration when you're deciding which plants deserve precious garden space. Select foliage as a backdrop for flowers or as a focal point on its own.

In addition to a plant's appearance, consider its growing requirements. Plants adapted to your climate usually thrive with only routine care. Cold hardiness isn't a factor when selecting annuals, although some perform better during the fall and winter in warm-winter areas. However, cold hardiness is of considerable importance for perennials. They must be able to survive the lowest temperatures common in your region. (See the USDA Cold Hardiness Zone Map, Chapter 1, page 17.) Knowledgeable staff at a nursery or garden center can offer valuable help in identifying plants well adapted to your region.

Choose plants with lovely foliage to set off your flowers.

Creating a Cutting Garden

Part of the fun of growing flowers is cutting them for indoor display. You can, of course, mix flowers for cutting into any garden bed. But if you don't want to ravage your outdoor displays, plant a separate cutting garden.

A cutting garden doesn't need to be "designed." Lay out your rows for convenience, with taller plants placed to the north so that they don't shade the shorter ones. If you have space, plant at least one rose bush—hybrid tea, floribunda, or shrub type. Most of the annuals and perennials grown for cutting thrive on being picked—the more flowers you cut, the more they produce. In fact some, like cosmos, will stop flowering if blooms aren't removed. The accompanying box, "Plants for a Cutting Garden," lists a selection of easy-to-grow annuals and perennials that produce excellent cut flowers.

Plants for a Cutting Garden

Annuals:

Ageratum (tall cultivars)
Calendula (pot marigold)
Celosia
China aster
China pinks
Cosmos
Gloriosa daisy
Larkspur
Pansy
Shirley poppy
Snapdragon
Statice
Stock
Sweet pea
Sweet William
Zinnia

Perennials:

Artemisia
Baby's breath
Balloonflower
Bellflower, peach-leaved
Black-eyed Susan
Butterfly weed
Coral bells
Cottage pinks
Feverfew
Globe thistle
Japanese anemone
Obedient plant
Purple coneflower
Yarrow

Spring- and summer-flowering bulbs:

Calla lily
Camassia
Crocosmia
Daffodil
Dahlia
Gladiolus
Grape hyacinth
Lily
Lily-of-the-valley
Ranunculus
Tuberose
Tulip

Cutting gardens are generally laid out in straight rows to make routine care and harvesting fast and efficient.

Container gardens require variety as much as any others. Choose plants that complement each other's form, texture, and color.

Container Gardening

Many annuals and tender perennials make excellent plants for container gardens. Grown in pots, window boxes, or even a pair of old boots, container plants can transform any area of your home or yard. Though hardy perennials, shrubs, and even trees may be grown in containers, keeping them healthy for many years requires special care. Seek advice at a local nursery if you're interested in this type of container gardening.

Pretty Plant Combinations

Mixing plants in a garden takes imagination, skill, and a bit of daring. Look at other people's gardens to find combinations you like—and those you don't. Select plants with varied heights, shapes, textures and colors, and plan for harmonious or complementary color schemes. Note time of bloom so that you will know how the garden will look through the season. Remember that foliage with interesting texture or color can carry a garden through times when no perennials are in bloom. Well-chosen annuals will give color through the season, too. Group at least three of the same plants together. Groupings or specimen plants can be repeated in large areas. Gardens evolve over time. No matter how much you like your initial plan, you're sure to change it and add to it over the years.

Variation in color and form gives interest to this Southeastern garden.

Groupings of ajuga and rhododendrons light up a shady corner.

Cottage gardens are noted for the diversity of plants they contain.

Harmonious colors make this garden feel calm and restful.

Grouping container plants can provide needed variety.

Nurseries and garden centers carry a good selection of annuals and tender perennials that grow well in containers. Choose from pansies, petunias, snapdragons, cockscombs, lobelias, geraniums, daisies, spike plant, and dusty miller. Finding interesting containers is part of the fun. Buy containers, or use a favorite pot or unusual found object. Make sure the container has drainage holes; if not, drill one-half-inch holes in the bottom.

Potting soil should have a crumbly texture and retain moisture without becoming soggy. While it's possible to make your own, many gardeners get the best results by purchasing bagged potting soils. Most types work well for annuals and tender perennials.

You can display one plant or many in a single pot. Don't be afraid to crowd a pot. Dense displays look better than sparse ones, and commonly used container plants perform well when crowded if well-watered and fertilized. Good container combinations mix colors, textures, and heights just as in gardens, but on a smaller scale.

Planting Containers. Begin by moistening the soil mix until it is damp. Add some slow-release fertilizer if you wish, in recommended quantities. Place screening or old nylon stocking material over the drainage holes, and fill your pot to within two to three inches of the rim. Insert the plants into the soil, working from the center out. Keep individual root balls as intact as possible, but disentangle roots that have wound around themselves. The tops of the root balls should be about ½ to 1 inch below the rim of the pot. As you add plants, fill in around them with potting soil. Water the pot deeply.

Caring for Container Gardens. Caring for container plants requires more vigilance than work. Plants in well-fertilized potting soil usually perform well if you keep them watered. Check moisture levels daily. In hot, breezy summer weather, the small amount of soil in a pot, particularly one made from porous terra-cotta, can dry out quickly. You may need to water several times a day. Flexible-tube drip-irrigation systems designed for containers can save you time and plants, particularly if you're away for a few days in hot weather.

Commercial potting mixes ordinarily contain few, if any, nutrients, so you'll have to fertilize from the beginning. What kind of fertilizer, how much to use, and how often to use it depend on the plant, the container, and the conditions on your site. In general, you're safe following dosages recommended on fertilizer packages. If you're uncertain, ask at your nursery.

Starting Plants

You can start annuals and perennials from seeds or purchase plants from a nursery or garden center. Starting from seeds is less expensive than buying plants but takes more time and effort. Many hybridized perennials must be purchased as plants, because seed-grown plants may not produce the desired characteristics. Such plants are usually produced commercially by root division or stem cuttings. Division is an easy process and is discussed later in this chapter.

Annuals and a few perennials are sometimes sown directly where they are to grow; in fact, some plants do best when direct-sown. Seed packets are dependable sources of basic information on planting—when and how deep to plant, and how long until germination.

Flowers for Direct Seeding

- Bachelor's button
- Blanketflower
- Cosmos
- Larkspur
- Lupine, annual
- Marigold
- Mexican sunflower
- Morning glory
- Nasturtium
- Shirley poppy
- Stocks
- Strawflower
- Sunflower
- Sweet alyssum
- Sweet pea
- Zinnia

Direct Seeding

Tools & Materials: Rake, water sprinkler, seeds, sand, row cover material (or burlap or straw), scissors **Difficulty:** Easy

1 Prepare the soil as described in Chapter 2. (See pages 34–37.) Rake it smooth, and sow the seeds evenly on the surface if you're carpeting an area with plants. If you wish to grow a single plant, sow three to five seeds in a spot, and thin to the strongest seedling after the first true leaves have expanded. When planting a group, sow two to three seeds for every desired plant and thin as necessary.

2 If you're carpeting an area with small seeds, such as those of sweet alyssum or poppies, mix the seeds with a few teaspoons of dry sand. The extra bulk will help you scatter the seeds more evenly. Some seeds require light to germinate and should be left uncovered (the packet will specify). Just press them firmly into the soil. Cover larger seeds with a fine layer of soil, if recommended, and then water thoroughly.

3 The key to success is keeping seeds moist until they germinate. You may need to check the site several times a day and water as necessary. Apply water as a gentle sprinkle so that you don't dislodge the seeds. To conserve moisture, cover the seeded area with a thin layer of straw, row cover, or burlap, and water through the material. Remove burlap or row cover material after the seedlings have germinated.

4 When the plants are several inches tall, thin them to the recommended spacing. To thin, carefully snip off unwanted plants; pulling or digging risks disturbing the roots of those left in place. Continue to water regularly, even if the plants are drought-tolerant, until growth is well established. For perennials, supplemental water may be needed throughout the first season.

Starting Summer-Blooming Bulbs & Tubers

The bulbs and tubers of lilies, dahlias, gladiolus, cannas, and similar plants can be planted directly into the garden or started indoors in pots for later transplanting. (See the planting suggestions that accompany each season.) In cold-weather climates, tender summer-blooming bulbs such as gladiolus and dahlias are planted in spring each year. Lilies are planted in spring or fall.

Plant bulbs or tubers in the garden after danger of frost has passed. Be sure to plant them at the depth recommended by the supplier, and don't let the soil dry out while they are sprouting underground. Plant as many bulbs or tubers as you want plants.

To get a head start on bloom time, plant bulbs or tubers indoors a few weeks before the last frost. Plant in four-inch pots, using one bulb or tuber to a pot. Keep the potting soil moist at all times. When shoots or leaves appear, put the pots in a warm bright window or under lights as described below in "Starting Seeds in Containers." Water and fertilize regularly as the plants grow, and carefully transplant the started plants into garden beds or display containers after all danger of frost has passed.

Gardeners in cold-winter areas will need to dig up tender corms and tubers in the fall and store them indoors. When you place these plants in a garden bed in the spring, be sure they're accessible and positioned so that the fall dig-

Starting Seeds in Containers

1 Sow seeds in containers filled with moist soil mix. Shake the seeds onto a piece of paper, and use the tip of a pencil to space them correctly. Depending on the size of the seeds, you can sow from 4 to 12 in each 4-inch pot. In flats, allow up to an inch between seeds. Cover the seeds with soil unless the packet says they need light to germinate. Wet the sown seeds gently by misting with water from a household spray bottle, and set the pots out of direct sunlight in a warm indoor spot. You can also buy heating mats to keep the soil mix warm.

2 Keep the soil moist by misting and covering with a plastic dome or by enclosing the containers in plastic bags. Use sticks to keep the bag from sagging onto the soil. When the seeds germinate, remove the plastic and gradually expose the containers to bright light. If possible, place them beneath a fluorescent fixture with ordinary tubes, suspended a few inches above the seedlings. Keep it lit for 12–16 hours a day. Setting seedlings on a sunny windowsill provides light but also heat. Make sure the seedlings don't dry out or roast.

3 Bottom water the containers by using a propagation unit with a wicking mat or by setting containers in a shallow, water-filled tray until the top surface of the soil mix glistens. Bottom watering minimizes fungal diseases and encourages deep rooting. Feed the seedlings once or twice a week with a water-soluble fertilizer, diluted to one-half the ordinary rate. If your plants are under fluorescent lights, keep the tubes raised about 2 inches above the top leaves. If the seedlings are in a window, turn the containers frequently to keep stems growing straight.

ging won't disturb neighboring plants. Because of this disruption, some gardeners prefer to grow tender bulbs in separate beds or cutting gardens or replace them annually.

Good garden hygiene discourages pests and diseases that live in debris both during the season and over the winter months.

Tools & Materials: Seed containers, soil mix, water mister, soil heating mat (optional), small sticks, plastic bags, fluorescent light fixtures (optional), water soluble fertilizer, plant pots, pencil **Difficulty:** Moderate

4 After the plants have developed their second set of leaves, transplant them into individual containers. You can transplant small plants into four- or six-cell plastic packs; use 4-inch pots for plants that grow large quickly. Fill the cells or pots with fresh, moistened potting soil. Holding a seedling gently by a seed leaf, prick its roots out of its pot with a sharpened pencil taking care not to disturb the roots and attached soil—or gently remove all the plants and carefully tease apart roots of plants growing close together.

5 Use a pencil to poke a hole in the soil of the new cell or container. Holding the seedling by the root ball or leaves, place it in the pot, and fill around it to bury the roots. Suspend larger seedlings in an empty cell while you add moistened potting soil around their roots. Gently firm but do not pack the soil mix; seedling roots need oxygen as much as they need water. Place the cell packs or individual containers under lights or on the windowsill again. Water and feed as before. Turn plants in a window a quarter turn each day to keep the stems straight.

6 When the seedlings are large enough to put in the garden, they need to be "hardened off," or acclimated to conditions outdoors. Begin by setting the plants outside for a few hours every day, in a spot protected from direct sunlight and wind. Over the period of a week or so, gradually increase the time and exposure to sunlight and wind. Leave them out all night if there is no frost danger. Transplant tender plants after all danger of frost has passed. Cold-hardy seedlings often tolerate light frosts but can be stunted by them.

Transplanting Outdoors

Transplanting to the garden is a simple procedure, as long as you follow a few guidelines. Always space the plants according to their mature size, following recommendations. You can fill the spaces between slow-growing perennials with annuals for the first one or two seasons. Make sure the annuals are shorter than the perennials so that they don't retard the perennials' growth. Water is crucial for new plants. If nature doesn't oblige, provide an inch per week throughout the growing season—even for drought-tolerant plants—until they are established. Mulch around the plants to retain water, keeping the mulch back from the stem to avoid disease problems.

Transplanting outdoors during the summer can be hard on seedlings. Cover them with shade cloth, or erect a temporary lath house for filtered light.

Steps for Transplanting

Tools & Materials: Trowel or shovel, water **Difficulty:** Easy

1 If you're transplanting into a new bed, prepare the soil as described in Chapter 2, on pages 34–37. If you're transplanting into an old bed, amend the soil with compost where the new plant will go. Water the container, and let it drain. Before you remove the plant from its pot, use a trowel or shovel to dig a hole in the bed a few inches wider than the plant's root ball and not quite as deep.

2 Gently slide the plant from the container, keeping the root ball as intact as possible. Don't pull on the stem. Instead, slip your fingers on either side of it, and turn the container upside down. Tap on the container with the other hand or a trowel to loosen the root ball. If your plants are in packs, squeeze the bottom of each cell, and push from the bottom to slide the root ball out of the pack.

3 Gently loosen congested roots on the bottom and lower sides of the root ball; unwrap any that encircle the ball. Place the plant into the hole, firm the soil around it, and water thoroughly. For large plants, set the plant in the hole, and fill the hole about halfway with soil. Then soak the root ball with water, and let it drain. Add the remaining soil, firming it gently around the stem. Water thoroughly.

Propagating Perennials

The easiest method for increasing your perennials, aside from starting seeds, is division. Many perennial plants form a dense concentration of stems, called a crown, at their base. As the number of stems increases each year, the plant increases in diameter. You can produce two or more new plants from a single plant by dividing the crown and its attached root and top growth. Some plants, such as daylilies, hostas, and irises, have thick stems and roots that are easy to imagine as separate plants when you look at the root ball. Other plants, such as yarrows, asters, and Shasta daisies, have finer roots and stems that appear as a more-or-less undifferentiated mass. But they will still form new plants when divided. Although small plants can be divided, you'll get a better show more quickly if you divide mature plants into several good-size clumps.

Divide perennials in the early spring or early fall. In cold-winter climates, spring division offers new plants a full growing season to become established. In mild-winter climates, fall division provides months of mild weather for establishment and avoids subjecting divisions to hot, dry summer weather. Before you divide plants, prepare the areas where the divisions are to be transplanted.

Division isn't just a solution for increasing your plants. Some perennials become unhealthy when they grow too large. Division helps to rejuvenate these plants.

Steps for Dividing

Tools & Materials: Scissors, garden fork or spade, knife, trowel, mulch **Difficulty:** Moderate

1 The day before you intend to divide the plant, water it well to make the soil easier to dig. If necessary cut back the foliage to 6 to 10 inches to make the plant more manageable.

2 Using a garden fork or spade, dig up the whole plant with as many of its roots intact as possible. This is easier if you work in a circle around the plant.

3 Pull the roots apart by hand, cut them with a knife, or pry them apart with two garden forks. Divide them so that each piece has a stem or growing point and a supply of roots.

4 As quickly as possible, plant the new divisions. Position the crowns at the depth they were previously growing. Water and mulch well, and fertilize if necessary.

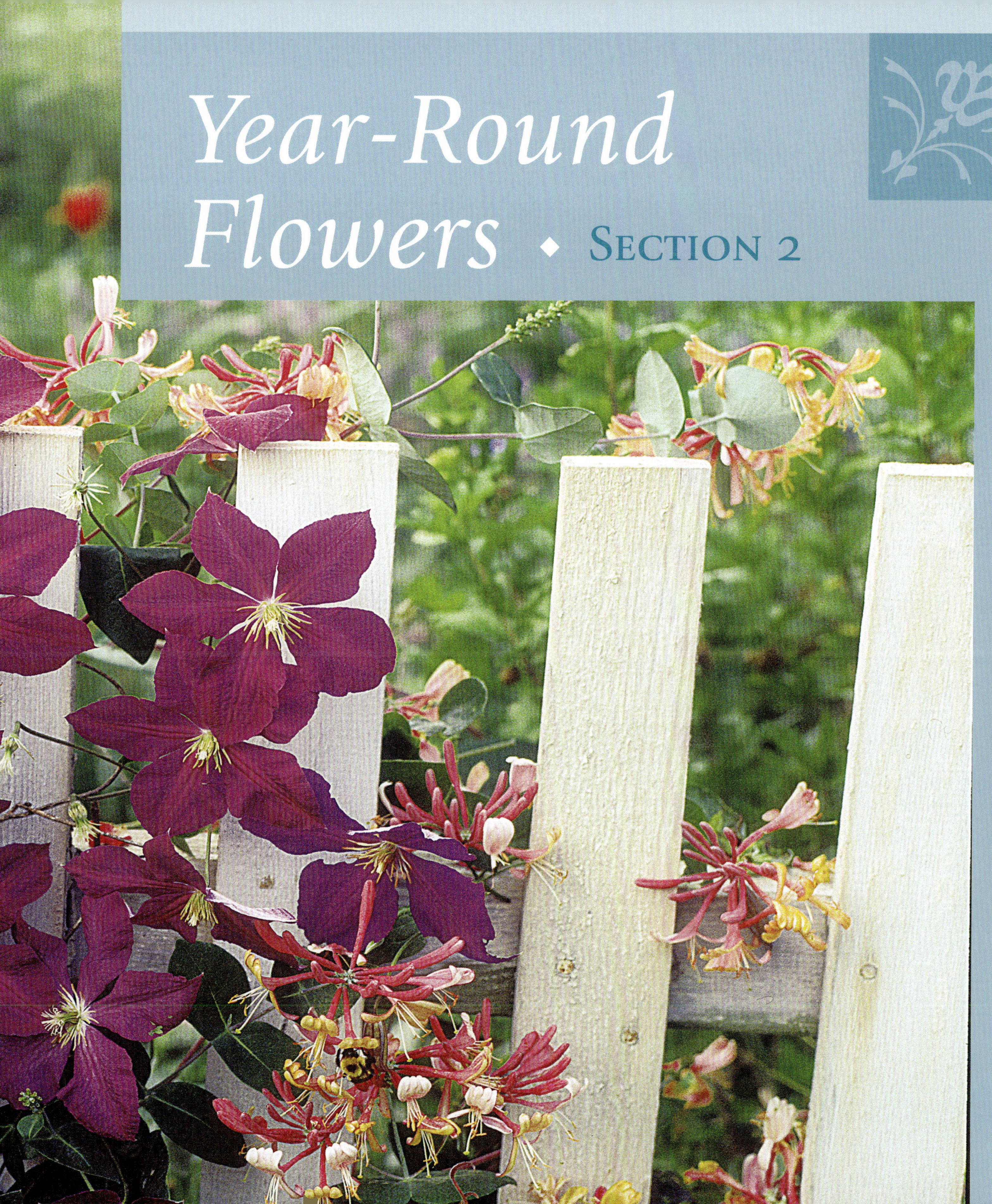

Year-Round Flowers ◆ Section 2

Chapter 5 *Spring*

All gardeners' hearts beat faster in spring. Buds swell on trees and shrubs as the days grow longer. And gardeners everywhere rouse themselves from winter's lethargy, eager for the first day the garden soil is dry enough to work.

In the flower garden, spring is the season of bulbs and perennials. It begins with snowdrops, crocuses, daffodils, and narcissus and finishes with peonies and poppies. As spring melts into summer, perennial gardens are washed with color that increases and intensifies as the season advances. The perennial garden reaches its peak in late spring and early summer and becomes the focus of most gardeners' attention. Much of the information in this chapter concerns perennial flowers, although flowering shrubs such as azaleas, forsythias, rhododendrons, pieris, and lilacs also contribute color to spring landscapes.

Although most spring gardening activity occurs outdoors, the indoor garden also needs some care at this time of year. Houseplants that have been dormant over the winter begin to grow actively again and so need more water, light, and fertilizer than they did during the winter. Then too, some houseplants come into bloom in the spring.

It's an understatement to say there's plenty to do, indoors and out, as the spring season gets under way.

Blue forget-me-nots and white peony- flowered tulips make a lovely spring combination, opposite.

Spring Colors

Outdoor gardening really begins in late winter, when the first crocuses and snowdrops poke their heads above the snow. Those late-winter bulbs bloom mostly in white, yellow, or purple. Yellow and white remain much in evidence as spring's palette progresses with an assortment of soft lavenders, blues, pinks, and roses. Many spring colors are light and soft, with pastels in abundance. Most gardens also offer some strong reds (tulips, for example), bright yellows (daffodils and forsythias), and violets. But spring is also a time of gentler colors—entirely fitting for a world newly reborn.

Daffodils and forsythias bring spring indoors.

Bulbs and shrubs of late winter are joined by early spring bloomers—daffodils and narcissus—and then succeeded by tulips and hyacinths. After the bulbs' glowing rivers of color fade, herbaceous perennials take over. Irises, columbines, peonies, poppies, and other perennials supply color between bulbs and roses and summer annuals in many gardens. In warm climates, cool-weather annuals bloom in a host of bright colors in early spring.

Of course, to show spring flowers for best effect it helps to start with a well-designed garden. Before you begin gardening, first consider where to locate your garden and how to design and lay it out, referring to the descriptions on pages 14–27. With those design principles in mind, you can then begin considering spring flower colors.

Flowers in Gardens & Arrangements

Spring's soft colors can be mixed and matched in many ways. If you decide on a single-color garden, you might consider a small all-white bed of white cultivars of dianthus, bleeding heart, and hyacinth. If your taste runs more to blues and purples, try deep purple pansies with sky blue forget-me-nots—a combination that is especially lovely beneath the branches of pale purple lilacs or wisterias. Many pink-and-blue partnerships are possible, such as salmon pink Oriental poppies with purple clustered bellflowers or deep blue irises in late spring, or lavender blue Jacob's ladder with the dainty pink lockets of bleeding heart. You can create a heavenly pink-and-purple garden with pink varieties of Oriental poppies, lupines, and bearded irises. If you like blue-and-yellow schemes, try forget-me-nots with yellow tulips and johnny-jump-ups, perhaps, or light yellow narcissus behind sky blue Siberian squills. If you like red and yellow together, consider mixing the red-and-yellow flowers of American columbines with basket-of-gold or the rich golden yellow of globeflowers.

Yellow abounds in many spring gardens, opposite. In addition to this exuberant mass of basket-of-gold, this garden contains purple rockcress, multicolored tulips, and red and pink azaleas.

Bouquets & Arrangements. Spring colors can also be combined in innumerable ways in bouquets and indoor arrangements. Classic spring flowers for arrangements include daffodils, tulips, irises, Oriental poppies, peonies, and lilacs. Small branches from flowering shrubs and ornamental and fruit trees make nice additions. Besides the popular forsythias and lilacs, try blossoms of flowering quince, viburnum, apple, cherry, dogwood, apricot, plum, or magnolia. A beautiful spring bouquet can be as simple as a big bunch of daffodils and narcissus, or pansies or sweet peas in assorted colors. Later in the season you can make lavish, sweetly fragrant arrangements using the large flowers of peonies and lilacs. Or try creating charming miniature bouquets in tiny vases filled with purple and white violets, blue grape hyacinth, sprigs of pink bleeding heart, and fragrant white lily-of-the-valley.

The "Spring Palette" table beginning on page 76, lists spring flowers by color. Use it to help you select plants that bloom in your favorite colors and to decide upon different color combinations. The table also shows you which kinds of flowers come in more than one color. The "Seasonal Blooming Schedules," beginning on page 284, will give you more information on these same plants and many others, including when they bloom and how tall they grow.

Seeking Inspiration

Looking at other people's gardens is one of the best ways to get ideas for your own. Visit public gardens, too, and analyze the color schemes and plant groupings. Although the plantings in public gardens are usually on a grand scale, you can still find plant pairings to scale down and adapt for your own backyard. Some public gardens have "idea gardens" full of small-scale plantings designed to inspire home gardeners.

The Spring Palette

Plants noted below in ***boldface*** type are described in full detail in "Flowers for Spring Gardens," page 78. Some plants listed here flower in late spring and well into summer and so are profiled in "Flowers for Summer Gardens," page 136. In all plant listings in this book, plants are arranged alphabetically by scientific (botanical) name.

RED FLOWERS

Oriental poppy

Abutilon (flowering maple)
***Anemone* (windflower)**
***Aquilegia* (columbine)**
Bougainvillea
Centaurea (sweet sultan)
Chaenomeles (Japanese quince)
***Dianthus* (garden pinks)**
***Episcia* (flame violet)**
Euphorbia (crown of thorns)
Fritillaria (crown imperial)
Fuchsia
Geum
***Heuchera* (coral bells)**
Hibiscus
Iris
Ixora (flame of the woods)
Lathyrus (sweet pea)
Manettia (firecracker vine)
***Papaver* (Oriental poppy)**
Ranunculus (Persian buttercup)
Rhododendron (azalea and rhododendron)
Saponaria (soapwort)
Tulipa (tulip)
***Viola* (pansy)**

PINK FLOWERS

'Guy Yerkes' rhododendron

***Anemone* (windflower)**
***Aquilegia* (columbine)**
Arabis (rockcress)
Armeria (sea pink)
Astrantia (masterwort)
Bergenia
Bougainvillea
Catharanthus (Madagascar periwinkle)
Centaurea (bachelor's button, sweet sultan)
Clematis
***Dianthus* (garden pinks)**
***Dicentra* (bleeding heart)**
Epimedium
Erica (heath)
Erythronium
Euphorbia (crown of thorns)
Fuchsia
***Geranium* (cranesbill)**
***Hatiora* (Easter cactus)**
***Heuchera* (coral bells)**
Heucherella
Hibiscus
Hyacinthoides (Spanish bluebell)
***Hyacinthus* (hyacinth)**
Incarvillea (hardy gloxinia)
Iris
Ixora (flame of the woods)
Justicia
Lathyrus (perennial pea, sweet pea)
Lonicera (honeysuckle)
***Malus* (crabapple)**
***Paeonia* (peony)**
Pelargonium (geranium)
Phlox
***Primula* (primrose)**
Ranunculus (Persian buttercup)
Rhododendron (azalea, rhododendron)
Saponaria (soapwort)
Saxifraga (saxifrage)
Thalictrum (meadowrue)
Tradescantia (spiderwort)
***Tulipa* (tulip)**

ORANGE FLOWERS

'Ballerina' tulip

Clivia
Epimedium
Geum
Hibiscus
Iris
***Papaver* (Oriental poppy, Iceland poppy)**
Ranunculus (Persian buttercup)
***Rhododendron* (azalea)**
Trollius (globeflower)
***Tulipa* (tulip)**
***Viola* (pansy)**

YELLOW FLOWERS

Marsh marigold

Acacia
Adonis
Alchemilla (lady's mantle)
***Aquilegia* (columbine)**
***Aurinia* (basket-of-gold)**
Caltha (marsh marigold)
Centaurea (sweet sultan)
Chrysogonum (goldenstar)
Cornus (cornelian cherry)
Crocus
Doronicum (leopard's bane)
Draba
Epimedium
Erythronium
Euphorbia (crown of thorns)
Forsythia
Fritillaria
Hemerocallis (daylily)
Hibiscus
***Hyacinthus* (hyacinth)**
Iris
Jasminum (winter jasmine)
Lachenalia (cape cowslip)
Lathyrus (sweet pea)
Linaria (toadflax)
Lonicera (honeysuckle)
Lysimachia
Meconopsis (Welsh poppy)
Moraea (butterfly iris)
***Narcissus* (daffodil, narcissus)**
Nemesia
***Papaver* (Iceland poppy)**
Potentilla (cinquefoil)

***Primula* (primrose)**
Ranunculus (Persian buttercup)
Stylophorum (celandine poppy)
Thermopsis (Carolina lupine)
Trollius (globeflower)
***Tulipa* (tulip)**
Tussilago (coltsfoot)
Uvularia (merrybells)
***Viola* (pansy)**

BLUE FLOWERS

Siberian squill

Amsonia (blue star)
***Anemone* (windflower)**
***Aquilegia* (columbine)**
Baptisia (false indigo)
***Brunnera* (Siberian bugloss)**
Centaurea (bachelor's button, mountain bluet)
Chionodoxa (glory-of-the-snow)
***Geranium* (cranesbill)**
Hyacinthoides (Spanish bluebell)
***Hyacinthus* (hyacinth)**
Ipheion
Iris
Jacaranda
Mertensia (Virginia bluebell)
Muscari (grape hyacinth)
***Myosotis* (forget-me-not)**
Nemesia
Nigella (love-in-a-mist)
Omphalodes (navelwort)
Phlox
Polemonium (Jacob's ladder)
***Primula* (primrose)**
Pulmonaria (lungwort)
Puschkinia
Rosmarinus (rosemary)
Scilla (Siberian squill)
Veronica
Vinca (periwinkle)
***Viola* (pansy)**

PURPLE FLOWERS

'Universal True Blue' pansy

***Anemone* (pasqueflower, windflower)**
Campanula (bellflower)
Centaurea (sweet sultan)
Clematis
Crocus
Daphne
Erica (heath)
Erythronium
***Geranium* (cranesbill)**
Helleborus (Lenten rose)
***Hyacinthus* (hyacinth)**
Iris
Lathyrus (sweet pea)
Mertensia (Virginia bluebell)
Nemesia
Phlox
***Primula* (primrose)**
Pulmonaria (lungwort)
Rhododendron
Syringa (lilac)
Thalictrum (meadowrue)
Tradescantia (spiderwort)
***Tulipa* (tulip)**
Valeriana (valerian)
***Viola* (violet, pansy)**
Wisteria

WHITE FLOWERS

'Winter Gold' crabapple

Abeliophyllum (Korean forsythia)
Allium (flowering onion)
***Anemone* (windflower)**
***Aquilegia* (columbine)**
Arabis (rockcress)
Astrantia (masterwort)
Baptisia (false indigo)
Bougainvillea
Calochortus
Catharanthus (Madagascar periwinkle)
Cerastium (snow-in-summer)
Clematis
***Convallaria* (lily-of-the-valley)**
Crocus
***Dianthus* (garden pinks)**
***Dicentra* (bleeding heart, Dutchman's breeches)**
Dodecatheon (shooting star)
Epimedium
Erica (heath)
Fothergilla
Fritillaria (fritillary)
Fuchsia
Galium (sweet woodruff)
Gardenia
***Hatiora* (Easter cactus)**
Helleborus (Lenten rose)
Hepatica
Hesperocallis (desert lily)
Hibiscus
Hyacinthoides (Spanish bluebell)
***Hyacinthus* (hyacinth)**
***Iberis* (candytuft)**
Iris
Lachenalia (cape cowslip)
Lathyrus (sweet pea, perennial pea)
Ledebouria
Leucojum (snowflake)
Lilium (Easter lily)
Lonicera (honeysuckle)
***Malus* (crabapple)**
Magnolia (star magnolia)
***Narcissus* (narcissus, daffodil)**
Nemesia
Nigella (love-in-a-mist)
Ornithogalum (star of Bethlehem)
***Paeonia* (peony)**
***Papaver* (Iceland poppy)**
Philadelphus (mock orange)
Phlox
Polygonatum (Solomon's seal)
***Primula* (primrose)**
Pulmonaria (lungwort)
Rhododendron (azalea, rhododendron)
Rosa (Cherokee rose)
Saponaria (soapwort)
Saxifraga (saxifrage)
Shortia (Oconee bells)
Smilacina (false Solomon's seal)
Syringa (lilac)
Thalictrum (meadowrue)
Trillium
Tulipa (tulip)
Viburnum
***Viola* (violet, pansy)**
Weigela
Wisteria
Zantedeschia (calla lily)
Zephyranth

Peony

Flowers for Spring Gardens

In a book this size there are far too many springtime flowers to mention, let alone describe. This chapter presents profiles on the stars of spring throughout most parts of the continental United States and southern Canada. Other excellent plants are mentioned in the "Spring Palette" and in the book's Appendix, "Seasonal Blooming Schedules," beginning on page 284.

The following spring-flowering plants are listed alphabetically by their scientific (botanical) names. For each plant you'll find descriptive information, suggestions for using the plant in the garden, and basic guidance on planting and care. Most plants adapt to a range of acidity or alkalinity. For plants with a special need for a particular pH range, the preference is noted.

Anemone / **Windflower**

Grecian windflower

Anemones belong to the buttercup family, and different species open their bright red, pink, purple, or white flowers in spring or fall. Grecian windflower (*Anemone blanda*) has tuberous roots, with pink, blue, or white flowers on 6- to 8-inch plants in early spring. Give it full sun and a spot in the front of a bed or border in Zones 6–10. Snowdrop anemone (*A. sylvestris*) is 12 inches tall, with white flowers in spring; it's a good plant for woodland gardens in Zones 3–9.

Anemones grow best in well-drained soil that contains plenty of organic matter. They do not tolerate drought well, so water them during spells of dry weather. Start Grecian windflower in fall; soak the dried, buttonlike tubers before planting at a depth of 2 to 3 inches. Set out plants of snowdrop anemone in spring in cooler climates, in either spring or fall in warm climates.

Another anemone, the late-blooming Japanese anemone, is described in Chapter 7.

Aquilegia / **Columbine**

Gracefully spurred columbines bloom for four to six weeks in late spring and early summer. The flowers are borne atop slender stalks arising from a low mound of scalloped leaves. Hybrids are available in many shades of purple, blue, pink, rose, red, and deep yellow. Grow columbines in the middle of beds and borders. The plants are perennial but tend to be short-lived and so need to be replaced after a few years. Often they will self-sow and hybridize with one another. Columbines vary in their hardiness. Most species are hardy in Zones 3–10, hybrids often in Zones 5–10.

'McKana Giant' Columbine

The American columbine (*Aquilegia canadensis*) is a lovely native wildflower in the eastern part of North America. The dainty flowers have yellow sepals and red spurs, and dance on top of slender 1- to 2-foot stems. The plants self-sow readily and tend to spread each year.

The Rocky Mountain columbine (*A. caerulea*), Colorado's state flower, has blue blossoms with white centers and grows about 2 feet tall.

Grow columbines in full sun to partial shade, in moist but well-drained soil. They average 2 to 3 feet tall and should be spaced 10 to 18 inches apart. Sow seeds or purchase plants locally or through the mail.

Aurinia / **Basket-of-Gold**

Basket-of-gold (*Aurinia saxatilis*) is a standard of the spring rock garden and a lovely edging plant for beds and borders. It is also handsome in containers. A low, creeping plant about 6 to 12 inches tall, basket-of-gold has gray-green foliage and bright yellow flowers in early spring. A few cultivars

Basket-of-gold

offer flowers in more delicate pastel shades. These plants are hardy in Zones 4–9.

For best results, grow in full sun and well-drained soil of average fertility. Space plants 8 to 12 inches apart.

Brunnera / **Siberian Bugloss**

Siberian bugloss (*Brunnera macrophylla*) is a tough, undemanding perennial that produces sprays of heavenly little sky blue flowers that resemble forget-me-nots. The flowers bloom in mid- to late spring but leave behind them the plant's interesting mounds of large, deep green, heart-shaped leaves. The stems are covered with bristly hairs, so you might want to wear gloves when working around the plants. Siberian bugloss grows 1 to 1½ feet tall, spreads rapidly, and is hardy in Zones 3–10.

Plant Siberian bugloss 1 to 1½ feet apart in full or partial shade or in full sun; provide deep, moist, well-drained soil containing lots of organic matter. Propagate new plants in spring or fall by division, root cuttings, or from seed.

Siberian bugloss

Convallaria / **Lily-of-the-Valley**

Lily-of-the-valley

Lily-of-the-valley *(Convallaria majalis)* is a carefree perennial with sweet-scented white flowers. Its waxy bell-shaped flowers dance along slender little stems in late spring. The large, elliptical leaves, about 8 inches tall, remain after the flowers are gone and hold up until late in summer, when they begin to turn brown and die back.

Lily-of-the-valley is hardy in Zones 3–9 and quite easy to grow, spreading rapidly once established. Grow it as a ground cover, especially in shady areas. Lily-of-the-valley thrives in woodsy conditions—moist (but well-drained) humusy soil in partial shade or filtered sunlight. Plant the little pointed pips horizontally, approximately 2 inches deep and about 4 inches apart. Unlike most spring-blooming bulbs, the lily-of-the-valley is best when planted in the spring.

Crocus / **Crocus**

Dutch hybrid crocuses bloom in early spring, a bit later than the earliest spring-blooming crocuses. Their chalice-shaped flowers are larger than most of the species, but the color range is typical of all crocuses: deep purple, lavender, lilac, golden yellow, yellow-orange, white, and white striped with purple. The plants grow 4 to 6 inches tall; they are hardy in Zones 3–9.

Grow crocuses at the front of beds or borders, beneath the branches of spring-flowering trees and shrubs, or indoors for winter flowers. The corms spread quickly if the grassy leaves are left in place until they die back naturally. Crocuses need lots of sun; if you place them in a spot that is sunny and protected, they will bloom a couple of weeks earlier than normal.

Plant crocuses in early fall in any average garden soil. Set the corms 4 inches deep, in groups of six or more. When the plants become crowded after several years and produce fewer flowers, lift and divide the corms in early fall or late spring after the foliage has died back.

Crocus

Dianthus / **Garden Pinks**

Garden pinks

The clove-scented flowers of the genus *Dianthus* are versatile and delightful in the garden. Various species are annual, biennial, or perennial. Collectively they are known as garden pinks, and most bloom in late spring or early summer. All the garden pinks make fine cut flowers with their spicy-sweet scents and cheerful combinations of colors. Flowers bloom in shades from deep rose and various pinks to white; petals are often marked with contrasting colors. Hardiness varies, but most are hardy in Zones 4–10. If you live where winters are severe, protect your pinks with a covering of evergreen boughs or other loose mulch.

Plants range in height from 6 to 18 inches, and can be spaced 10 to 15 inches apart. Generally speaking, they need well-drained soil with a slightly alkaline pH and full sun. Start from seed or purchase plants. The perennials are relatively short-lived and should be propagated every few years by dividing the clumps in spring, or by layering, or by taking cuttings midsummer. Shearing or cutting off dead flowers sometimes coaxes garden pinks into blooming a second time.

Dicentra / **Bleeding Heart**

Bleeding heart

The familiar, old-fashioned bleeding heart *(Dicentra spectabilis)* produces distinctive rosy heart-shaped flowers that dangle from their slender stems like a string of lockets. (An all-white form is also available.) This plant blooms from late spring into early summer and is hardy in Zones 3–9. The plants grow 2 to 2½ feet tall and should be planted 2 feet apart.

Fringed bleeding heart

Fringed bleeding heart *(D. eximia)* produces a neat clump of lacy foliage. It starts blooming in late spring and continues sporadically in summer and fall. The flowers are usually cherry pink; different cultivars offer a range of colors from crimson to white. Fringed bleeding heart grows to about 1½ feet tall. Space plants 12 inches apart.

Both species prefer partial shade and rich, moist, humusy soil. The plants appreciate a topdressing of compost or manure in fall. Propagate by division in early spring or from root cuttings taken in early summer.

Flame violet

Episcia / Flame Violet

Flame violets belong to the same plant family as their better-known relatives, the African violets. Decorative foliage makes the many cultivars of flame violets handsome houseplants all year, but in spring they burst into bloom, producing lots of tube-shaped flowers that flare into five petals. The plants have a semitrailing habit and look good in either hanging baskets or standard flowerpots.

Give flame violets an indoor location with bright light but no direct sun, plenty of humidity, and warm temperatures: 70° to 75°F during the day, with a 5°F drop at night.

Plant them in a mix of equal parts of vermiculite, perlite, and peat moss, or use a soilless potting mix designed for African violets. Keep the soil mix evenly moist but not soggy. Place the pots on a "pebble tray" to help keep the humidity level high around the plants. (A pebble tray is a shallow tray with a layer of pebbles in the bottom; keep water in the tray below the pebbles, not deep enough to submerge the stones.) When the plants are growing actively in spring and summer, feed them every two weeks with a diluted all-purpose houseplant fertilizer. Plants are easily propagated by rooting leaf cuttings or separating offsets.

Gardenia / Cape Jasmine

A classic florist flower that is a popular gift on Mother's Day, the gardenia (formerly *Gardenia jasminoides*, now *G. augusta*) is grown outdoors in the South and California and indoors in cooler climates. A woody shrub growing 2 to 5 feet tall, its glossy dark green leaves beautifully set off the large, creamy-white, intensely fragrant flowers. Outdoors, they bloom all spring and summer; indoors they may bloom in either season, but mostly in spring.

Outdoors, plant gardenias 4 to 5 feet apart in rich, moist soil with an acid pH. Feed the plants every other month during the growing season with the same kind of fertilizer used for azaleas and camellias. (This fertilizer, specially formulated for acid-soil plants, is widely available at garden centers.) Gardenias make good foundation plants in warmer climates.

Growing gardenias indoors can be tricky but is richly rewarding, especially when the flowers waft their sweet perfume all through the house. Indoor gardenias like cool temperatures (60° to 65°F), bright light without direct sun, even moisture, and ample humidity when the plants are setting buds. They cannot tolerate drafts or sudden sharp changes in temperature, both of which cause the buds to drop before they have a chance to open. The plants generally tend to bloom better when their roots are potbound.

A good potting mix for gardenias is one part potting soil, two parts compost or peat moss, and one part perlite, or use a soilless mix for African violets. Add about a teaspoon of rock phosphate to the soil in each pot and feed with an all-purpose fertilizer or a fertilizer for acid-soil plants every two weeks during spring and summer when they are actively growing.

After an indoor plant finishes blooming, prune it back and allow it to rest over the winter. Stop fertilizing, and gradually cut back on watering to let the soil become dry to the touch between waterings.

Outdoors, fertilize once a month during the growing season with a fertilizer for acid-soil plants. Do any necessary pruning after the plant finishes blooming. Plants flower in the summer when grown outdoors.

Cape jasmine

Cranesbill

Geranium / Cranesbill

Hardy geraniums, also called cranesbills, are perennial flowers—not to be confused with the tender geraniums so popular in the summer garden and as houseplants, which belong to the genus *Pelargonium*. If you want to read about that kind of geranium, see page 99. The plants discussed here are hardy outdoor perennials.

Cranesbills are hardy, adaptable plants, most of them relatively low-growing. Many make good ground covers or additions to a rock garden. They are also attractive in the front of beds and borders. Most cranesbills start blooming in early to midspring and continue through most of the summer. A range of pretty colors is available, and they harmonize beautifully with many other spring and summer flowers.

Hardy geraniums are widely grown in Europe and are becoming better known in North America. Their durability and ease of cultivation make them worthy additions to any garden. Hardy in Zones 4 or 5 to 9 or 10, depending on species, cranesbills tolerate hot weather as well as colder conditions.

Most cranesbills will bloom in either full sun or partial shade. They are not fussy about soil—they thrive in any well-drained soil of average fertility. Plants can generally withstand dry spells, so long as the drought is not too prolonged or severe. Set plants 8 to 12 inches apart. Propagate cranesbills by division in early spring or in autumn.

Hatiora / Easter Cactus

For spring bloom, you can count on houseplants in the Easter cactus genus (*Hatiora gaertneri* and *H. rosea*, formerly *Rhipsalidopsis gaertneri* and *R. rosea*). The Easter cactus has jointed stems made up of flat, oval segments. The stems form many branches, growing upright when young and then drooping over as the stems grow longer. The plant as a whole has a gracefully arching form. Cultivars are available with flowers in various shades of pink, rose, and red.

Grow Easter cactus in a potting mix that is one part potting soil, two parts peat moss, and one part perlite or builder's sand. Add a tablespoon of rock phosphate to each quart of potting mix. The plant does well in an east or west window, with a temperature around 70°F. When the plant is growing actively, it needs abundant moisture and high humidity. Feed with a balanced all-purpose fertilizer once a month except when the plant is dormant. When flower buds form, fertilize with a high-potassium plant food throughout the blooming period.

After Easter cactus has finished blooming, it enters a brief dormant period for about a month. During this time stop fertilizing, and water only enough to keep the plant from shriveling. Repot the plant in fresh potting mix when it begins to grow again. Propagate after the plants finish blooming in the spring or summer by rooting pieces of the stem.

Easter cactus

Coral bells

Heuchera / Coral Bells

Airy, graceful coral bells (*Heuchera sanguinea*, *H.* × *briziodes* and hybrids) come into bloom in very late spring, and most keep flowering until midsummer or even later. The plants are characterized by tall, slender stems of tiny bell-shaped flowers, usually red, arising from low mounds of rounded, ivy-shaped leaves. An exciting, relatively new group of hybrids has been bred for colorful and beautifully variegated leaves; these usually have small white flowers. Plant coral bells in beds and borders, rock gardens, or massed as a ground cover. The red-flowered varieties are attractive to butterflies. These plants are hardy in Zones 3–10.

Coral bells grow in either full sun or partial shade, but most cultivars prefer a bit of shade. They make themselves at home in a variety of soils, though they prefer a slightly acid pH and good drainage. Plant coral bells a foot apart, and be sure to cover the whole rootstock, leaving only the crown exposed. The plants appreciate a topdressing of compost once a year and a mulch in winter to prevent heaving. Propagate them by division every four years or so, in the autumn or early spring.

Hyacinthus / Hyacinth

Most hyacinths found in North American gardens are Dutch hybrid bulbs (grown in the Netherlands) and bred from the common garden species, *Hyacinthus orientalis*. The color range for hyacinths has expanded beyond the traditional pink, white, and blue to include red, yellow, deep purple, and even apricot. The intense, sweet fragrance of the flowers provokes decided reactions—you either love the scent or quite the contrary.

Dutch hyacinths reach slightly less than a foot in height. Plant them in beds and borders, or in containers.

Hyacinths are easy to force into bloom indoors. (See page 187 for information on forcing bulbs.) They can be grown for midspring flowers in the outdoor garden in most areas except northern New England and high altitude locations. In cold regions the bulbs should be lifted and stored indoors during the winter, then replanted in early spring. Gardeners elsewhere can plant the bulbs in midautumn, about 9 inches apart and 4 to 6 inches deep. The plant will grow in any well-drained soil of average fertility.

'Blue Delft' hyacinth

Iberis / Candytuft

Candytuft comes in both annual and perennial forms, both of which are versatile, easy-to-grow plants with a variety of uses in the garden. Annual candytuft (*Iberis umbellata*) bears flat-topped or rounded clusters of dainty flowers in white or shades of pink and lavender. It blooms lustily from spring right through summer. The perennial species (*I. sempervirens*) is hardy in Zones 3–10; its bright white flowers appear in late spring into early summer. Use candytufts in the front of a bed or border, in the rock garden, to edge sidewalks and paths, or next to driveways.

Candytufts prosper in full sun and rich, well-drained soil. They grow 6 to 12 inches tall, and can be spaced 1 to 1½ feet apart. Although they can tolerate some dryness, they bloom better with plenty of moisture. Water them during dry spells to maintain the best display. Shearing back annual candytufts after the first flush of flowers fades (there are too many to pick off individually) will prompt them to bloom again. Sow seeds of annual candytuft outdoors in early spring; purchase plants of the perennial type.

'Fantasia' annual candytuft

Iris / Iris

For centuries, elegant irises have been a favorite among gardeners and artists. The best known and most widely grown irises are the bearded, Dutch, Siberian, and Japanese types; southern gardeners also grow Louisiana irises. Early-blooming bulbous irises, which can be forced indoors for winter flowers, are discussed on page 188. Generally, irises bloom in spring to early summer, and they are a feature of many late spring gardens. Most grow from rhizomes, some from bulbs, and all are distinguished by their straight, tall, swordlike or grassy leaves that remain an attractive feature throughout the entire summer.

Many irises grow best in the North, some only in the South, and a few others—like the flamboyant Pacific Coast iris—are generally grown only on the West Coast where they are native.

Individual types and varieties have a short blooming period—one to three weeks—so plant several types to extend the season. Plant irises in their own beds, along walks or driveways, in front of a hedge or wall, or in clumps in mixed flower gardens. The shapes of the flowers are bold, so use them carefully.

All irises are heavy feeders and like well-drained soil that's rich in organic matter and nutrients. They need full sun for at least six hours a day.

'Stellar Lights' bearded iris

Siberian iris

'Inner Beauty' Louisiana iris

Bearded irises, the most widely grown types, have been extensively bred to provide a stunning range of colors including white, pale ivory to deep yellow and gold, apricot, orange, pink, magenta, maroon, brownish-red, lavender, orchid, blue, blue-violet, purple, and deep purple-black. Some, called reblooming bearded irises, flower in spring and again in summer if conditions are right. In an open garden, shorter bearded types are easiest to work with. The tall bearded cultivars, which may grow 4 feet or taller, need to be next to a wall or other windbreak or their stems may snap in high wind. Border and intermediate types are perfect for small gardens. Bearded irises will grow in Zones 3 to 10, though they need partial shade in hot climates. Lousiana irises are often a better choice in the Southeast.

Plant bearded irises when the blooming season is over in midsummer in the North; in the South, wait until the hottest part of the summer has passed. This is also the time to divide and replant crowded clumps. To plant, dig a deep hole and make a mound of soil in the center. The top of the mound should be level with the surrounding soil. Set each rhizome horizontally on top of the mound and spread the roots down over the mound. Fill the hole with soil, firm it around the roots, and water thoroughly. After planting, you'll need to water only during prolonged dry spells. Plant tall bearded irises 2 to 2½ feet apart, standard dwarfs 1 foot apart, and miniature dwarfs 8 inches apart. Tall bearded iris-

Types of Iris

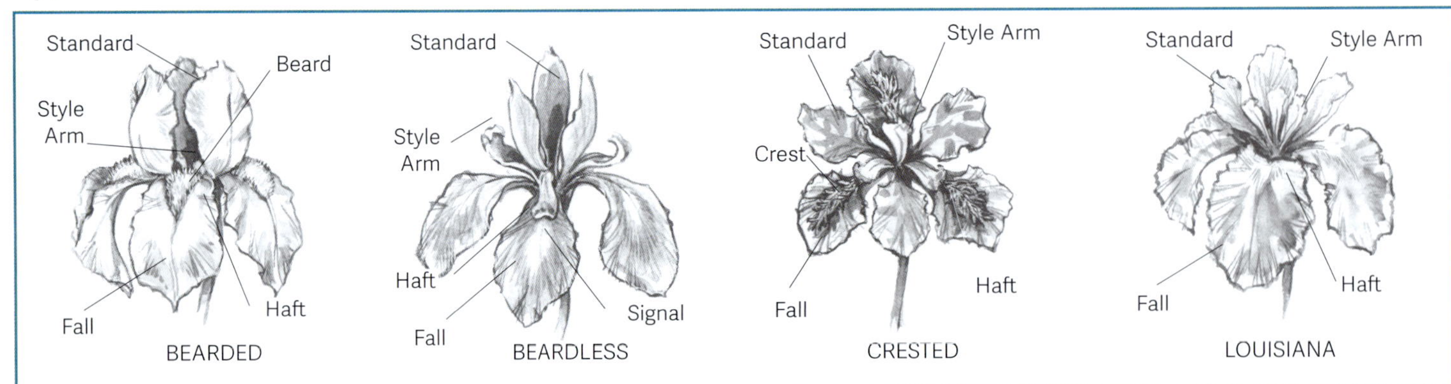

es need to be divided after three or four years. When dividing old clumps, discard the old central parts of the rhizomes and replant just the younger outer parts.

Siberian irises (*I. sibirica*) are late-blooming beardless types in shades of blue, violet, purple, rose, and white. The plants grow 2 to 3 feet tall. Siberian irises combine beautifully in the garden with peonies, Oriental poppies (especially in shades of pink and salmon), campanulas, foxgloves, and early-blooming daylilies in yellow or apricot shades. They are hardy in Zones 4–10, easy to grow, and don't need to be divided often. The plants have vigorous root systems, so plant them in deep holes with compost in the bottom. Firm the soil well around the rhizomes when planting, and keep the bed watered until the plants establish themselves. Be sure to pick off spent flowers to prevent the formation of seed pods, which are a favorite residence of various insect pests.

Louisiana irises, hardy in Zones 4–9, are native to wetlands in the southern United States and are especially popular there. They are beardless, and hybrids bloom in an extensive color range, including white and shades of yellow, orange, red, pink, blue, violet, purple, and brown. The plants grow from 6 inches to 4 feet tall, depending on cultivar, and thrive in moist to wet soils. Plant the rhizomes in the fall, about 2 inches deep, and propagate new plants by division.

Japanese irises (*I. ensata*) are also beardless, with large, wide-petaled flowers somewhat resembling orchids or peonies. The color range for hybrids is limited to blues, purples, and white, but the flowers may be beautifully patterned with contrasting veins, spots, splashes, or flushes of color. They bloom in late spring and early summer. Most grow 2½ to 4 or more feet tall. The plants are hardy in Zones 5–10 but may need winter protection in the North. Japanese irises like rich, slightly acid soil that is moist to wet in summer, but they do not like wet conditions in winter. Where summers are hot or when grown in beds and borders with other plants, they will need to be watered. Plant them so their crowns are 2 inches below the soil surface. Japanese irises need to be divided every three or four years. When dividing, keep three or four fans of leaves in each division.

Lupinus / Lupine

Lupine

Lupines belong to the pea family. So if you grow vegetables, the shape of the lupine flower will look familiar to you. Unlike peas, though, lupines gather their flowers into dense upright spikes and produce them in late spring to early summer in an assortment of pretty shades of pink, red, purple, lavender, blue, yellow, and white. Lupines grow 3 to 5 feet tall. Most are hardy in Zones 4–9.

Give lupines full sun, plenty of moisture, and well-drained soil that is reasonably rich in nutrients and organic matter. They tend not to like lime or manure. Space them 1 to 2 feet apart. If you live in an area buffeted by hot winds during the summer, shield your lupines from their drying effects with a good windbreak, and stake the tall stems.

Forget-me-not

Myosotis / Forget-Me-Not

The true forget-me-nots (*Myosotis* species) are the source of one of the most beautiful true blues in the plant world. They are all the more welcome because their dainty spring flowers combine handsomely with daffodils, tulips, azaleas, and other favorites of the season. They start blooming in mid- to late spring and continue into summer. There are both biennial and perennial species and several cultivars in different colors. Annual *M. sylvatica* often self-sows and is a biennial in many gardens. It grows 9 to 12 inches tall. The perennial species *M. scorpioides* is hardy in Zones 5–9 and grows 6 to 18 inches tall.

Forget-me-nots can be grown from seed or purchased plants; space 6 to 10 inches apart. You can grow them in either full sun or in partial shade, wherever the soil is damp.

Trumpet narcissus

'Molten Lava' small-cupped narcissus

There are many kinds of narcissus. Daffodils and narcissus can be grown in most climates, but different types do better in different places. In the far North, small-cupped, poeticus, and jonquil types work best. In the South, try small-cupped, jonquilla, triandrus, and tazetta types. Stay away from late-blooming varieties if you live in a warmer climate, because the weather will be too hot for them when they bloom.

Narcissus and daffodils are divided into 12 divisions according to flower type. The most popular of the 12 divisions are described below.

1. Trumpet narcissus are those with the classic "daffodil" shape—the central trumpet, the corona, is as long as, or longer than, the length of the outer petals (called the *perianth*). The flowers may be all yellow, all white, bicolored, or may have a yellow trumpet and white outer petals.

2. Large-cupped narcissus have central cups that are large, but not as long as trumpets. Flowers come in the full range of narcissus colors, including varieties with salmon, pink, or bright orange cups. Often the outer petals are a color different from the central cups.

3. Small-cupped narcissus come in the same colors and color combinations as large-cupped narcissus. In these cultivars the cup is smaller and substantially shorter than the length of the petals.

4. Double narcissus have either an extra set of outer petals or a double cup, or both.

5. Triandrus narcissus produce two or more flowers on each stem. Usually, their central cups are short and the outer petals curve backwards.

6. Cyclamineus narcissus are distinguished by their backward-curving petals. Their central cups are usually longer than those of triandrus types, and they produce only one flower per stem.

7. Jonquilla narcissus, the jonquils, often resemble the small-cupped types. They may produce one or more flowers per stem, and many are fragrant. These cultivars take hot weather better than other narcissus.

8. Tazetta narcissus have several to many (usually small) flowers per stem. This group includes the paperwhite narcissus that is so popular for indoor forcing, along with its relatives. Most are good for southern gardens. Several cultivars, including paperwhites, don't require chilling to bloom; these aren't hardy outdoors except in Zones 8–9.

9. Poeticus narcissus include both species and hybrids, all of them recognizable by large flat white petals and a contrasting small, flat central cup.

Plant narcissus bulbs in fall, at least a month before you expect the first frost, in soil with good drainage. Plant them one and one-half times as deep as the height

Types of Narcissus

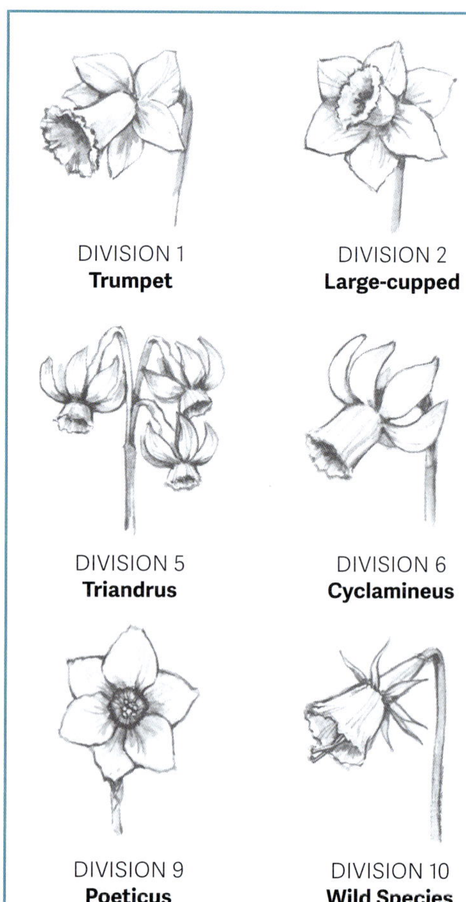

of the bulb. When in doubt, plant deeper rather than shallower. If you want the plants to naturalize without needing to divide the bulbs often, set them deeper than normal—the plants won't spread as fast and will stay maintenance-free for a longer time. Feed the plants once a year with compost or an all-purpose fertilizer.

In beds and borders, narcissus need to be lifted and divided every four years or so. Dig the bulbs after the foliage dies back in late spring or early summer. Let them dry in the shade and don't divide them until the offsets break off easily. (Otherwise you risk damaging the bulbs.) You can replant the divided bulbs right away or store them until autumn in a cool, dry, well-ventilated place.

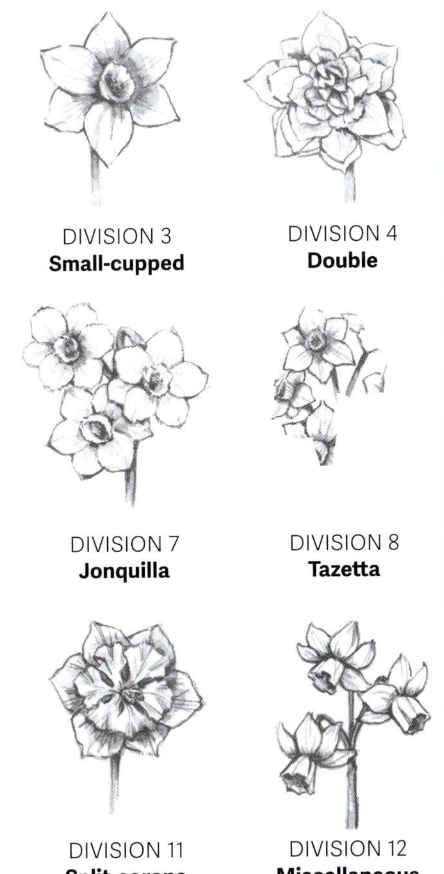

Paeonia / Peony

Peonies come in two forms—the familiar herbaceous kind (*Paeonia lactiflora*), which dies back to the ground each winter, and the less well known tree peony (*P. suffruticosa*), which has woody stems. Herbaceous peonies are among the most beloved garden flowers in cooler climates. They bloom in late spring to early summer, with huge single or double blossoms that are showy and often sweetly fragrant. Their flowers come in many shades of red, rose, and pink, as well as cream and white. Peonies are easy to grow, dependable bloomers that live long and ask little of the gardener. Because of their hardiness, peonies are good choices for northern gardeners. And because of their tenacity, they're good choices for lazy gardeners.

Peonies make marvelous cut flowers. When you cut peonies for indoor display, take the buds that are just beginning to open. If you notice ants crawling on the buds, don't be alarmed. They are there to eat a sweet syrup carried on the buds. Shake them off any flowers you cut to bring indoors.

'Festiva Maxima' peony

'Anne Rosse' peony (left) and 'Bowl of Beauty' peony (right)

Give your peonies full sun if you can, although they will perform reasonably well in partial shade. The flowers can be damaged by high winds, so put the plants in a sheltered spot. Peonies grow well in just about any average to good garden soil. The one thing they can't tolerate is wet feet; the soil must be well drained. They prefer a pH that is slightly—but not strongly—acid. Enriching the planting bed with compost, manure, and other sorts of organic matter will help to ensure good texture, drainage, and nutrition.

To plant new peonies, first dig the soil to a depth of 1½ feet and dig in some organic matter. Add a handful of rock phosphate or superphosphate for each plant. Position the plant so its crown is 1 to 2 inches below the soil surface. Avoid planting peonies too deep or they will not bloom, regardless of how much you fertilize them. Peonies resent being moved, so plant them where you'll want them for the long term. The only care they need is an annual feeding in early spring with a balanced, all-purpose fertilizer and perhaps staking to keep the heavy blossoms from bending their stems toward the ground. In autumn, cut back the stems to ground level. In northern gardens, a loose winter mulch is a good idea, particularly during the plants' first winter in the garden.

Propagate peonies in autumn by digging and dividing established plants. Dig the large, fleshy roots with a garden fork and cut them into pieces with three or more eyes. If you then replant the pieces at the recommended depth, you will enjoy more peonies the following spring.

Papaver / **Poppy**

There are both annual and perennial kinds of poppies; all of them are useful in the flower garden. The perennials, Iceland and Oriental poppies, are classic late spring to early summer flowers, blooming in a wide range of lovely colors. Iceland poppies may be red, pink, salmon, yellow, ivory, or white, and Oriental poppies come in shades of red, pink, orange, salmon, and rosy purple, as well as white. Annual Shirley poppies bloom a bit later, in shades of red, rose, pink, and salmon, with the petals shading to white.

Poppies are generally easy to grow in full sun or some light shade. They need well-drained sandy or loamy soil with plenty of organic matter. The plants do not like to be crowded. Poppies make lovely, long-stemmed cut flowers, their silky, ruffled petals resembling tissue paper. (See page 127 for information on searing stems of cut flowers.)

Iceland poppy

Oriental poppy

'Eighth Wonder' corn poppy

Iceland poppy *(Papaver nudicaule)* should be planted in early spring in most climates and in autumn in the South and Pacific Southwest. Sow seeds where plants are to grow, or space purchased plants 1 to 1½ feet apart. Plant bare-root Oriental poppies *(Papaver orientale)* 1 to 3 inches deep in the garden in late summer to early fall; plant container-grown plants in spring. Space them 1½ to 2 feet apart. They prefer a richer soil than Iceland poppies, but they, too, need good drainage. The tall plants may need staking too. Don't move or divide the plants for several years after planting in order to allow them a chance to establish themselves and develop their full beauty. Mulch the plants in fall with compost or well-rotted manure; in spring dig the old mulch into the soil to add nourishment.

Shirley poppy, or corn poppy *(P. rhoeas),* is a hardy annual that grows 1½ to 2 feet high. Shirley poppies don't take well to transplanting, so plant them directly in the garden where you want them to stay. Sow the seeds shallowly in autumn, except in the far North, where you should sow them in early spring. Although the plants will grow in poor soil, they'll do beautifully in good soil.

Phlox / **Phlox**

The best-known spring phlox is moss pinks *(Phlox subulata),* hardy in Zones 4–8. This low-growing ground cover spreads its cheerful magenta, pink, lavender, or white flowers over rock gardens and slopes in gardens all over North America. Trim back the plants after they finish blooming to maintain a neat shape.

Blue phlox or wild sweet William *(P. divaricata)* is hardy in Zones 4–9 and blooms with or just a bit later than moss pinks—in midspring. It grows 15 to 18 inches tall and, in addition to flowers, produces creeping stems that root and cause the plants to spread quickly. This species likes some shade and needs little or no attention.

Creeping phlox *(P. stolonifera),* as its name implies, has a creeping habit and spreads rapidly. Its flowering stems are about a foot high, and flowers appear in mid- to late spring. This species and its cultivars are hardy in Zones 3–9. Given a fairly rich, humusy soil that is moist but not soggy, creeping phlox will bloom vigorously. It is a good companion for spring bulbs and a handsome ground cover under both trees and shrubs.

Spring-blooming forms of phlox are generally fairly easy to grow. Most kinds

'Candy Stripe' moss pink

'Scarlet Flame' moss pink

will grow and bloom in any reasonably fertile garden soil, but for the strongest plants and best flowers, give them rich soil and plenty of water during dry spells. Start from purchased plants; all can be propagated by division or by rooting stem cuttings.

Primula / Primrose

Botanists have given primroses a family all their own, and it is a large one. There are more than 300 kinds of primroses. There are many hardy and delightful perennial cultivars to choose among, though some are certainly difficult to grow.

The key to growing primroses successfully is to remember that they are woodland natives. As such, they like partial shade and rich, moist soil with an acid pH. Give them plenty of humus (leaf mold and peat moss are good sources). Primroses are lovely planted under trees, alongside a stream or pool, and in the rock garden. In cooler climates, they bloom in early to midspring; in warmer climates, they are wonderful in winter gardens. Hardiness varies with species.

Lift and divide the plants every few years as soon as they finish blooming. You can also propagate new plants from seed in early to midautumn or in early spring. Sow the seeds indoors or in a cold frame, and move transplants to their permanent garden location once the danger of frost is past in spring.

There are many lovely primroses worthy of a place in the garden. Following are just a few choices. *Primula denticulata* grows 10 to 15 inches tall and produces clusters of lilac to purple flowers in early spring. *P. japonica* is a vigorous, hardy plant that reaches a height of about 2 feet. Sometimes called candelabra primrose, its clustered purple, pink, or white flowers are borne atop the tall stems in late spring. Polyanthus primroses *(P. × polyantha)* are the most widely grown of all. Their distinctive clustered flowers bloom in a spectrum of rich colors—golden yellow, pink, rose, red, magenta, blue-violet, and white—and most have a bright yellow eye. The small, broadleaved plants grow just 6 to 8 inches tall and bloom in early spring. They can also be grown indoors in cool, bright rooms for winter flowers.

'Gold Laced' polyanthus

Tulipa / Tulip

Tulips are available in thousands of cultivars. A tremendous selection of heights, colors, and blooming times is available, and there are several different flower forms. Most nursery catalogs divide tulips into groups according to their blooming time and flower form.

Unfortunately, many hybrid tulips are not reliably perennial or are short-lived, especially in warmer climates. So many gardeners prefer to treat them as annuals, digging and discarding the bulbs when they finish blooming, and replanting the space with summer annuals. Species tulips often last longer in the garden. Check nursery catalogs to learn more about the many kinds of tulips available.

Plant tulip bulbs in midfall (October in most places) in deep, rich, well-drained soil with a neutral to slightly alkaline pH. Give them lots of sun. Planting depth varies with the type and size of bulb. Follow the directions that come with the bulbs you buy.

The 15 official divisions of tulips are described below and are illustrated on the next page spread.

1. Single early tulips have classic, cup-shaped flowers in a host of colors, blooming in early to midspring; plants grow 6 to 18 inches tall.

2. Double early tulips bear full, double flowers in shades of red, pink, orange, yellow, and white. Despite their name, they bloom a little later than the single early types, though still early in the tulip season; plants grow 12 to 16 inches tall.

3. Triumph tulips bloom right in the middle of the tulip season, in midspring. Their color range is mostly red, white, and shades of pink. Many of the flowers have a second color flamed onto the petals. Plants grow 14 to 24 inches tall.

4. Darwin hybrids are large-flowered, tall-growing plants that bloom in midspring in a wide range of bright colors.

5. Single late-flowering tulips, which used to be called cottage tulips, are generally tall (24 to 30 inches) and usually have pointed petals and long stems. Confusingly, this group also includes what used to be called Darwin tulips, which are not the same as the newer Darwin hybrids.

6. Lily-flowered tulips have pointed petals and a gracefully curving shape. They come in colors representing the entire tulip range, except for dark purples and maroons. The plants are 18 to 26 inches tall and bloom late.

7. Fringed tulips bear cup-shaped flowers having petals with fringed edges. Colors include lavender, red, pink, yellow, and white; 14 to 26 inches tall.

8. Viridiflora tulips have flowers flushed with green, and sometimes mostly green and edged in a contrasting color; 16 to 21 inches tall.

9. Rembrandt tulips have streaked or variegated colors caused by a virus; true Rembrandts are no long grown in North America, but some similar-looking hybrids are available.+

'Golden Emperor' fosteriana tulip

'Angelique' double late tulip

Tulip

Fringed tulip

Types of Tulips

DIVISION 1 **Single Early**

DIVISION 2 **Double Early**

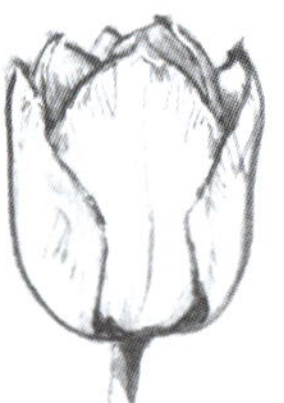

DIVISION 3 **Triumph**

DIVISION 4 **Darwin Hybrid**

DIVISION 5 **Single Late**

DIVISION 8 **Viridiflora**

DIVISION 9 **Rembrandt**

DIVISION 10 **Parrot**

DIVISION 11 **Double Late**

DIVISION 12 **Kaufmannia**

10. Parrot tulips are late blooming and are distinguished by fringed petals. Many of the flowers are streaked with a contrasting color. They are large and sometimes droop on the stems.

11. Double late tulips (peony-flowered) have large, full flowers resembling peonies, in many colors. They bloom late in the tulip season and grow 14 to 24 inches high.

12. Kaufmannia tulips are sometimes called waterlily tulips because of the way most open their flowers wide. These short tulips bloom closer to midspring.

13. Fosteriana tulips also bloom in midspring. The plants grow 12 to 18 inches tall, and their flowers are quite large.

14. Greigii tulips are low-growing and have foliage that is streaked and mottled with purple. They bloom in midspring, after Kaufmannia hybrids.

15. Miscellaneous tulips do not fit into any of the other categories.

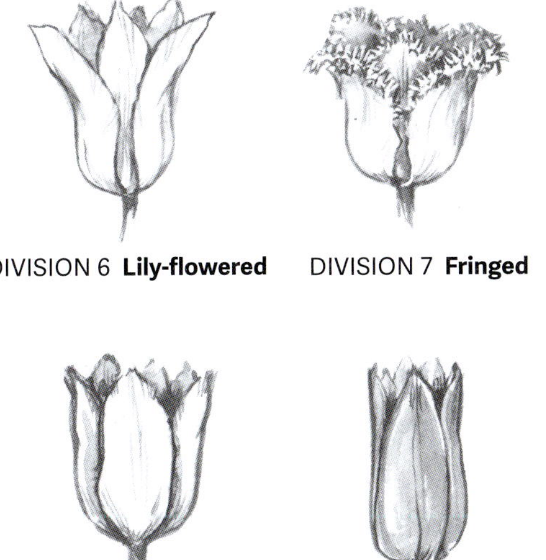

Viola / Violet, Pansy

This genus includes annuals, biennials, and perennials. Some of its members are garden favorites: pansies, johnny-jump-ups, sweet violets, violas, and horned violets (also called tufted pansies). Pansies and sweet violets grace the spring garden. Johnny-jump-ups and horned violets bloom into summer (horned violets also may bloom again in fall, with the return of cooler weather).

Sweet violets *(Viola odorata)* are diminutive plants, with small, fragrant flowers in various shades of purple or white carried above 6-inch mounds of heart-shaped leaves. The plants spread rapidly and can become invasive. Try them as a ground cover, to edge a bed or border, or in the rock garden. Hardy in Zones 6–10, they prefer rich, moist, humusy soil and some shade.

Pansies *(V. × wittrockiana)* can be either annual or biennial. Their distinctive flowers with or without the clown-face dark markings are available in many colors, including red, rose, maroon, pink, lavender, true blue, deep blue, purple, orange, gold, yellow, and creamy white. Most pansies grow 6 to 10 inches tall. Pansies bloom best in cool weather. They work well planted above bulbs; a combination of bright yellow daffodils and blue and violet pansies is a showstopper. Pansies are also fine plants for containers.

Johnny-jump-ups *(V. tricolor)* look like small pansies in shades of purple, blue, and yellow. They bloom in spring and summer in the North, all winter in the South. They can behave as biennials or short-lived perennials, hardy in Zones 4–9. They also self-sow readily.

All *Viola* species and cultivars do best in rich, moist soil. They like full sun but will bloom nicely in partial shade. Keeping faded flowers picked off and pinching back the plants will encourage continued bloom.

Sweet violets

Start from seeds or purchased plants. Northern gardeners can plant seeds indoors in early winter and set out transplants in early spring, as soon as the threat of heavy frost is gone. Plants can tolerate light frost. To get flowers even earlier, sow seeds in midsummer and help the plants get through winter with a cold frame or insulate them under a good layer of mulch. Warmer-climate gardeners can plant pansies in fall for late winter flowers.

'Accord Clear Primrose' pansy

Spring Activities

Spring's the time to work the soil, and to prepare new planting beds and rejuvenate old ones. It's the time to plant: to set out transplants of hardy annuals and perennials and to sow seeds of summer annuals, outdoors or indoors.

Spring is also a time to enjoy outdoor flowers, especially in the perennial garden. Most perennial gardens reach their peak bloom in late spring and early summer in the north, earlier in warmer climates. More color is available in late spring than at any other time of the year.

As the wonderful symphony of bloom reaches its crescendo, there's work to be done. Dying flowers need to be deadheaded, early blooming plants may need to be pruned or trimmed and reshaped. Dried foliage must be removed from spring bulbs. Lilies and tender bulbs such as dahlias and cannas need to be planted out for flowers in summer and early fall.

This chapter gives you a rundown of planting techniques and basic garden maintenance chores for spring.

If sown indoors and planted outdoors in late spring, this biennial hollyhock will flower in summer, as if it were an annual.

Digging a New Garden Bed

Fall is usually a better time than spring to dig a new bed. That's because fall digging allows the soil time to mellow and gives weed seeds a chance to sprout for your removal of at least some weed plants before spring planting. Besides, spring is chock full of other gardening tasks. Yet because most people don't get around to digging new beds until spring gardening fever sets in, this digging section appears in this spring activities chapter.

Digging new beds and borders is the hardest work in gardening. While digging,

Digging a New Garden Bed

Tools & Materials: Garden spade (to cut sod), round-nose shovel for digging, garden fork, perhaps a mattock or crowbar if soil is hard or rocky, and a tarp on which to place soil and turves **Difficulty:** Moderate

1 If you are making a new garden in an area that is now lawn, you first need to remove the sod. After slicing manageable-sized squares into the sod with a spade, slice and slide the spade's blade horizontally under the grass roots, cutting them off. Then lift out the turves for removal.

2 Pile the turves outside the garden before removal. If you store them in an undisturbed place, layering them with like sides together as shown—grass to grass and root to root—they will break down into a nicely textured compost. Or place turves, thus layered, at the bottom of your dig.

3 To double dig, remove the topsoil to a spade's depth. Then work compost, aged manure, peat moss, or leaf mold into the trench before amending removed topsoil and returning it to the bed. If you piled soil on a nearby tarp, simply raise the far side of the tarp to dump soil back into the hole.

you accomplish several goals. First and foremost, you loosen the soil so that plant roots can push through more easily. To help keep the soil loose, fluffy, and easy to work, it's essential to mix in ample quantities of organic matter as you dig. If you mix in fertilizer at the same time (or amendments such as lime recommended by a soil test), you'll be distributing the nutrients evenly to ensure they'll be within reach of all the plants in your garden.

Organic Matter. The importance of organic matter to a healthy garden soil can't be overemphasized. Compost, partially decomposed leaves, and well-aged animal manures are all excellent sources of organic matter, which is simply formerly living plant material in a stage of partial decay. Compost is also called humus, which refers to organic material in an advanced stage of decay. Organic matter particles act like little sponges—creating air spaces between soil particles, while simultaneously absorbing and holding moisture and nutrients and then releasing both slowly for roots.

Organic matter corrects problem soils such as sand and clay, improving drainage in clay soils and increasing the water-holding capacity of sandy soils. Also, it nourishes beneficial soil organisms that break down nutrients for plant use and help make the soil a healthy environment for roots. It's easy to add organic matter while you're digging a new garden; the easiest way to keep the soil well-supplied in existing gardens is to keep the soil surface covered with a mulch of compost, shredded leaves, or shredded bark.

Digging. For most gardens, simple but thorough digging is all you need. Remove any existing turf or weeds. Then spread about 3 inches of compost or well-aged manure over the entire bed, and dig it into the soil with a shovel or tiller. Loosen and turn over the soil to a depth of at least 12 inches—18 inches deep is even better. Then rake the soil smooth before planting.

If you suspect drainage problems or have very heavy soil, you may need more elaborate soil preparation, called *double digging.* This produces a beautifully porous, fine-textured planting area. But it is comparatively heavy work, and unless your soil is severely compacted it's probably not necessary. Double digging involves removing the top layer of soil from the garden about a spade deep, loosening the subsoil below to another spade's depth with a garden fork while working in amendments there, and enriching the topsoil with compost, manure, or another form of organic matter before returning it to the bed.

Power Tilling. A power tiller can be a labor-saving device for turning over new ground. But most power tillers won't dig 12 inches deep, so you'll still need to loosen deeper soil with a garden fork.

Stop tilling as soon as you have clods the size of a golf ball; you can level these with a rake before planting. *Note:* Grinding soil to a fine powder with a tiller destroys the vital air channels needed for good drainage. Also, using a power tiller routinely every spring to prepare annual and vegetable beds can bring many weed seeds nearer the surface and encourage their germination.

Watching Your Step. Once the soil is prepared, try not to walk on planting areas, or to drive a tiller in them. Otherwise, you run the risk of compacting the soil. Create paths to keep traffic out of planting areas. Make beds small enough to reach into easily for maintenance chores. For this, some strategically placed stepping-stones will help you get to larger areas without compacting the soil.

Maintaining Good Soil. Once the garden is established—especially if you are growing perennials, you will be able to do less digging and rely more on annual topdressings of organic matter and fertilizers and the work of soil-improving organisms, such as earthworms, to maintain good soil quality.

Established gardens benefit from the addition of a 1-inch thick layer of compost each year. When working compost and fertilizers into these planting beds, scratch them in lightly around plant roots and crowns (where roots meet stems). Do not disturb the roots themselves, and be very careful not to get chemical fertilizers on the crowns, because the concentrated materials could injure delicate plant tissues.

Starting Plants from Seed

Growing your own seedlings affords you a greater choice of plants and varieties for your garden than purchasing plants from your local garden center. And seeds are much cheaper than plants sold by mail-order nurseries. Seeds for hardy plants can be sown directly in the garden. But tender plants and slow-growing ones can be started indoors to produce plants that flower earlier than they ordinarily would if sown outdoors.

Before you plant any seeds, be sure the containers and tools you plan to use are clean. Seedlings are easy prey for disease-causing organisms. It's better to start seeds in a sterile growing medium.

Watering

Bottom watering helps keep visible portions of the plant dry and thereby less susceptible to moisture-borne fungal diseases. Bottom watering also ensures an even distribution of moisture and encourages deeper root growth. Still, top watering is often more convenient and helps wash down harmful salts that can accumulate if you use synthetic rather than organic fertilizers.

A number of commercial seed-starting mixes are available, or you can make your own mix from equal parts of peat moss, vermiculite, and perlite. (See pages 116–117.)

Sowing Seeds

Most seed packets carry instructions on planting depth and spacing for the seeds. A general rule of thumb is to plant seeds at a depth that is two to three times their diameter. Tiny seeds (those of begonias, nicotiana, snapdragons, or African vio-

Soil Squeeze Test

All gardeners are anxious to get into the garden in spring, but digging while the ground is still half frozen or wet can break down soil structure and cause compaction. To tell if your soil is ready to work in spring, scoop up a handful of dirt and squeeze it into a ball inside your palm. Then open your fingers. If the soil ball sticks together when you poke it gently, the ground is still too wet to work. But if the ball crumbles easily when you poke it, you can start digging. If it's really powdery, run a sprinkler on the area and wait a few hours so you won't be working in a cloud of dust.

Soil too moist holds a fingerprint.

Soil too dry won't hold together.

Soil just right holds together...

...then crumbles at a touch.

lets, for example) can be mixed with sand to help separate them and generally make them easier to distribute. Sprinkle this sand mixture on top of the potting mix. Cover the surface with milled sphagnum moss, which helps prevent fungal diseases, or vermiculite, which helps keep tiny seeds from washing about upon misting. Plant larger seeds in individual holes, or make furrows as you would in the outdoor garden.

Some gardeners cover their seeds with a thin layer of milled sphagnum moss to protect the seedlings from damping off (a lethal fungal disease). Sphagnum moss has fungicidal properties. If you use it in your seed flats, make sure it stays moist at all times. Otherwise, when the moss dries out it becomes hard and stiff, and tender seedlings may have difficulty penetrating it. It's also a good idea to wear gloves when you work with sphagnum moss, because it can cause skin irritations if it gets into cuts or scratches.

Temperature, Light & Water

The best temperature for germination varies from plant to plant. Generally speaking, flowering houseplants usually sprout best in warm temperatures of 70° to 75°F. Cool-season flowers germinate better in cooler temperatures around 60° to 65°F. Shrubs and perennials often need even cooler temperatures—55°F or so—to sprout.

Seedlings need plenty of light as soon as they break through the soil surface. Fluorescent fixtures are the best way to supply light for indoor seedlings. Their light is very even, and the plants don't need to be turned in order to grow straight. You can use special "grow light" tubes, full-spectrum daylight tubes, or a combination of warm white and cool white lights. Set the lights on a timer so they're on for 16 hours a day. The tops of the seedlings should be no more than 3 or 4 inches below the lights for the first couple of weeks; then you can gradually raise them to 6 or more inches above the leaves. Start out with the seedling flats elevated on some sort of stand that can be gradually lowered as the plants grow

These calendula seedlings didn't get enough light upon germination and are becoming leggy as they reach toward the window to get more light.

Sowing Seeds in a Flat

Tools & Materials: Seeds, sand to help distribute tiny seeds, milled sphagnum moss, mister, plastic cover, water pan **Difficulty:** Easy

1 If seeds are as tiny as sand grains, making them hard to distribute evenly, mix sand into the seed packet and sprinkle the mixture in even rows over the soil.

2 Cover with milled sphagnum moss to keep seeds from washing about during initial misting and to help prevent damping off (a fungal disease).

3 Mist well and then enclose the flat in a plastic bag to retain moisture. Keep the flat away from sunlight until first leaves appear through the sphagnum.

4 When first leaves appear, remove the plastic bag, provide bright light, and sprinkle as shown or bottom-water. Then thin the seedlings.

Feeding Seedlings

Since the soilless mixes sold for seed starting contain almost no nutrients, you'll have to supply some as soon as seedlings develop a couple of sets of leaves. But don't go overboard; overfertilizing your seedlings will result in weak, floppy plants more prone to problems. Young seedlings can't handle full-strength fertilizer. Dilute liquid fertilizers to one-quarter the strength recommended on the label (or, if you use fish emulsion, half strength); use this diluted food once a week for the first three or four weeks. Then you can gradually work up to using full-strength fertilizer.

elevated on some sort of stand that can be gradually lowered as the plants grow taller (a pile of books works nicely). Or suspend the light fixture on chains that allow it to be raised as the plants grow.

If you want to try growing seedlings without lights, your best bet is in a south window that's covered by sheer curtains (to keep the heat from becoming too intense) or a bright, unshaded east or west window. Turn the flats of seedlings every day so the stems grow straight.

Seeds and young seedlings need to be watered carefully so seeds aren't washed out of the soil and delicate new roots aren't disturbed. The best approach is to water from below, setting the flats or pots in lukewarm water in a sink or special watering tray. Another technique is to mist the soil surface with a plant mister until the soil is thoroughly moistened.

Make sure your seedlings don't dry out; water stress can set them back permanently at this stage, when plant tissues are young. But don't overwater, either. Constantly soggy soil encourages root rot, damping off, and other problems. Water your seedlings when the soil is somewhat dry.

Flats of young seedlings are protected in a cold frame. Plastic bottles help keep tender seedlings warm. Such bottles are called **cloches**.

Thinning & Transplanting

When the seedlings develop their first true leaves (the first leaves that have the characteristic shape of that plant; usually the second set of leaves to actually appear on the plant), it is time to thin them. You can thin by pulling up unwanted seedlings individually, snipping off the stems at soil level with nail scissors, or carefully lifting and transplanting the young plants to other containers.

Spacing for seedlings depends on the size of their leaves. The leaves should not touch, so that air can circulate freely around the plants (good air circulation helps to prevent disease problems). Three inches is considered a good average spacing distance for many seedlings at this stage. Crowding seedlings together in-creases root competition, encourages the spread of damping off and other diseases, and causes plants to shade each other, which in turn makes them spindly.

When the leaves touch again, the plants are probably big enough to go into individual pots or outdoors into the garden, if weather conditions are right. (See "Planting Outdoors," page 97.)

If you grew your seedlings in peat pots, water them well from the bottom before transplanting, to soften the pots. Tear the sides of the pot when putting plants out into the garden, so the roots can easily grow through the pot walls as they're

Thin the seedlings after the second set of leaves appears, using a pair of narrow-pointed scissors, such as a nail scissors, to clip off unwanted seedlings at soil level.

This marigold seedling has both its seed leaves **(cotyledons)** and the first pair of true leaves. On most flower plants, seed leaves are smooth-edged.

supposed to. Sometimes peat pots are so stiff that roots have difficulty breaking through them. When planting, make sure the rims of the peat pots are below the soil surface; you may need to tear off the top half inch or so. If the pot rims stick out of the soil they can dry out; they then act as wicks, drawing moisture out of the soil and evaporating it into the air. On a sunny, breezy day this wicking action could cause serious water stress for young plants.

Hardening Off

Seedlings started indoors need to adjust gradually to the harsher environment outdoors. Before you move seedlings out to the garden, harden the plants over a two-week period by exposing them to increasingly colder temperatures and by cutting back slightly on watering. Or you can harden plants by setting them outdoors in a sheltered spot for an hour or two; then bring them back inside. Move them outside for a longer time each day, eventually leaving them out overnight. By the end of the second week the plants should be ready to move into the garden. Plants can be hardened off in a cold frame if you open the lid a little bit farther each day, then removing it entirely for the last few days.

Planting Outdoors

Outdoor planting is largely governed by weather conditions. Still, some planning is needed to prepare the seedlings for transplanting. Seedlings in unsegmented flats can be blocked to separate their roots for a few days before transplanting.

The best day for transplanting is a cloudy, calm one, ideally late in the day. Bright sun and wind can dry out transplants and newly arrived nursery plants. Even on a cloudy, humid day it is important to dig the planting hole before you remove a plant from its pot or flat. The hole should be big enough to comfortably accommodate all the roots and deep enough to allow the plant to sit at the same depth as it did growing in its container. If the garden soil is dry, pour some water into the hole before planting. Set the plant in the hole and fill in around its roots with soil. Firm the soil gently; don't pack it down hard. Then water the plant thoroughly to help it settle in. Providing some shade for the first few days will help the young plants adjust to their new surroundings. Floating row covers, described below, are convenient to use and effective for shading.

In addition, if spring brings windy weather to your area, protect young plants with cloches or floating row covers (lightweight spun polyester fabric specially made to protect plants from frost, wind, and insects).

Transplanting Seedlings

Tools & Materials: Transplant container, soil, trowel, watering device **Difficulty:** Easy

After seedlings have developed their true leaves (second set of leaves), gently replant them in a somewhat larger container.

After plants have developed robust leaves, harden them off. Then transplant them to the garden.

Annuals to Start in Spring

These annuals grow quickly and should bloom outdoors in summer if you start seeds indoors in early spring, several weeks before the last frost.

Ageratum (flossflower) *Browallia*
Callistephus (China aster) *Celosia* (woolflower) *Clarkia*
Dorotheanthus (ice plant)
Iberis (candytuft)
Lobelia
Lobularia (sweet allyssum)
Myosotis sylvatica (Forget-me-not) (annual)
Nemesia
Nicotiana (nicotiana)
Petunia
Phlox drummondii (phlox) (annual type)
Tagetes (marigold)
Thunbergia
Tithonia

Early Spring

Cooler Climates

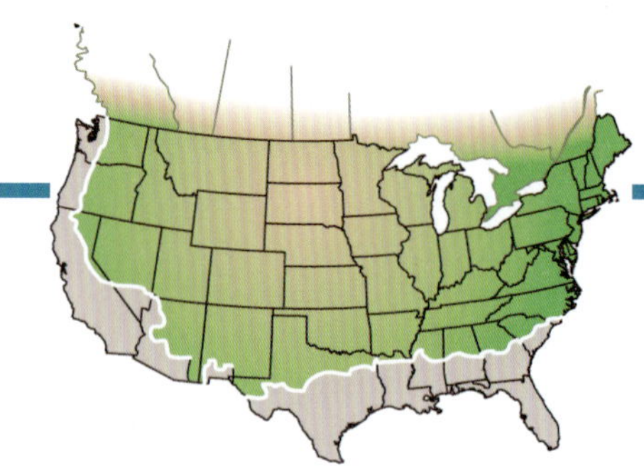

As shown on accompanying maps, if you live where winters are cold—from the mid latitudes to southern Canada—use the information on the "Cooler Climates" pages as your guide. If you live in the South, Southwest, or mild regions along the West Coast, you'll find the information on the facing "Warmer Climates" pages more useful.

Established Plants

For gardeners in cooler climates, one of the first springtime chores is to remove the mulch that covered perennial beds and rose plantings over the winter. Depending on weather conditions in your area, the mulch can start coming off perennial beds when the danger of hard frost is over (or when local forsythia starts to bloom). Rake up all the leaves that have blown into your hedges and shrubs over the winter; use them to start a new compost pile. Shredding leaves will make them break down faster. If you don't have a shredder, spread the leaves in a layer on the lawn and run over them a few times with a power lawn mower to shred them.

Fertilize established perennials, bulbs, and shrubs with an all-purpose blend of organic or synthetic fertilizer. Liquid fertilizers can simply be watered in; powdered and granular fertilizers need to be scratched into the soil around plant crowns. Be careful not to damage young shoots when you scratch in fertilizers.

Divide perennials that bloom in late spring or summer. Daylilies, lilies, and early chrysanthemums fall into this category. Daylilies don't need dividing often, but if yours didn't bloom very heavily last year, it probably means they are crowded and ready to be divided. Chrysanthemums and Shasta daisies, on the other hand, need to be divided every couple of years in order to remain vigorous. Dig up the root clumps, throw away the old, woody central part, and replant the healthy younger roots from the outside of the clump. Replant new divisions from whatever perennials you are propagating in loose, fertile soil that has been enriched with compost or well-rotted manure, along with a helping of high-phosphorus fertilizer (rock phosphate or a standard formula with a high middle number such as 5-10-5).

Divide daylilies in spring or early fall. Cut back stems before digging up root clumps.

To repot a potbound plant back into the same container, trim the outer roots.

Sharpen pruning shears and other tools, if you haven't done so already, before you need to use them for deadheading and other maintenance.

Prune spring-blooming shrubs early in the season just to remove weak or damaged branches and to shape the bushes. Wait to give them their real pruning after they finish flowering later in the spring.

Repair or paint arbors, trellises, and other structures that need attention.

Planting

In milder areas, you can sow seeds of hardy annuals (those early bloomers that tolerate some frost and flower best in cool weather) and perennials directly in the garden as soon as the soil can be worked.

Warmer Climates

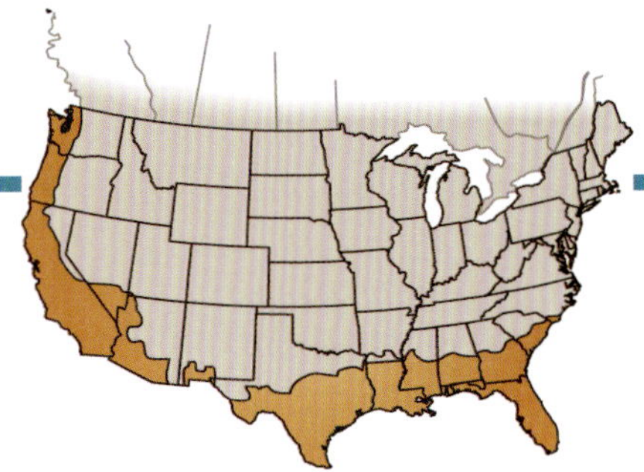

In milder areas, you can sow seeds of hardy annuals (those early bloomers that tolerate some frost and flower best in cool weather) and perennials directly in the garden as soon as the soil can be worked. Good candidates for early planting include calendulas, annual candytuft, columbines, garden pinks, larkspur, lupines, Shirley and Iceland poppies, sweet alyssum, and sweet peas. Pansies and snapdragons are also cool-weather flowers. If you started seeds indoors in late winter, you can plant out the seedlings when the soil is workable.

Established Plants

The hardy annuals planted in fall are coming into bloom now. Deadhead and water: larkspurs, Shirley poppies, bachelor's buttons, pansies, garden pinks, and others as needed.

Begin preparing soil in beds and borders for summer flowers. (See pages 92–94.) Dig in plenty of compost or well-aged manure and, if you like, a balanced or slow-release fertilizer. You can feed established plants with compost or manure, too; heavy feeders will appreciate a bit of fertilizer as well. Fertilize perennials, shrubs, and vines, such as clematis and jasmine. Fertilize spring bulbs when they finish blooming with compost, rock phosphate, bulb fertilizer, or an all-purpose formula such as 5-10-5.

Divide crowded plantings of summer- and fall-blooming perennials. Likely candidates include chrysanthemums and Shasta daisies (see facing page for information), dahlias, daylilies, hostas, marguerites, and summer phlox. Replant the divisions in loose, fertile soil enriched with compost or well-aged manure, along with some high-phosphorus fertilizer (rock phosphate, or a standard formula with a high middle number such as 5-10-5).

Mulch around your perennials and roses in anticipation of the hot weather ahead. Also, drive stakes for long stemmed late spring and summer bloomers that need them.

Prune any summer-flowering shrubs that bloom on new growth, such as crape myrtle, butterfly bush, abelia, hydrangeas, hypericum, and rose-of-Sharon. After they finish blooming, clip or pinch back azaleas, camellias, and rhododendrons to shape them. Feed them afterward with an all-purpose fertilizer. (Give azaleas, camellias, and rhododendrons a product formulated for acid-loving plants.)

Planting

Fast-growing cold-tolerant flowers can be sown directly in the garden if you didn't plant them last fall. Sweet peas, alyssum, and nemesia are good candidates.

Plant pansies if you didn't plant them last fall. If you started late spring and summer annuals and perennials from seed indoors, you can start moving the seedlings out to the cold frame to harden them off before planting in the outdoor garden. Plant out purchased plants or hardened-off seedlings of asters, baby's breath, columbines, garden pinks, larkspurs, snapdragons, oxalis, and phlox.

Set out (in mild areas) ageratum, cockscomb, zonal geraniums, portulacas, annual salvias, zinnias, and other bedding plants once danger of frost has passed. All these plants like lots of sun. In shady beds plant impatiens and torenia.

Stakes & Supports for Tall Plants

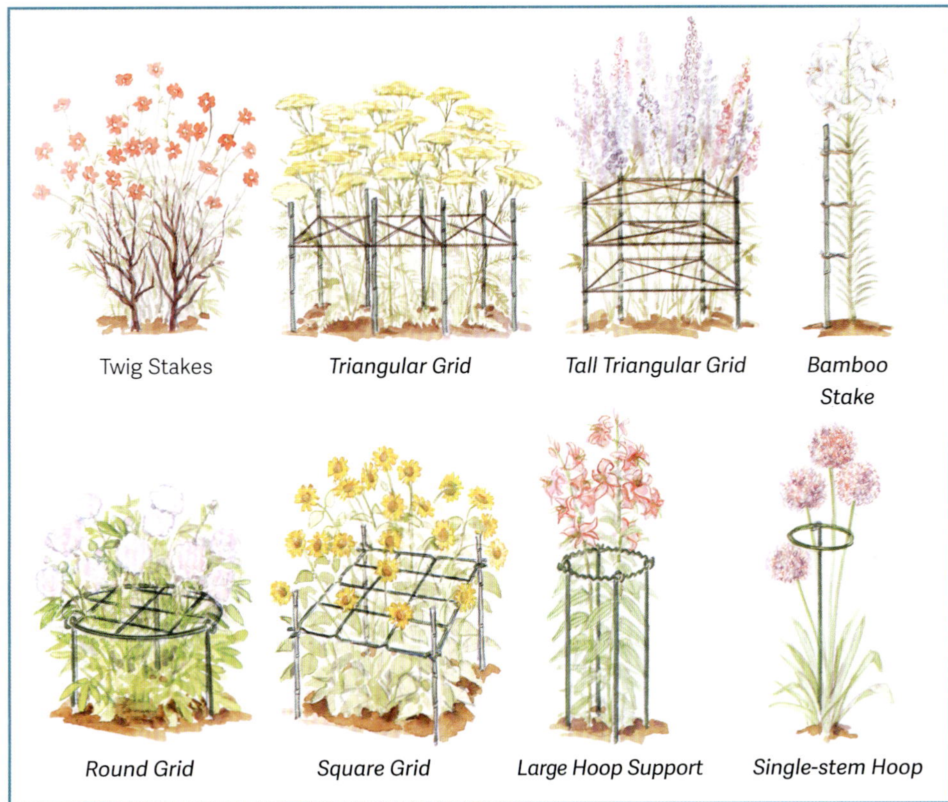

Mid Spring

Cooler Climates

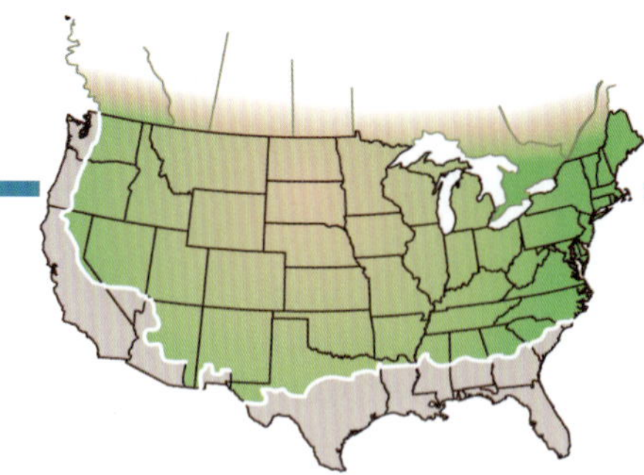

Established Plants

In the far North, finish removing mulches from perennials and roses.

Topdress (lightly fertilize) perennials as their new shoots appear aboveground. In this case, apply well-rotted manure or compost, perhaps supplemented with an all-purpose formula like 5-10-5. Very gently scratch these materials into the soil between plants. As early spring bulbs end blooming, feed them with rock phosphate, superphosphate, or bulb fertilizer.

Clip off dying flowers of spring bulbs, but leave the foliage to mature.

Begin fertilizing roses once a month as their flowering season approaches; follow directions on the fertilizer label.

Harden off seedlings grown indoors in a cold frame before planting in the garden. Open the lid a little farther each day (then close it at night).

Continue dividing summer and fall-blooming perennials that are crowded or have spread beyond their intended areas.

Planting

As the weather grows warmer, begin moving annual and perennial seedlings you started indoors to the outdoors (or to a cold frame) to begin hardening off before transplanting. Ventilate the cold frame on sunny days and whenever the outdoor temperature rises above 45°F. Close it at night.

Sow seeds of hardy annuals and perennials directly in the garden as soon as the soil can be worked in cooler areas. Such plants include columbines, garden pinks, larkspur, lupines, poppies, sweet alyssum, and sweet peas. Set out pansies and other cold-tolerant bedding plants purchased from the local garden center.

Plant bare-root roses or other shrubs while still dormant, as soon as the soil can be worked. When the danger of heavy frost is past, plant out new perennials and hybrid lilies. New hardy water lilies can be planted now, too.

Planning

As you work on spring maintenance chores, think ahead to summer and decide what you'd like to grow in containers on the patio or in other places this year. For the best results, plan container groupings just as you plan beds and borders, mindful of plant forms and growth habits, heights and textures, flower colors and fragrances, and blooming times.

Clean out plant containers. Scrub off any loose dirt or accumulated fertilizer salts with a stiff brush; then sterilize by soaking the pots in a solution of 1 part liquid chlorine bleach to 9 parts water. Rinse with clear water before filling the pots with soil. By the middle of spring, you can plant container flowers that tolerate some cold weather.

Note empty spots in your bulb beds and decide what to order for fall planting to fill the gaps.

Planting Bare-Root Roses

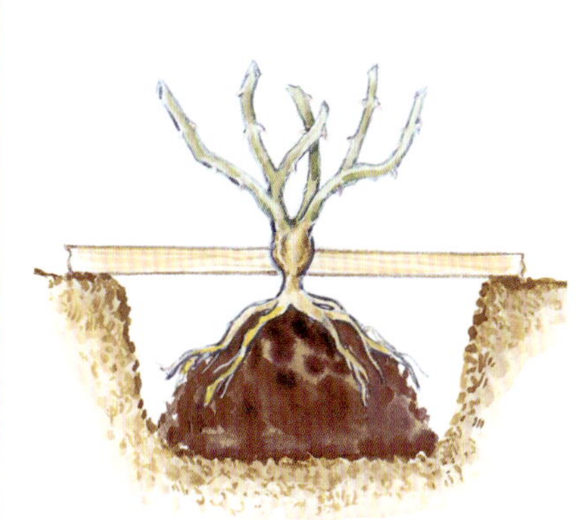

Plant bare-root roses atop a mound of soil. Position the knobby graft union on the stem 1 to 2 inches below soil level in cool climates—slightly above in warm climates.

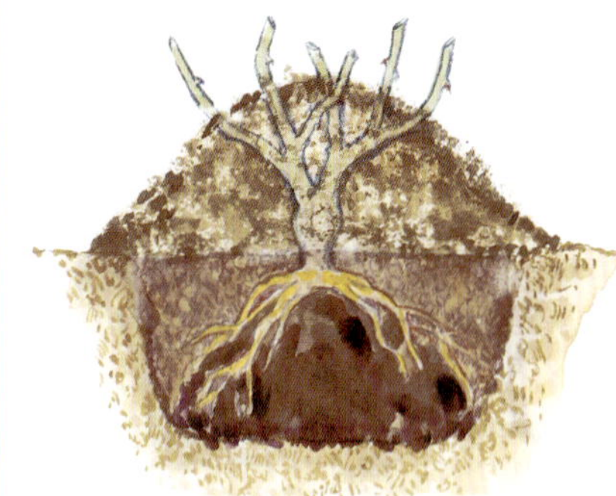

Water well. In the coldest climates, mulch the new plants for a few weeks to protect them from late freezes.

Warmer Climates

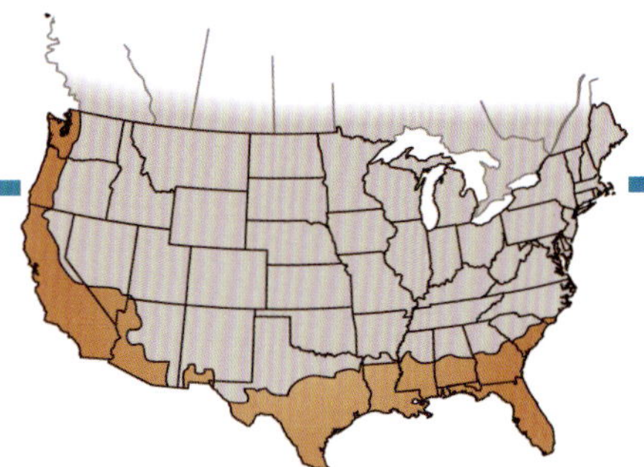

Established Plants

As spring progresses, continue to fertilize emerging perennials (lightly), bulbs (after blooming), and roses (monthly).

Remove the dead flowers of spring bulbs, but leave the foliage to mature. Don't remove the leaves until they have turned brown and dried out.

Pinch the tops of asters and chrysanthemums once a month after the plants are 6 inches tall. This promotes bushier plants with more buds.

Prune spring-blooming shrubs that flower on old wood, such as forsythia and lilac, when they finish blooming. Begin staking tall-growing perennials when they are up and growing. (See "Stakes and Supports for Tall Plants," page 99.) You can also begin setting up soaker hoses and drip irrigation systems, especially in arid regions, in preparation for the onset of hot weather. Inspect watering systems already in place to make sure they are still functioning properly.

Planting

If you started summer annuals from seed indoors, continue moving the seedlings outdoors or to the cold frame for hardening off. To ensure vigorous, well-nourished plants, feed the seedlings with a diluted, balanced water-soluble fertilizer.

Leave the cold frame uncovered, now that the sun is stronger, except on especially windy days.

Plant mail-order perennials as soon as you receive them from the nursery. Also plant hardened-off seedlings and purchased plants of annuals, summer-blooming perennials, summer bulbs, tropical water lilies, and container plants. Water new transplants regularly if spring rains don't oblige.

Transplant summer annuals started from seed indoors.

Plant annuals among and around the bulbs so you'll have flowers throughout the summer. Daylilies are another good companion for spring bulbs, particularly daffodils—their foliage hides the yellowing leaves of the bulbs.

Pinching & Pruning Chrysanthemums

Pinch tips of chrysanthemum stems monthly to promote bushier growth.

Disbud mums to promote larger flowers from remaining buds.

Late Spring

Cooler Climates

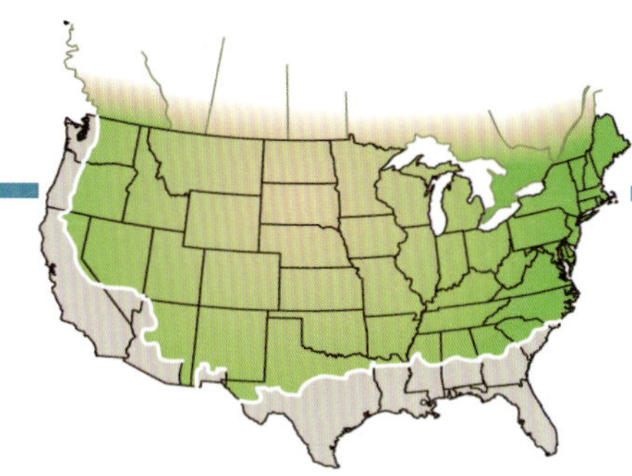

Established Plants

When early perennials finish blooming in late spring, you can divide and replant those that need it. Divide chrysanthemums and other autumn-blooming perennials, if you haven't already taken care of this.

Continue deadheading tulips and other late spring bulbs. Gardeners in cooler climates can now start to pinch back fall-blooming asters and mums once a month after they become 6 inches tall. Pinch back summer phlox in order to make it bushier.

Prune forsythias, lilacs, and other spring shrubs when they finish blooming. If you wait until later in the season to prune these shrubs, you may cut off next year's flower buds.

Apply a thick mulch of acid plant matter under azaleas and rhododendrons if your summers are hot. Acid plant matter (such as pine needles or chopped oak leaves) keeps the soil acidic enough and conserves moisture.

Water all new seedlings, transplants, shrubs, and trees regularly until the plants become established. New plants need tender loving care as they settle into the garden. After danger of frost, you can set out soaker hoses.

Fertilize summer-blooming perennials, annuals, and container plants with a fertilizer that is rich in phosphorus and potassium—use a formula with a proportionately smaller first number, such as 5-10-10.

Install stakes for delphiniums, lilies, and other tall summer bloomers that need the support. And as you go about your garden chores, clip off dead flowers from pansies, violets, and other early plants to prolong blooming.

Set out soaker hoses after danger of frost is past. Protect the hose from solar deterioration by covering it with a layer of mulch.

Stake main stems of plants that will grow tall and top heavy. Place the stake about an inch from the stem, and tie them together with twine in a figure 8 pattern that allows the stem to flex in the wind.

Planting

There's still plenty of planting to do. Northern gardeners can set out perennials newly arrived from the nursery, such as bleeding hearts, columbines, delphiniums, irises, lupines, peonies, and primroses. If the plants are dry when they arrive from the nursery, soak them in water before you plant them.

After the danger of frost, plant tropical water lilies, outdoor containers, and windowboxes. Also plant out seedlings of China asters, petunias, snapdragons, and other flowers started indoors a couple of months earlier. Harden off the seedlings before you plant them in the garden. Also set out purchased plants of tender annuals such as impatiens. Keep an eye on the weather, though, and cover the plants if an unexpected late frost threatens.

Overplant spring bulbs with annuals to have color all summer. Sow summer annuals directly in the garden if you didn't start seeds indoors. This will give you more flowers from a limited space. Good candidates for direct-sowing include the following: bachelor's buttons, clarkias, calendulas, cosmos, marigolds, nasturtiums, melampodium, painted tongue, sunflowers, and zinnias.

Plant out tuberous begonias, cannas, dahlias, gladiolus, and other tender bulbs, placing a little compost in the bottom of each planting hole.

Plant annuals, such as dianthus, around and among spring bulbs to hide their yellowing foliage.

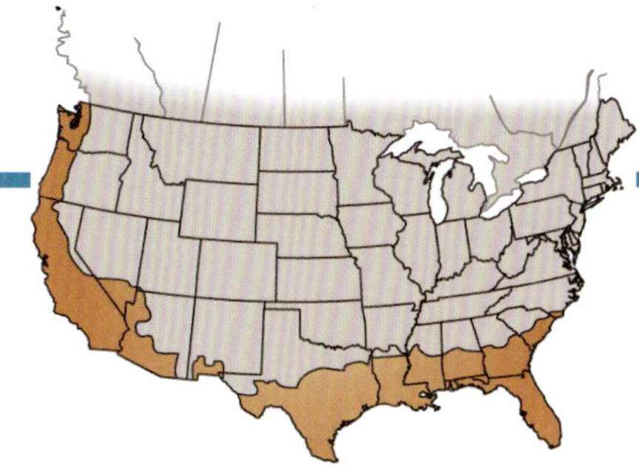

Established Plants

Thin the annuals that you seeded directly in the garden last month. Replace pansies and other cool-weather annuals with heat-tolerant annuals such as impatiens.

Thin direct-seeded plants after they've begun to develop their true leaves (usually a second pair).

Continue deadheading perennials and annuals as the flowers fade. Deadhead spring-blooming shrubs, too, and prune them when their blooms have finished. When impatiens and other annuals with long blooming seasons start to flower, pinch them back to encourage bushier growth and more blossoms.

Fertilize annuals and perennials for continued healthy growth and prolific flowering. Sidedress with compost, or scratch some all-purpose fertilizer into the soil in a ring around the plant stems. Be careful not to let the fertilizer come in contact with plant stems, though, or it could burn them. Or apply a liquid fertilizer (either a synthetic formula or a solution of fish emulsion or seaweed extract) to the soil above the roots or as a foliar spray.

Mulch perennials and ornamental shrubs to help them withstand summer's hot, dry weather. Annuals also benefit from mulching. If you wait to mulch until the plants show signs of water stress, it may be too late. The best time to mulch is before the summer heat sets in.

Continue dividing and replanting early-blooming perennials after they finish flowering. As early annuals finish blooming, pull them up and replace them with summer flowers.

Dig tulips and hyacinths that have finished blooming, after the leaves turn yellow if you want to save them. Refrigerate bulbs to replant in fall. Otherwise discard them.

Planting

Before the weather gets too hot, finish planting perennials, annuals, and containers. When you set out annuals, pinch back the main stem by about one-third so the plants produce more flowers over a longer time. Protect new plants with shade cloth for several days if the weather is hot.

Plant tropical water lilies, lotus, and water cannas, and any remaining summer bulbs, such as dahlias, tuberous begonias, gladiolus, and tuberoses. Staggering your bulb plantings ten days to two weeks apart will give you a succession of bloom in summer.

Plant summer annuals, such as zinnias, over daffodil bulbs to fill the bare spot and provide a second season of bloom.

Indoor Gardens — All Climates

These windowsill flats hold a mix of seedlings, including blooming marigolds, herbs, and vegetables—nicely complementing the vase of cut daffodils.

Early Spring

Many houseplants resume active growth in spring as the lengthening days bring the end of a winter's dormant period.

Light Levels

If you moved any plants to western or northern windowsills to reduce light levels during the winter, move them back to bright eastern or southern windows when they start to put forth new growth.

Fertilizing

Watch for signs that your indoor plants are breaking dormancy. When they break dormancy, begin to water them more often and feed them with an all-purpose houseplant fertilizer.

If you garden organically, feed houseplants with fish emulsion or seaweed extract. Plants in active growth can be fertilized once a month. As flowering time approaches, feed plants every two weeks with a dilute liquid fertilizer that is high in phosphorus.

Seedlings

If you started annuals or perennials from seed indoors in late winter, fertilize the young plants lightly every two weeks from now until it is time to plant them in the garden. Use a more dilute fertilizer solution than you are using to feed mature houseplants.

Overfeeding seedlings makes them grow too fast, and they may become weak and spindly. Compact, sturdy seedlings survive the stress of transplanting much better; they will make the transition to the outdoors more quickly and will suffer less transplant shock than weak, overstimulated seedlings. If your indoor seedlings start to look straggly, they may be getting too much fertilizer, too high temperatures, not enough light, or a mix of the above.

Most seedlings do best when the temperature is between 50° and 65°F, and they need as much light as you can give them. Keep seedlings in a bright southern window, or if you are raising them under fluorescent lights, keep the tops of the plants only a few inches below the lamps.

Planting

In cooler regions, early spring is the time to start summer annuals from seed indoors. You can sow ageratum, asters, bachelor's buttons, calendulas, celosia, cosmos, dusty miller, gazania, hollyhocks, impatiens, lisianthus, marigolds, nasturtiums, nicotiana, nierembergia, petunias, phlox, portulacas, salvia, snapdragons, strawflowers, and verbena. As soon as the seeds germinate, move the seedlings to a bright, cool windowsill, to a place under fluorescent lights, or outdoors into the cold frame. Warmer-climate gardeners who started sowing annual seeds in late winter should finish the planting early in spring, so plants will be big enough to move outdoors before the weather begins to get too hot.

In cool climates, sow summer annuals, such as these bachelor's buttons, indoors in early spring.

Propagation

Early spring is also the time to propagate summer annuals overwintered as houseplants. You can take stem cuttings from begonias, geraniums, and impatiens and root them in pots or flats of vermiculite, perlite, or a soilless potting mix.

Pot up tubers of caladiums, dahlias, and tuberous begonias so you will have plants ready to set outdoors in late spring when the weather is warm. If the tubers were stored in their pots over winter, remove the top 2 inches of soil from each pot, replace it with fresh potting mix, and water to start the sprouting process.

African violets that have developed long "necks" can be divided now and repotted in fresh soil mix. See "African Violets," page 222, for information on rejuvenating plants that have developed necks.

Start begonia tubers concave side up.

Mid Spring

No matter where you live, continue watching houseplants for signs that dormancy is over. If houseplants have outgrown their pots, repot in fresh potting medium. Either move them to larger pots or, to maintain the plant in the same size pot, prune back the roots and top growth by about one-third. To prune roots, remove the plant from its pot, carefully untangle as much of the rootball as you can, and trim off the outer roots along the bottom and sides of the rootball.

Planting

Gardeners in cooler zones should finish sowing indoors any annual seeds still not planted. In warmer climates, Mid Spring is too late to start annuals indoors, but you can plant trailing plants in hanging baskets so they can establish themselves and begin to fill the basket before you move them outdoors later in spring.

Late Spring

When nighttime temperatures stay above 55°F, you can start moving houseplants to a shady spot outdoors for a summer vacation. Put out cool-loving plants first: azaleas, camellias, Christmas cactus, cyclamen, gardenias, and others. Tender tropical plants should stay indoors until summer, when temperatures won't drop below 60°F.

Repotting

Tools & Materials: Trowel, newspaper, larger pot, watering can **Difficulty:** Easy

1 Spring is a good time to repot root-bound houseplants. Begin by removing the plant from the old pot.

2 Loosen some of the roots around the outside of the rootball with your fingers, and gently spread them apart.

3 Put some potting mix in the bottom of the new pot, after covering the drainage hole with a piece of broken clay pot or paper towelling.

4 Set the plant in the pot and fill around it with fresh potting mix to within ½ inch of the pot rim. Water well.

Chapter 6 *Summer*

In summer, annuals combine with perennials and summer bulbs to provide a nonstop show of color. And this can be an almost instantaneous show if you buy annuals as nearly full-grown plants from a garden center. Many perennials flower lavishly in late spring and early summer, and some, such as coreopsis, will continue blooming sporadically through much of the summer if you regularly deadhead them (remove their spent flowers). Summer is the time when the cutting garden is at its height. Pots, planters, and window boxes spill over with the glorious hues of easy-to-grow geraniums, marigolds, and other annuals. You can group lots of containers on a deck, patio, or other outdoor living space to create a lush garden right where you like to picnic, read, or entertain in pleasant weather.

Summer is also the season for special kinds of gardens. If you like to spend time in your garden in the evening, you can plant some flowers that open or release their fragrance when the sun goes down. Or you can create a garden for a particular location, that's dry or shady, by planting flowers that thrive in those conditions.

Summer offers a whole palette of brilliant as well as softer colors for the garden and for fresh bouquets. This chapter first looks at summer colors and a selection of the plants that make up the color palette for outdoor plantings and indoor arrangements. It also addresses special kinds of gardens—in containers, for fragrance, for nighttime enjoyment, for shade. And because annuals play a special role in the summer garden, you'll find guidance for them, too.

A hot-colored combination of (clockwise from right) golden yarrow, coppery coneflower, rosy red beebalm, and red helenium is perfect for summer.

Chapter 6 Summer

Summer Colors

Summer carries over spring's rosy reds of peonies and introduces those of roses and hollyhocks along with the blazing colors of annuals—yellow and orange marigolds, scarlet salvias, hot magenta or salmon impatiens, gold celosias. This is also the time for geraniums in a whole range of warm tones and petunias in just about every shade of pink, red, and purple, along with white and pale yellow. Deep blues are also in evidence. For example, purply blue mealycup sage is a wonderful companion for some of the gold, white, and melon-colored flowers. Bachelor's buttons in their classic blue are delightful in bouquets, where they seem to bring a bit of the sky indoors.

The bright colors of summer flowers seem to reflect the warmth and intensity of the season. Many gardeners like to tone down the brilliance of summer colors by mixing off-white or cream-colored flowers and silver-leaved plants into beds and borders. Yet, all in all, the richness and abundance of summer colors are good for the soul.

A cool blend of two different purples in the foreground, is enlivened by a gorgeous pink. Additionally, white as pure as clouds adds a refreshing note.

Combining Summer Flowers

If you like pink and blue combinations, you might grow a pink cultivar of perennial phlox (*Phlox paniculata*) with one of the blue salvias. Or you could plant tall, steel blue globe thistles (*Echinops* 'Taplow Blue') behind a pink beebalm cultivar such as 'Marshall's Delight'. If pink and purple is your fancy, you can mix pink and purple petunias with pink phlox, purple salvia, and pink cultivars of sedums. Early in the season you could pair purple campanulas with pink and mauve foxgloves. Another pretty combination is blue delphiniums or violet-blue larkspur, perhaps with some lavender, and a pink cultivar of coral bells (*Heuchera sanguinea*). You can brighten the scheme with some golden 'Gold Plate' yarrow or pale yellow 'Moonbeam' coreopsis.

A wide range of blue-and-yellow color schemes is also possible. Consider, for example, blue-violet larkspur or blue balloon flower (*Platycodon grandiflorus*) with pale yellow 'Moonshine' yarrow or low-growing golden marigolds. Or try 'Moonshine' with the rich yellow of another yarrow cultivar, 'Coronation Gold', and a violet-blue salvia such as 'Victoria' or 'May Night'.

An especially beautiful combination is blue mealycup sage with zinnias, early dahlias, or daylilies in soft shades of melon, salmon, and peach. Shasta daisies or other white flowers add sparkle to this color scheme.

If you like warm color schemes, you might plant yellow marigolds, scarlet salvia, orange dahlias, and golden rudbeckias or yellow-and-red gaillardias. Or grow tall annual snapdragons in shades of yellow, apricot, bronze, and pink with early mums or dahlias in gold and bronze tones.

Bright, strong colors can be especially good choices for warm-climate gardens. They hold up under the blazing summer sunlight in southern gardens—they don't appear pale and bleached out as lighter colors can. (But bear in mind that many summer flowers need full sun in cool climates and fare better with some afternoon shade in hot climates.)

To give your garden a softer, cooler look, use lots of pastels or blues and violets in your color scheme. If you're looking for a cool oasis to beat the heat, the sight of a clean, crisp, all-white garden can be refreshing. As you can see in the table "The Summer Palette" (pages 110–111) there are lots of white flowers to choose from. To spice up the color, add some pink or melon-colored zinnias.

If you've always wanted a cottage garden with a riot of richly colored flowers, try a combination of campanulas, columbines, delphiniums, foxgloves, hollyhocks, and garden pinks. A cottage-style garden consisting entirely of annuals might include bachelor's buttons, cosmos, larkspur, nicotiana, pincushion flower (*Scabiosa*), and Shirley poppies. For another pleasing mixture of several colors, try red and pink snapdragons with orange and yellow calendulas, yellow irises, and blue marguerites (*Felicia amelloides*), and scaevola.

Warm colors harmonize beautifully in this border of red, yellow, and orange daylilies, red-and-yellow gaillardia, and bright yellow rudbeckia, above.

An all-white garden can be refreshingly simple, left, like this mass of cosmos surrounding a bench at the edge of a lush, manicured, green lawn.

The Summer Palette

Plants noted below in **boldface type** are described in detail in "Flowers for Summer Gardens," page 136. In all listings in this book, plants are arranged alphabetically by scientific (botanical) name. When scientific and common names are the same, just one name is shown.

RED FLOWERS

'Europeana' rose

***Alcea* (hollyhock)**
Astilbe
***Antirrhinum* (snapdragon)**
***Begonia* (wax and tuberous begonias)**
Bougainvillea
***Callistephus* (China aster)**
Campsis (trumpet vine)
Celosia
Clematis
Cosmos
Crocosmia
Dahlia
Dianthus (garden pinks)
Fuchsia
Gladiolus
Gomphrena (globe amaranth)
Hibiscus
Impatiens
Kniphofia (red-hot poker)
***Lilium* (lily)**
Lobelia (cardinal flower)
Lupinus (lupine)
Lychnis (Maltese cross)
Monarda (beebalm)
Nicotiana (flowering tobacco)
***Pelargonium* (geranium)**
Penstemon
Petunia
***Rosa* (rose)**
Salpiglossis (painted tongue)
Salvia
Tanacetum (pyrethrum)
Verbena
Zinnia

PINK FLOWERS

Petunia

Abelia
Acanthus (bear's breech)
***Achillea* (yarrow)**
***Alcea* (hollyhock)**
Allium (flowering onion)
***Antirrhinum* (snapdragon)**
Armeria (sea pink)
Astilbe
***Begonia* (wax and tuberous begonias)**
Bougainvillea
***Callistephus* (China aster)**
Celosia
Centaurea (bachelor's button)
***Chelone* (turtlehead)**
Clematis
Cleome (spider flower)
***Consolida* (larkspur)**
Coreopsis
Cosmos
Dahlia
Delphinium
Dianthus (garden pinks)
Digitalis (foxglove)
Erigeron
Eustoma (lisianthus)
Filipendula
Fuchsia
***Geranium* (cranesbill)**
Gladiolus
Gomphrena (globe amaranth)
Gypsophila (baby's breath)
***Hemerocallis* (daylily)**
Hibiscus
Hydrangea
Iberis (annual candytuft)
Impatiens
Lagerstroemia (crape myrtle)
***Lilium* (lily)**
Limonium (statice)
Lupinus (lupine)
Lychnis (rose campion)
Malva (mallow)
Monarda (beebalm)
Nicotiana (flowering tobacco)
Oenothera (showy primrose)
***Pelargonium* (geranium)**
Petunia
***Phlox* (garden phlox)**
Physostegia (false dragonhead)
Potentilla (cinquefoil)
Rhododendron (azalea)
***Rosa* (rose)**
Salpiglossis (painted tongue)
Saponaria (soapwort)
Scabiosa (pincushion flower)
Sedum
Sidalcea (prairie mallow)
***Stokesia* (Stokes' aster)**
***Tanacetum* (pyrethrum)**
Tradescantia (spiderwort)
Tropaeolum (nasturtium)
Verbena
Veronica
Zinnia

ORANGE FLOWERS

'Cosmic Orange' cosmos

***Alcea* (hollyhock)**
***Antirrhinum* (snapdragon)**
***Asclepias* (butterfly weed)**
Bougainvillea
Calendula (pot marigold)
Celosia
Cosmos
Dahlia
Gladiolus
Gomphrena (globe amaranth)
Helenium (sneezeweed)
***Hemerocallis* (daylily)**
Impatiens
Kniphofia (red-hot poker)
Ligularia
***Lilium* (lily)**
Petunia
Rhododendron (azalea)
***Rosa* (rose)**
***Tagetes* (marigold)**
Tropaeolum (nasturtium)
Zinnia

YELLOW FLOWERS

'Stella de Oro' Daylily

***Achillea* (yarrow)**
Allium (flowering onion)

Anthemis (golden marguerite)
***Antirrhinum* (snapdragon)**
Artemisia
Calendula (pot marigold)
***Callistephus* (China aster)**
Celosia
Centaurea (globe centaurea)
Coreopsis
Cosmos
Dahlia
Eremurus (foxtail lily)
Gaillardia (blanket flower)
Gladiolus
Helenium (sneezeweed)
Helianthus (sunflower)
Heliopsis
***Hemerocallis* (daylily)**
Kniphofia (red-hot poker)
***Lilium* (lily)**
Limonium (statice)
Linum (golden flax)
Lupinus (lupine)
Oenothera (evening primrose, sundrops)
Opuntia (prickly pear)
Petunia
Potentilla (cinquefoil)
Rhododendron (azalea)
***Rosa* (rose)**
Rudbeckia (black-eyed Susan)
***Tagetes* (marigold)**
Tropaeolum (nasturtium)
Verbena
Zinnia

BLUE & VIOLET FLOWERS

Bachelor's button

Aconitum (monkshood)
Adenophora (ladybells)
Agapanthus (lily-of-the-Nile)
Ageratum
***Alcea* (hollyhock)**
Baptisia (false indigo)
***Callistephus* (China aster)**
***Campanula* (bellflower)**
Centaurea (mountain bluet, bachelor's button)
Clematis
***Consolida* (larkspur)**
Delphinium
Echinops (globe thistle)
Eryngium (sea holly)
Eustoma (lisianthus)
Gentiana (gentian)
***Geranium* (cranesbill)**
Hydrangea
Impatiens
Iris
Limonium (statice)
Linum (blue flax)
Lobelia
Lupinus (lupine)
Petunia
Salpiglossis
Salvia
Scabiosa (pincushion flower)
Stokesia (Stokes' aster)
Tradescantia (spiderwort)
Veronica

PURPLE FLOWERS

'Purple Prince' zinnia

Acanthus (bear's breech)
Allium (flowering onion)
Aster
Bougainvillea
Buddleia (butterfly bush)
Centaurea (bachelor's button)
Clematis
Cleome (spider flower)
***Consolida* (larkspur)**
Dahlia
Delphinium
Digitalis (foxglove)
Echinacea (purple coneflower)
Fuchsia
***Geranium* (cranesbill)**
Gladiolus
Hesperis (dame's rocket)
Hosta
Iberis (annual candytuft)
Iris
Lavandula (lavender)
Liatris (gayfeather)
Limonium (statice)
Lupinus (lupine)
Petunia
***Phlox* (garden phlox)**
Physostegia (false dragonhead)
Salvia
Scabiosa (pincushion flower)
Tanacetum (pyrethrum)
Thalictrum (meadowrue)
Zinnia

WHITE FLOWERS

'Sonata' cosmos

Abelia
Acanthus (bear's breech)
***Achillea* (yarrow)**
Agapanthus (lily-of-the-Nile)
Ageratum
***Alcea* (hollyhock)**
Anaphalis (pearly everlasting)
Anthericum (St. Bernard's lily)
***Antirrhinum* (snapdragon)**
Armeria (sea pink)
Artemisia
Aruncus (goatsbeard)
Astilbe
Begonia
Bougainvillea
***Callistephus* (China aster)**
***Campanula* (bellflower)**
Centaurea (bachelor's button)
Chelone (turtlehead)
Cimicifuga (bugbane)
Clematis
Cleome (spider flower)
Clethra (sweet pepperbush)
Consolida (larkspur)
Dahlia
Delphinium
Dianthus (garden pinks)
Dictamnus (gas plant)
Digitalis (foxglove)
Eustoma (lisianthus)
Filipendula (meadowsweet)
Gladiolus
Gypsophila (baby's breath)
Hibiscus
Hydrangea
Iberis (annual candytuft)
Impatiens
Lagerstroemia (crape myrtle)
Leucanthemum (Shasta daisy)
Liatris (gayfeather)
***Lilium* (lily)**
Limonium (statice)
Lonicera (honeysuckle)
Lupinus (lupine)
Lysimachia (gooseneck loosestrife)
Macleya (plume poppy)
Malva (mallow)
Nymphaea (water lily)
***Pelargonium* (geranium)**
Petunia
***Phlox* (garden phlox)**
Rhododendron (azalea)
***Rosa* (rose)**
Saponaria (soapwort)
Scabiosa (pincushion flower)
Tanacetum (pyrethrum, feverfew)
Tropaeolum (nasturtium)
Verbascum (mullein)
Verbena
Veronica
Yucca
Zinnia

Gardening in Containers

Plants in pots are a great means of dressing up a window, providing front-door welcome, or creating the perfect setting for relaxing on a deck or city rooftop. Place large tubs of bright flowers next to the front door, or set smaller pots with just one or two plants on all or some of the steps leading up to your front porch.

Porches are another good place for containers of flowers, if you place them where they'll get some light. Hanging baskets can be suspended from the underside of a porch roof at varying heights to create a pleasant effect. You can also train climbing plants in pots on trellises, or let long trailers dangle from hanging baskets to create a living privacy screen or to shade the porch.

Out in the yard or on a patio or rooftop, tubs of trellised climbing plants can screen off unsightly areas, divide space, create privacy, or provide shade.

Other good places for container plants include balconies and fire escapes, the pavement around swimming pools, and edges of driveways and paths. If you have

For a lush, romantic look, place petunias, ivy geraniums, and bidens in hanging baskets and window boxes above a bed or border of blossoms.

Create a garden with pots and tubs of plants in different heights. (Left) Tubs of ornamental grasses and pots of coleus. (Above) Place containerized plants for a welcome—shown are geranium, begonia, browallia, and coleus.

Plants for Pots and Other Containers

Here are some good plants for pots, tubs, and window boxes.

Sunny Locations

Begonia (wax begonia)
Browallia
Cleome (spider flower)
Dahlia (dwarf dahlia)
Dianthus (garden pink)
Fuchsia
Iberis (annual candytuft)
Impatiens (New Guinea impatiens)
Lobelia (edging lobelia)
Lobularia (sweet alyssum)
Pelargonium (geranium)
Portulaca (rose moss)

Johnny-jump-up

Rosa (miniature rose)
Salvia
Tagetes (marigold)
Tropaeolum (nasturtium)
Verbena
Viola (pansies, including Johnny-jump-ups)
Zinnia

Note: Add trailing foliage plants, such as sweet potato vine (***Ipomoea batatas*** 'Blackie' or chartreuse 'Margarita') or silvery ***helichrysum*** for texture and color.

Shady Locations

Begonia (wax begonia, tuberous begonia)
Browallia
Impatiens (bedding impatiens)
Lobelia (edging lobelia)
Nicotiana
Vinca major 'Variegata' (variegated vinca)

Geraniums

Hanging Baskets

Arctotis (African daisy)
Begonia (tuberous begonia)
Cobaea (cup-and-saucer vine)
Convolvulus (dwarf morning glory)
Fuchsia
Lantana montevidensis (trailing lantana)
Lobelia (edging lobelia)
Petunia (cascading petunia varieties)
Pelargonium (ivy-leaved geranium)
Phlox (annual phlox)
Thunbergia (black-eyed Susan vine)
Tropaeolum (nasturtium)
Vinca major 'Variegata' (variegated vinca)

Purple lobelias (center) with yellow bidens, tuberous begonias, and red and pink petunias

several plants in small individual pots, group them in a fern stand window box or tub to create a massed effect. Cover the tops of the pots with unmilled sphagnum or peat moss to hide them.

Finally, don't overlook window boxes, which can be colorful and charming, especially if seen from the street.

If you plant in removable plastic liners sized to fit neatly into your window boxes, you can create seasonal displays that pop in and out of the boxes quickly and keep the window boxes looking great all year. For example, you might plant bulb plants for spring, followed by summer annuals, then mums for fall, and then conifers with small lights for the winter holidays.

Window boxes overflowing with flowers soften house facades and add a touch of romance to urban street scenes. Ivy geraniums cascade beautifully over the sides of window boxes or hanging baskets.

A well-designed window box, left, combines taller flowers, such as these red, white, and pink nicotianas, with shorter and cascading plants, such as pink petunias and variegated English ivy.

Classic terra-cotta pots, below, come in many sizes and a variety of shapes suited for almost every type of plant.

Designing Container Gardens

Planning a container garden is just like planning a garden bed or border, but on a smaller scale. A well-planned container garden, whether it consists of many different containers of plants or several plants in a large tub or window box, still takes into account variation of plant heights and compatibility of forms, textures, and colors. The most successful color schemes for container gardens are generally built on just a few colors. Polychromatic schemes can be too chaotic in the confines of a container garden. Yet containers encourage experimentation, allowing you to try different color combinations that you can easily change for the next year.

The main difference in growing plants in pots is that the plants are much more dependent on you to supply certain needs than are plants in the ground. For one thing, the soil in containers dries out more quickly than garden soil—because there is less of it and because moisture evaporates through the sides and bottom of the pot, as well as from the soil surface. That means you need to water a container garden more often. On the other hand, it's far easier to achieve an ideal soil for container growing than in garden beds because you can quickly create your own.

Types of Containers

Containers come in many shapes and sizes, and in a variety of materials. Three of the most versatile and widely used materials are clay (terra-cotta), plastic, and wood. Consider the merits of each type before choosing the right container for your needs.

Whatever material you choose, make sure the container has adequate drainage holes. If it doesn't have holes, you can use it as a *cachepot*; in this case, put your plant in a clay pot and set that on a layer of gravel or sphagnum moss inside the fancy cachepot to ensure sufficient drainage.

Many people prefer plain pots in their gardens because plain pots don't distract from the plants. But if you like more decorative containers, consider colors and designs that harmonize with the colors of the flowers growing in them as well as with the surroundings. Indoors especially, it's smart to ensure that the design on the pot is not too bold or too busy for the room.

Glazed pots, without drainage holes are called cachepots, designed to hold a liner pot with a hole. Glazed pots with holes need a saucer.

Clay (Terra-Cotta) Pots. The traditional container, and still the favorite of many gardeners, is an unglazed clay pot. Clay pots are porous, allowing air and moisture to pass through their walls. This is usually an advantage because well-drained, well-aerated soil promotes healthy roots. However, the porosity of a clay pot can be a drawback in hot, dry climates where you need to conserve soil moisture to keep plants from drying out.

Porosity has another potential drawback. If you grow your plants in standard clay (or plastic) pots indoors, or in an outdoor area, where you need to protect furniture or surroundings from runoff water, you'll need saucers under the pots. Plastic saucers are waterproof, but those made of unglazed clay are not. If you want to use clay saucers, you'll need a waterproof mat or coaster underneath to keep water from slowly seeping through. (Fortunately, you can now get plastic saucers that look very much like terra-cotta.)

Clay pots come in a broad range of sizes, from 2½ to 15 inches in diameter at the top. In addition to the familiar round tapered shapes, the pots may be square or cylindrical, or textured on the outside. There are also wider, shallower clay pots designed for forcing bulbs and growing orchids.The drainage hole in the bottom of most clay pots allows excess water to drain off, decreasing the chance of root rot. For traditionally-shaped pots, the rim around the top makes pots easy to pick up, and tapered sides allow you to easily remove a plant from the pot.

On the negative side, clay pots are heavy, especially when full of damp soil, and they are also breakable. They cannot withstand freezing temperatures and are likely to crack if left outdoors over winter.

Still, clay pots are quite versatile and dependable.

Plastic Pots. Like clay pots, plastic pots are available in a wide assortment of sizes and in even more shapes. And they have many advantages over clay pots. They are cheaper, lighter in weight, and more resistant to breakage. Unlike clay pots, plastic pots also come in different colors. Some are even designed to look just like terra-cotta. White or light-colored pots are best in warm climates because they reflect the sun's heat and can be selected to coordinate with the colors in their surroundings and with plant colors.

Because plastic isn't porous, plastic pots retain water longer than clay. While this means you won't have to water them as often, it also means you need to be careful to keep plants from getting waterlogged. A light, well-drained soil mix and multiple drainage holes in the bottom of plastic pots are essential for healthy plants in most climates.

Wooden Containers. Window boxes are often made of wood, and large wooden barrels and tubs are ideal for holding big plants or several smaller ones planted together. Wooden containers are attractive and slower to heat up in hot weather. Unfortunately, wooden containers are heavy, and moist soil will eventually cause them to rot. Redwood planters are by far the most durable, but also the most expensive. Oak barrels and half barrels also make perfectly serviceable containers for plants.

Wooden tubs can hold one or two large plants, like these tuberous begonias, or several smaller plants of varying heights.

Besides standard flowerpots, tubs, and boxes of wood, there are many sorts of fancy wooden containers with various patterns and designs painted on them.

Container Maintenance

Containers do need a certain amount of maintenance. Clean them every year or so, as soon as deposits begin to build up around the rim. Deposits are caused by the salts contained in fertilizers and by the minerals contained in hard water. These deposits can harm plants if you don't remove them periodically. Cleaning containers isn't difficult. Just scrub the empty pots in soapy water and rinse them thoroughly. If the deposits are from hard water, you'll probably need to soak the pots first; adding a bit of vinegar to the water will help make the deposits dissolve. If you want to reuse a pot that has held a diseased plant, soak it for several hours after cleaning in a solution of one part liquid chlorine bleach to nine parts water; then rinse it thoroughly. Clay pots can also be disinfected by boiling them in water for about 20 minutes. Scrub out wooden containers with a solution of one part liquid chlorine bleach to nine parts water, then rinse them well.

Clean fertilizer salts from pots. Take extra care if the pot held a diseased plant.

Plants and Soil

The relationship between plants and soil is complex, but a basic understanding of this relationship will help you to better appreciate what plants need to grow well. Plant roots don't really grow in soil; they grow in the spaces between soil particles. Air and water also travel through these spaces. Water is the medium that carries the nutrients plants need to grow, and air is important to the survival of the soil microorganisms that assist in the transfer of moisture and nutrients from soil to plant roots.

Plant roots need oxygen, too, which is why all but specially adapted plants die when roots are waterlogged for too long. When soil is watered from rain or from a hose, some or all of the air between the soil particles is replaced by the water. If excess water can't drain away, new air can't enter, and eventually roots will suffocate. Root rot is caused more by the presence of too little air than by too much water. In heavy, dense soil, the particles are so close together that there is little room for air, water, and roots.

Seedlings do best in light, aerated soils. This nasturtium seed germinated with 3-inch roots in just over a week.

Potting Mixes for Containers

The best growing medium for plants in containers—indoors or outdoors—is one that is light, loosely textured, well aerated, and well drained. The loam that works well in garden beds is too heavy for containers. Watering tends to settle and compact soils in containers more than soils outdoors; plus there are no earthworms in the containers to help keep the soil loose and aerated. That is why a light soil mix is so important for plants in pots.

These days, good potting soils and soilless blends for containers are readily available. It's also easy to mix your own.

If you use commercial potting soil, choose a brand that does not contain any fertilizers. The fertilizers that some manufacturers add to potting soil are sometimes too strong for young seedlings and delicate plants.

A good homemade container mix often contains soil, a lightening agent (usually vermiculite, perlite, or builder's sand), organic matter (peat moss, leaf mold, or compost), and additional nutrients from fertilizers of either natural or manufactured origin. You can use a packaged potting soil (but not a soilless mix) or garden soil in your homemade potting mixes. If you use garden soil in your containers, you should first pasteurize it by baking it at a low oven temperature for half an hour to kill disease organisms and other pathogens that may be present. (This doesn't smell pleasant.)

Soilless potting mixes are useful whenever soilborne diseases could be a problem, such as for starting seeds or cuttings. A soilless mix is generally sterile, and because it contains no nutrients, you rely exclusively on fertilizers to control the amount and kinds of nutrients your plants receive. Soilless mixes are sold at garden centers, or you can make your own mix from vermiculite, shredded peat moss, and builders sand or perlite.

When planting in containers, some gardeners like to put a layer of gravel or horticultural charcoal in the bottom of each pot to promote drainage. Others say it's unnecessary. People have success both ways. One thing gravel will do is keep soil from leaking out the drainage hole in the pot. A small piece of paper towel or newspaper placed over the drainage hole serves the same function—it allows runoff water to drain out but keeps the soil from escaping with it.

Potting Mix Recipes

Soilless mixes are ideal for starting seeds and cuttings, which are susceptible to soilborne diseases when young.

Although you can buy special blends of potting mixes for given plants and growth stages, you can save money by buying in bulk and mixing your own.

All-Purpose Mix #1

1 part potting soil
1 part builder's sand
1 part peat moss
1 tablespoon rock phosphate (or bonemeal*) per quart of mix

All-Purpose Mix #2

2 parts potting soil
1 part compost
1 part sand
1 tablespoon rock phosphate (or bonemeal*) per quart of mix

Richer Mix for Humus-Loving Plants

1 part potting soil
2 parts compost
1 part sand, perlite, or vermiculite

Soilless Potting Mix

3 parts peat moss
1 part each of sand, perlite, and vermiculite

Note: Unless you are growing acid-loving plants, add ¼-cup of horticultural lime to each bushel of mix to neutralize the acidity of peat moss.

**Some authorities feel that bonemeal is a potential carrier of Mad Cow disease.*

Soil Conditioners, Fertilizers, and More Used in Soil and Potting Mixes

To improve soil, you can use a variety of amendments, shown here about two-thirds of their actual size.

Soil Conditioners are used primarily to improve aeration and drainage. Compost also slowly releases a range of nutrients. Gypsum also adds calcium. Horticultural polymers regulate moisture by absorbing it from wet soil and releasing it back slowly as the soil dries.

Soil Fertilizers (listed below) are used to anticipate basic nutrient needs of plants and address deficiencies. All are commonly used fertilizers and the nutrients they supply.

- *Cow manure, cottonseed meal, blood meal*: nitrogen, promotes vigorous growth, photosynthesis, and good leaf color (see caution*)
- *Rock phosphate*: phosphorus, promotes ripening of fruit and seeds, and root growth (symbolized as "*P*" in fertilizers)
- *Greensand*: potassium, for growth of fruits and uptake of other nutrients, as well as photosynthesis (symbolized as "*K*" in fertilizers)
- *Sul-Po-Mag*: **sul**phur, **po**tassium, **mag**nesium
- *Horticultural lime*: calcium carbonate, sweetens acid soil (reducing pH), thereby helping plants absorb nutrients. Also adds calcium and improves the structure of clay soils
- *Bonemeal*: phosphorus (see caution*)
- *Synthetic fertilizers*: blends of the following, always listed in this order: Nitrogen (N), phosphorus (P), potassium (K)
- *Superphosphate*: phosphorus

* *Some authorities feel bovine-based fertilizers are potential carriers of Mad Cow disease.*

Soil Conditioners

Potting soil | Builder's sand | Peat moss | Compost (also a nutrient)

Perlite | Vermiculite | Pelletized gypsum (also a nutrient) | Polymer

Soil Nutrients

Dehydrated cow manure

Black rock phosphate

Greensand

Sul-Po-Mag (lagbinite)

Horticultural lime

Bonemeal

5-10-10 fertilizer

Superphosphate

Drainage Aids in Containers

Horticultural charcoal | Pot shards | Pea gravel

Mulches

Peat moss (also a conditioner)

Sphagnum peat moss

Milled sphagnum moss

Cedar mulch

Summer Beds and Borders

Most perennial gardens slow down as summer progresses, but annuals can fill in empty spots in perennial beds and borders. Most gardeners mix annuals and perennials—a tradition that goes back to the English cottage garden style. Some people find the mixture of plant forms, heights, colors, and growing habits that characterizes the cottage garden to be unsettling, busy, and chaotic. Others find the style exuberant and charming. In any case, more and more gardeners are trying their hand at cottage gardens.

In addition to choosing plants for their color and shape, you can plan gardens for special purposes, such as for fragrance or nighttime viewing, or to produce flowers for cutting or drying. You may need to plan your garden to fit particular environmental conditions, such as hot, dry weather or shade. No matter what your needs and desires, there are plenty of ways to fill your garden with color all summer.

This border of annuals, is planted in flowing drifts of flowers, like a perennial garden. Here are yellow marigolds, scarlet salvia, and geraniums.

Annual Borders

Using annuals in a border makes it easy to change your garden every year. If you don't like aspects of this year's plant combinations, next year you can change them without digging and moving established plants. You can change your color scheme, too, especially if you have an all-annuals garden.

If you want to create an annual border with the rich look of a perennial garden at peak bloom, choose plants according to their height, color, form, and growing conditions.

For tall annuals at the back of the border, include the larger cultivars of several popular plants: zinnias, African marigolds, snapdragons (especially the Rocket series), nicotianas, dahlias, and cosmos.

In a pink and blue cottage garden, tall globes of allium stand above masses of blue forget-me-nots.

Middle-of-the-border annual plants include petunias, impatiens, salvias, geraniums, anemones, calendulas, daisies, coreopsis, gaillardias, compact nicotiana cultivars, gloriosa daisies, dwarf forms of sunflowers, begonias, and coleus.

Low-growing plants for the front of the border include sweet alyssums, lobelias, portulacas, dwarf zinnias, sanvitalia, annual verbenas, and ornamental peppers.

It is important to match plants to growing conditions, as well as choosing them for visual appeal. If your summers are cool, you'll have better luck with snapdragons, penstemons, and lobelias. Where summers are very hot, you can rely on portulacas and ornamental peppers. Tips for growing annuals in shade or in dry climates are given in the following sections.

In this annual border, tall sunflowers provide vertical accents, with mid-height zinnias and candytuft, and edgings of sweet alyssum and nasturtiums.

Fragrant Gardens

Flowers that are deliciously scented as well as colorful are a special pleasure in the garden. Scents are often strongest in flowers with waxy petals or a lot of petals.

Good plants for a fragrance garden include sweet alyssum, balsam, carnations and clove pinks, nicotiana, petunias, sweet sultan, heliotrope, mignonette, lavender, garden phlox, scented geraniums, stocks, and verbena. There is also an uncommon species of gladiolus that releases its perfume at night (*G. tristis*). And, of course, roses. Many old-fashioned shrub roses and the newer Austin English roses are wonderfully scented, and some modern hybrid tea roses, such as 'Fragrant Cloud', are also especially fragrant. All of these flowers bloom in summer, when the hot, heavy air intensifies their scents. Vines such as sweet peas, honeysuckle, and wisteria can perfume a trellised gazebo or arbor.

Warm-climate gardeners can grow Carolina jessamine (*Gelsemium sempervirens*), tuberose (*Polianthes tuberosa*, which blooms in fall), heliotrope, and Madagascar jasmine (*Stephanotis floribunda*). Earlier in the growing season, you'll find fragrance in some peonies and shrubs such as lilac, mock orange, and Russian olive in cold climates or frangipani (*Plumeria*) and jasmine in hot climates. Scented spring-blooming bulbs and corms include hyacinths, irises, and lily-of-the-valley.

If you want fragrance indoors, you could add a gardenia, Persian violet (*Exacum affine*), wax plant (*Hoya carnosa*), or various kinds of jasmine to your houseplant collection.

Masses of lavender perfume the air with their rich fragrance.

Night Gardens

If you will be spending time outdoors at night, why not plan your garden to put on a good show when the sun goes down? One type of evening garden contains white and pastel flowers that are visible at night. As the twilight deepens, the vivid reds, blues, oranges, and purples that stand up so well to strong sunlight start to fade and disappear. But flowers of white, pale pink, cream, and pale yellow begin to glow in the fading light. Night gardens can also include some of the palest silver-leaved foliage plants such as beach wormwood or dusty miller.

The other way to choose plants for night gardens is to include flowers that don't open until sunset and those whose fragrance intensifies after dark. Most night-blooming flowers are white, and many are sweetly scented to attract the night-flying moths that pollinate them. Be sure to include some of the night-blooming flowers listed below in your after-dark garden.

You should also consider lighting, both for safety reasons and for added drama. The type you choose will depend on the effect you want to achieve. For example, floodlights mounted in trees cast a soft light on paths or garden beds on the ground; at the same time they cast interesting shadow patterns from tree limbs and foliage. This kind of lighting can create a mysterious quality as well as being functional. Lamps can be mounted on posts or poles of various heights to light different areas of the garden from above. These fixtures can illuminate areas, such as a patio used at night for dining or entertaining, or a recreation area.

Along pathways, you might consider downlights in short, fat posts (*bollards*) that have lamps built into them. There are also low-voltage light systems for this purpose; low-voltage kits are easy to install and may not require a licensed electrician.

To highlight night-blooming gardens or particular plants, install swivel-mounted fixtures at ground level to cast light upward. You can also install lamps recessed into the ground to provide uplighting. Spotlights trained on plants create very dramatic effects; you can also light plants from behind to silhouette them.

Night-blooming flowers (all blooming in summer) include the following:

***Datura innoxia* and *D. metel* (datura).** Vining or bushy annuals that produce huge, white, trumpet-shaped flowers with an intense, sweet scent. Not recommended for households with children and pets because they are extremely poisonous.

***Nicotiana alata* (nicotiana).** These annuals are fragrant at night; cultivars come in many colors. Two other, taller species—*N. affinis* and *N. sylvestris*—have more fragrant tubular white flowers. You should grow them as annuals.

***Ipomoea alba* (moonflower).** This morning glory relative is a vigorous annual vine that produces fragrant white 4- to 6-inch flowers that open in the afternoon and close the next morning.

***Oeonothera caespitosa* and *O. pallida* (evening primrose).** *Oeonothera caespitosa*, the gumbo lily, grows well in clay soils, opening its fragrant white blossoms late in the day. It is biennial or a short-lived perennial but will bloom the first year if you start seeds early indoors. *O. pallida* is a perennial hardy in Zones 5 to 8; it has fragrant white cup-shaped flowers and grows about 18 inches tall.

***Matthiola longipetala* (night-scented stock).** Unremarkable during the day, at night this hardy annual opens strongly scented pink to purple flowers. The plant will bloom all summer long.

Flowers in the night garden begin to glow in the fading light. Those with fragrance are particularly alluring.

Gardening in Dry Climates

Gardeners in climates where summers are dry (or those in other areas who are looking for low-maintenance plants) can still have plenty of flowers. Choosing the right location for the garden will help. Here are some tips:

- Site the garden where it will get some shade during the hottest part of the afternoon.
- Avoid planting your flowers on sloping ground that drains quickly.
- Don't choose a location with very windy conditions.
- Plant as far as possible from trees with shallow root systems, such as maples, which steal moisture and nutrients from the surrounding soil.
- Add mulch to help conserve moisture and keep the soil cool.
- Position the thirstiest plants closest to the water source.

Some plants that ordinarily grow best in full sun when the soil is rich and moist will manage in drier soil if they receive some shade during the day. The hotter the climate, the more these sun lovers will appreciate some shade, especially in the afternoon. Some of the perennials that behave this way are lady's mantle, Japanese anemone, bergenia, columbine, purple coneflower, peach-leaved bellflower, snakeroot, bleeding heart, cranesbills, and daylilies.

In hot, dry climates choose plants that thrive with little attention, such as the spiky yucca, yellow ice plant, and red valorian shown here.

Plants for Dry Gardens

Perennials especially good for dry, sunny gardens include yarrow, butterfly weed, coreopsis, globe thistle, amethyst sea holly, gaillardia, Oriental poppy, penstemons, balloon flower, black-eyed Susan, and sedum 'Autumn Joy'. Hollyhocks, golden marguerite, artemisia, baby's breath, candytuft, rose campion, sundrops and other evening primroses, lamb's ears, and yucca can also resist a fair degree of drought.

Annuals that can withstand hot, dry conditions include annual coreopsis (*C. tinctorea*), bachelor's buttons, cosmos, Dahlberg daisy (*Dyssodia tenuiloba*), morning glory, portulaca, snow-on-the-mountain, sunflower, California poppy, Mexican sunflower (*Tithonia rotundifolia*), strawflower, spider flower, and zinnia.

Gaillardia tolerates dry conditions.

This shady garden is full of soft color from the airy pink and white wands of foamflower (Tiarella wherryi).

Gardening in Shade

Shade gardens hardly need to be the colorless, boring places that many of these are. Many colorful flowers need or can tolerate varying degrees of shade. Because the plants are not seen in the blinding glare of full summer sun, their colors appear richer, and subtleties of plant texture and form are more obvious. In a shade garden, you are more likely to notice the many tones of green foliage, yellow-green to bright green to blue-green to deep green; the subtle interplay of textures, feathery against bold, fuzzy against glossy; the ever-changing patterns of sunlight and shadow that dance over leaves and ground when the breeze blows. If you have shade on your property, think of it as an opportunity rather than a liability.

The first step in planning a shade garden is to evaluate the kind of light you have to work with. Shade is not a simple concept. Shade cast by buildings is different from shade cast by trees. The shade beneath a tall, open tree like an elm is brighter than the shade under a lower, denser tree like a maple. There is deep shade, partial shade, and light shade. Morning sun is easier on plants than the same number of hours of midday or afternoon sun, which is hotter.

When assessing the shade in your garden beds, consider its quality and duration—how dense the shade is, the time of day when it blankets your garden, and for what amount of time. Also consider how the shade changes from season to season; shadows fall in a different place in July than in April. Consider reflected light, too. For example, does a white or very glossy wall near your garden bounce additional light onto the plants?

Unless your garden is in full shade—that is, it receives no direct light all day (which is unlikely unless you live in the middle of a forest or surrounded by tall buildings)—there are flowers you can grow. In fact, you may be surprised at how many flowers will bloom happily in the shade. When planning your shade garden, choose white or pastel flowers for the areas of deepest shadow because dark-colored flowers will become lost where light is most dim.

Types of Shade

If your garden is shady, it's important to understand that there are different types of shade.

Partial Shade (sometimes called semi-shade or open shade) is found where plants receive 3 to 6 hours of sun a day, in the morning or afternoon, or receive lightly dappled shade with shafts of sunlight reaching the ground all day. Many plants will thrive in partial shade, including those on the list in "Flowers for Shade" listed at right.

Light Shade (also called thin shade) is deeper than partial shade but is still a brightly lit environment. Plants may receive unobstructed sun for an hour or two a day, or they may be brightly lit with shifting patterns of sun and shadow from lightly leaved branches above. Another definition of light shade is a location receiving full shade for a couple of hours a day and partial shade the rest of the time. The plants listed at right all grow in light shade.

Medium Shade (also called half shade or high shade) occurs under trees with light foliage high above the ground. Sun may strike the ground early or late in the day, but the garden is shaded during the peak sunlight hours between 10 a.m. and 2 p.m. Woodland wildflowers such as the wood anemone (*Anemone nemorosa*), foamflower (*Tiarella* species), amd wild sweet William (*phlox divaricata*) bloom in medium shade, as will wax and tuberous begonia, fuchsia, daylily, and some other flowers; consult your local garden center for additonal suggestions.

Full Shade describes a location where no direct sun strikes the ground. It is found underneath mature trees with dense foliage, such as maples and oaks. Woodland wildflowers are the best choices for a fully shaded location. Try trilliums, hellebores, and violets.

Dense Shade is too dark and cool for a garden, unless you grow flowers in pots and rotate them into and out of the garden every few weeks. Dense shade is the year-round shadow cast by mature conifers and tall buildings.

Remember, too, that you can plant sun-loving crocuses and other spring bulbs in places that are shaded in summer by deciduous trees, which don't get their leaves until after the bulbs have bloomed. Some summer lilies, such as the turk's-cap lilies, don't mind a bit of shade at all. Autumn-blooming colchicums, lycoris, and hardy cyclamen will also grow well in light shade.

Flowers for Shade

The plants listed below tolerate partial to light shade. Keep in mind that brighter light produces more flowers.

Annuals

Ageratum houstonianum (ageratum)
Begonia hybrids (begonias, wax and tuberous)
Browallia speciosa (browallia)
Catharanthus roseus (Madagascar periwinkle)
Fuchsia × *hybrida*
Impatiens species (impatiens)
Lobelia erinus (edging lobelia)
Lobularia maritima (sweet alyssum)
Mimulus species (monkey flower)
Myosotis sylvatica (annual forget-me-not)
Nicotiana species (nicotiana)
Torenia fournieri (wishbone flower)
Viola × *wittrockiana* (pansy)

Bleeding heart

'White Senator' begonia

Perennials

Aconitum species (monkshood)
Alchemilla mollis (lady's mantle)
Anemone × *hybrida* (Japanese anemone)
Aquilegia species (columbines)
Astilbe species (astilbe)
Bergenia cordifolia (bergenia)
Brunnera macrophylla (Siberian bugloss)
Chrysogonum virginianum (golden star)
Dicentra spectabilis, D. eximia (bleeding heart)
Digitalis species (foxglove)
Doronicum species (leopard's bane)
Epimedium species (epimedium)
Galium odoratum (sweet woodruff)
Geranium species (cranesbills)
Hemerocallis species (daylilies)
Hesperis matronalis (dame's rocket)
Hosta species (hosta)
Myosotis species (forget-me-not)
Phlox divaricata (wild blue phlox)
Polemonium caeruleum (Jacob's ladder)
Polygonatum species (Solomon's seal)
Polygonum aubertii (silver lace vine)
Primula species (primroses)
Pulmonaria species (lungwort)
Smilacina racemosa (false Solomon's seal)
Tiarella cordifolia (foam flower)
Trollius species (globe flower)
Vinca minor (periwinkle)
Viola species (violets)

Solomon's seal

Plan a cutting garden for maximum flower production, and choose flowers in colors that will harmonize with your indoor decorating scheme.

Cutting Gardens

One of the greatest rewards of flower gardening is having lots of blossoms to cut for bouquets and arrangements. If you enjoy bringing fresh flowers indoors, consider a cutting garden—most useful when its primary function is production rather than display.

The best location is in an out-of-the-way corner of your property, out of sight from visitors, because a cutting garden is meant to be productive rather than decorative. You'll want to plant the flowers in easy-to-access rows, and to include all the colors and flower types you'll want to combine for arrangements inside the house. Most people put their cutting gardens along the borders of their property or out behind the gardens that are meant for viewing.

If you're not concerned about appearance, you could plant a small cutting garden close to the house—perhaps right outside the back door—so upkeep will be easier. Vegetable gardeners often plant a few rows of cutting flowers in the food garden where their color is a welcome addition. Herb gardeners sometimes mix flowers and herbs in the same plot.

Siting the cutting garden in full sun will give you the greatest selection of plants. If your garden site gets less than five or six hours of sun a day, concentrate on growing shade-tolerant flowers. Even shade gardeners may have a wider range of choices than they realize.

Planning a Cutting Garden

There are several factors to consider. To keep things easier for yourself, plan the layout with the plants' growing conditions and maintenance needs—rather than the garden's appearance—in mind. Put plants with similar growing needs together, and be sure to leave enough space between rows or blocks of plants to allow room for you to get in to cut flowers, pull weeds, and perform other routine chores. Some gardeners lay out their cutting gardens by flower color, planting in blocks or rows of red, purple, yellow, and so forth.

Put the tallest plants at the back, which is ideally the north side of the garden so they won't shade shorter plants. Place

How to Plan

Group together plants with similar needs for water, light, and fertilizer. To allow the plants to get maximum sun exposure, put the tallest plants at the back, which is ideally the north side of the garden so they won't shade shorter plants. Place medium-size plants next and the shortest ones in front.

A cutting garden planted in neat, short rows looks attractive, and the blossoms are readily accessible for cutting and gathering.

medium-size plants next and the shortest ones in front. In between the rows or beds, plant grass or cover pathways with a good layer of mulch to keep down weeds and make it easy to get in and cut flowers without getting your shoes dirty. For fine-textured mulch materials such as cocoa bean hulls, a layer 1 inch deep should suffice; for coarser materials such as wood chips, put down as much as 2 inches.

If the garden includes perennials, try to plan for bloom in different seasons. Stagger plantings of annuals two weeks apart to provide a succession of flowers to cut throughout the season.

In selecting flowers to grow, of course include the colors you like best. But also consider colors that will go with your decorating scheme indoors. And think about the forms of the flowers and the sorts of shapes you will need for composing bouquets and arrangements for your home. Traditional arrangements call for three basic plant forms: tall, spiky flowers; rounded shapes; and small, airy "filler" blooms. Most cutting flowers are long-stemmed, but you can use diminutive blossoms in charming miniature arrange- ments. A characteristic all good cutting flowers share is the ability to retain their freshness for at least several days indoors.

Flowers for Cutting Gardens

Perennials and bulbs to consider growing in a cutting garden include anemones, asters, astilbe, baby's breath, liatris, penstemons, coral bells, coneflowers, coreopsis, daffodils, dahlias, gladiolus, globe thistles, hollyhocks, Jacob's ladder, lilies, lavender, lupines, peonies, phlox, carnations, garden pinks, poppies, tulips, yarrow, and, of course, roses.

Annuals that make good cut flowers include bachelor's buttons, gaillardias, calendulas, California poppies, China asters, candytuft, celosia, cleome, cosmos, globe amaranth, gloriosa daisies, love-in-a-mist, nicotiana, salpiglossis, Shirley poppies, salvias, snapdragons, statice, stocks, sweet peas, verbena, and zinnias.

This variety of cutting flowers, front to back, includes yellow pansies, rose lisianthius, pink lavatera and larkspur, and blue larkspur.

Harvest & Care of Cut Flowers

Flowers respond differently to cutting, and knowing how to handle them will prolong their lives in vases and arrangements indoors.

The best time to cut flowers is early in the morning before the dew has dried. That's when plants contain the most water, and stems, leaves, and flowers are full and turgid. The next best time is early evening. Although the blossoms will contain less water after spending the day in the sunshine, the plants will have been manufacturing food for themselves throughout daylight hours. So blossoms cut in the evening will be well supplied with nutrients, which will help them survive in the vase.

Take a pail of lukewarm (110°F) water out to the garden with you and plunge the flowers into it as you cut them. Be sure your cutting tools are sharp—dull tools can crush the capillaries in stems, making it difficult for the flowers to

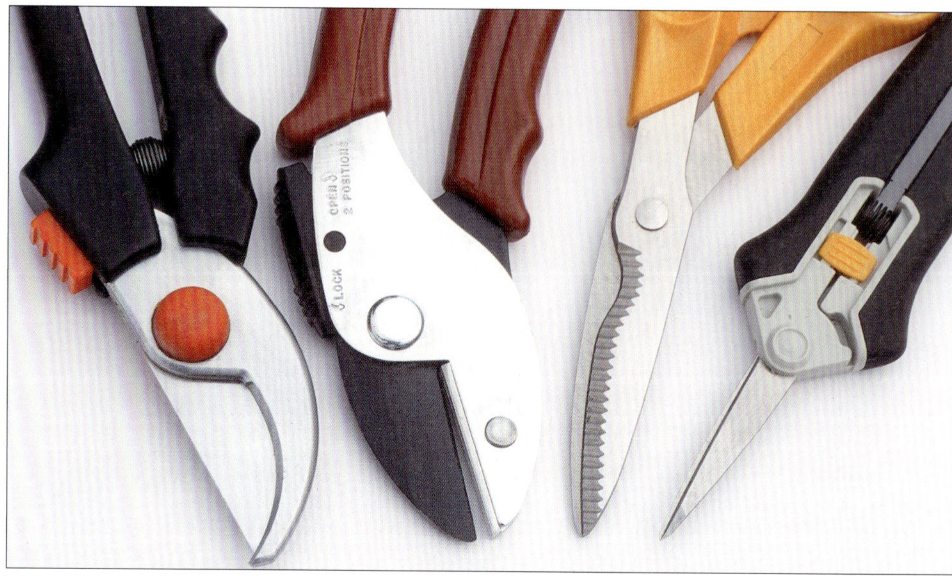

Pruners for tough stems and branches up to ⅜ in. diameter, include **(left to right):** ***bypass pruners*** with a blade that slices cleanly past a stem-gripping blade and ***anvil pruners*** with a blade that presses stems against a flat anvil. Bypass pruners make cleaner cuts without damaging bark or squashing water capillaries. Yet anvil pruners are efficient for quick rough cuts of weeds and overgrown plants. ***Pruning scissors*** (orange handles) serve well on soft stems and flat leaves. ***Needle-nosed shears*** allow precise cuts in tight quarters.

Cut soft stems, such as tulips, underwater with a sharp knife. Do this underwater because exposure to the air closes capillaries.

When cutting stems, whether soft or tough, cut diagonally to create a larger surface for water intake. To make your flowers last as long as possible, change their water every day, and cut about ½ in. off stem bottoms.

draw up water. Use a sharp knife to cut soft-stemmed flowers. Branches of trees and shrubs and woody-stemmed plants such as chrysanthemums are best severed with bypass, rather than anvil, pruning shears.

When and Where to Cut. Don't cut tightly closed buds or fully opened flowers. Most flowers last longest if cut when the buds are about half open and showing color. Some exceptions to the rule are asters, mums, marigolds, and zinnias, which should be cut when they're fully open. In all cases, take only flowers that are in perfect condition; those damaged by disease or insects probably won't last long. It's best for the plant if you cut the stem right above a bud, or the point where two stems meet; that way, the plant will be able to send out a new shoot.

***Remove all leaves** that will be underwater in the display. Otherwise they will decay and foul the water.*

Care After Cutting. When you get your flowers into the house, they will benefit from having their stems recut underwater. When flowers are out of water for even a few seconds, their stems seal off. Recutting the stems allows your delicate flowers to again draw up water.

Extend the display life of flowers that bleed sap. Seal stem ends by searing them slightly over a lighted candle or dipping them quickly in boiling water. This will stop the outflow of sap, yet the capillaries will still be able to draw water upward.

Some flowers bleed a milky sap or clear fluid when they are cut. Seal these stems, as shown in the photo above, to prevent petals from dropping, or the water from becoming discolored. Flowers that need to be sealed include poppies, buttercups, and poinsettias and other euphorbias, or spurges. Daffodils also bleed, but you can condition them in a container by themselves before arranging them with any other flowers.

The ends of woody stems, such as those of lilacs, mock orange, rhododendrons, and other shrubs, may be split (not mashed) with a hammer or slit with a sharp knife, or you can simply cut them at the bottom with a sharp knife.

Woody stems, such as this mock orange, can be split by tapping lightly with a hammer, or more laboriously, by splitting them with a sharp knife.

Conditioning Cut Flowers

For a longer-lasting arrangement, condition (or harden) your cut flowers before you put them on display. Stand the flowers loosely in a big container of water so that air can circulate around the stems. Most flowers can be conditioned in lukewarm water, but some—daffodils, dahlias, forget-me-nots, hydrangeas, poinsettias, and poppies, among them—should be conditioned in cold water. (There is no need to keep the water warm; just start with warm water if recommended in the list opposite.) Leave the flowers in the dark at room temperature for a couple of hours or overnight. Then move them to a cool location.

Flowers are conditioned in the dark so that their stomata (tiny openings in the leaves and stems) will close, reducing the amount of water that would be lost by transpiration. Very delicate flowers or those with limp stems, such as tulips, can be wrapped in paper before you put them into the conditioning water. Florist's tissue is the best paper to use—it is lightly waxed and will not fall apart underwater. You can purchase this paper at a florist supply or crafts store, but you can also use newspaper or plain tissue paper.

Wrap weak-stemmed flowers for hardening the same way a florist would wrap a bouquet: lay the flowers diagonally across a sheet of florist's tissue, roll the paper around them, and secure the tissue with florist's tape. Be sure to leave the ends of the stems exposed.

Condition lilies in warm water; snapdragons don't need warm water, but many other flowers do.

Arranging Cut Flowers

When you are ready to arrange your flowers, start with a clean vase. Wash it first in water to which a little ammonia or chlorine bleach has been added, to eliminate any bacteria that might have collected in the vase from previous bouquets. Rinse it thoroughly. To minimize the growth of new bacteria—which would shorten the life of your flowers—remove all leaves and thorns that would be underwater in the vase. You can leave some foliage above the water level for most flowers, but for lilacs, mock orange, and zinnias, strip off all the leaves. If your flowers look a little stark with so much of their foliage removed, you can fill some space with a few leaves from long-stemmed houseplants or good-looking greenery from the garden.

Fill the vase with lukewarm water (very hot or very cold water can shock your flowers). You can extend the life of the arrangement by adding a flower preservative to the water. Or you can use lemon-lime soda in place of the commercial preservative (use 12 ounces of soda per gallon of water). If you will

When arranging flowers, position the largest flowers first, then work in the smaller ones.

Florist's foam allows precise positioning of stems. Soak it in water with preservative before you insert the stems.

be arranging your flowers in a metal vase that is not lined with glass, plastic, or ceramic, skip the preservative. Otherwise the preservative may react with the metal and lose its effectiveness.

If you are anchoring flowers in a block of florist's foam, soak the foam in water to which preservative has been added before you put the foam in the vase.

Caring for Fresh Flowers

When the arrangement is finished, put it in a cool, airy but draft-free place. Keep cut flowers away from fireplaces, lamps, sunny windows, and other heat sources because heat will draw moisture out of the petals. For best results, change the water in the vase every day, and cut about ½ inch from the bottoms of the stems. These two simple steps will really extend the life of your cut flowers. Short-lived flowers such as primroses, violets, and forget-me-nots will especially appreciate a daily misting treatment.

When the flowers begin to fade, removing spent blossoms from the vase will let you get more mileage out of your arrangement.

Cutting & Conditioning A Select List

Here are specific directions for cutting and conditioning some popular flowers.

Achillea species (yarrow). Cut when half the flowers in the cluster are open. Condition overnight in cold water.

Aconitum species (monkshood). Cut when half the flowers on the spike are open. Condition overnight in cold water.

Alcea rosea (hollyhock). Cut in late afternoon or early morning, when three or four flowers on the stem are open. Split the stem ends 4 to 6 inches, and sear the ends over a candle. Condition in warm water to the base of the buds. Double-flowered varieties generally last longer in the vase than single-flowered types.

Anemone species (anemone). Cut when the buds show color, but before they open. Condition annual anemones in warm water to the base of the buds; perennial anemones in cold water.

Antirrhinum majus (snapdragon). Cut spikes when the first flowers open. Strip off excess leaves. Condition overnight in water to the base of the remaining leaves.

Aster species (aster). Cut when flowers are half to fully open. Strip off excess leaves; split the stems and recut them underwater. Condition the plants in warm water up to the base of the leaves.

Astilbe species (astilbe). Cut when half the flowers in the feathery head are open. Split the stems and condition them overnight.

Buddleia species (butterfly bush). Cut spikes when half the flowers are open. Strip off excess leaves, and split the stems. Condition them in warm water up to the base of the remaining leaves. Limp flower spikes can be revived by placing the stems in hot water before conditioning them.

'Moonshine' yarrow

Calendula officinalis (calendula). Cut when the flowers are three-quarters to fully open. Remove excess leaves; then condition the flowers in warm water to the base of the remaining leaves. Recut the stems underwater before conditioning to make the flowers last longer.

Cleome

Callistephus chinensis (China aster). Cut when the buds are three-quarters to fully open. Recut stems underwater before conditioning; then condition them overnight. Remove the leaves before arranging—they wilt quickly.

Campanula medium (Canterbury bells). Cut when the flowers are one-quarter to half open. Condition them overnight in warm water.

Celosia argentea (celosia). Cut when the flowers are fully developed; cool weather intensifies their colors. Strip off all excess leaves. Condition overnight or until both the stems and flowers are firm.

Centaurea cyanus (bachelor's buttons). Cut when the flowers are fully or nearly open; buds will not open in water. Condition overnight.

Chrysanthemum × grandiflorum (chrysanthemum). Cut when half to fully open. Strip off all foliage below the water level; leave foliage on the stems above the water level to help the flowers last longer.

Cleome hassleriana (cleome). Cut the flower when clusters are half open. Split the stems and condition overnight in warm water. Cleomes wilt when cut, but usually revive quickly during conditioning.

***Consolida ambigua* (larkspur).** Cut when the first flowers on the spike are open. Condition for two or more hours in cold water with ½ teaspoon of denatured alcohol or two tablespoons of white vinegar added per quart.

***Convallaria majalis* (lily-of-the-valley).** Cut stems when the first flowers open. Dip the stem ends in hot water; then condition them in cool water up to the base of the flowers.

***Coreopsis* species (coreopsis).** Cut when the flowers are fully open but the centers are still tight. Condition overnight in cold water to the base of the flowers.

***Cosmos* species (cosmos).** Cut when the flowers are open and the heads are still tight. Condition overnight in cold water to the base of the flowers. Blooms may drop pollen as they mature.

***Dahlia* cultivars (dahlia).** Cut when the flowers are just fully open. Condition in cold water. Revive prematurely wilted flowers by recutting the stems and placing them in warm water.

'Fascination' dahlia

***Delphinium* cultivars (delphinium).** Cut the large spikes when the first flowers open, and strip off any excess leaves. Condition in cold water.

***Dianthus caryophyllus* (carnation).** Cut when the flowers are half open. Strip off excess leaves; then condition in warm water to the base of the remaining leaves.

***Digitalis* species (foxglove).** Cut the stems when the first flowers are open. Split the stem ends an inch or more. Condition in warm water to the base of the flowers.

***Freesia* cultivars (freesia).** Cut when several flowers on the stem have opened. Submerge stems and flowers entirely in cold water overnight.

***Gaillardia* species (blanket flower).** Cut when the petals are open but the centers are still tight.

***Gardenia augusta* (gardenia).** Cut when the flowers are nearly open. Split the woody stems and condition the flowers overnight in cold water. Handle with care; gardenia petals bruise easily.

***Gladiolus* cultivars (gladiolus).** Cut the flower spikes when in bud. Split the stems and condition overnight in warm water to the base of the leaves.

***Gomphrena* species (globe amaranth).** Cut when the flowers are at least three-quarters open. Remove excess foliage and split the stems. Condition overnight in warm water.

***Gypsophila* species (baby's breath).** Cut sprays when half the flowers are open. Condition overnight in cold water to the base of the lowest flowers.

***Helianthus* species (sunflower).** Cut when the flowers are fully open. Strip off excess leaves and condition overnight in warm water to the base of the remaining leaves. Giant sunflowers need heavy wire inserted in each stem to support the weight of the flower.

***Heliotropium arborescens* (heliotrope).** Cut when half to three-quarters of the flowers in the cluster are open; include part of the woody stem if possible. Condition overnight in warm water. Be sure to keep foliage above the water level.

***Hemerocallis* cultivars (daylily).** Cut stems with several well-developed buds; they will open in water. Condition overnight in cold water. Remove flowers from the stem as they fade.

***Heuchera sanguinea* (coral bells).** Cut when half the flowers on the spray are open; buds will not open in water. Condition overnight in cold water.

'Role Model' daylily

***Hydrangea* species (hydrangea).** Cut the big flower heads when in full bloom. Strip off excess leaves and condition in warm water to the base of the remaining leaves.

***Iberis* species (candytuft).** Cut when half the flowers in the cluster are open. Condition overnight in cold water.

***Iris* species (iris).** Cut Dutch irises as the first flower on the stem opens. Cut bearded, Japanese, and Siberian irises when the first bud begins to unfold. Condition all irises in room-temperature water to the base of the flowers.

***Lathyrus odoratus* (sweet pea).** Break off the stems of annual types when they are almost completely in bloom. Cut perennials when the clusters are half open. Condition them overnight at room temperature.

***Lavandula* species (lavender).** Cut when the buds are fully colored but before they open. Strip off excess foliage and split the stem. Condition in warm water to the base of the flowers.

***Leucanthemum* × *superbum* (shasta daisy).** Cut when the flowers are just fully open. Condition overnight in warm water.

***Lilium* species and cultivars (lilies).** Cut when the first flowers on the stem open. Split the stem an inch or so and condition overnight in warm water to the base of the buds. Remove the anthers (the six narrow, orange shapes in the flower center, attached to long slender filaments) to keep pollen from dropping onto nearby furniture. Lily pollen can stain fingers, furniture, and clothing.

***Limonium* species (statice).** Cut flower clusters when they are half open. Condition overnight in cold water.

***Lupinus* species (lupine).** Cut spikes when the first flowers open; leave as much foliage on the stem as possible. Condition in warm water to the base of the remaining leaves.

***Narcissus* species (daffodil, narcissus).** Cut when buds are beginning to open. Condition overnight in cold water in a container by themselves.

***Nicotiana* species (nicotiana).** Cut when one or two flowers in the cluster are fully open. Condition overnight in warm water to the base of the flowers. Each flower lasts only a few days, but the buds continue to open for up to a week.

***Paeonia* species (peony).** Cut when the buds show color. Remove excess leaves and split the stems. Condition in warm water to the base of the remaining leaves.

***Papaver nudicaule* (Iceland poppy).** Cut when the buds are still tight. Seal the stem ends over a candle or in boiling water. Condition overnight in cool water in a cool, dark place. The flowers open quickly in warm water.

***Papaver orientale* (oriental poppy).** Cut when the buds are still tight. Sear the base of the stem over a candle. Condition in cool water up to the base of the bud.

***Petunia* × *hybrida* (petunia).** Cut when the flowers are nearly open. Flowers and leaves may wilt when cut, but they revive with conditioning. Strip the leaves below the water level and condition them overnight in water.

***Phlox paniculata* (garden phlox).** Cut when half the flowers in the cluster are open. Split the stems and condition overnight in cold water.

***Primula* species (primrose).** Cut when the flower clusters are half- to three-quarters open. Condition overnight in cool water.

***Ranunculus asiaticus* (ranunculus, Persian buttercup).** Cut when the flowers are opening but the centers are still tight. The flowers wilt when cut, but revive when conditioned. Condition overnight in warm water.

***Rosa* species and cultivars (rose).** Cut roses when in bud, ideally in late afternoon. Recut the stems underwater before conditioning, just below a leaf node. Strip the leaves from the bottom of the stem, but leave as many as possible. Submerge most of the stem in cold water overnight; wrap the buds in tissue before conditioning.

'Champagne Cocktail' rose

***Rudbeckia* species (coneflower).** Cut when the flowers are open but the centers are still tight. Condition overnight in cold water. Remove leaves as they wilt.

***Salpiglossis sinuata* (salpiglossis).** Cut as soon as flowers are fully open. Condition overnight in cold water to the base of the flowers.

***Salvia* species (salvia).** Cut blue salvia when the flowers on the lower half of the spike are open. Cut scarlet salvia when half to three-quarters of the flowers on the spike are open. Condition both types of salvia overnight in warm water.

***Scabiosa atropurpurea* (scabiosa).** Cut when the flowers are almost fully open. Split the stems and condition overnight in cool water to the base of the flowers. Scabiosa buds won't open in water unless they are fully developed.

***Syringa* species (lilac).** Cut when the first flowers in the head are open. Remove all the foliage and make several splits in the stem. Condition in cool water to the base of the flowers.

'Mme Lemoine' lilac

***Tagetes* species (marigold).** Cut when the flowers are just fully open. Strip off excess leaves; then condition overnight in cool water to the base of the remaining leaves. The flowers last a week or two.

***Tanacetum coccineum* (pyrethrum).** Cut when the first flowers open. Split the stems and condition them in warm water.

***Tanacetum parthenium* (feverfew).** Cut when half the flowers are open. Condition them overnight in warm water if you wish (they last well even if not conditioned).

***Tropaeolum* species (nasturtium).** Cut as soon as the flowers are fully open, with large buds ready to unfold. Split the stems. Condition them overnight in cold water. Nasturtium leaves are also nice in arrangements; condition them for 24 hours in warm water.

***Tulipa* cultivars (tulip).** Cut when the buds show color. Wrap stems and flowers in florist's tissue; then condition overnight in cold water to the base of the buds.

***Viola* × *wittrockiana* (pansy).** Cut when flowers are fully open. Leave foliage attached to make the flowers last longer. Condition in cool water to the base of the flowers.

***Zantedeschia* species (calla lily).** Cut at any stage from bud to full bloom. Submerge most of the stem and leaves in cold water for an hour or two. Then shake off the excess water and arrange the flowers.

Air-dry flowers by hanging them upside down in bunches. Fasten the stems together with rubber bands as shown on the next page. This holds the stems securely as they shrink during drying.

Flowers for Drying

Dried flowers remind us of the glories of the summer garden long after the winds have turned biting cold and the garden is buried under snow. Because drying your own flowers adds so much to the enjoyment of having a summer flower garden, here are some basic directions to help you get started.

Although most of the classic everlastings (flowers that air-dry very easily) are annuals, quite a few perennials also dry well. The list on page 135 focuses on flowers that can be dried easily and successfully. Many more flowers besides these can be dried, but this list includes good candidates in a range of forms and colors.

How to Dry Flowers

Harvest flowers meant for drying on a sunny, warm day when the plants are dry. For the best results, pick most flowers for drying just as they mature. To air-dry flowers, strip off the leaves and tie the stems in small bunches with twine or rubber bands. Hang the bunches upside down in a dark, dry, airy place.

If you want to preserve more of the flowers' color and to keep petals from curling up, try using silica gel (a desiccant in the form of small granules sold in garden centers and craft shops). To dry flowers in silica gel, begin by conditioning them. Stand the stems of the cut flowers in water for several hours, which will

Yarrow dries well. To preserve the most color, try using silica gel as a desiccant, explained on the next page.

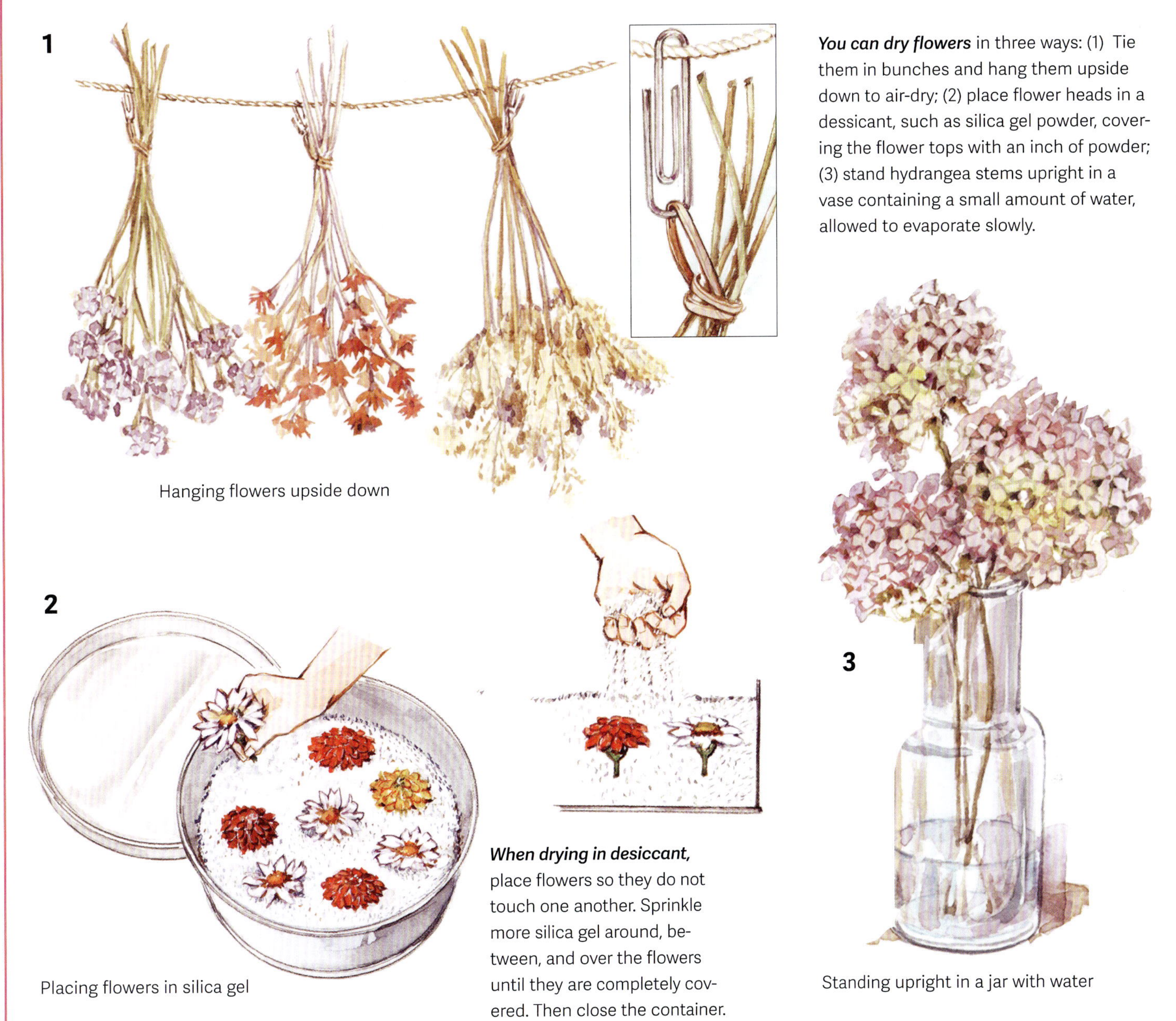

You can dry flowers in three ways: (1) Tie them in bunches and hang them upside down to air-dry; (2) place flower heads in a dessicant, such as silica gel powder, covering the flower tops with an inch of powder; (3) stand hydrangea stems upright in a vase containing a small amount of water, allowed to evaporate slowly.

Hanging flowers upside down

Placing flowers in silica gel

When drying in desiccant, place flowers so they do not touch one another. Sprinkle more silica gel around, between, and over the flowers until they are completely covered. Then close the container.

Standing upright in a jar with water

allow them to send water throughout the plant, making the petals firm. However, don't get the flowers wet. Then cut off the stems to leave only an inch or so before placing them in silica gel.

Dry the flowers in airtight plastic or metal containers. Put a ½-inch-deep layer of silica gel in the bottom of the container if the flowers are to be dried facedown; use more silica gel if you dry the flowers as shown in accompanying illustrations.

Dry flowers in a single layer, making sure the petals don't touch one another. (If they touch, flowers won't dry properly and could rot.) Dry flat, daisylike flowers facedown; most other flowers dry best faceup. Insert a piece of green florist's wire into the short stem (See page 134.) For faceup flowers, bend it into a sharp angle so the other end of the wire protrudes from the silica gel (this makes it easy to remove the dried flowers from the container). Long sprays and spikes of flowers can be laid horizontally to dry and don't need to be wired.

Lay the flowers carefully on top of the silica gel. Then sprinkle more desiccant around and over them until they are completely covered. Put the lid on the container, label it with the type of flower and the date, and set the container in a warm, dry place.

Flowers in silica gel take anywhere from a couple of days to a week to dry. Once the flowers feel dry and papery, they have dried sufficiently. Carefully pour off the desiccant and remove the flowers.

Silica gel isn't cheap, but it's clean and effective and can be reused. When the crystals turn pink, they can't absorb any more moisture. To prepare them for reuse, spread them in a shallow layer in a baking pan and place it in an oven set at 250°F until the crystals turn blue again, which will require half an hour or longer. Then remove the pans from the oven, and put the crystals in an airtight container while they're still hot. Don't use them until they have cooled. It's a good idea to oven-dry and cool the crystals just before you are ready to use them, so you don't run the risk that they will have absorbed moisture during storage.

Baskets of dried flowers are a delightful way to brighten your home in winter. When the colors fade, discard the flowers.

To stiffen weak stems, insert florist's wire up the stem, forming a hook using needle-nose pliers. Gently pull the hook into the flower head.

Caring for Dried Flowers

One problem with dried flowers is that thin stems are brittle and tend to break easily. To avoid broken stems, cut the stems short when you prepare the fresh flowers for drying, and insert a piece of heavy-gauge green florist's wire through each stem and into the head of the flower. If the wire tends to slip out, try the following trick: insert one end of the unbent wire through the stem and into the flower until it pokes out the center. Then make a tiny hook using your fingers or needle-nose pliers and gently pull the hook back through until it catches and hides itself in the center of the flower. For long stems you can either insert a wire into the stem before drying or spiral-wrap fine florist's wire around the stem later on.

Bugs sometimes chew small holes in dried flower arrangements and ruin their appearance, occasionally also causing them to shatter. The simplest preventive measure is to put the arrangement in your freezer for a day or two a few times a year. The cold won't damage the flowers, but it will kill any beetle larvae or other bugs that may be hiding in the arrangement. If some of your dried flowers do shatter, you can save any undamaged petals to add color to potpourris and discard the rest.

Finally, dried flowers will not last forever. After several months or a year, the flowers start to look dusty (they're almost impossible to clean), and the colors begin to fade. Enjoy them as winter reminders of summer's bounty, and replace them when their quality starts to decline.

Here Is A List of Ideal Flowers to Dry

Insert stems of dried flowers into a foam block to hold them in place in the container.

***Achillea* species (yarrow).** Pink, yellow; air-dry.

***Ageratum houstonianum* (ageratum).** Blue-violet, purple; dry in silica gel.

***Allium aflatunense, A. giganteum* (ornamental allium).** Purple; dry the seed heads that form after the flowers fade; air-dry.

***Artemisia* species (artemisia).** Foliage; air-dry.

***Astilbe* species (astilbe).** White, pink, red; the feathery flower plumes turn beige when dried; air-dry.

***Celosia argentea* (celosia).** Red, crimson, magenta, pink, orange, apricot, gold; air-dry.

***Consolida ambigua* (larkspur).** Purple, blue-violet, pink; air dry or use silica gel.

***Echinops* species (globe thistle).** Steel-blue, globe-shaped flowers; air-dry.

***Eryngium* species (sea holly).** Metallic blue flowers, unusually shaped but somewhat like thistles; air-dry.

***Gomphrena globosa* (globe amaranth).** Small, round purple, magenta, pink, white, orange flowers; air-dry.

***Gypsophila* species (baby's breath).** Sprays of tiny white flowers; air-dry.

***Helichrysum bracteatum* (strawflower).** Red, crimson, rose, pink, salmon, bronze, yellow, gold, white; pick before fully open; air-dry.

***Hydrangea* species (hydrangea).** The big flower heads fade eventually to beige as they dry. To dry, stand stems upright in a vase with a little water in the bottom; let the flowers dry in this position.

***Lavandula* species (lavender).** Light to deep purple; air-dry.

***Liatris* species (liatris).** Tall, rosy purple flower spikes; air-dry.

***Limonium sinuatum* (statice).** Purple, pink, yellow, white; air-dry.

***Nigella damascena* (love-in-a-mist).** The unusual seed pods resemble bird nests; air-dry.

***Rosa* species and cultivars (rose).** Shades of red, pink, yellow, orange, white; dry buds in silica gel or air-dry; individual petals can be air-dried.

***Sedum spectabile* (sedum 'Autumn Joy').** Flower heads turn beige, rust, or brown when dried; air-dry.

***Tagetes* species (marigold).** Yellow, gold, orange, mahogany, bicolors; dry in silica gel.

***Xeranthemum annuum* (xeranthemum, immortelle).** Pink, lavender, purple, white; air-dry or use silica gel.

***Zinnia* species (zinnia).** Many shades of red, orange, yellow, salmon, pink, rose, cream; dry in silica gel.

Strawflowers and baby's breath

Statice and strawflowers

Flowers for Summer Gardens

Summer's palette is rich and varied. There are so many colors to choose from, so many kinds of plants, and so many places to grow them. This chapter offers basic directions on how to grow some of summer's classic flowers.

The following summer-flowering plants are listed alphabetically by their scientific (botanical) names. These plants are readily available in local nurseries and from mail-order catalogs. They are also reliable and easy to grow if you provide the recommended conditions. For each plant you'll find descriptive information, suggestions for using the plant in the garden, and basic guidance on planting and care. Most plants adapt to a range of pH (acidity or alkalinity); for plants with a special need, the preference is noted. For an explanation of the plant naming system, see page 31.

Achillea / Yarrow

'Inca Gold' yarrow

This perennial is grown for flat-topped flower clusters of white, pink, yellow, red, salmon, and other warm shades. German Galaxy hybrids offer the rose and salmon colors. 'Fanal' is a popular cultivar.

The flowers bloom in early to midsummer, and some cultivars will continue into late summer if deadheaded regularly. Most species and cultivars grow 1 to 4 feet tall; their foliage is fernlike, in some species very finely divided and feathery looking. Often the leaves are aromatic when crushed, and some yarrows are grown in the herb garden for their historical healing applications. Yarrow flowers can be cut for fresh arrangements or dried. Most yarrows are hardy in Zones 3–10.

Yarrow is generally easy to grow, and the taller species are handsome in perennial gardens. There are lower-growing species also, usually grown in rock gardens.

Yarrow tolerates hot, dry conditions and does well in dry, exposed places. The plants are not particular about soil, but they will grow best in a well-drained, loamy soil of average fertility. Start them from seed, or purchase plants locally or by mail. Plant them 1 to 1½ feet apart. Divide established plants every three years or so, in either spring or fall.

'Blue Horizon' flossflower

Ageratum / Flossflower

This popular and easy-to-grow annual (*Ageratum houstonianum*) belongs to the daisy family. Low-growing cultivars form compact mounds and are favorites for window boxes and edging flower beds. Plants grow from 6 to 18 inches tall, depending on the culitvar, and have dark green leaves that are almost hidden by the fluffy flowers. Ageratum blooms from early summer until frost. The most common color is a purplish blue, but there are also pink- and white-flowered forms. The flowers of taller cultivars are useful for both cutting and drying.

Grow ageratum in average garden soil in either full sun or light shade. The plants can't tolerate frost, so don't plant them out in spring until all danger of frost is well past. Plants will also bloom indoors during the winter from seeds sown in September if you give them lots of sun.

Alcea / Hollyhock

Hollyhock

The charming, old-fashioned hollyhock (*Alcea rosea*) has been a favorite of flower gardeners for generations. This short-lived perennial is often grown as a biennial, because it is prone to a number of diseases. Hollyhocks grow in tall, slender spikes with showy flowers in midsummer to late summer in a range of warm colors in either single- or double-petaled forms. The plants are hardy in Zones 3 to 8, and gardeners farther south can grow them as biennials, setting out young plants in fall for bloom the following year.

Because they grow so tall (to 6 feet), you may wish to give hollyhocks a place of their own in the garden, rather than trying to fit them into a mixed border. A row of hollyhocks can look just right next to a white picket fence or a stone wall, or you can plant them in clumps next to the house. If you want to grow hollyhocks with other flowers, try them in a cottage garden or at the back of a bed or border.

The plants will thrive in almost any garden soil, as long as they get plenty of sun and moisture. To establish new plants, sow seeds in spring, mulch the plants to winter them over, and transplant the young plants the following spring to their permanent location. Hollyhocks self-sow readily, so you need not start new plants every year. Because of their height, the plants need to be staked or grown in a spot protected from wind.

Antirrhinum / Snapdragon

The colorful spikes of snapdragons (*Antirrhinum majus*) are splendid both in the garden and as cut flowers. They bloom in a host of colors—shades of red, pink, orange, yellow, white, and purple, as well as bicolors. Snapdragons can be either annual or perennial, depending on where you live. Though perennial in warm climates, they are best grown as annuals, because they can develop diseases when left to winter over. In most parts of North America, snapdragons bloom in early summer, but in mild climates they bloom in late winter or early spring.

Snapdragons range in height from 9 to 36 inches and space requirements vary by cultivar. Plants will grow in either full sun or partial shade, and they do best in cool weather, in moderately rich soil. In northern regions, start seeds indoors 8 to 12 weeks before the last expected spring frost, and set out seedlings as soon as you can work the soil. You can extend the blooming period by sowing seeds in batches several weeks apart and by keeping faded flowers picked off. If you cut off entire spikes when the flowers fade, the plants may bloom again in fall.

'Rocket Mix' snapdragons

Artemisia / Wormwood

'Silver Mound' artemisia **(A. schmidtiana)**, left, and dusty miller **(Senecio cineraria)**.

Artemisias belong to a large genus of aromatic plants grown primarily for their foliage, and they are extremely useful in flower gardens. Their silvery white foliage is excellent for moderating bright color combinations that might otherwise tire the eyes. Artemisias can grow from 1 to 3 feet tall, depending on the species or cultivar. Most artemisias are hardy in Zones 4–10; farther north, grow them as annuals.

Artemisias are easy to grow and do best in well-drained, sandy soils of average fertility. They need full sun. Plants may start to look straggly in hot, humid weather; if this happens, cut back the plants by half or more to clean them up and to stimulate new growth.

A similar silver-leaved annual that's widely available in garden centers is dusty miller (*Senecio cineraria*), a small plant that is a good choice for the front of the garden.

Astilbe / Astilbe

Astilbe

This lovely, feathery perennial garden favorite is native to China and Japan. Tall, airy plumes of tiny fluffy flowers arise from a mass of glossy green, toothed foliage in early to midsummer. Astilbes make good cut flowers, too. The most widely grown are cultivars of *Astilbe* × *arendsii,* with flowers of white, carmine red, or various shades of pink and rose. Plants grow 1½ to 3 feet tall. There are dwarf astilbe cultivars that grow just 1 foot high. Astilbes are hardy in Zones 4–8.

Astilbe grows well in any good garden soil, as long as it is moist and rich in organic matter. Plants do best in partial shade; full sun may burn the foliage and bleach out the flowers. Use astilbes in the perennial border or massed by themselves in damp, shady spots. Space plants 1 to 2 feet apart. Propagate by division in spring or fall.

Begonia / Begonia

Several begonias are widely grown as houseplants and as outdoor bedding and container flowers. None of the common ones can tolerate frost. Hundreds of species and varieties are available—the selection so vast that some aficionados become collectors and specialize in growing nothing but begonias. Some begonias are grown for their decorative foliage, but the best-known garden types are favored for their flowers. The two most widely grown types are wax begonias (*Begonia* Semperflorens-Cultorum Hybrids) and tuberous begonias (*B.* Tuberhybrida Hybrids).

Wax begonias have glossy, rounded leaves 2 to 4 inches long in varying shades of green and bronze. (As a rule, green-leaved varieties can tolerate more shade than bronze-leaved types.) The inch-wide flowers can be either single or double (depending on the cultivar) and come in shades of pink and red as well as white. Plants grow 6 to 12 inches tall.

Wax begonias bloom continuously all summer. They are excellent bedding plants and work beautifully in containers and window boxes. Wax begonias make good houseplants, too. In autumn, before the first frost, you can dig up plants or take cuttings to root and pot up for bloom indoors during the winter.

Wax begonias are readily available as plants, but you can also grow your own from cuttings from a friend's plant or from seeds. To start wax begonias from seed, sow seeds indoors in midwinter (January or February) to plant outdoors in spring. Transplant out after all danger of frost is past, spacing plants 6 to 12 inches apart. Wax begonias grow in either sun or shade but do best in light shade. Plants grown in medium to deep shade will not produce as many flowers as those in brighter light, but they will bloom.

Tuberous begonias are strictly for shade. They produce large, splashy blossoms in brilliant warm colors and show them off against contrasting dark green leaves. The flowers of some varieties resemble camellias, roses, or carnations in form. The plants bloom from midsummer to fall, and may be 8 to 18 inches tall, depending on the cultivar. Many are cascading in habit. Tuberous begonias grow and bloom beautifully in shady or partly shady gardens or in pots, tubs, window boxes, or in hanging baskets on shady porches or on patios.

The plants grow from tender bulbs that must be dug up and stored in fall (even in mild climates) and replanted the following spring. The plants need a long growing season; if you live in a

'Kalinka Red' and 'Kalinka Rose' wax begonias

Tuberous begonia

cold climate, start the tubers indoors in February or March. Plant only tubers that are firm and free of disease. Start them in pots of a porous, well-drained potting mixture that contains some compost or peat moss, making sure the rounded side of the tuber is down and the concave, depressed side is facing upward. Barely cover the tubers with potting mixture. Keep the soil evenly moist but not sopping wet (about as damp as a wrung-out sponge). The temperature should be about 75°F during the day, with a small drop at night. When the sprouts push their way through the soil, make sure the plants get strong light or even direct sun for part of the day. Less light will give you weak, gangly plants.

When all danger of frost has passed, plant outdoors in rich, moist soil that is well drained and deeply dug. Plants need shade for at least part of the day. Fertilize monthly with an all-purpose fertilizer until blooming begins and a low-nitrogen fertilizer after that. Organic gardeners can simply keep the soil well-supplied with nutrients from compost and all-purpose organic fertilizer blends worked into the soil in advance of planting, or give plants an extra boost during blooming with liquid seaweed or fish emulsion. Because the flowers are large and heavy, tuberous begonias usually need staking.

Cold-climate gardeners should dig their begonia tubers after the first frost; warm-climate gardeners can wait until the leaves yellow and start to turn brown at the end of the season. Spread out newly dug tubers and let them dry in the sun for a few days. Then cut off the tops an inch above the tubers. Shake off the soil, lay the tubers in a shallow box or tray, and cover them with peat moss or dry sand. Keep tubers of the same color flower together and label the boxes, so you know what you're planting in spring. The best storage temperature is 40° to 50°F.

Callistephus / China Aster

China aster

The annual China aster (*Callistephus chinensis*) is a dependable garden flower that is terrific for cutting as well. It blooms from midsummer until frost. Native to China and Japan, the China aster is available in a range of cultivars growing from 6 to 36 inches tall. Flowers come in white, purple, blue-violet, and in a variety of shades of pink and rosy red.

China asters are tender annuals. Start seeds indoors about six weeks before your last expected spring frost, or direct-seed outdoors after the danger of frost has passed. Space plants 1 to 1½ feet apart in the garden. China asters thrive in rich, well-drained soil in full sun. They need to be watered during dry spells. Avoid planting them where other asters grew the previous year; this helps prevent the diseases to which asters are prone.

Campanula / Bellflower

Known for their bell-shaped flowers, bellflowers come in a large assortment of annual and perennial forms with a host of uses in the flower garden. There are tall, upright species for beds and borders, diminutive forms best suited to rock gardens, and trailing species perfect for hanging baskets. They range in height from 8 inches to 4 or more feet. Bellflowers bloom in early to late summer, depending on the species, with flowers in various shades of violet-blue or white. Many species are grown and loved.

Bellflowers are generally easy to grow in average garden soil that is moist but well-drained; most like full sun. Hardiness varies with species, but many are hardy in Zones 4–8. Space plants 6 to 18 inches apart, depending on the species. Give them full sun to partial shade.

'Blue Chips' Carpathian bellflower

Rocket larkspur

Consolida / **Larkspur**

The annual, or rocket, larkspur *(C. ambigua)* is a lovely cut flower and can be dried as well. It grows from 1 to 4 feet tall and produces spikes of flowers in shades of violet, blue, pink, and white in early to late summer. The plant is a hardy annual and grows best in cool weather.

Give larkspur full sun to partial shade, and rich, humusy soil that's well drained but moist. It's a lovely addition to most any flower border or cutting garden. Sow seeds outdoors in autumn in warm climates, or in the early spring elsewhere.

Coreopsis / **Tickseed**

The yellow daisylike flowers of coreopsis are a mainstay of the summer flower garden. The plants are easy to grow and bloom abundantly through much of the summer, if deadheaded regularly. Most coreopsis flowers are golden yellow, but there are also pink and bicolored cultivars, as well as the lovely pale yellow 'Moonbeam', which mixes beautifully with blue and violet flowers. There are both perennial and annual species; the annuals are sometimes called calliopsis. The perennials are more widely grown. Though hardiness varies with species, many are hardy in Zones 3–9. Perennials and annuals alike hold up well in hot weather.

Coreopsis grows in practically any garden soil. All it asks is full sun. The plants are seldom bothered by pests and diseases, and the flowers are excellent for cutting, lasting a long time in the vase. Various kinds grow from 1 to 3 feet tall and make attractive additions to the front or middle of the flower garden. Picking off spent flowers will keep the plants producing plenty of new ones.

Set out purchased plants in spring, 15 to 18 inches apart. Propagate new plants by dividing established clumps in spring or fall.

Annual coreopsis

Dahlia / **Dahlia**

Members of this genus of tender tuberous plants native to Mexico and Central America have been extensively bred into thousands of flamboyant, large-flowered varieties.

The American Dahlia Society recognizes 17 distinct classes of dahlias, based on the form and size of the flowers. Some of the most popular kinds are shown on the next page. Dahlias grow from 10 inches, for dwarf types, to 7 feet tall. Dahlias bloom in temperate climates in late summer and well into autumn. In many gardens they put on their finest show in September. Dahlias flourish in loose, rich, loamy soil with excellent drainage. They like lots of moisture, but the plants do not like soggy conditions. They need at least six hours of sun a day to produce the best flowers. Prepare soil for dahlias by digging in a 2-inch layer of compost or manure in the autumn before planting. In spring, turn the soil again and incorporate some rock phosphate or superphosphate, and wood ashes, or an all-purpose fertilizer such as 5-10-5.

In cold climates, plant out dahlia tubers as soon as the danger of frost is past, or start them indoors in pots to get earlier flowers. In warm climates, plant out in early spring. Space the tubers 2 to 3 feet apart. All but dwarf varieties will need staking; set the stakes in place before planting to avoid damaging the tuberous roots. Plant the tubers 6 inches deep. Lay the root horizontally in the hole with the eye, or growing point, facing upward and toward the stake. Cover the tuber with 2 to 3 inches of soil at planting, leaving a depression in the soil. As the shoots grow, gradually fill in around them with more soil, until just a very shallow depression is left (it will hold water for the plant).

Allow only one or two of the strongest shoots to develop on each plant—cut back the rest at ground level. Culti-

'Hillcrest Albino' dahlia

'Claire de Lune' dahlia

'Jaldec Jolly' dahlia

Dahlia Classes

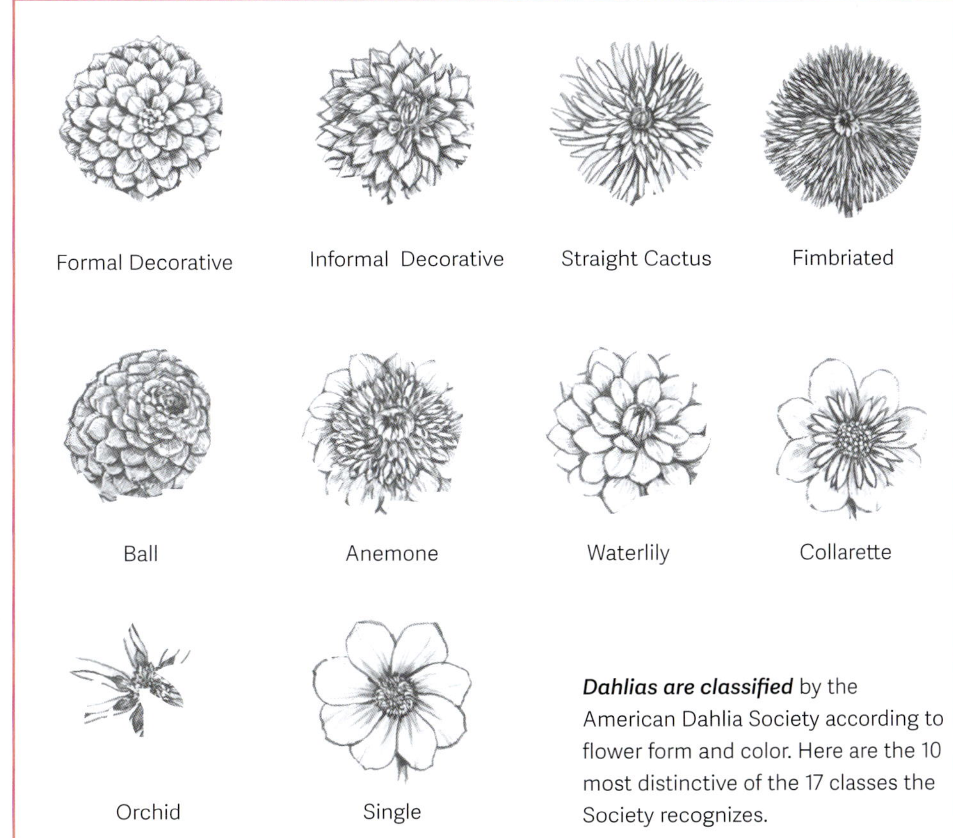

Dahlias are classified by the American Dahlia Society according to flower form and color. Here are the 10 most distinctive of the 17 classes the Society recognizes.

vate lightly once a week to keep the soil well aerated until the end of summer. Scratch a handful of fertilizer into the soil around each plant about the middle of August to give the flowers a boost.

In warm parts of Zone 7 and south, dahlias can be overwintered in the ground under a thick mulch. Elsewhere, in autumn after a heavy frost has blackened the plants, cut back the stems to 4 inches above ground level. Dig up the clumps of tubers and store them indoors over winter as described on page 184. Divide the clumps before replanting in spring so that each division has both roots and growth buds.

Delphinium / **Delphinium**

Delphiniums are highlights of the midsummer flower garden for two reasons: their glorious shades of blue and the sheer size of their flower spikes. At 6 or 7 feet, they tower over most other perennials. Almost everyone who sees delphiniums in their full glory wants to grow them, but the tall hybrids are hard to grow; you have to be able to meet their demands in order to succeed. There are also some smaller, less finicky delphiniums, such as the Belladonna hybrids, which top out around 4 feet tall and are easier to grow. Besides blue, delphiniums also come in white, pink, and bicolors.

Delphiniums don't take kindly to hot climates, and they don't generally grow well in hot soils. They generally grow best in Zones 3–7.

Choose a site in full sun, far away from tree roots and protected from wind. The tall, hefty flower spikes are likely to break in strong wind or heavy rain. Stake the plants before they bloom to avoid trouble.

Delphinium

Delphiniums must have extremely rich soil that is loose to a depth of at least 2 feet. Set purchased plants 2 to 2½ feet apart. Putting a handful of compost or slow-release fertilizer in the bottom of each planting hole is a good idea. Position the plants at the same depth at which they were growing in their nursery container.

After plants begin to grow, scratch a handful of fertilizer into the soil around each one (or spread additional compost on top of the soil). Water regularly, irrigating the soil rather than sprinkling from overhead because the crowns are prone to rot. As the season progresses, keep an eye out for blackspot fungi on the leaves, a delphinium nemesis along with crown rot. At the first sign of black spot, remove and destroy any affected leaves. If blackspot is a problem in your area, you should definitely be on the lookout for its presence. If the disease strikes, spray the plants with a sulfur-based fungicide, or look for a product that is labeled as a control for black- spot and is safe to use on delphiniums.

After the first year, you'll need to thin the flower stems every spring. Each plant will send up lots of them, but it can only support four or five. Wait until the shoots are several inches tall; then save only the strongest, sturdiest ones. Cut off the others at ground level. Given this painstaking care, your delphiniums should reward you with stately spires of the showiest flowers imaginable.

Gladiolus / Gladiolus

The bold, brightly colored flower spikes of gladiolus are a familiar summertime sight in backyards, flower stands, and farmer's markets. The color range of today's gladiolus hybrids includes practically every warm color imaginable, plus various shades of lavender, an unusual lime green, white, and bicolors. Gladiolus spikes grow quite tall (3 to 6 feet) and often need staking. There are also smaller miniature varieties.

'Tiny Tot' gladiolus

Gladiolus need deep, loose, rich soil to grow well. Incorporate plenty of organic matter into the bed and put some all-purpose fertilizer in the bottom of planting holes or trenches.

The plants grow from tender corms planted in spring, dug up in fall, and stored indoors over winter. For a succession of bloom, plant gladiolus in batches two weeks apart from early spring (after the last frost) until midsummer. The plants will flower from midsummer until early fall. Planting depth depends on the size of the corms: plant corms larger than 1 inch across from 6 to 8 inches deep, medium-size corms (½ to 1 inch) 4 to 5 inches deep, and smaller corms 3 inches deep. Set corms about 6 inches apart.

Keep the bed watered as the plants grow. When the flower spike appears, make sure the plants get plenty of water. During dry weather you'll need to water deeply every two or three days.

Since the corms are tender, they need to be dug before frost in cold climates; warm-climate gardeners often lift them, too, to control their weedy growth. You can start lifting the corms a month to six weeks after the plants finish blooming. Unlike spring bulbs, gladiolus corms can be dug before their leaves die. As soon as you dig the corms, cut off the leaves to the top of the corm. Destroy the old foliage because it can harbor pests and diseases to which glads are prone. Spread the corms in an open container to dry; separate the smaller offsets when you can pull them off easily. Store them over the winter in a cool, dry, well-ventilated place. If you live in a warm climate, place the corms in cold storage to ensure that they enter dormancy.

Gladiolus in mixed colors

Hemerocallis / Daylily

'Charles Johnston' daylily

'Kindly Light' daylily

Daylilies are incredibly easy to grow, come in a huge (and ever-expanding) range of colors, and require practically no care. How could any gardener go wrong with such a plant? There are cultivars that bloom in early, mid, and late summer—careful selection can give you daylilies in flower most of the summer. Some cultivars, such as 'Stella de Oro' and 'Happy Returns', bloom for much of the summer. A range of heights is available too—daylilies grow from 1 to 5 feet. They are hardy in Zones 3–10.

Daylilies grow vigorously in any soil that's damper than a desert and drier than a swamp. They'll make themselves at home in any ordinary garden soil. Daylilies bloom in either full sun or partial shade, although they will bend toward the light if you put them in a shady spot. They are seldom bothered by pests and diseases and don't even need to be watered except during a severe drought.

Plant your daylilies in clumps in the flower garden or at the back of the border. They are handsome when massed in front of a fence or beside a driveway.

Daylilies are tuberous plants that spread rapidly and are easily propagated by division. The plants don't need dividing very often, but when after several years you notice that the plants are crowded and not producing as many flowers as they once did, divide them. Dig up the clumps with a spading fork in late summer or early fall, when the plants have finished blooming. Shake off the loose soil and cut apart the clumps. Replant the outer portions, leaving about three tubers in each division, and throw out the old central parts. Replant the divisions in loose soil to which you have added some compost or aged manure.

Impatiens / Impatiens

Colorful, free-blooming impatiens are among the most widely grown flowers. Their flower-covered mounds light up shady beds and borders throughout North America. They come in many shades of pink along with reds, violets, oranges, and white. These easy annuals bloom from early summer until killed back by frost.

The hybrids grown today are in two basic forms: the low-growing bedding type, which bears many individual flowers on plants 4 to 12 inches tall, and the somewhat-harder-to-find balsam type, which grows taller (to 3 feet) and carries its flowers in clusters in the axils of the leaves. A third type, the New Guinea impatiens, grows 12 to 24 inches tall, with flowers in shades of orange, red, or violet. Many of them have variegated leaves.

Although best recognized as a shade-loving plant, impatiens also grows well in sunny places, as long as you give it plenty of water. The plants do fine in average garden soil that is moist but well drained. The balsam and New Guinea types do best with more sun and richer soil.

Balsam impatiens is hard to find in garden centers, so you may want to grow this type from seed. Start seeds indoors four to six weeks before you expect your last spring frost. Plant out seedlings when all danger of frost is past, spacing plants 6 to 8 inches apart.

'Showstopper Rose' bedding impatiens (left) and double-flowered impatiens (right)

New Guinea impatiens

Lilium / Lily

'Enchantment' lily (Asiatic hybrid)

Unlike daylilies, with which they are sometimes confused, true lilies have traditionally been considered hard to grow. Yet today's hybrids are sturdier and more disease-resistant than their predecessors and bloom beautifully if you give them the growing conditions they prefer. Lilies grow from 2 to 8 feet tall, depending on the species or cultivar, and their flowers, while basically trumpet-shaped, take a variety of forms. Hybrid lilies are divided into eight classes according to their form. Some of the more popular types are shown in the illustration below. The color range includes shades of pink, red, yellow, orange, purple, and white, and some are spotted, flushed, or striped with a second color. Many lilies are deliciously fragrant. Most lilies are hardy in Zones 4 or 5 to 8, depending on the species or cultivar. Gardeners farther south can dig and refrigerate the bulbs for two months before replanting them each spring, thereby giving them the cold period they need in order to bloom. Lilies flower in early to late summer, again depending on the species or cultivar.

Chief among the needs of lilies is light, loamy soil with absolutely perfect drainage. Lilies can't tolerate moisture standing around the bulbs. They also don't like hot soil, so you need to either mulch them or overplant them with annuals or ground covers to shade their roots and help keep the soil cool. Most lilies grow best in not-quite-full sun. A spot where the plants get bright, filtered sun for most of the day is ideal.

Most lily bulbs are planted in fall, but some of the late-blooming types can be planted in spring. Plant the bulbs three times as deep as the bulbs are tall, usually from 4 to 8 inches. You can also purchase lilies as container-grown plants in spring; plant these at the same depth that they're growing in their pots. The plants are heavy feeders and benefit from one to two applications of an all-purpose fertilizer in spring. During dry weather, water the plants once a week until they bloom. After they finish flowering, the plants like drier conditions. Many lilies grow tall—4 feet or more—and so need to be staked. In fact, it's a good idea to stake all cultivars that grow taller than 3 feet. The stakes need to be far enough away from the plants so they don't touch the bulbs and should be set in place just before the first flowers open. Tie the plants loosely to the stakes so the stems will not be damaged, as shown on pages 154.

Every few years, when the plants become crowded, you should lift and divide the bulbs. After the plants have finished blooming and the foliage has died back in fall, carefully dig up the clumps, leaving as many of the roots intact as you can. Very gently separate the bulbs, and replant them immediately. Keep the bulbs out of the soil for only the briefest possible time so they don't dry out.

Longiflorum lily

Lily Flower Classes

Hybrid lily classes include these four, plus Candidum, American, Aurelian (Trumpet), and other hybrids.

Asiatic hybrid

Oriental hybrid

Martagon

Longiflorum

Pelargonium / **Geranium**

The common garden geraniums belong to the genus Pelargonium. Native to South Africa, they are tender perennials, usually grown as annuals in North America. Geraniums are handsome in summer gardens, especially in containers. Cuttings taken late in the season will give you flowers indoors in winter if you grow them on a sunny but cool windowsill or under fluorescent lights.

Zonal geraniums (*Pelargonium* × *hortorum*) are the most widely grown. These plants have round, medium green leaves with scalloped and slightly fluted edges, sometimes marked with a dark band. They are excellent plants for tubs or pots on patios and rooftops and for the back of a window box. Zonal geraniums grow 1 to 3 feet tall and bloom in assorted shades of red, pink, orange, and white from early summer well into autumn. These geraniums like lots of sun, although they can tolerate a little shade. They do not like wet feet.

'Pink Harry Hieover' zonal geranium

The ivy geranium (*P. peltatum*) has trailing stems 2 to 3 feet long that make it perfect for hanging baskets and window boxes. As its name suggests, this plant's leaves resemble those of English ivy. The flower clusters are looser than those of other geraniums, and the overall plant has an airy, gracefully cascading look. The flowers bloom all summer until fall, in shades of burgundy, red, rose, pink, lavender, and white. Give it full sun in cold climates and partial shade in warm climates.

Ivy geranium

Geraniums thrive in any ordinary garden soil as long as it's well drained and not too rich in nitrogen, which causes the plants to produce too many leaves and too few flowers.

Gardeners in the warmest climates can grow zonal geraniums outdoors all year and sow seeds in either spring or fall. Cooler-climate gardeners can start plants from seed indoors or in a cold frame 10 to 12 weeks before the last heavy frost is expected in spring. Transplant the seedlings outdoors after the danger of heavy frost is past. Space your transplants or purchased plants about a foot apart.

Take cuttings in late summer to root for indoor flowers later on, or to overwinter for the following year. Make the cuttings 3 to 5 inches long and take them from young, green, sturdy shoots. Root them in a mixture of two parts sterile potting soil, one part sand, and one part vermiculite. Transplant them to individual pots when new leaves start to appear, a sign that roots have formed. Although the plants are tender, they grow best indoors where temperatures are cool—50° to 60°F. Give them as much light as possible and plenty of air circulation. Water them sparingly, though, or else the stems may rot.

Petunia / Petunia

'Strawberry Daddy' and 'Daddy Blue' petunia

Another tremendously popular summer annual—seen everywhere in flower beds, pots, and window boxes—is the petunia *(P. × hybrida)*. The color range is concentrated in reds, purples, pinks, and whites, but there are many shades of these colors, along with some unusual colors such as yellow. Petunias can also be bicolored, striped, or edged or ruffled with white.

The basic petunia flower is funnel-shaped, but breeders have developed frilled, ruffled, wavy, and doubled flowers in larger and larger sizes. There are upright petunias and cascading varieties bred for hanging baskets and window boxes, as well as trailing varieties to use as ground covers. Petunias grow 8 to 15 inches tall (except for the trailers, which creep along the ground) and bloom all summer long until frost.

Petunias are widely available in garden centers and are also fairly easy to grow from seed. In either case, don't put plants out in the garden until all danger of frost is past and the weather is warm. Petunias can't tolerate cold.

Start seeds indoors 6 to 10 weeks before you expect the last spring frost. Keep the growing medium moist and give the seedlings plenty of light on a sunny windowsill or under fluorescent lights. Transplant outdoors when frost danger is past, spacing plants 10 to 12 inches apart.

In temperate gardens, petunias bloom happily all summer in average garden soil as long as they get full sun, or at most some afternoon shade. Pick off faded flowers to keep the plants flowering lavishly. Southern gardeners can cut back plants by half in July for renewed bloom (except for trailers, such as 'Purple Wave'). Petunias may self-sow, but the new generation of plants won't look like its hybrid parent.

Phlox / Phlox

Summer phloxes bloom lavishly and from mid- to late summer and sometimes into autumn. Many cultivars are available in various shades of pink, purple, and white, plus bicolors.

Garden phlox *(Phlox paniculata)* is a perennial and grows from 2 to 4 feet tall, depending on the variety. Use taller cultivars in the back of the garden and shorter ones in the middle. The flowers are fragrant and good for cutting. Plants are hardy in Zones 3 to 9. Space the plants 1½ to 3 feet apart.

They need full sun in cold climates (partial shade in hot climates), rich, loamy soil, and lots of moisture. The plants are quite hardy but prone to attack by mold and mildew in hot, humid weather. To help prevent this, space the plants to allow air to circulate between them, and water them at ground level rather than sprinkling the leaves from overhead. Thinning the plants, and allowing just three or four shoots to remain on each plant, will promote good air circulation, strong growth, and large, abundant flowers. Propagate new plants from cuttings taken from the tips of new shoots late in the summer.

Lift and divide perennial phlox about every three years, when the plants finish blooming, in order to maintain the vigor of the plants. Cut off the flower clusters as the blossoms fade to keep the plants blooming longer. Phlox is a heavy feeder and appreciates an annual topdressing of compost or well-rotted manure. Scratch some all-purpose fertilizer into the soil around the plants when they start growing in the spring.

Annual phlox (*P. drummondii*) grows up to 1½ feet tall and blooms all summer. Dwarf cultivars grow just 6 to 8 inches tall and are good for edging. Space plants 6 to 12 inches apart.

Garden phlox

Rosa / Rose

There are thousands of rose cultivars, with many new ones introduced every year. While information on rose types and culture fills entire books, they are so popular that a brief survey is worth including here.

Bush roses include hybrid teas, floribundas, grandifloras, miniatures, and old-fashioned (heirloom) varieties. Bush roses can grow anywhere from 1 to 6 feet tall, and they produce the majority of their flowers on the tops of the plants.

Climbing roses have long canes that should be fastened to trellises, arbors, fences, and other supports. Large-flowered climbing roses bloom repeatedly or continuously through summer and even into early fall. Rambler roses have longer, thinner canes and smaller flowers and bloom only once in late spring or early summer.

Shrub roses have an upright growth habit, and their canes arch gracefully. They can be trained as hedges or massed in groups. They include ground cover types, polyantha roses, and groups of modern hybrids based on old garden roses (hybrid musks, hybrid rugosas). They also include Austin English roses, which combine the large, full, fragrant flowers of old-fashioned roses with the durability of modern hybrids. Shrub roses grow 4 to 12 feet tall (except for the low ground-cover types) and bear flowers in a variety of forms and colors. Some of them bloom all season; others bloom only once in spring.

Nurseries sell roses either in dormant, bare-root form or in containers. Bare-root roses are usually packaged in special plastic bags with their roots wrapped to keep them moist. Sometimes they come in cardboard boxes that are theoretically (but not always actually) biodegradable and meant to be planted right along with the plants. Inspect roses carefully before

'Martha's Vineyard' rose (shrub)

'Roman Holiday' rose (bush)

you take them home from the garden center, or when they arrive from the mail-order nursery. The canes should be firm, smooth, and green or reddish in color. Top-quality plants have at least three sturdy canes about ⅜-inch in diameter.

Bare-root roses are planted while the plants are still dormant, as illustrated on page 100. Cooler-climate gardeners plant them in early spring, once the soil has dried out enough to be worked and no more heavy freezes are expected. Warm-climate gardeners plant their bare-root roses in the fall.

Container-grown roses can be planted anytime during the growing season.

'Apothecary's' rose (shrub)

'Blaze' rose (climber)

They are more convenient to plant, but they are also more expensive and don't come in as broad a selection as bare-root roses do.

Plant roses where they will get at least four hours of sun a day, preferably in the morning. Good air circulation is essential, for roses are subject to fungus diseases. They need deep, well-drained, loamy soil that contains substantial amounts of organic matter. A straw mulch can help deter blackspot fungi by keeping soil from splashing onto leaves (spores of black spot and several other diseases overwinter in soil). Keep roses away from vigorous-rooted trees, suchas maples, that compete with neighboring plants for water and nutrients.

In subsequent years, feed the plants right after you prune them in early spring, spreading a ring of compost plus a handful of fertilizer (either an organic blend or a standard 5-10-5 formula) around the plant. Feed the plants again when they have set buds and a third time a couple of months before the first fall frost. Unless you have gotten an inch of rain during the week, water roses thoroughly once a week.

Roses are subject to aphids, spider mites, Japanese beetles, and several fungal diseases. If you notice any of these problems, treat them at once; for a safe homemade spray, see page 151. Your local garden center can recommend appropriate organic controls or synthetic sprays.

Roses need to be pruned severely in early spring just as their buds begin to swell. During the growing season, prune off any diseased foliage or damaged canes, and cut off faded flowers just above the uppermost five-part leaf. If you discover any suckers growing from the rootstock, cut them off at ground level.

Climbers are an exception. Along with old-fashioned roses, they mostly bloom on wood formed from the previous year's growth. They need less severe pruning and should receive their major pruning as soon as the plants are finished blooming, to avoid cutting off this year's flower buds.

Winter protection for roses in cold climates is described on page 194.

Perennial salvia

Salvia / **Sage**

There are annual, biennial, and perennial sages grown for their flowers. They are easy to grow. Their spikes of flowers enliven the garden in summer and early fall, in strong colors of the most flaming scarlet to shades of deep blue and violet or white.

Annual salvias—scarlet salvia *(Salvia splendens)* and mealycup sage *(S. farinacea)* bloom all summer into fall and can be 8 to 36 inches tall, depending on the cultivar. Perennial species, such as the widely grown *S.* × *superba*, will bloom in early to midsummer and grow 1½ to 3 feet tall. They are hardy in Zones 5 to 10.

Plant salvias in beds and borders and in pots on the patio. Plant dwarf types in window boxes. All salvias need lots of sun and light, plus well-drained soil. Most tolerate some dryness.

Annual salvias grow quickly from seed sown indoors about eight weeks before the last expected spring frost. Set the plants out in the garden after all danger of frost is past. Annual types grow best in warm soil.

Perennials thrive in any good garden soil, and their flowers are welcome additions to summer flower gardens and cut flower arrangements. (White and rosy pink cultivars are also available.) Plant the perennials 1 to 2 feet apart. New plants are easily propagated from cuttings or divisions. Take cuttings in early fall or early spring. Crowded plants can be dug and divided in early fall or early to midspring. Water the perennial salvias during dry weather.

Tagetes / **Marigold**

Marigolds are tender annuals, appreciated for their cheerful yellow, orange, and mahogany flowers (there are also bicolors). They are easy to grow, asking only full sun and well-drained soil of average fertility to bloom all summer long until hit by frost. You can start plants from seed indoors in late winter or buy plants at garden centers in spring. Marigolds thrive in hot weather. Don't plant them out in the garden until all danger of frost is past.

'Seven Star Red' marigold

African marigolds (*Tagetes erecta cultivars*) grow from 10 to 36 inches tall, depending on the cultivar, and have lemon yellow, gold, or orange flowers 2 to 4 inches across. The hybrids and cultivars on the market today are often called American marigolds. They are cheerful additions to beds and borders, and the taller varieties are good for cutting.

'Snow Drift' African marigold

Signet marigold

French marigolds (*T. patula cultivars*) and signet marigolds (*T. tenuifolia cultivars*) are compact plants with small flowers. French marigolds grow 6 to 18 inches tall, with flowers of golden yellow or orange, in some cultivars striped with mahogany red. Signet marigolds top out at about 12 inches and have yellow or orange flowers. Their foliage has a citrusy scent, and the plants keep blooming without deadheading. They are ideal for window boxes, the front of the garden, or edging sidewalks and driveways.

Veronica / **Speedwell**

'Shirley Blue' veronica

Veronicas are handsome, easy-to-grow, hardy perennials whose spikes of little blue, purple, pink, red, or white flowers have a multiplicity of uses in flower gardens. They bloom in early to midsummer, and some flower again in late summer to fall if you deadhead them promptly. The taller-growing kinds (which reach 2 to 4 feet) are excellent in the middle of flower beds and borders. Low-growing types (1 to 1½ feet tall) work well in the front of the garden, in rock gardens, and as edgings.

Veronicas need full sun and appreciate a moderately fertile, moist but well-drained soil, although they will grow in most average soils. The plants tolerate both heat and drought. Space low-growing types 10 to 12 inches apart, taller cultivars 18 inches apart. Though theoretically hardy in Zones 3 or 4 to 10, they're not always entirely hardy in very cold winters. If you live in Zone 3 or 4, you might want to dig up the plants in fall and put them in a cold frame over winter, just to be safe.

Order plants from a nursery for spring planting, or grow them from seed. Cool-climate gardeners can propagate new plants by lifting and dividing established plants in spring or by taking cuttings in the summer. Warm-climate gardeners can divide the plants in early fall, after they finish blooming.

Zinnia / **Zinnia**

There are tall, large-flowered zinnias (2 to 3 feet tall) for the back of the garden, dwarf sizes (6 to 12 inches tall) for the front of the garden and for edging, and medium-height plants to use in between. The palette contains many shades of red, orange, pink, and yellow, along with creamy whites and an unusual light green. Zinnias make wonderful, long-lasting cut flowers.

Zinnias thrive in hot weather and can tolerate dryness and intense sun. They'll grow in just about any soil and bloom quickly from seed. In fact, they are good plants to include in a child's first garden. The plants are seldom troubled by pests and diseases except in humid climates, where they sometimes get mildew. Cultivars of the narrow-leaved zinnia *(Z. angustifolia)* resist mildew, and their small, star-shaped single blossoms are charming.

Sow the seeds directly in the garden after all danger of frost is past in spring, or, if you want earlier flowers, start seeds indoors several weeks earlier. You can sow seeds in successive batches, three or four weeks apart, until the end of June to have zinnias blooming continuously until the first fall frost.

'Profusion Orange' zinnia

Watering is especially important during the summer. Water established perennials, annuals, and shrubs regularly and deeply during dry weather to prevent heat stress.

Summer Activities

Besides maintenance, summer gardeners everywhere are busy cutting flowers for bouquets and arrangements and, later in the season, for drying. At this time, it's also vital to cut off faded blossoms—a process called *deadheading*, as explained on the next page.

Then too, summer's the time to treat houseplants to an outdoor vacation. Good summering spots for houseplants can be a deck or patio; an arbor, gazebo, or lath house; or a protected corner of the garden in which the plants are sunk in their pots. Choose spots that match the light requirements for each plant.

Watering

Water is especially important in summer. Try to water established perennials, annuals, and shrubs regularly and deeply during dry weather to prevent heat stress. It is essential to water new plantings to help them get established. Roses and delphiniums are especially sensitive to drought, so keep them well watered. Late-blooming shrubs such as hydrangeas and crape myrtles also need plenty of water as their buds develop.

Finally, don't forget about plants in containers and window boxes. Container soil dries out far more quickly than garden soil, and in hot, dry weather you'll probably need to water containers at least once—and sometimes twice—a day. Check soil moisture by sticking a finger into the pot, and water plants whenever the top inch feels dry. Remember that unglazed clay pots allow water to evaporate through their walls and dry out faster than plastic containers. Don't wait to water until plants go limp, for by that time they will already be suffering from water stress. One exception to the watering rule is geraniums—they bloom best if allowed to dry a bit between waterings.

Overhead vs. Ground Level. The most efficient way to deliver water to plants is to water them at ground level, with soaker hoses or a drip irrigation system. This equipment allows water to trickle out slowly into the ground, where it is absorbed and made available to roots with no runoff or waste.

Watering overhead, with sprinklers or a handheld hose, allows some of the water to be lost to evaporation, and is likely to deliver too much water to some plants and not enough to others. However, overhead water offers benefits. It cleans dust and dirt from foliage and cools the air around plants on a hot day.

Deep vs. Shallow. Whichever watering method you use, try to water deeply and infrequently. That is, instead of giving the garden a quick sprinkling every day, water once or twice a week for a few hours, so the water soaks deeply into the soil.

Cover soaker hoses with mulch to prevent deterioration in sunlight and to reduce evaporation of surface water. Rain gauges let you monitor rainfall, but a more reliable check of watering needs is soil moistness two inches below the surface.

Benefits of Deadheading

Deadheading, the removal of spent flowers, serves two purposes: It keeps your garden looking its best and often promotes more flowers. With perennials, deadheading may stimulate a second bloom. With annuals, it encourages continued blooming, rather than production of seeds (which hastens a plant's shutting down for the year). Sharp shears leave a clean cut, less vulnerable to disease. Pinch off tender or thin stems with your fingertips.

This will encourage plants to send some roots deeper into the ground instead of concentrating them in the top few inches of soil, where they will be more vulnerable to heat and dryness.

The old rule of thumb was to ensure that the garden got an inch of water a week from all sources. But the amount of moisture needed varies with soil type, the plants in the garden, and weather conditions. In cool, cloudy weather, or in heavy clay soil, your plants may be fine with less water. In hot, dry weather or with sandy, porous soil, plants may need more water and more frequent watering.

When to Water. To tell when it's time to water, poke a finger into the soil in various parts of the garden. When the soil feels dry an inch or two below the soil surface, it's probably time to water.

Mulch. Mulching the garden in summer helps conserve soil moisture (slowing the rate at which it evaporates) and decreases the frequency of watering necessary. To mulch well, spread an inch or two of a fine-textured mulch such as cocoa bean hulls, or 2 to 3 inches of coarser materials such as shredded bark or wood chips.

Planning

As summer draws to a close, think about ordering bulbs for fall planting, making notes for changes in next year's beds and borders. Take time to assess which plants are thriving and which aren't, which combinations of flower colors and plant forms please you and which don't, and whether your color scheme is working. When planning, record your thoughts in a gardening journal, rather than trying to file loose sheets of paper here and there. When inspiration strikes, write it down, lest you lose it in the summer haze. (For more on starting a journal, see page 27.)

Safe Spraying with Baking Soda

To prevent black spot on roses and prevent or control powdery mildew on roses, garden phlox, zinnias, bee balm, lilacs and other susceptible plants, mix 1 tablespoon baking soda per gallon of water. To help the spray stick to foliage, add a few drops of insecticidal soap, Ivory soap, or horticultural oil. Spray every four to seven days.

Early Summer — Cooler Climates

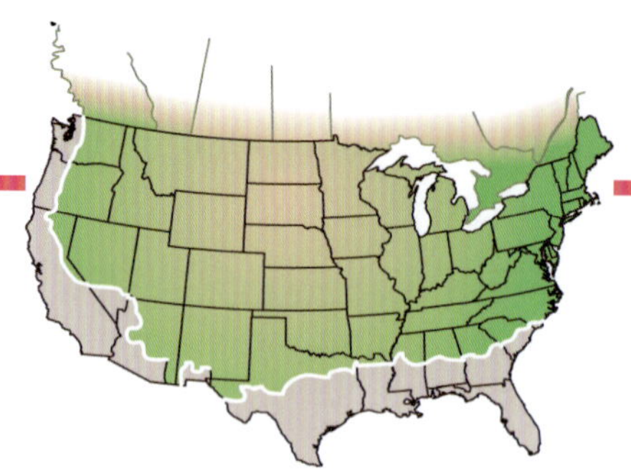

As shown on accompanying maps, if you live where winters are cold—from the mid latitudes to southern Canada—use the information on the "Cooler Climates" pages as your guide. If you live in the South, Southwest, or mild regions along the West Coast, you'll find the information on the facing "Warmer Climates" pages more useful.

Established Plants

Summer means maintenance in gardens everywhere. It's time to deadhead peonies and other spring perennials as their flowers fade. Don't forget to trim off the dead flowers from lilacs and other spring-blooming shrubs, too. Pinching off the faded flowers from early-blooming annuals encourages them to keep blooming. Also remove the foliage from spring bulbs as it yellows and dries.

Weed perennial beds and mulch them to keep new weeds from growing and to conserve soil moisture. Also fertilize, mulch, and—if necessary—weed early-blooming annuals such as sweet alyssum, China asters, candytufts, and nasturtiums. Fertilize and mulch lilacs and other spring shrubs when they are finished blooming. Also, if they need it, prune lilacs and other spring-blooming shrubs that bloom on old wood; these plants set their buds in summer for next year, so pruning later would remove some of the next year's flower buds.

Deadhead spent flowers, such as this peony, so the plant's energy isn't diverted to producing seeds.

Fertilize and mulch floribunda and hybrid tea roses after they complete their first flush of blooms. Cut back the flower stems to the closest five-leaflet stem when the blossoms start to fade in order to prolong bloom. Ramblers (a special type of climber) are treated differently from other roses; cut their blooming canes back to the ground once they finish flowering. And keep an eye out for aphids and blackspot on your roses; any such problems are easiest to control at the first sign of trouble (See box on page 151 for an easy homemade preventive spray.) Wash off aphids with a strong spray of water from a hose, or spray with insecticidal soap. If blackspot strikes, spray with a fungicide that controls blackspot.

Lightly fertilize container plants throughout the summer. Feed once a month with a seaweed and fish emulsion product, or a half-strength solution of a concentrated liquid all-purpose fertilizer. Don't overfeed—too much fertilizer causes weak, too rapid growth that is easy prey for pests and diseases.

Mulch sweet peas in early summer to keep their roots moist. Sweet peas are touchy in most climates. Be sure to water them during periods of dry weather.

Pinch back bushy annuals to produce compact growth and lots of flowers. Pinching tall chrysanthemum and aster varieties will promote bushier plants. Fertilize them now as well. As summer begins, stake delphiniums and other tall-growing summer-blooming perennials.

Thin phlox and bee balm to increase vigor and improve air circulation to reduce the chance of powdery mildew and fungus diseases. In crowded clumps, cut back some stems to the ground.

Planting

Plant gladiolus, dahlias, cannas, and tuberous begonias, if you haven't already done so. Sow seeds of fast-growing annuals such as sweet alyssum, morning glories, moonflowers, marigolds, nasturtiums, and zinnias for late summer flowers.

Set out annual bedding plants—begonias, impatiens, and other annuals. Feed the transplants with a balanced fertilizer and water well after planting.

Sow seeds now of spring and summer perennials for flowers next year. Sow in a nursery bed or open cold frame. You can also sow these seeds in midsummer, or even late summer in Zones 6 and 7. Columbines and primroses are candidates for early summer sowing.

Propagation

Create more of your own plants from established specimens, if you like, by taking cuttings from lavender and chrysanthemums and by layering azaleas, forsythias, and roses. Consult a good book on plant propagation for details.

Warmer Climates

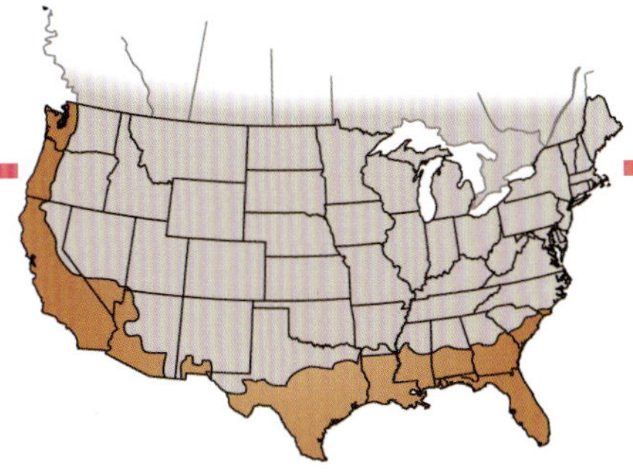

Pinch off the dead flowers of annuals in early summer to keep the plants blooming. Pruning or shearing back the plants will promote bushier, more compact growth. Also remove the dead foliage from spring bulbs, if you haven't already done so. Early summer is the time to give early-blooming shrubs such as azaleas and forsythias a light pruning. Summer-blooming shrubs, such as butterfly bush (Buddleia) need their spent flowers trimmed off regularly.

Pinch back chrysanthemums and tall asters for the first time to make them bushy and produce more flowers.

Cut gladiolus for indoor arrangements. When cutting, remove the least possible amount of foliage with each flower spike so the foliage can nourish the bulb for next year.

Mulch your gardens to help hold moisture around the plants' roots during the stressful hot weather ahead. Annuals, perennials, roses, and shrubs—especially broadleaved evergreens such as azaleas, rhododendrons, and camellias—should all be mulched for summer.

Water plants when they need it to prevent stress (see pages 150–151 for information on efficient watering).

Fertilize and water shade-loving plants, such as fuchsias and tuberous begonias, and keep them in light shade.

Fertilize roses after their first blooming is over.

Stake tall varieties of lilies and other tall plants that will be coming into bloom soon. Staking provides necessary support.

Lightly fertilize container plants throughout the summer. Feed them once a month with a liquid seaweed and fish emulsion product or a half-strength solution of a concentrated liquid all-purpose fertilizer. Don't overfeed potted plants, because too much fertilizer causes weak, too-rapid growth that is an easy target for pests and diseases to attack.

Dig up (in the warmest climates) spring bulbs and store them in a refrigerator over the summer to replant in fall. Or, in climates where bulbs survive outdoors all year, dig and divide offsets from mature bulbs. Transplant the divisions as soon as you make them. Most gardeners dig and discard hybrid tulips when they finish blooming. Most irises, too, are finished blooming by now in warm regions and so can be dug, divided, and transplanted.

Dig clumps of spring bulbs, such as these narcissus, and separate the young offset bulbs.

Replant the divided bulbs immediately and water them after planting.

Planting

Replace early plantings of annuals and spring bulbs with heat-tolerant flowers such as cosmos, marigolds, gaillardias, pentas, portulacas, tithonias, and zinnias. In all warm climates, it is also time to set out bedding plants in shady places. There is still time to plant the last of your dahlias and gladiolus. And you can still plant tropical water lilies in ponds or tubs.

Cover the soil surface of submerged water lily pots with gravel to keep the soil from floating away.

Continue direct-seeding of ageratums, celosias, marigolds, nasturtiums, globe amaranths, sunflowers, and zinnias for late summer and autumn flowers. Plant seeds or transplants of annuals in, among, or over tulips, narcissus, and other early-blooming bulbs to hide the dying foliage. You can also sow seeds of marigolds, zinnias, and annual verbenas for late summer replacement plants in the garden. Sow the seeds outdoors in an out-of-the-way spot in a protected area where they will get some shade.

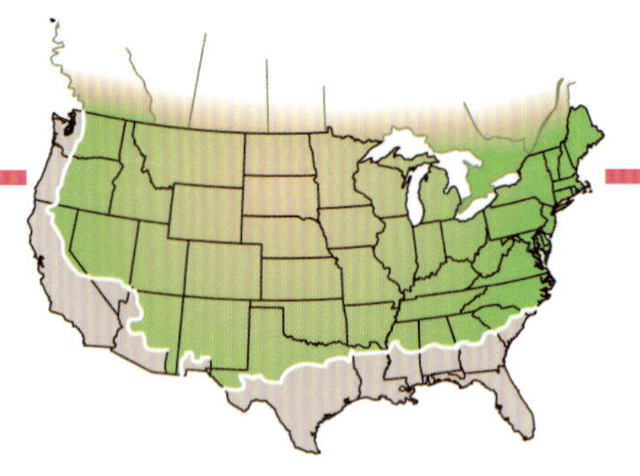

Established Plants

Continue to focus on basic maintenance chores in midsummer. It is such a pleasure to be outdoors in the garden surrounded by all the flowers in bloom that the work doesn't seem so bad. Most gardeners find that weeding, watering, and deadheading are enjoyable, soothing activities if attended to regularly so they don't get out of hand. Keep an eye out for any problems; it's easier to prevent pests and diseases than to fight them after they've established a foothold among your plants.

Deadhead as shown on pages 151 and 152.

Continue removing faded flowers from perennials and roses. Remember that cutting off rose blossoms in spring is also pruning the plants, so do it carefully. Use sharp pruners and cut back to an outward-facing bud above a shoot that has five leaves. Deadhead your annuals, too. Plants that produce too many flowers to be picked off individually, such as sweet alyssum and lobelia, can simply be sheared back and shaped, and a new flush of blossoms will follow. Bachelor's buttons and petunias tend to look straggly in midsummer; if you cut back the plants by 6 inches after the first flowering is over, they may bloom again.

Stop pinching chrysanthemums and tall asters by the middle of July; otherwise flowering will be delayed in fall.

Lightly fertilize container plants through the summer, as described on the previous page.

Hand-weed or else lightly cultivate the unmulched beds of annuals and perennials to keep weeds down. Remove the damaged or diseased leaves plus matted leaves on the ground. Keeping the garden clean is the best preventive action against pests and diseases.

Stake delphiniums, tall lilies, tall dahlias, garden phlox, and other tall summer flowers before they come into bloom.

Remove suckers from flowering trees and shrubs. These are leafy shoots that sprout below the graft swelling on grafted roses and trees, small branches that sprout low down on the trunk of flowering trees, or spindly shoots growing from the rootstock near the main part of the plant on lilacs and other flowering shrubs. Cut off any suckers to direct the plant's energy into its main branches.

Staking Tall Summer Flowers

Tie tall plants to individual stakes as they grow. Clustered plants can be held upright by means of perimeter stakes and a network of crossing twine supports.

Planting

In areas where there are at least ten weeks remaining before the first expected fall frost, you can sow seeds of short-season annuals for fall flowers. Annual phlox, portulacas, salpiglossis, sanvitalia, and sweet alyssum are good candidates.

Sow outdoors in a nursery bed or cold frame seeds of such perennials and biennials as coreopsis, delphiniums, foxgloves, perennial gaillardias, lupines, campanulas, hollyhocks, shasta daisies, pansies, sweet Williams, and dianthus for flowers next summer.

Plant colchicums and autumn crocuses for fall flowers.

Sow seeds for winter houseplants in outdoor pots, which you can bring indoors when the weather turns cold. Good prospects include browallias, calendulas, cinerarias, primroses, snapdragons, schizanthus, stocks, and salpiglossis.

Propagation

Other plants can be propagated from cuttings at this time of year. You can take cuttings from begonias, geraniums, and gloxinias to start new plants.

Planning

Order new daylilies and irises from nursery catalogs, to fill in gaps in your plantings or to add some new colors for the next year. Also order spring-blooming bulbs and perennial plants for autumn planting and winter forcing.

Warmer Climates

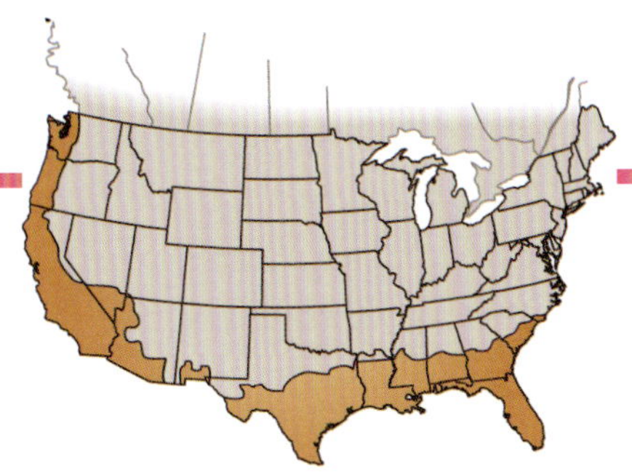

Established Plants

Even if you only venture out in the cool of morning or evening, maintenance is the name of the game in midsummer. If you still have some spring bulbs in your garden, dig them up when the foliage has died and store them to replant in fall. You can leave narcissus bulbs undisturbed for a few years, but tulips perform better in the South when they are dug up and replanted every year.

Deadhead perennials and either deadhead or shear back annuals to keep them blooming and to keep the garden looking its best. Many plants will rebloom if you keep picking off faded blossoms; in addition to most annuals, some perennials, such as coreopsis, coral bells and cranesbills will keep on blooming if deadheaded regularly. Prune wisteria when it finishes blooming.

Pinch back chrysanthemums one last time in early July. Disbud dahlias and late-blooming roses if you want to have fewer but larger flowers.

Water plants whenever they need it. (See pages 150–151.) As temperatures soar, keep a close watch on all plants in pots, tubs, window boxes, and hanging baskets. You'll need to water them once or even twice a day in midsummer.

Mulch the garden to conserve soil moisture. Mulching will also keep weed growth in check. Make sure your annuals, perennials, and roses, in particular, are well mulched to help get them through summer with a lot less stress.

Fertilize heavy-feeding perennials such as delphiniums, Shasta daisies, and chrysanthemums. Annuals also like a midsummer feeding, especially ones you've cut back to encourage a new flush of flowers. Fertilize all your container plants, too, as indicated on page 152, but be careful not to overfeed them.

Fertilize reblooming roses now to encourage them to bloom again in late summer and autumn. Although suckering is less likely in warm climates where roses are planted with the graft union aboveground, it can occur. Check your roses for suckers, and cut any off.

Stake tall-growing lilies, gladiolus, dahlias, hardy asters, and chrysanthemums before they come into bloom.

Keep garden beds free of weeds, dead foliage, and plant debris. Not only will this allow the beauty of your plants to show through, it will also help prevent pest and disease problems.

Planting

Plant now for flowers in seasons to come. Plant seeds of marigolds, melampodiums, salvias, verbenas, zinnias, and other fast-growing annuals for fall flowers.

Continue planting dahlias and gladiolus until the middle of August for autumn flowers. In addition, this is the time to plant colchicums, autumn crocuses, and spider lilies.

Propagation

Take cuttings from shade-loving plants such as impatiens and begonias and root them so you will have new plants that will bloom in the fall. You can also take some cuttings from your azaleas, bougainvilleas, camellias, hydrangeas, jasmines, and lilacs.

Enclose individual pots or entire flats in plastic bags to make sure that cuttings get plenty of humidity while they are forming roots. The plastic should not come in contact with the plant leaves. Keep plastic-covered pots out of direct sunlight.

Planning

Order spring-blooming bulbs and perennials for fall planting and winter forcing.

Taking Cuttings

Tools & Materials: Knife, stakes, plastic bags, horomone powder (optional) **Difficulty:** Easy

1 Take cuttings from healthy stems, just above a node. Then insert them firmly into potting soil (rooting hormone powder optional).

2 Place cuttings in moist soil and cover them loosely with stake-supported plastic bags. Remove the bags if condensation forms.

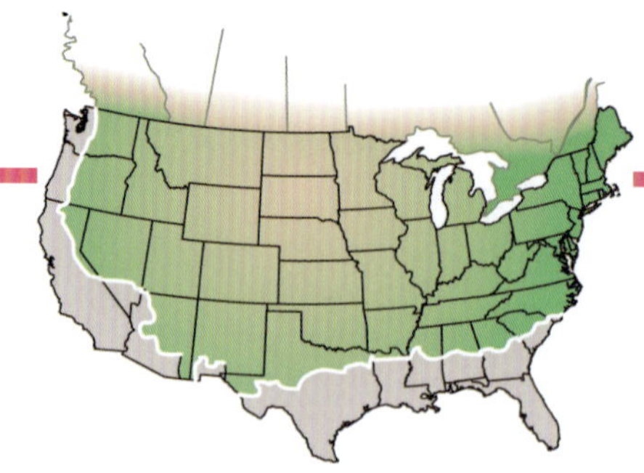

Established Plants

Harvest everlastings—baby's breath, celosias, globe amaranth, statice, strawflowers, and other flowers—to dry for winter arrangements.

Continue deadheading perennials and annuals and pinching back begonias, impatiens, and other shade plants that have gotten leggy. Don't let biennials like foxgloves and sweet Williams go to seed unless you want them to self-sow (and volunteer in unexpected places). When hollyhocks finish blooming, cut them back to the ground and dispose of all tops and leaves to minimize disease problems in future years.

Stake late-blooming tall dahlias, glads, hardy asters, and mums that need it.

Rake up and get rid of fallen leaves and other plant debris in the garden. Keep the garden weeded. Especially don't allow any weeds to go to seed, or you'll have many more to contend with the following year.

Continue watering (See guidance beginning on pages 150–151.) By all means continue to closely monitor plants in containers, and water them as often as they need it, testing soil moisture with your finger.

Divide iris rhizomes so they have time to become established before freezing temperatures set in.

Stop feeding perennials, roses, and shrubs so they will have time to harden for winter. But continue to fertilize container plants that will bloom into the fall, as indicated on page 152.

Dividing Iris

Tools & Materials: Pruning Shears, digging fork, knife, water source and pan, chlorine bleach **Difficulty:** Moderate

1 Cut away all but one-third of leaf lengths, leaving a compact fan that doesn't demand excessive nutrients.

2 Using a spading fork, carefully loosen soil around the clump of rhizomes and then remove each.

3 Cut young rhizomes away from older, spongy ones as shown, discarding older and diseased portions.

4 Soak rhizomes in a 9:1 solution of water and chlorine bleach for 30 minutes if borers infest irises. Let dry for several hours.

Planting

Finish sowing seeds of biennials and perennials outdoors for spring bloom. For example, campanulas, forget-me-nots, foxgloves, hollyhocks, and sweet Williams can all be sown before the end of summer so the seedlings have a chance to establish themselves before the ground freezes in late fall.

Planning

As summer's end approaches, order spring-blooming perennial plants and bulbs for autumn planting and winter forcing if you haven't already done so.

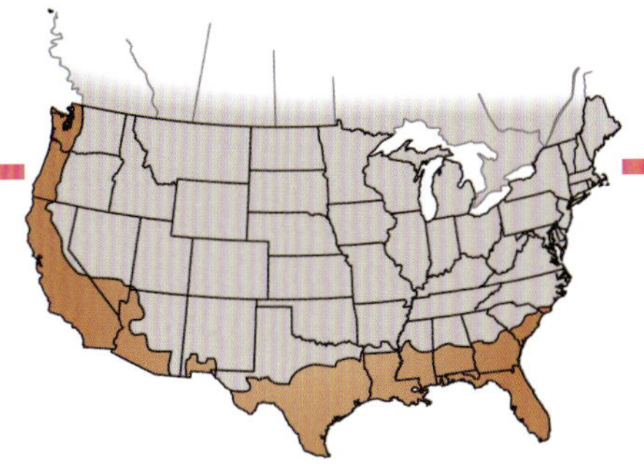

Established Plants

Continue to remove dead flowers in late summer from annuals and perennials and from summer-blooming shrubs, such as hydrangeas. It's an appropriate time to prune your summer shrubs when they have finished blooming.

Water and mulch flower beds and borders well during the intense heat of late summer (see Watering guidance on pages 104–105). Be sure to water container plants as often as they need it.

Continue fertilizing. In particular, fertilize and stake tall lilies that have not yet bloomed. Be careful when working in areas where spider lilies and magic lilies (Lycoris) are planted. Though their foliage has died back, their flower stems will come up soon. Water them deeply to get them started.

Watch for fungus in beds and borders if you live where late summer brings heavy, humid air; fungus is especially problematic on mums, roses, crape myrtle, verbenas, and zinnias. As soon as you see spotted leaves or a powdery gray coating, signs of fungus or mildew, get rid of any affected leaves. If necessary, spray with fungicidal soap, sulfur, or other fungicide listed for use on the affected plant. (Or try the homemade spray described on page 151.)

Feed dahlias and reblooming roses in early August to encourage them to bloom in the fall. You can feed chrysanthemums one last time as they get ready to flower.

Planting

Set out transplants (or in the warmest climates, plant seeds) of ageratums, sweet alyssums, calendulas, cosmos, marigolds, nemesias, sunflowers, zinnias, and other annuals to bloom in fall—there's still time. You can also plant seeds of Iceland poppies, pansies, and snapdragons for flowers in late winter and early spring. And sow biennials and perennials such as columbines, dianthus, hollyhocks, and primroses outdoors to bloom next year. Gardeners in the Southwest can also sow calendulas, forget-me-nots, snapdragons, stocks, violas, and sweet peas for winter bloom.

Plant calla lilies, spider and magic lilies, Dutch irises, freesias, Madonna lilies, oxalis, crocosmias, and other bulbs in mild areas of the South. You can also still plant colchicums and autumn crocuses for fall flowers.

Propagation

Divide and replant crowded daylilies, Madonna lilies, spider and magic lilies, irises, poppies, primroses, marguerites, and Shasta daisies when they finish blooming. This is also the best time to take cuttings from azaleas, rhododendrons, camellias, and other shrubs to start new plants.

Planning

Think ahead to flowers you will want to have in coming seasons. Start by renewing the soil in beds where you will plant in the fall. Dig in compost or leaf mold to improve soil structure. Also spread some fertilizer, following the application rates listed on the label. Use either a standard 5-10-10 or 5-10-5 formula or an organic blend (which will supply many trace elements not found in standard fertilizers).

Order spring-blooming bulbs and perennials for fall planting and winter forcing if you have not already done so. Ordering early gives you a wide choice.

Dividing Daylilies

Tools & Materials: Two digging forks, sturdy knife, water source **Difficulty:** Moderate

1 After lifting overgrown clumps of daylilies, minimize damage to roots and fans by driving two digging forks in, rather than slicing through with a spade.

2 Rinse soil from the clumps so you can see connections before you begin prying the fans apart, either with your hands or with a sturdy knife.

Prune back *houseplants, such as this geranium, before you take them outdoors.*

Don't neglect your houseplants in summer, even though your focus is on the outdoor garden. Now that the weather is quite warm, you can move tender and tropical houseplants outdoors for the season. Prune back any plants that need it when you take them outdoors. Sink all but the largest pots into the garden, or transplant the plants directly into the soil outdoors. If you have problems with slugs and other pests, slip an old nylon stocking over pots to keep pests from crawling in through the drainage holes.

Provide houseplants summering outdoors with the degree of light they need. Plants needing indirect light should get a shady spot outdoors. Start sun-lovers in the shade, too; gradually expose them to more light (to avoid sunburned leaves). In fall, the plants will need the reverse process to give leaves time to adapt to lower light levels indoors. In warmer climates, most houseplants will do best outdoors with at least afternoon shade.

Pinch back poinsettias if you are growing them for Christmas display; this encourages branching. Be sure to fertilize the plants regularly.

Before sinking a pot *for summer, a nylon stocking can prevent soil-dwelling critters from crawling up the pot drain hole.*

Early Summer

Plant chrysanthemum cuttings now for plants that will bloom indoors in autumn. You can also sow seeds of fairy primroses and cinerarias in order to have indoor flowers in winter.

Midsummer

Water and fertilize your houseplants regularly, both those spending the season outdoors and the ones still indoors. In warm climates, put heat-sensitive houseplants in a lath house or in the shade. Begonias, fuchsias, and primroses are especially prone to heat damage.

Fertilize poinsettias if you've moved them outdoors for the summer in preparation for winter color.

Potted cyclamens, freesias, and oxalis that have been resting can be started

A lattice panel *can protect houseplants summering outdoors if the plants need partial shade.*

Before bringing houseplants indoors that were sunken in the garden, break off roots that have grown through drain holes.

growing again to bloom indoors in autumn and winter.

Planting and Propagation

Start seeds of snapdragons for indoor flowers in late autumn; wax begonias, calendulas, and other flowers to bloom in winter; kalanchoes to bloom in late winter; and calceolaria for flowers next spring. (For winter flowers, see "Sow Now for Winter Flowers," above.)

Root the cuttings of chrysanthemums for flowers in late fall.

Late Summer

Start preparing your houseplants for winter. Pinch back plants that are spending summer outdoors so they will be bushy and well shaped when you bring them back indoors in the fall.

Sow Now for Winter Flowers

The following plants will bloom indoors in winter if you sow seeds in summer:

Begonia Semperflorens Cultorum Hybrids (wax begonia)
Calendula officinalis (pot marigold)

Pot Marigold (**Calendula**)

Callistephus chinensis (China aster)
Celosia cristata (woolflower)
Clarkia amoena (satin flower)
Cuphea ignea (cigar plant)
Exacum affine (Persian violet)
Heliotropium arborescens (heliotrope)
Impatiens wallerana (impatiens)
Lantana species (lantana)
Pelargonium × *hortorum* (geranium)
Pentas lanceolata (Egyptian star cluster)
Salpiglossis sinuata (painted tongue)
Tagetes species (marigold)
Thunbergia alata (black-eyed Susan vine)
Torenia fournieri (wishbone flower)
Tropaeolum majus (nasturtium)

'Patriot Honeylove' lantana

Pinch back chrysanthemums for the last time if you are growing them for use as indoor plants in fall and winter.

Propagation

Take cuttings from geraniums, lantanas, poinsettias, and other plants that can be grown to bloom indoors in winter. For faster rooting, you can dip the end of each cutting in rooting hormone. (Rooting hormone is sold in many garden centers, often in the form of a powder. Follow package directions for use.)

When taking a cutting, you can dip the cut end in hormone to hasten rooting.

Chapter 7 *Autumn*

For most gardeners, autumn means the fiery colors of fall leaves—glowing gold, red, orange, rust, bronze, and brown. These colors, along with the vibrant purple that also typifies fall, are echoed in the colors of the most classic of autumn flowers—chrysanthemums.

Autumn gardens can be full of color until frost. In early fall, several perennials, along with a host of annuals, are still flowering. Dahlias reach their peak, and some types of roses send up a second flush of bloom. Asters also burst forth, blooming well into the season. Some bulbs bloom in autumn. And many garden centers sell pansies to plant for fall flowers.

Long-stemmed grasses, as well as pods and berries, can lend softness and interest to bouquets and arrangements. If you add purple asters, you have a concert of color that captures the very essence of the season.

Very importantly, autumn marks the start of the indoor gardening season. Cuttings taken from garden annuals can be potted for indoor flowers later on. It's also time to pot up spring bulbs for forcing indoors in winter.

Autumn Flowers

This chapter addresses the variety of colors available in fall flower gardens and provides suggestions for combining them. Here you'll also find guidance on arranging freshly cut or dried flowers. Because autumn is also the beginning of the indoor gardening season, there are also tips on using houseplants.

Flowers in Gardens & Arrangements

Lots of summer annuals and some perennials continue to fill flower gardens with color in early fall. Annuals still blooming include sweet alyssum, impatiens, marigolds, nasturtiums, petunias, stocks, lobelia, and geraniums. Dahlias, gladiolus, and early chrysanthemums that started blooming in summer continue into autumn, with dahlias putting on their finest show in many gardens in September. Summer perennials still blooming include Michaelmas daisies (especially the New England asters, many of which come into bloom in September), sunflowers, salvias, veronicas, yarrows, turtleheads, coneflowers, coreopsis, gaillardias, hardy ageratums, daylilies, goldenrods, tiger lilies, sedums, statice, garden phlox, and Shasta daisies.

Yet autumn has its own stars in the garden. In addition to the bright and hot colors of dahlias, the warm earth tones of chrysanthemums; the blues and violets of monkshoods; and the soft roses, pinks, and white of Japanese anemones can each serve as the basis on which to build color schemes. Autumn

Autumn gardens can be lush with blossoms. Sweet autumn clematis **(Clematis terniflora)** festoons this arbor, opposite. Inside the garden, chrysanthemums, dahlias, gladiolus, and a wide variety of other annuals and perennials continue blooming from summer.

crocuses can be combined with other fall bulbs in gardens of their own or planted among autumn perennials.

If you like the pink-and-blue color schemes, there are numerous possibilities.

For example, the lavender-blue flowers of Aster × frikartii combine beautifully with the pinks and rosy pinks of New England aster cultivars. Or grow the blue-violet monkshood with 'Autumn Joy' sedum. The flowers of 'Autumn Joy' are pink when they first open in late summer and deepen gradually to an unusual salmony bronze color.

Try adding a touch of yellow to pink-and-blue fall gardens if you want more brightness. Sunflowers are still blooming in fall and marry well with the purply blue New England asters. An autumn bulb garden might combine autumn

'Autumn Joy' sedum (front), golden rudbeckia, and ornamental grasses will last well into autumn.

This autumn cart arrangement combines flowers with ornamental grasses and bright orange pumpkins.

crocuses in lilac-blue and violet with lavender and mauve-pink colchicums and golden yellow sternbergias.

Another direction to go with autumn colors is to mix white flowers with a second color. You might try growing white boltonia with asters in shades of rosy red and rosy pink, with perhaps a lavender-blue cultivar as well. Globe amaranth is still blooming in many gardens, and it makes a handsome display in mixed shades of red, red-violet, and white.

In southern gardens, fragrant white tuberoses combine well in autumn gardens with a white cultivar of mealy-cup sage (actually a slightly grayish shade) and red-violet globe amaranth. Camellias are a late autumn and winter highlight in many warm-climate gardens,with their large flowers in shades of red, rose, pink, and white.

As the transitional time between outdoor and indoor gardening seasons, autumn offers opportunities for displaying the products of both environments. You can still create varied bouquets and arrangements from the outdoor garden, and you can display fall-blooming houseplants on windowsills or as table centerpieces. Fall arrangements can combine fresh garden flowers with wildflowers, long-stemmed grasses, pods, and berries and dried everlastings.

It's better to avoid leaves from deciduous trees because their fiery colors don't last indoors. They will simply turn brown. Peony leaves are a good substitute. They develop wonderful autumnal shades of burgundy and bronze and last longer.

Autumn colors are warm and earthy. 'Blue Star' asters, 'September Glow' sedum, and yellow chrysanthemums provide this spectacular display.

The Autumn Palette

Plants noted here in ***boldface type*** are described in detail in "Flowers for Autumn Gardens" on page 172. In all listings in this book, plants are arranged alphabetically by scientific (botanical) name. When scientific and common names are the same in such lists, just one name is mentioned. *Note:* This list includes a few of the best annuals for fall color as a reminder that many summer annuals keep blooming until frost. Also, a few types of roses—especially some of the newer varieties—rebloom in fall most years.

RED FLOWERS

'Pam' chrysanthemum

Antirrhinum majus (snapdragon)
Arumitalicum (Italian arum), red berries
Aster species
Camellia, early cultivars
***Chrysanthemum* × *grandiflorum* (garden mum)**
Dahlia cultivars
Gomphrena species (globe amaranth)
Impatiens cultivars
Pelargonium cultivars (geraniums)
Rosa cultivars (roses), some rebloom in autumn
Salvia splendens (scarlet salvia)
Schizostylis coccinea (crimson flag)
Schlumbergera truncata (Thanksgiving cactus)

PINK FLOWERS

'Autumn Joy' sedum

***Anemone* × *hybrida* (Japanese anemone)**
Antirrhinum majus (snapdragon)
Aster species
Boltonia asteroides
Callistephus chinensis (China aster)
Calluna vulgaris (heather)
Camellia, early cultivars
Celosia cristata (crested cockscomb)
***Chrysanthemum* × *grandiflorum* (garden mum)**
Colchicum species and cultivars
Cosmos bipinnatus
Cyclamen hederifolium (hardy cyclamen)
Dahlia cultivars
Gomphrena species Impatiens cultivars
***Lycoris species* (magic lily, spider lily)**
Nerine species (nerine lily)
Oxalis species
Pelargonium cultivars (geraniums)
Pentas lanceolata (Egyptian star cluster)
Petunia cultivars
Phalaenopsis cultivars (moth orchid)
***Schlumbergera truncata* (Thanksgiving cactus)**
Sedum 'Autumn Joy' (Autumn Joy stonecrop)

ORANGE FLOWERS

'Hy Luster' dahlia

Antirrhinum majus (snapdragon)
Celosia cristata (crested cockscomb)
***Chrysanthemum* × *grandiflorum* (garden mum)**
Dahlia cultivars
Helenium autumnale (sneezeweed)
Lilium lancifolium (tiger lily)
Tagetes cultivars (marigold)

YELLOW FLOWERS

'Yellow Sandy' chrysanthemum

Antirrhinum majus (snapdragon)
Celosia cristata (crested cockscomb)
***Chrysanthemum* × *grandiflorum* (garden mum)**
Cosmos sulphureus
Dahlia cultivars
Helenium autumnale (sneezeweed)
Helianthus annuus (sunflower)
Rudbeckia species (coneflower)
***Sternbergia lutea* (winter daffodil)**
Tagetes species (marigold)

'Danum Foxy' dahlia

BLUE & VIOLET FLOWERS

Crocus

***Aconitum species* (monkshood)**
Ageratum houstonianum
Aster species
Callistephus chinensis (China aster)
Caryopteris species (bluebeard)
Ceratostigma plumbaginoides (leadwort)
Conoclinium coelestinum (hardy ageratum)
Echinops ritro (globe thistle)
Exacum affine (Persian violet)
Gentiana species (gentian)
Salvia species

Korean hybrid chrysanthemum

PURPLE FLOWERS

'Primetime Blue' petunia

Ageratum houstonianum
Antirrhinum majus (snapdragon)
Aster species
Callistephus chinensis (China aster)
***Chrysanthemum × grandiflorum* (garden mum)**
Colchicum species and cultivars
***Crocus species* (autumn crocus)**
Dahlia cultivars
Elsholtzia stauntonii
Eupatorium purpureum (Joe Pye weed)
Gladiolus cultivars
Gomphrena species (globe amaranth)
Impatiens cultivars
Lespedeza species (bush clover)
Liatris species (gayfeather)
Oxalis species
Pentas lanceolata (Egyptian star cluster)
Petunia cultivars
Salvia species and cultivars
Veltheimia bracteata (forest lily)
Veronia noveboracensis (ironweed)
Veronica cultivars
Viola × wittrockiana (pansy)

WHITE FLOWERS

'Blanche Poitevene' chrysanthemum

Abelia × grandiflora (glossy abelia)
***Anemone × hybrida* (Japanese anemone)**
Antirrhinum majus (snapdragon)
Aster species
Boltonia asteroides
Callistephus chinensis (China aster)
Calluna vulgaris (heather)
Camellia, early cultivars
***Chrysanthemum × grandiflorum* (garden mum)**
Cimicifuga species (snakeroot)
Clematis terniflora (sweet autumn clematis)
Colchicum species and cultivars
Cosmos bipinnatus
***Crocus species* (autumn crocus)**
Dahlia cultivars
Helianthus annuus (sunflower)
Myrtus communis (myrtle)
Nipponanthemum nipponicum (Nippon chrysanthemum, Montauk daisy)
Osmanthus species (sweet olive)
Oxalis species
Pentas lanceolata (Egyptian star cluster)
Petunia cultivars
Phalaenopsis cultivars (moth orchid)
Polianthes tuberosa (tuberose)
Polygonum aubertii (silver lace vine)
Salvia cultivars
***Schlumbergera truncata* (Thanksgiving cactus)**
Tricyrtis species (toad lily)
Yucca species

Mums, asters, goldenrod, tansies, zinnias, and nasturtiums

Room decor, left, can be greatly enhanced by houseplants that are thoughtfully placed. In this bright room, the plants bring the feeling of the garden indoors.

Fall-blooming orchids, below, make an elegant display, backed by tropical foliage plants and ferns. Left to right are lady's slipper orchids, moth orchids, pansy orchids **(Miltonia)**, and more moth orchids.

Indoor Display & Decorating

As the outdoor garden winds down in fall, you can find plenty of ways to grow flowers indoors. Beginning in late summer, you can take cuttings of garden annuals and pot them up for indoor bloom later on, and you can lift some plants entirely and pot them for bloom on a sunny windowsill. Fall is also the time to pot spring flowering bulbs for a forcing process that will provide indoor color in winter.

Houseplants that have spent the summer outdoors are brought back inside, and those that bloomed in spring and summer enter a period of dormancy when they will need less care. Some classic houseplants begin their own show in fall: Thanksgiving cactus, for example, and Jerusalem cherry, with its bright red fruit. Sweet olive (*Osmanthus fragrans*) will bloom indoors from September to May in a cool, bright spot, perfuming an entire room. In addition, many orchids that are suited for indoor growing bloom during autumn.

To use plants effectively as part of indoor decor, consider the characteristics of the plants themselves as they relate to one another, as well as the qualities of the rooms in which you want to place them. Consider plants in terms of their color, texture, and form. For flowering plants, color is the most important factor. Also consider how plants relate to room size, style of furnishings, color scheme, and plant environment (light, humidity, and temperature).

Flower & Room Colors

Flowers, growing in pots or cut for a vase, are a delightful way to enhance any decor. The spots of color they provide can be used to harmonize with or complement the overall color scheme, to pick up an accent color that occurs in upholstery or wallpaper, or to provide a dash of dramatic contrast in a neutral room.

If the room is decorated in a monochromatic scheme, the flowers should probably be a shade of the same color. If the room is neutral—decorated in grays or browns or whites—flowers in a bright, clear color will add life to the space.

When choosing flowers to blend comfortably with walls and furnishings, consider not only the colors themselves, but also the warmth or coolness of the colors. Stay within the same temperature range for harmony. For example, pink can be either warm, tending toward a salmon or peach tone, or it can be cool, with a bluish or purplish cast. When selecting a red geranium to match the pink in a drapery pattern, if the pink is warm, pick an orangey red geranium because a cherry red or magenta geranium flower would clash with the pink. With a purply pink, red that contains a hint of blue—a cherry red, perhaps, or red-violet—looks best.

Whatever the colors of the flowers you are working with, they will undoubtedly look better when viewed against a background of foliage. Many indoor gardeners like to display flowering houseplants in a verdant setting of large foliage plants; palms, dracaenas, ficus, and dieffenbachias are some favorites.

Texture, Form & Scale

Indoor foliage has other benefits besides color. It softens sharp lines of architecture and furnishings. In front of a window, the leaves of tall plants can filter the sunlight streaming into the room, creating a pleasantly dappled effect. To fully integrate flowering plants into interior decor, you would do well to think about a few other design qualities as well. Because you'll most likely be displaying your plants in groups for greater impact, be aware of the texture of each one. Texture is a twofold quality. There is the texture of individual leaves—glossy, fuzzy, smooth, waxy, wavy, toothed—which we notice at close range. Whereas, the texture of the plant as a whole—delicate and lacy, or bold and angular—becomes apparent from across a room.

A variety of textures usually results in a more interesting display.

If you have difficulty "seeing" the texture of the plant as a whole, try looking at the shadow it casts on a wall when a light shines on it. When you plan plant groupings, try to place similarly textured plants together if you want to create a unified, integrated look.

The shapes and growing habits of plants also play an important part in indoor displays. You can use plant shape as an architectural element, to create or alleviate tension in the design or to direct a viewer's eye toward a prominent fea- ture in the room. Plants have these four primary styles of growth: upright (vertical or spiky), bushy (mounded or ball-shaped), horizontal or spreading, and trailing or climbing. Using plant shapes to influence the way our eyes travel around a room

Plant Silhouettes

Combine different forms to create a more interesting plant display.

This plant arrangement leads the eye from one plant or group to another.

makes it possible to create either bold, dramatic, or subtly integrated effects with plant displays.

Along with texture and growth habit, also consider scale. Both size and texture affect how well a plant fits into a room. In a small room with a subdued color scheme, finely textured, soft-colored plants work better than boldly textured, bright-colored ones. Bright and bold plants fit best in larger or boldly decorated rooms. In a small office, a collection of African violets looks better than would a big, shrubby gardenia. On the other hand, those same violets would disappear in an open-plan loft space, where larger shrubs would be far more appropriate. Think about using large plants in large open rooms, alcoves, or hallways, or to divide or screen off parts of rooms. Use smaller plants on windowsills, shelves, bookcases, end tables, desks, or dining tables. Combine them with candles for centerpieces. Elevate them on pedestals or plant stands to view them at eye level.

Plants should also work with the style in which the room is furnished. A boldly shaped succulent or bromeliad that has a contemporary look might seem out of place in a Victorian-style parlor with lace curtains and chintz-covered sofas.

Grouping Houseplants for Display

There are limitless ways to group plants indoors to show them off. One effective approach is to group several plants of the same type. For example, indoor favorites such as begonias and African violets come in many sizes, growing habits, and colors. A selection of different begonias makes a nice display. You may find yourself becoming a collector of a type of plant that does particularly well for you.

To design a really effective and interesting grouping, think about your indoor garden as if it were an outdoor flower border. Think three-dimensionally; arrange the plants with shorter ones in front and taller ones in back, with a background of tall foliage plants taking the place of trees and shrubs that form the backbone of the outdoor garden. Create depth with tiered plant stands or low stands placed in front of a windowsill.

If you have a big picture window or sliding glass doors onto a deck, patio, or lawn, you can achieve wonderful effects by relating your indoor plants to the outdoor landscape, creating a visual transition from outdoors to indoors. Choose houseplants that echo the landscape plants in your region—perhaps cacti and succulents in a desert climate; bromeliads, hibiscus, gardenias, and tropicals in the South; or bulbs and azaleas in a wooded setting.

If so inclined, you can even try a few decorator's tricks to create added impact. By spotlighting plants, you can create drama and interesting shadow patterns on a nearby wall. And plants in front of a mirror are multiplied for a striking effect. You can even set your potted plants in fancy cachepots in styles and colors that relate to the rest of the room.

This picture window afforded a chance to relate a display dominated by cacti to the dry outdoor landscape.

The Indoor Environment

Most homes offer an assortment of growing conditions that suit flowering plants in varying degrees. You don't necessarily need to show off your flowering favorites in the same place where you grow them. Most plants can stand a dim spot for a few days, so they can take center stage for a dinner party or family gathering. Also, try well-placed room lighting to supplement natural light and create a more hospitable environment for plants. You can buy plant lights that fit into standard track-mounted fixtures as well as full-spectrum fluorescent tubes that fit into compact, inconspicuous fixtures to attach above dark shelves and in dim corners.

Well-chosen lights make it possible to grow plants without a nearby window.

If you have no decent window exposures, you can set up a light garden in the basement or a back room. Rotate plants in and out of the growing area; move them into living spaces for display during their peak blooming periods.

What Plants Need to Bloom Indoors

The key to success with indoor plants is to choose plants that grow well in the type of environment you have to offer them. For example, without lots of sun and some cool nighttime temperatures, many cacti will grow but will not bloom indoors no matter how much fertilizer you give them. But the ideal conditions for cacti to bloom are too bright and too dry for African violets to thrive. African violets prefer bright (but not direct) light, such as that in a north-facing window. While they don't grow well in hot drafts, African violets like warmth and some humidity; they need temperatures to stay above 55°F at night to keep their leaves from rotting. On the other hand, African violets are doomed to failure in a cool, dry room. If you choose plants whose requirements match the conditions available in your house, you will have spectacular flowers. Plants suited to their surroundings are almost guaranteed to succeed.

To begin making choices, start with a basic understanding of what indoor flowering plants need to grow well. The factors you need to understand and manage to keep indoor plants thriving are water, humidity, light, fertilizer, ventilation, and pruning.

Plants Available from the Florist

To augment the supply of flowers from your indoor garden, you can rely on seasonal bloomers from the florist. Florist plants, such as cinerarias and calceolarias, are usually forced by commercial growers; it's often very difficult to get these to rebloom under home conditions. Paperwhite narcissus forced for indoor display are similarly difficult repeaters. These plants are generally discarded after they finish blooming, freeing you from further responsibility for their upkeep.

Water. First, all plants need water. Tropical plants need constant moisture, while others, such as succulents and cacti, need long dry periods to stimulate bloom. What no plant likes is too much water—overwatering is the biggest cause of houseplants' untimely demise. It is best to water most plants thoroughly (until you see water accumulating in the saucer

Paperwhite narcissus and African violets in pretty pots bring color to a bright—but not sunny—windowsill.

beneath the pot) and let them dry out between waterings. Giving plants a little bit of water every day or two may result in the surface roots getting waterlogged and eventually rotting, while deeper roots dry out and cease functioning. Less frequent but thorough watering ensures that all the roots receive moisture. Wait half an hour, and then empty any water remaining in the saucer. Letting it sit in water for a long time can eventually cause roots to rot.

Watering plants from the bottom (pouring water into the plant saucer) is effective for small plants. Watering from the top works for most plants so long as you're careful to keep from spilling water on the leaves. Top-watering also flushes excess fertilizer salts from the pot. If you water from the soil surface, continue until you see water accumulating in the saucer beneath the pot.

Humidity. In fall and winter most homes tend to become drier because of central heating. This is a problem for plants because low humidity can cause buds to dry out or drop off. Most flowering plants like a relative humidity of 40 to 50 percent. But in winter a centrally heated house can dry out to a relative humidity of 20 percent or less; in desert climates the humidity gets even lower. To increase humidity for your plants, mist them regularly and group them on pebble trays filled with water, which evaporates and increases humidity around the plants. Operating room humidifiers and using containers of water placed on top of nearby radiators will also help to boost humidity levels.

To increase humidity around plants, group them on a pebble tray. Keep the water level below the top of the pebbles, so the pots don't sit in water.

Light. Another essential is light. Indoor plants need lots of light to survive and even more light to flower. South-facing windows get the most light and north windows the least. Eastern exposures are generally brighter than western ones. Many—but not all—flowering plants do best in a window facing toward the south, especially in winter when the sunlight is much less intense.

If you don't have a bright, sunny windowsill, you'll need to supplement the available natural light with fluorescent fixtures placed above the plants. Special daylight tubes or a combination of cool white and warm white tubes make the best *grow* lights. Incandescent lights are helpful, too, but they give off substantial amounts of heat, lack blue-spectrum wavelengths plants need to manufacture carbohydrates, are costlier to operate than fluorescents, and don't by themselves supply the right kind of light. Daylight tubes, or a combination of cool white and warm white tubes, supply the full spectrum of light (blue, red, and far-red wavelengths) plants need to grow and bloom.

Fertilizer. Flowering houseplants should be fertilized more often than foliage plants. A balanced, all-purpose plant food is fine most of the year, but switch to a formulation with more phosphorus and less nitrogen as flowering time approaches. Look for a formula with a lower first number (which refers to nitrogen) and a higher middle number (which refers to phosphorus); this may also be labeled as a formula for flowering plants or African violets. Lots of nitrogen is good for foliage plants, but it will make your flowering plants produce nice leaves and no blooms. A formula such as 5-10-5 or 12-36-14 will promote blooms as well as healthy growth.

Ventilation. Indoors you need to make sure plants get adequate ventilation, because they don't have the benefit of the breezes and constant airflow outdoors. Still air indoors can trap pollutants from building materials and gas used for cooking and heating. This is particularly true in tightly insulated homes. Also, the air in the immediate vicinity of groups of plants tends to hold water vapor. Once you follow the recommendations to increase humidity (text at left) around plants, ventilation becomes even more important. Still, humid air can encourage various plant diseases, so it's important to keep the air moving. A slow fan can do the job nicely. Though plants need good air circulation, you should keep them out of cold drafts. Also keep plants away

Fluorescent lights are an excellent source of light for indoor gardens. See "Light" in text at left.

from heaters, which create hot and drying drafts.

Pruning. Woody-stemmed plants may usually need occasional pruning to produce better flowers and to maintain their overall vigor, as well as to keep an attractive shape. In general, prune right above a bud or node (where a leaf, flower, or another branch joins); there a new shoot can grow from the shortened stem. If you want the plant to grow outward in a more open form, prune above an outward-facing bud; if you want the plant to grow inward (for a more compact shape), cut above an inward-facing bud. Also prune away any dead or yellowing growth and any water sprouts (fast-growing, weak, tender shoots).

Pruning Woody & Herbaceous Plants

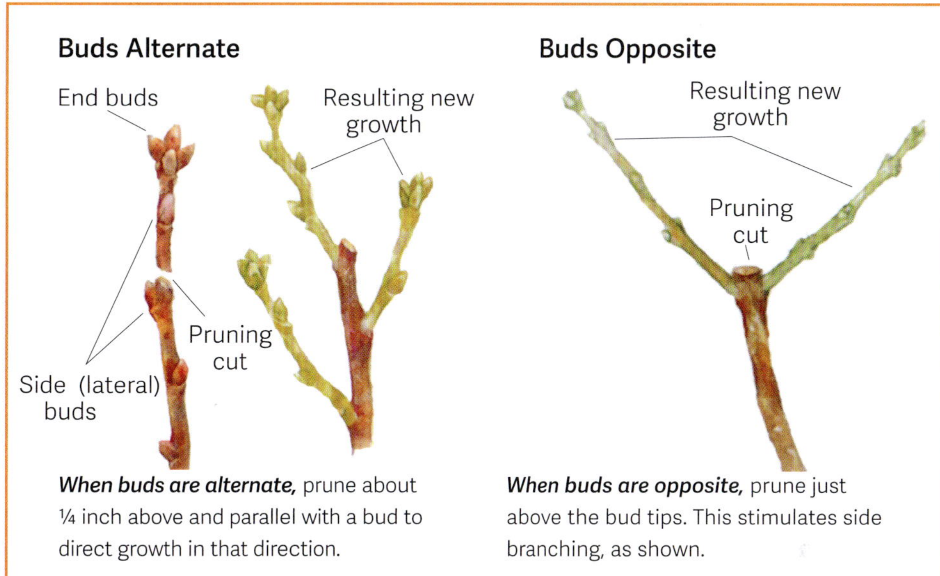

When buds are alternate, prune about ¼ inch above and parallel with a bud to direct growth in that direction.

When buds are opposite, prune just above the bud tips. This stimulates side branching, as shown.

Why Houseplants Don't Bloom

If your plants refuse to flower, here are some questions to ask yourself. For remedies, refer to related sections on, opposite.

- First, is the plant old enough to bloom? Some plants, especially woody ones, need to reach a certain age before they flower. If your reluctant bloomer is a woody-stemmed perennial that's less than a year old, it might not yet be ready to bloom.
- Is the plant getting the right amount of light? Many plants need a bright south window—one not shaded by trees—in order to bloom indoors. If your plant isn't getting enough light, all the fertilizer in the world won't make it bloom. If you can't move the plant to a sunnier window, to install grow lights.
- Is the plant getting the right duration of light (daylength)? Some plants, called short-day plants, only bloom when given a specific amount of darkness. Some short-day plants, such as Christmas cactus and kalanchoe, need short days and long nights in order to set buds. Some gardeners limit the daylength of such plants by covering the plants (or placing them in a closet) in the evening and removing the cover in the morning. In most cases it's important to cover these plants even though the outdoor daylength may be short, because even electric lights burning in the same room with short-day plants are bright enough to disrupt the darkness. Conversely, long-day plants such as geraniums, tuberous begonias, and spring-blooming orchids, can be tricked into blooming if natural light is supplemented with grow lights for several hours at night to create a longer "day." Fortunately, most houseplants are day-neutral and will flower without a particular number of hours of light or darkness.
- Is the temperature too warm or too cool? Some houseplants need to experience a change of temperature before blooming. Spring bulbs, for example, need a pronounced cold period in order to flower, as do a lot of cacti.
- Is the plant getting too much nitrogen and not enough phosphorus? If your plant is producing lots of leaves but no flower buds during its normal flowering season, you may be giving it too much nitrogen and not enough phosphorus and potassium.
- Are buds dropping off the plant rather than opening? If so, your plant is probably getting too much or too little water or humidity. Low humidity and overwatering or underwatering can cause flower buds to fall.
- Finally, is the pot too large or too small? Lots of plants, including amaryllis and clivia, bloom best when they're potbound. These plants won't bloom if the pot is too big. Other plants, such as begonias and dianthus, won't bloom if their roots are confined in too small a pot.

Flowers for Autumn Gardens

Autumn gardens can still be full of color, even in cold climates. Some of the plants discussed in this chapter actually begin blooming in summer, but all of them make their most important contribution to the garden in fall. In addition to the outdoor plants, you'll find a few autumn-blooming houseplants here.

The plants here are listed alphabetically by their scientific (botanical) names. These plants are readily available in local nurseries and from mail-order catalogs. They are also reliable and easy to grow if you provide the recommended conditions. For each plant you'll find descriptive information, suggestions for using the plant in the garden, and basic guidance on planting and care. Most plants adapt to a range of pH (acidity or alkalinity); for plants with a special need, the preference is noted. For an explanation of the plant naming system, see page 31.

'Splendens' Japanese anemone

Aconitum / Monkshood

'Arendsii' monkshood (or aconite)

The aconites are members of the but-tercup family. Two species of interest to flower gardeners are monkshoods (*Aconitum napellus* and *A. carmichaelii*), which are available in several cultivar forms. Monkshoods are the source of the drug aconite, and the plants are poisonous to ingest. However, they are lovely additions to perennial beds and borders, sporting attractive, glossy deep green leaves that are lobed and divided like fingers on a hand.

The plants grow to 5 feet tall. Their blue-violet to purple helmet-shaped flowers are borne in spikes beginning in mid- to late summer and continuing later into fall. They are useful in early autumn for bridging the gap between summer flowers and autumn chrysanthemums. Most species and cultivars are hardy in Zones 3–8, throughout most of the United States and into southern Canada.

Monkshood needs deeply dug, fertile soil that retains moisture but does not become waterlogged. The plant grows best in sun or partial shade. Space the plants 2 ½ to 3 feet apart.

Anemone / Japanese Anemone

Japanese anemones (*Anemone* × *hybrida*) are marvelous in late summer and early fall gardens, and not enough gardeners grow them. They bloom abundantly into September and even October, filling the garden with their pastel flowers until heavy frost brings down the curtain on their show.

Most Japanese anemones grow from 2 to 4 feet tall with sturdy stems that form many branches. The flowers come in various shades of pink, rose, and white. And the plants are hardy in Zones 5 or 6–9.

Japanese anemones grow well in any average garden soil, as long as it is well drained. You can plant them in either full sun or partial shade. The plants do need generous amounts of moisture, so remember to water them regularly and deeply during hot, dry summer weather. In colder climates, give the plants a good covering of loose mulch (such as salt hay or shredded leaves) over the winter.

Cool-climate gardeners should plant Japanese anemones in spring; warm- climate gardeners can plant in either spring or fall. Space the plants 8 to 12 inches apart in the garden.

Aster / Michaelmas Daisy

The best perennial asters for gardens belong to three different species. All three are loosely grouped under the common name Michaelmas daisy. They bloom from late summer into fall and are at their best in autumn gardens.

Michaelmas daisies are undemanding in terms of care; they'll grow in just about

'Alma Potschke' New England aster

any soil, as long as they get lots of sun and plenty of water. To maintain top blooming quality, dig up your aster crowns every few years in very early spring, cut off the

'Chequers' New York aster

vigorous outside growth and replant it, and then throw away the old center part of the crown. As the asters grow, either stake them to support the stems, or pinch back the plants to keep them more compact. Although the cultivated forms of Michaelmas daisies have been bred from wild asters native to North America, they are far more widely grown by English gardeners. Certainly they deserve to be better known in the United States.

Aster × frikartii grows 2 to 3 feet tall, with fragrant, lavender-blue flowers 2 to 3 inches across. This reliable species blooms from midsummer until frost, and plants are hardy in Zones 5–8.

A. novae-angliae, the New England aster, grows 3 to 5 feet tall and starts blooming in late summer. The plants are hardy in Zones 4–8. New England asters are seldom troubled by the mildew that can plague other asters. Many cultivars in pinks and purples have been developed, including 2-foot 'Purple Dome'. (Flowers of this and the next species are smaller but more abundant than *A. × frikartii*.)

A. novi-belgii, the New York aster, blooms in late summer and fall, and is hardy in Zones 4–8. Of all the Michaelmas daisies, this species produces the best cut flowers. Extensive breeding work has provided cultivars with a range of flower colors from white through pink to purple and plant heights from 1 to 4 feet.

Boltonia / Boltonia

Boltonia

Sometimes known as the thousand-flowered aster, boltonia deserves to be better known. It is virtually maintenance-free, and its masses of starry white or pink flowers make an excellent companion for asters and mums in the autumn garden. The species form of the plant, *Boltonia asteroides*, bears white or purple flowers and is seldom grown in gardens, little wonder since it grows an ungainly 6 or 7 feet tall. The white-flowered cultivar 'Snowbank' and pink 'Rosea' are the boltonias offered in nursery catalogs.

Both cultivars grow best in full sun, but they aren't at all fussy about soil. They thrive in practically any soil of average fertility, in either a moist or a dry place that's not too extreme in either direction. The plants branch freely and practically cover themselves with flowers from September until October or November, depending on the climate. The flowers can withstand several light frosts and hold up well in hot, humid late summer weather. The plants are hardy in Zones 3–9.

Boltonia is best grown in beds and borders, although you can also grow it as a hedge if you set the plants close together (about 2 feet apart instead of the usual 2 ½ to 3 feet). The plant's blue-green leaves are attractive throughout the growing season. The sturdy 3- to 4-foot flower stems don't need staking.

Chrysanthemum **(C. × morifolium)**

'Salmon Fairie' chrysanthemum

'Big Top' chrysanthemum

'Pennine Magnet' chrysanthemum

Chrysanthemum / **Chrysanthemum ("Mum")**

The chrysanthemum, or "mum" as it's commonly called, is the undisputed queen of the fall garden and a staple of the cut-flower and gift plant market as well. Commercial greenhouses are able to force mums into bloom year-round. But, to gardeners, chrysanthemums and autumn are pretty much synonymous.

Despite their popularity, chrysanthemums are not the easiest plants to grow. They need pinching to keep the plants bushy, they need to be divided often, and they are subject to a number of diseases. Still, their rich, earthy colors are unbeatable in fall, and it's worth the trouble to grow at least a few. Or you can treat mums as annuals and buy new ones each year. (If you have less than full sun, less than excellent drainage, or little patience for repeated pinching and annual dividing, treating mums as annuals is your best bet.) Individual plants bloom for three or four weeks, but choosing cultivars with different blooming periods can give you flowers from late summer well into fall, through several frosts. There are thousands of cultivars on the North American market alone, with a large assortment of plant heights, flower forms, and flower sizes. New cultivars are being developed all the time.

Pick a place for mums where you will be able to see and really appreciate their color in fall. Full sun is crucial, for even a little bit of shade will interfere with the plant's performance.

Spider mum

'Naomi' chrysanthemum

'Improved Mefo' chrysanthemum

'Rosedew' chrysanthemum

Rich, well-drained soil is another requirement. Start preparing the soil for mums a couple of months or even a season before you intend to plant them. Dig plenty of compost, leaf mold, or well-rotted manure into the bed. Because chrysanthemums are subject to root rot in wet soils, it is vital that the soil be light, loose, and very well drained. If your soil is heavy, you may need to make raised beds for your mums to give them better drainage.

A few weeks before planting time in spring, fertilize the planting area with an all-purpose fertilizer plus a good source of phosphate (superphosphate or a fertilizer with a higher middle number such as 5-10-5). If you garden organically, incorporate rock phosphate and greensand, or an all-purpose organic fertilizer blend, into the soil when you dig in the compost or manure.

Start your chrysanthemum bed with plants or rooted cuttings from a nursery. Hybrid varieties of mums will not come true from seed, and plants from the florist do not often survive in the garden. Spacing distance will vary according to the sizes of the cultivars you are growing.

During the growing season, feed the plants weekly with fish emulsion, or less often with a commercial time-release fertilizer (check the label; most are only applied once at the beginning of the growing season). Make sure the plants get plenty of moisture, especially during hot weather. Many gardeners like to keep their plants mulched as they grow, to conserve moisture.

Most chrysanthemums need to be pinched back to promote a nice, mounded shape and lots of flowers. When the plant is at least 5 inches tall, pinch out the growing tip to force the plant to branch. Pinch the plant at least once more as it grows, and pinch the tips evenly all over the plant in order to give it a symmetrical shape. If you live in a cold climate, stop pinching around midsummer so that the plants will bloom before the cold weather sets in. (For more information on pinching, see page 101.)

In cold climates, a good winter mulch is important, because the plants are not always entirely hardy. As an alternative to mulching, you can dig up the plants after they have bloomed and place them in a cold frame during the winter.

Divide your mums every year in order to maintain vigorous plants that bloom well. Dig up the plants in spring, discard the woody central parts of the root clump, and then replant the fleshy outer parts.

Colchicum / Colchicum

Colchicum

Colchicums bloom with autumn crocuses and have similar chalice-shaped flowers, although colchicum flowers are larger. Though not widely grown in North America, they should be because they are reliable and easy to grow, and the beautiful flowers are a welcome addition to fall gardens. Colchicums grow 4 to 6 inches tall and bloom in shades of pink, rose, lilac, and white. They are lovely when naturalized in a lawn. You can also plant them in beds and borders or in rock gardens. These plants are hardy in Zones 4–9. It's best to try to position them so their rather coarse foliage will be hidden by other nearby plants when they come up in the spring.

Colchicum plants grow from corms that are planted in late summer and burst into bloom just a few weeks later. Most species send up their autumn flowers on leafless stems; the foliage doesn't appear until the following spring. The leaves grow about a foot tall and die back in late spring or early summer, along with the foliage of spring bulbs.

Colchicum bulbs are shipped from mail-order nurseries in July or August when they are dormant. You should plant them as soon as you receive them. Any well-drained soil of average fertility will do. Plant the corms so their tops are 3 to 4 inches below the soil surface and 4 to 6 inches apart.

Perhaps the most stunning of all the colchicums is the hybrid called 'Waterlily'. Its large double flowers have pointed petals that, when fully open on a sunny day, look incredibly like water lilies. The flowers are quite beautiful. Their color is a hard-to-describe shade of soft, warm rosy pink, with a sort of golden glow to it. The plants grow 6 inches tall.

Crocus / Autumn Crocus

Like their spring-blooming relatives, autumn crocuses are good flowers for rock gardens, for the front of beds and borders, and for naturalizing in lawns. They bloom in shades of lavender, lilac, and purple. These colors lend a welcome contrast to the more typical golds, oranges, and russets that are so much a part of most autumn gardens. Wherever you plant autumn crocuses, plant lots of them. The carpet of blue or purple their flowers create when planted in masses is a stunning sight against the warm earth colors, the soft beiges and deep browns of the autumn landscape—a reminder of springs past and a harbinger of springs to come.

The autumn-blooming crocus species and cultivars available include, *Crocus goulimyi*, *C. kotschyanus*, *C. laevigatus*, *C. medius*, *C. sativus*, (saffron crocus), and *C. speciosus*. All grow about 4 inches tall and bloom in early to mid autumn. Hardiness varies with species, from Zones 3 or 5 to 8.

Autumn crocuses are grown like colchicums. The corms are shipped from suppliers in August. Plant them right away, and the flowers will bloom in September, October, and November. For the best flowers, plant your crocuses in full sun, in any average, well-drained soil. Plant the corms 3 to 4 inches deep and 3 to 6 inches apart. Autumn crocuses spread like the spring ones do, so give them room to expand.

Autumn crocus (Crocus speciosus)

Leucojum / Autumn Snowflake

Autumn snowflake

The members of this genus of white-flowered bulbs are called snowflakes. The most commonly available species and cultivars bloom in the spring and summer, but there is also an autumn-flowering species, Leucojum autumnale. Autumn snowflake grows about 8 inches tall, and its flowering stems are followed by slender, shorter, glasslike leaves. Its little bell-shaped, white blossoms dangle from slender stems singly or in groups of two or three. The base of the flower is sometimes tinged with pink. As with other snowflakes, you can plant this in clumps in the rock garden, under and between shrubs, or in beds and borders. It also naturalizes well in a lawn.

The three common species of snowflakes are hardy in Zones 4–9. They grow best in rich, light, somewhat sandy soil, and bloom in either full sun or partial shade. Plant the bulbs 4 to 5 inches deep and about 4 inches apart. After that, they need little care. You won't have to divide them for quite a few years, unless you want to move them or propagate new plants from offsets.

When buying bulbs of *Leucojum*, be careful to purchase them from a reputable nursery that sells only propagated stock, rather than bulbs collected from the wild. Wild plants are endangered in their native habitats as a result of over-collection for sale.

Lycoris / Lycoris

Magic lily

These relatives of the amaryllis are sometimes called spider lilies or magic lilies, and magical their flowers certainly are. The funnel-shaped flowers closely resemble those of amaryllis but are more delicate in their size, shape, and colors. Their petals are long and narrow, and many of the flowers have long, spidery stamens that curve and twist out into space from the center of the flower. Best of all, both common species of lycoris bloom from late summer into autumn, when their fanciful, exotic forms lend a touch of grace to gardens or patios.

Only one species, magic lily (*Lycoris squamigera*), is hardy in the North (Zones 5–9). However, the tender spider lily (*Lycoris radiata*) can be grown in pots and then moved indoors for the winter in areas north of Zone 8, where it isn't hardy. You can plant lycoris in beds and borders, or you can grow them in pots on patios and terraces.

The straplike leaves appear in spring, and the plants need to be watered regularly during this active growing period. In summer the leaves die back, and the plant vanishes for its dormancy. But in late summer the flower stalks burst through the soil, springing up as if by magic. The stems of magic lilies grow 1½ to 2 to 3 feet tall and are topped by clusters of the most exquisite, fragrant flowers, mostly in shades of pink and lilac pink. Spider lilies grow to 1½ feet with rose to deep red flowers. The plants seldom need to be dug and divided unless you want to move them or propagate new plants.

Plant the bulbs during their summer dormant period. They appreciate a sunny spot and well-drained soil that tends to be dry in summer. Set the bulbs approximately a foot apart, with the tops of their necks just below the soil surface.

You need to treat lycoris differently from most other plants in one important respect. That is, do not water them in summer, because they need a dry dormant period rather than a cold one. Too much moisture at this time of year could rot the bulbs.

Polianthes / Tuberose

Tuberoses with dahlia

Tuberoses (*Polianthes tuberosa*) are among the most fragrant flowers on earth and have been an important ingredient in perfume formulas for generations. The plants bloom from late summer into autumn, when most other fragrant flowers are long gone. Though attractive, the flowers are not terribly striking. They are waxy, white, and borne in clusters near the tops of the 3-foot stems. Flowers of 'The Pearl' cultivar are semidouble and thus somewhat showier. The flowers bloom in late summer and autumn, and the long and grassy leaves appear before the flowers.

Tuberose rhizomes are not cold hardy, so cold-climate gardeners need to store them indoors over the winter along with dahlias and tuberous begonias. Warm-climate gardeners can grow tuberoses in beds and borders; northerners in areas with freezing temperatures may prefer to plant them in pots. In fact, containers are really where tuberoses belong, because they can perfume a patio or terrace close to the house where you can enjoy them most.

Tuberoses need full sun and plenty of moisture. It is important to water regularly when the leaves appear. The plants grow best in rich, well-drained soil that contains plenty of organic matter. Set the rhizomes 2 inches deep and 4 to 6 inches apart. Tuberoses grow best in soil with an acid to neutral pH. If your soil is alkaline, you should feed the plants as they grow with an acidifying fertilizer formulated for other acid-loving plants such as camellias, rhodo- dendrons, and azaleas.

The plants need a long, warm growing season in order to produce flowers. In cold climates, start the rhizomes growing indoors in spring, about six weeks before outdoor temperatures will be at least 50°F. Elsewhere, plant them directly outdoors in the spring after the last frost has occurred.

When the leaves start to turn yellow in the fall, stop watering the plants and let the soil dry out. When the leaves are dead, or after the first fall frost, dig up the plants or remove them from their pots. Cut off the dead leaves and let the rhizomes dry for two weeks in a dry, airy place.

Store the rhizomes as you do other tender bulbs in a cool, dark, dry location with good air circulation, where the temperature will not dip below 40°F. Pack them in boxes, if you like, wrapping them in tissue paper or filling the boxes with dry peat moss or sand. Or, place the rhizomes in mesh onion bags or spread the rhizomes out on a shelf. Check the rhizomes periodically for mold, decay, or damage, and discard any showing those signs.

Schlumbergera / Thanksgiving Cactus

Thanksgiving cactus

Thanksgiving cactus (*Schlumbergera truncata*) is an easy-to-grow houseplant that blooms dependably and lavishly every fall (and sometimes in the spring as well). There are numerous shades of red, pink, and white that are available, as well as salmon and pale pink that is flushed with gold.

Thanksgiving cactus stems are made of a series of jointed flat, basically oval segments. The edges of each segment are notched; and the notches (see photos next page) provide the easiest way to distinguish Thanksgiving cactus from Christmas cactus, which has scalloped edges. The stems grow upright at first, then nod over as they elongate. The stems also branch as they become longer. Eventually the plants will develop a gracefully arching shape. The plants grow slowly and need a few years before they branch and droop.

Like its other holiday-blooming relatives, Thanksgiving cactus is tender and is an epiphyte (a plant that grows on the trunks of trees or other surfaces, rather than with its roots in soil). Its roots are wiry and thin and grow best in a light, well-drained potting mix. A blend of one part potting soil, two parts peat moss, and one part perlite or builder's sand will serve nicely.

This cactus likes a warm room (around 70°F is good) and thrives in either eastern or western windows. Although most authorities suggest the plants need cool temperatures or exactly the right day length in order to set buds, that is not required. In the author's experience, these plants need no such special treatment to ensure bloom every year. Just put them outdoors in summer and leave them out through the first cool nights if you wish; then bring them indoors and keep them close by the window, where they get whatever light comes through the glass. Other lights in the room that are turned on at night (if not overly bright) don't apparently disturb the plants' bud setting or blooming.

Individual flowers last only a few days, but the plant sets many buds and continues to set more after the first flowers wilt. Picking off wilted flowers appears to extend the blooming period. After blooming is finished, the plant produces new leaves. Throughout this time, the plant appreciates a weekly or biweekly watering and an occasional dose of all-purpose plant food.

At some time in winter, growth stops and the plant rests. During this time, water it only when the leaves start to look a little shriveled. In late summer or early autumn, start to water more often and fertilize the cactus as it begins to set buds.

Thanksgiving cactus (left) vs. Christmas cactus

Sternbergia / Sternbergia

Sternbergia

This golden-flowered bulb (*Sternbergia lutea*) blooms with colchicums and autumn crocuses; it makes a good companion for their lavender and blue flowers. One of its common names, "winter daffodil," is a bit misleading because it is the plant's leaves, not the flowers, that are usually in evidence during winter. Also, its flowers are shaped more like crocuses than daffodils. In early fall, each plant sends up several flowering stems about 8 inches tall. The deep yellow flowers are chalice-shaped when they first open, but in bright sunlight they spread their pointed petals wide into a star. The flowers last into October.

Sternbergia is most valuable for its color, since most other fall bulbs bloom in purples, blues, or lavender-pinks. Another virtue of this plant is its toughness; both flowers and leaves are able to withstand weather conditions that would ruin the more delicate colchicums and crocuses. The bulbs are hardy in Zones 6–11.

The bulbs are shipped from mail-order nurseries in midsummer and should be planted right away for flowers beginning around the middle of September. Plant bulbs 4 inches deep and about 6 inches apart in well-drained soil in a sunny location. Good drainage is important—the bulbs may rot in soggy soil. The bulbs like a good baking in summer, so gardeners in cooler climates are wise to plant them next to a south-facing wall or in a similarly sheltered spot with plenty of sun.

Sternbergia bulbs need lots of moisture as they grow and bloom; you may need to water them in the fall if your weather is dry. In cold climates, the plants need a good mulch to protect them from the severe winter weather. When the ground freezes, cover the planting area with 6 inches of shredded leaves or other loose mulch, tucking it in around the leaves.

Be sure to purchase your bulbs from a reputable source that sells only propagated, rather than wild-collected bulbs, endangered in their native habitats as a result of over-collection.

After digging summer bulbs for the winter, you can wash them, which helps you see them clearly when you begin dividing them in spring. Let them dry thoroughly before storing.

Autumn Activities

Autumn is a great time to be out in the garden. In the North and at higher altitudes, the days are pleasantly cool—and in the South, pleasantly warm. At this time, you can work surrounded by the unique beauties of the autumn landscape with garden flowers still in bloom. In this season of harvest and completion, you can enjoy a sense of satisfaction in the garden's successes and begin to consider what to do differently next year. As you go about your garden chores, keep a little notebook handy to jot down ideas and inspirations about colors to try next year and what plant might look good in that empty spot next to the garage. And start thinking about revising your garden plans so you'll be ready to order seeds and supplies in winter.

Plan, too, for winter flowers you'd like to have blooming indoors this year, and for early spring flowers outdoors. Well before frost threatens, pot up or take cuttings of garden annuals to bring indoors. Buy daffodils, hyacinths, crocuses, and other hardy bulbs now to prepare them for forcing into bloom indoors during the winter. This is also the natural time to plant these bulbs in the outdoor garden for early spring flowers.

Besides the classic hardy bulbs, you can bring a whole host of other bulbs into bloom indoors over winter if you start the process now. Choices include the big trumpet-shaped flowers of amaryllis; brilliant red, pink, or blue-violet poppy anemones; elegant calla lilies; tuberous begonias; and exquisitely fragrant freesias.

Dividing & Transplanting Perennials

Division is the easiest way to increase your stock of plants. Division is also important for maintaining the health of most perennials. In climates where autumn weather is cool and frost comes early, perennials are best divided in early spring. But in most of the rest of the country, transplanting and division can be done in early to mid autumn for any plants that aren't blooming.

Transplant early enough to allow plants four or more weeks to send out new feeder roots before the ground freezes. If you transplant too late, plants won't have enough time to grow roots, and they'll probably die over the winter. In either spring or fall, the best time to transplant is when the weather is moist and cool. A cloudy day is ideal.

Two or three days before transplanting, thoroughly water the plants to be moved or divided. At this time, cut back the top growth of the plants by about one-third, to make the plants and divisions easier to handle. Some plants that form especially thick, tough clumps (such as bearded iris and daylilies that haven't been divided for quite a few years) can be cut back even further—by two-thirds, or to about 6 inches—before the clumps are dug up.

Divide crowded clumps of perennials into sections having both stems and roots. Then replant the divisions.

Dividing Bulbs & Bulblike Plants

Tools & Materials: Garden spade (to cut sod), round-nose shovel for digging, garden fork, perhaps a mattock or crowbar if soil is hard or rocky, and a tarp on which to place soil and turves **Difficulty:** Easy to Moderate

Narcissus

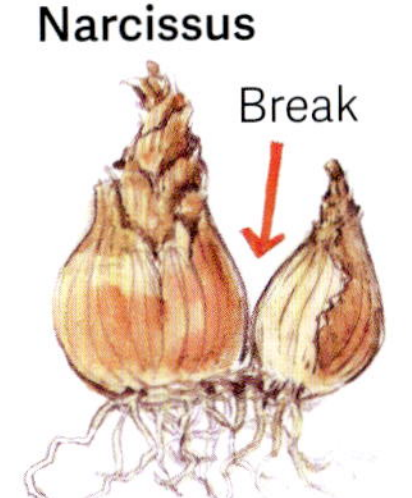

True Bulbs (narcissus, tulips, fritillaria, snowdrops, grape hyacinths, snowflake). Break double-nosed narcissus at the basal plate.

Lily

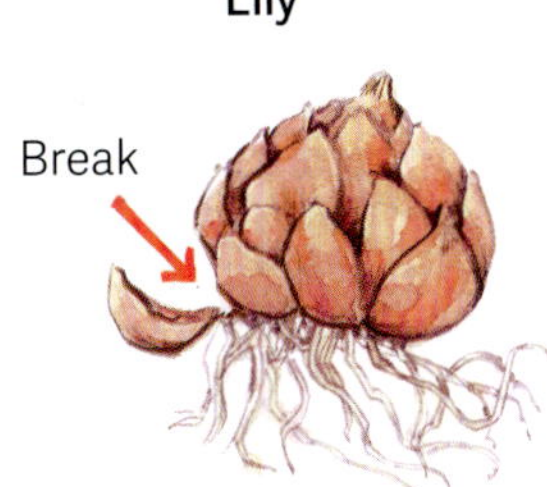

Scaly Bulbs (lilies). Separate the outer scales and plant them.

Dahlia

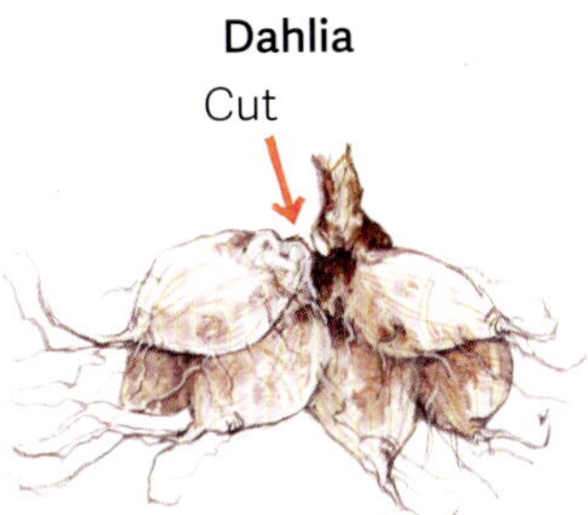

Tuberous Roots (dahlias). Cut individual roots or clusters of two to three from the plant's crown.

Begonia

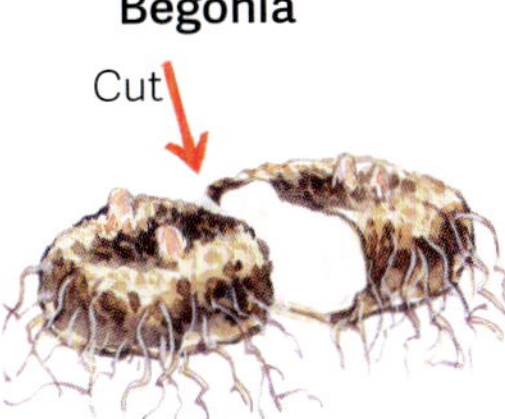

Tubers (tuberous begonias, cyclamen, winter aconite, Grecian windflower, poppy anemone). Cut each tuber into several pieces, making sure each new piece has at least one "eye," the point from which the new shoots will grow.

Iris

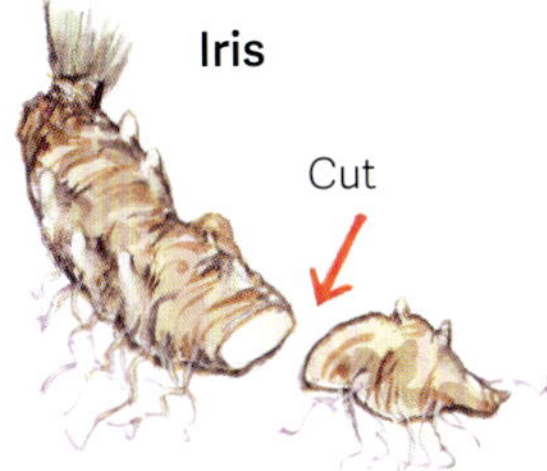

Rhizomes (bearded iris, Siberian and other beardless irises). Cut the smaller, rooted end away from the older, sometimes spongy main portion, making sure that all divisions have at least one "eye," the point from which new shoots grow.

Gladiolus

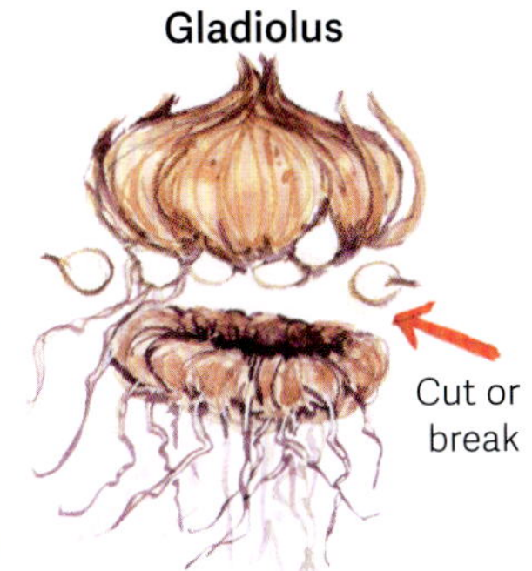

Corms (crocus, colchicum, gladiolus, freesia). Remove the offsets by hand or with a knife.

(See page 156 for illustrated steps on dividing bearded iris; see page 157 for dividing daylilies.)

On moving day, first dig the new holes for your new divisions (to minimize their time out of the ground). If you can't wait for a cloudy day, grab some newspapers or an old sheet to shade divisions while they're waiting to be planted. (Shade minimizes transplant shock and keeps plants from drying out too quickly.) When you are dividing several plants, it's a good idea to keep a pail of water handy so that you can dunk any divisions that start to dry out before you get them replanted.

Carefully dig around the outside of the clump of plants with a spade or spading fork to loosen the roots. Dig straight down until you are below the main part of the rootball; then angle the spade or fork underneath the plant. Be careful not to injure tuberous root structures and plant crowns (the growth point where stems join roots).

When the plant clump is out of the ground, divide it into sections, as shown in the photo on page 181. Pull apart loose clumps; cut apart an especially dense clump with a sharp knife, or use two pitchforks positioned back to back to pry apart a large clump. Divide the clump so that each division has roots and at least one healthy stem or growing tip (or, for dense plants, several stems). Before replanting the newly divided root clumps, carefully look over the roots and prune off any that are broken, shrivelled, or straggly.

When you're ready to transplant, plant your new divisions, add some water to the hole, set in the division, and gently fill in around the plant with good soil and compost. You should plant most root clumps at the same depth they originally grew, or with their crowns even with the soil surface.

It's important to give transplants a good watering to settle the soil. If the weather is dry, continue to water the transplants regularly throughout the dry spell. New divisions need plenty of moisture while they are establishing feeder roots. Keep an eye on them for a few weeks as they settle in. Since you've worked compost into the planting hole, you don't need to fertilize. Wait until spring to fertilize fall transplants; feed-ing plants in fall just makes them more susceptible to winterkill.

Finally, label the new transplants both in the garden and on your garden plan, so that you will remember next spring what you planted where. It's easy to forget the exact location of the plants when you get back into the garden next spring.

Fall Planting of Spring Bulbs

In colder climates, daffodils, tulips, and other hardy spring-blooming bulbs for the outdoor garden should be planted in early to mid autumn, before the first hard frost in your area. In warm climates, plant later in fall—November or even December where winters are very mild. (If you plant earlier, warm soil may cause spring bulbs to try to bloom.)

Hardy bulbs will thrive in almost any well-drained soil, in full sun or partial shade. To prepare the garden for bulbs, dig out the soil to whatever depth your bulbs need, as illustrated in "Bulb Planting Depths," below.

Place the bulbs in the soil where you

Bulb Planting Depths

True Bulbs & Corms

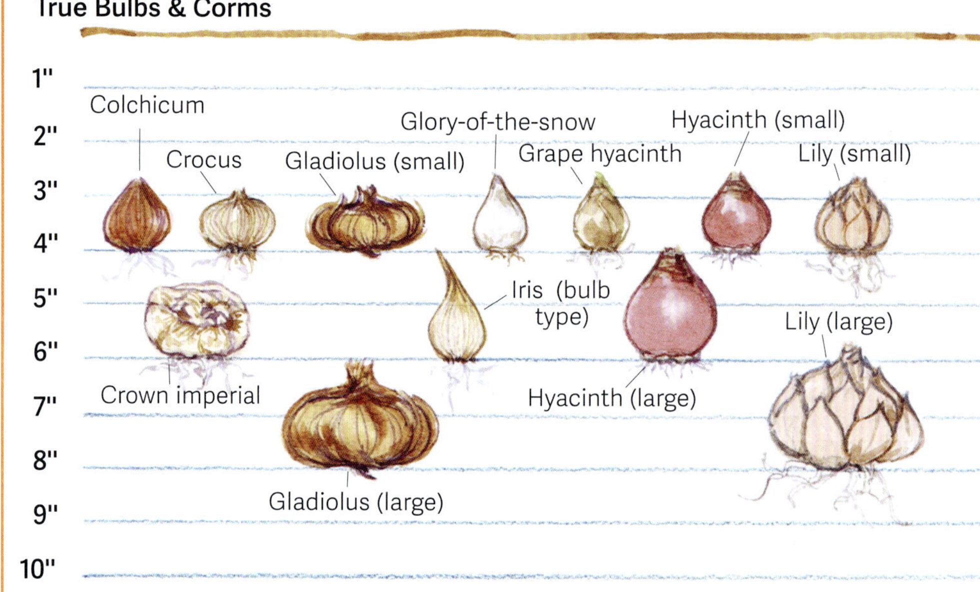

Tubers, Rhizomes & Tuberous Begonias

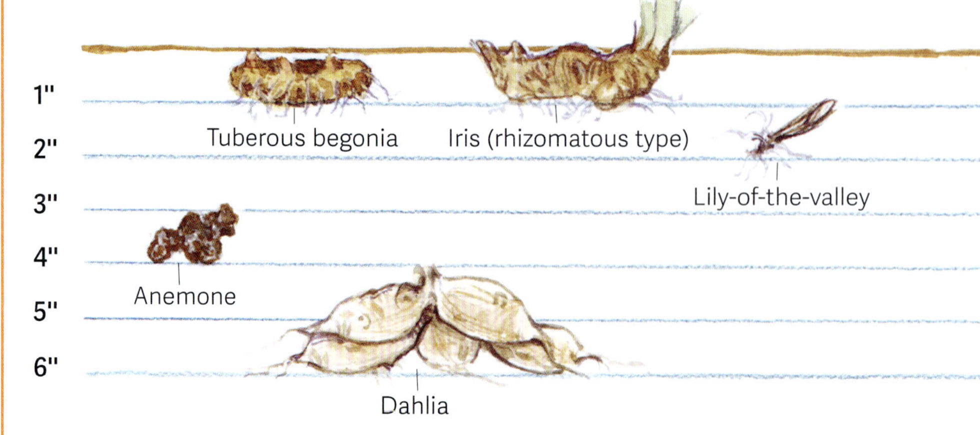

will plant them, with their pointed end up. For the best display, plant the bulbs in drifts or in clusters of 12 or more. Make sure the bulbs are set firmly in the soil, as indicated in "Planting Hardy Bulbs," at right. Then cover them with soil, water thoroughly, and after the ground is frozen, mulch the bed with a 2- to 3-inch layer of shredded leaves or other loose mulch.

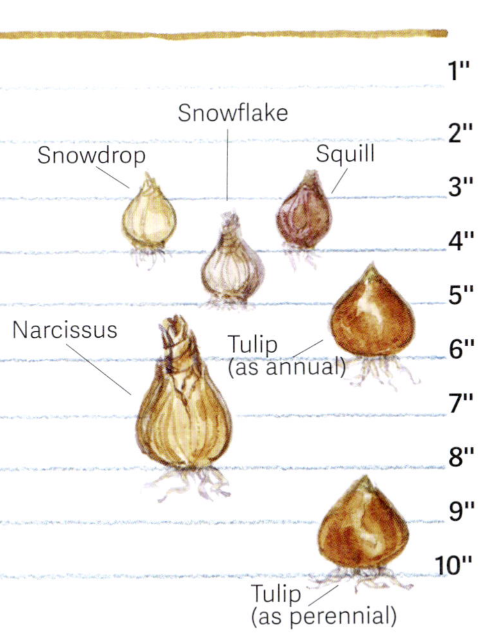

Depths & Sizes: Planting depths vary with sizes of bulbs. For bulbs shown in two sizes, plant the larger bulbs at the lower depth. Lacking this illustration, use this rule of thumb: Plant 2½ times as deep as the bulb diameter.

Exception: Hybrid tulips are shown in the same size, but at two depths, because hybrids are not reliably perennial in many localities. If you want to regard them as annuals, plant them about 6 in. deep. If you want them to have a better chance of becoming perennial, plant them 10 in. deep.

Planting Hardy Bulbs

The method shown employs "Fort Knox for Bulbs," a cage of ½-inch galvanized wire mesh designed to prevent tunneling rodents from getting to the bulbs. If tunnelers aren't a big problem for you, skip the cage. Still, surface marauders, such as squirrels and chipmunks, may dig up smaller bulbs unless you cover the soil with wire mesh until first shoots appear.

Tools & Materials: Shovel, digging fork, tarp, trowel, ½-inch mesh cage

Difficulty: Easy to Moderate

1 Dig a hole 4 to 5 in. deeper than the deepest planted bulbs. Determine this depth from "Bulb Planting Depths," shown at left.

2 Add soil with plenty of organic matter to promote drainage. If your soil is sandy or contains a lot of clay, dig in extra peat moss, leaf mold, or compost.

3 After raking the soil flat, place the cage and add a few more inches of soil with amendments, plus rock phosphate if soil tests indicate the need.

4 Place bulbs, such as these tulips, at recommended depths usually listed on packaging. Largest bulbs tend to be planted the deepest, explained at left.

5 Small bulbs are planted just a few inches deep. But this makes them more vulnerable to surface digging rodents, such as squirrels and chipmunks.

6 Cover your bulbs with ½-in. galvanized mesh. Mulch after the ground is frozen, and remove the mulch and mesh as first shoots appear.

ꟹ Preparing Tender Bulbs for Winter

When the first frost strikes, dig up tender bulbs and corms, and put them in storage for the winter. Wait to dig most bulbs until the foliage has started to turn brown or has been softened by frost. Exceptions are tuberous begonias and tuberoses, which can't tolerate even a light frost; dig them before frost arrives.

- After loosening the soil below the plant, such as the gladiolus below, carefully lift the entire plant with a spade or digging fork, retaining a good clump of soil around the bulbs. Sort the bulbs according to variety or at least by color as you dig them; tag them so you can keep track of which is which.

Gladiolus corms

- Let the bulbs dry in a cool, dark, ventilated but frostproof cellar. Remove foliage and stems when they fall off. A few days later, shake off dry soil. Always let bulbs dry on the surface before you store them or else they may mildew or rot.
- Sort according to variety or at least by color. Label the storage boxes so that you'll know what's what when replanting the next spring.
- Pack the bulbs in cotton, tissue paper, dry sand, or peat moss. Store in a dark, dry, airy place where the temperature will not drop below 50°F.

Planting bulbs for forcing indoors in autumn will give you flowers like these tulips, narcissus, and crocus in the depths of winter.

Forcing Bulbs Indoors Ω

Many bulbs that otherwise bloom outdoors in spring can be forced into bloom indoors in winter. Begin the process in autumn. Stagger planting times if you want to enjoy continuous bloom over a long period. As a rule of thumb, plant in September for late December or January flowers, in October for flowers in February, and in November for flowers in March. As you plant, label each pot with the type of bulb, flower color, and date of planting. When the bulbs bloom later on, make a note of the date to help you plan next winter's bulb display.

Selecting Good Bulbs. In autumn, buy bulbs from a reliable establishment and choose carefully. The better the bulb, the more rewarding the results. Because forcing is stressful for bulbs, weak, damaged, or diseased bulbs may bloom poorly or not at all.

Take the time to inspect newly purchased bulbs carefully. They should be firm, with no soft spots, moldy patches, or nicks. The basal plate (the flat bottom of the bulb from which the roots will grow) should also be firm. If you receive bulbs by mail that are damaged, ask the supplier to replace them.

Cool Storage

If it's not yet time to plant the bulbs when you get them, store them in the refrigerator if you live in a warm climate. In cooler climates you can also store them on an open shelf where air can circulate freely around them. Cool, but not freezing cold, temperatures are best for storing bulbs. Never put them in the freezer.

Pots

If you are reusing old pots, scrub the pots thoroughly and soak them in a disinfectant solution of one part liquid chlorine bleach to nine parts water before you plant them. Rinse well. Soak clay pots in water overnight before planting in them so that the porous pots don't absorb much soil moisture upon planting.

Planting Medium

Bulbs need loose, crumbly soil with good drainage. A potting mix of equal parts garden loam or potting soil, peat moss, and sand is ideal—or use a soilless potting mix. Most forced bulbs should be buried only to their tips, leaving the tips exposed, unless otherwise noted in the directions for individual bulbs, begin-

Methods of Forcing Bulbs

Plant most types of bulbs in pots or deep flats. Pots should have drainage holes in the bottom and be 5 to 6 inches in diameter; flats should be 4 to 5 inches deep. The number of bulbs per pot depends on the kind and size of the bulbs. A 6-inch pot will hold five to six tulip bulbs, three double-nosed daffodils, or three hyacinths. Use a 5-inch bulb pan (a wide, shallow pot) to force crocuses, irises, squills, or grape hyacinths. Leave about 1 ½ inches between the bulbs when you plant them. They should be close together but not touching.

Some bulbs such as hyacinths and paperwhite narcissus are commonly planted in bulb jars filled with just water.

Narcissus. You're safe in buying firm, healthy-looking paperwhite narcissus bulbs even if they've already begun sprouting, as shown at left. However, bulbs deteriorate quickly on the garden center shelves; the bulb shown at right isn't worth risking your money on.

Tulips. Plant tulip bulbs with their tips just above the soil surface. The 5-in. pot here accommodates four bulbs without their touching. Tulip bulbs require 14 to 16 weeks of cold storage before they will form roots, unless you buy bulbs labeled as "prepared" (ready for forcing).

Amaryllis. Plant amaryllis bulbs so the upper third of the bulb is above the soil line, one bulb per 5- to 7-in. pot. Allow about 1 in. between the top of the soil and the pot rim.

Hyacinths. Force prechilled, "prepared" bulbs immediately in bulb jars (as shown) or in pots. If the bulbs haven't been prechilled, you need to refrigerate them as explained on page 187.

ning on page 186. Leave ½ inch between the soil line and the rim of the pot to allow for watering. Water the bulbs thoroughly but gently when you finish planting.

Storage After Planting

After the bulbs are planted, they need many weeks of darkness and cold storage (at temperatures ranging from 35° to 48°F) before you can actually begin forcing them; this cold period allows the roots to form.

Place the potted bulbs in an unheated garage or shed or in an outdoor cold frame, or bury them in the garden and cover them with a layer of straw, sawdust, or wood chips. If you expect temperatures to dip below freezing, wrap with a couple of old towels to insulate the pots. You can also store a pot or two in the refrigerator, if you cover the pots to block out light.

It takes an average of 14 to 16 weeks for roots to form. During that time, you need to keep the soil moist but not wet. Check the pots once a week, and water them if the soil is dry.

When shoots appear, move the pots to a bright, warmer spot such as a windowsill. The warmth will stimulate growth, and bright light will keep the plants from getting too leggy. Once plants start to bloom they don't need as much light, so you can move them to wherever you'd like to display them.

Replanting Outdoors

Bulbs that are hardy in your area can be planted out in the garden after being forced, but they won't bloom again for a year or two. During this period they regain their strength, so any flowers will most likely be smaller than those you forced indoors. If you expect to plant bulbs outdoors after forcing them, feed them with a bulb fertilizer when you pot them up for forcing and again in spring when you plant them out in the garden. Note that bulbs can't be forced twice. After you have forced them once, you must either plant them outdoors or discard them.

Planting & Forcing Various Bulbs

The following bulbs are all reliable and rewarding for winter blooms. Hardiness zones are included for readers who wish to later replant bulbs outdoors for future flowers. Outdoor planting depths are shown on pages 182–183.

Anemone coronaria / Poppy (or Florist's) Anemone

'Saint Brigid' poppy anemone

When you buy these tubers, they should appear shriveled, as if all the life has dried out of them. Soak the tubers in lukewarm water before planting them in order to soften them a bit. When they are soft enough that you can dent them with your fingernail, they are ready to plant.

These bulbs need no cold period, but move the pots to a moist, cool location where the temperature is 45° to 50°F for six to eight weeks to allow roots to develop. Cover the pots with burlap, and keep the soil moist. Then uncover and move the plants to a bright, airy location, also with temperatures around 50°F. Water freely as the plants grow.

Zones 6–9 for planting outdoors.

Begonia Tuberhybrida hybrids / Tuberous Begonia

'Non Stop' tuberous begonia

Plant five tubers to a 12-inch pot, in a light, rich, well-drained potting mix. Set the rounded side of the tuber on the soil, with the concave side facing up. Lightly cover with soil. Tuberous begonias bloom in summer, so plant them in spring, not fall.

Set the pots in a cool place out of direct sun, and water thoroughly. Keep the soil evenly moist. Feed once a month with a flowering houseplant fertilizer. When shoots appear, move the pots to a sunny place where daytime temperatures are around 75°F. The plants need a 10°F drop in temperature at night.

When the plants finish blooming and the leaves die back, remove the tubers from their pots. Snip off any remaining leaves and let the tubers dry for two weeks. Then store them in dry peat moss in a cool, dark, dry place until planting time next spring.

Only in warm Zones 10–11 for planting outdoors.

Convallaria majalis / Lily-of-the-valley

Lily-of-the-valley

Lily-of-the-valley pips are usually shipped from mail-order houses in fall. You can buy them preplanted or plant them yourself. All you need to do is add water to preplanted pips and you'll have flowers in two or three weeks. If you plant your own, set them about 5 inches apart with their tips just below the soil surface. Put them in a cold location for 3 to 3½ months; then move them to a bright (not necessarily sunny) spot with temperatures in the 60s°F. As with bulbs, you can plant the pips in the garden in spring, and they will bloom in successive years.

Zones 3–8 for planting outdoors.

Crocus hybrids / Crocus

'Golden Yellow' and 'Purple Giant' crocuses

Plant Dutch crocus corms in mid- to late autumn, 1 to 2 inches deep and 1 inch apart. Six corms will fit in a 4-inch pot. The pot should be at least 3½ inches deep to accommodate the roots. Give the potted corms eight weeks of cold storage. Water sparingly until the plants are full grown; then keep the soil moist but not waterlogged. They bloom in about three weeks after completing the cold period.

Zones 3–8 for planting outdoors.

Freesia hybrids / **Freesia**

Freesia

Plant freesia corms in September or October, six to a 5-inch pot, or in shallow bulb pans or flats. Position the corms 2 inches apart and with their tops just below the soil line. Set the pot in a cool (50°F), dark place for six to eight weeks to allow the roots to develop. Keep the soil moist but not soggy; do not overwater. Feed once a month throughout rooting, growth, and blooming with a flowering houseplant fertilizer.

When the rooting period is past, move the pots to a bright, warmer (60° to 65°F) location. Make sure the temperature drops at least 10°F over night. The plants should bloom in three months—which would be midwinter if you planted the corms in September. The weak stems will probably need staking.

When the flowers finish blooming, keep watering and feeding the plants until late spring; then stop. When the foliage dies, store the pots on their side in a dark, dry place until it is time to replant in fall.

Zones 9–11 for planting outdoors.

Hippeastrum hybrids / **Amaryllis**

Amaryllis

Amaryllis is one of the easiest bulbs to force. Bulb sizes vary; larger bulbs will produce more flowers. For winter flowers, amaryllis bulbs can be purchased already potted, or planted potted as soon as you receive them from a mail-order supplier. Just be sure to plant them eight weeks before you want flowers. Amaryllis grows exceptionally well in a mix of equal parts soil, peat moss, and compost.

Because amaryllis doesn't need any cold period, the forcing process begins at once. Water the bulb well when you first pot it up or purchase it. Then water sparingly for 10 days, by which time root growth should have begun. Use lukewarm water; hot or cold water can shock the bulb.

When leaves are growing, water the plant more often and feed it once a month with a diluted, balanced fertilizer. Keep the plant where temperatures are between 60° and 70°F. Remove the leaves as they fade and die back. Then let the bulb rest (do not water) for at least a month before repotting and starting to water and feed it again. Then it should bloom again.

Zones 9–11 for planting outdoors.

Hyacinthus orientalis / **Hyacinth**

Hyacinths

For flowers in January and February, pot the bulbs in fall, water them well, and store in a cold frame or a wooden box placed against an outside wall of the house, covered with several inches of straw, until mid-December. Bulbs for early spring bloom should be potted in fall and kept outdoors all winter, covered with straw.

Hyacinths can also be forced in bulb glasses, as shown. Keep the bottom part of the glass filled with clean water. To give bulbs in glasses a cold period, fill the bottom part with water so it barely touches the bulb's basal plate. Put the glass in a paper or foil lined insulated bag, tie the top shut, and put the bag in your refrigerator. (The bag also shields the bulb from the refrigerator's light.)

Open the bag periodically to check progress. When the shoot is about 4 inches tall, you should bring the glass into bright but indirect light.

Buying prechilled hyacinth bulbs makes forcing in bulb glasses especially easy; simply place the chilled hyacinth bulb on top of the water-filled glass in a dimly lit corner of a cool basement until roots grow and a shoot appears.

Zones 3–7 for planting outdoors (or farther south in warmer climates if dug and refrigerated each year).

Iris species / Iris

Iris reticulata

The small bulbous irises are the best kind to force. *Iris reticulata* will give you violet-purple flowers, and *I. danfordiae* will give you yellow ones. Plant the bulbs in midfall to have flowers in mid- to late winter. Plant them 2 to 3 inches deep and 3 inches apart. Give the potted bulbs eight weeks of cold storage for roots to develop. When the plants bloom, keep them in a sunny but cool spot. Save the bulbs after blooming for planting outdoors in fall.

Zones 5–9 for planting outdoors.

Lilium 'Enchantment' / Enchantment Lily

'Enchantment' lily

This outdoor garden favorite, an Asiatic hybrid lily, can be flowered indoors as well. 'Enchantment' is a particularly vigorous lily, which is why it responds well to forcing. A single bulb will reward you with 10 or more of the stunning blossoms, which are bright orange with darker spots. The flowers are borne atop 2- to 3-foot stems.

Plant three small bulbs in a 12-inch pot that is twice as tall as the bulbs. Put a 2-inch layer of pebbles in the bottom of the pot before adding the soil—excellent drainage is critical. Plant the bulbs 1 inch deep. Water well and set the pot in a cool (60° to 65°F), dark place where there is some humidity—such as a basement. Keep the soil evenly moist.

Once shoots emerge, in about three weeks, feed the plants once a month with a flowering houseplant fertilizer. When the shoots appear, move the pot into full sun and keep the soil moist. The plants should bloom in about six weeks. Stake the tall stems to help them support the flowers.

When the last flowers die, cut off the stem right below the lowest blossom. Continue feeding and watering the plant, and keep it in a bright window so bulbs can build up strength for a repeat show. Once the leaves die, cut off the stem at ground level. Remove the bulbs from the pot, and store them in dry peat moss until planting time next year.

Zones 4–9 for planting outdoors.

Narcissus cultivars / Daffodil & Narcissus

'Topolino' daffodils

For winter flowers, pot the bulbs in early September. Put three bulbs in a 5-inch pot, four or five in a 6-inch pot. Double-nosed bulbs (those with a smaller bulb attached to the main bulb) will give you the most flowers. The top of each bulb should be just above the soil surface. Water thoroughly after planting. Place the pots in cold storage, as described on page 185, until late December or early January. Then move the pots to a cool, but sunny, location. Keep the soil moist, and feed with a flowering houseplant fertilizer after blooming. When the leaves die, save the bulbs to plant outdoors in fall.

Zones 3–9 for planting outdoors.

Narcissus papyraceus 'Paperwhite' (N. 'Paperwhite')/ **Paperwhite Narcissus**

Paperwhite narcissus

The small white blossoms of this narcissus are sweetly fragrant, the bulbs bloom quickly after planting, and the forcing procedure is practically foolproof. The flowers grow in clusters around the tops of the 12- to 20-inch stems, depending on the cultivar. A single bulb, if it is of good quality, will produce several flowering stems. Cream and yellow cultivars are also available.

Bulbs are available in autumn and can be planted any time after you get them. They need no cold storage period and don't even need soil. You can plant the bulbs in pots of soil or perlite, in bowls of pebbles, or in a bulb glass or other container of water. To plant in soil, perlite, or pebbles, fill the container halfway with the medium of your choice. Set the bulbs on top, about ½ inch apart. Add more of the medium until the bulbs are about one-third covered. Water the soil or perlite thoroughly, or add water to the pebbles until it just touches the bottom of the bulbs. If you are planting in water, fill the glass until the bottom of the bottom third or so of the bulb is in water.

Some gardeners like to set the containers in a dark place for two or three weeks to let the roots develop before moving the pots into a bright place. But you can have success without a dark period, simply by leaving your pots of paperwhites on a bright windowsill until they bloom.

The best thing about paperwhites is their speed—they give you flowers about four weeks after you plant them. They bloom readily anytime from November to April. Bulbs planted in December and January will bloom more quickly than bulbs planted in November. For continuous bloom, start new bulbs every two weeks. You can save some bulbs to force in late winter and early spring by keeping them cool to prevent sprouting.

After the plants finish blooming, gardeners in the warmest climates can plant the bulbs outdoors. Everywhere else they should be discarded.

Zones 8–10 for planting outdoors.

Tulipa hybrids / **Tulips**

'Flair' tulip

Hybrid tulips come in early, mid- and late-season forms; when forced, these forms provide early, mid- and late-winter bloom. Planting pots of each type will give you flowers for several weeks.

Plant five or six bulbs to a 6-inch pot, with the flat side of the bulb facing toward the outside of the pot. That way, the flowers will turn outward and give the nicest display. Plant the bulbs as soon as they arrive from the nursery. Handle carefully, because they bruise easily, and plant them with their tips just above the soil surface. Tulips need 14 to 16 weeks of cold storage to form roots.

To bring tulips into bloom, give them good ventilation and plenty of light, but keep them out of direct sun. Keep the soil moist but not soggy.

Zones 4–7 for planting outdoors (or farther south in warmer climates if dug and refrigerated each year).

Zantedeschia species and hybrids / **Calla Lily**

Calla lily

Plant the rhizomes in September, one to a 6-inch pot, for flowers in December and January. Barely cover the top of each rhizome when you plant it, and leave space in the pot to add more soil later when roots appear on the surface.

Water moderately until the roots are well established. When shoots appear, water thoroughly and often. A greater problem is dryness, which sends the plants into dormancy. Feed the plants every few weeks with an all-purpose houseplant fertilizer. Keep nighttime temperatures cool (55° to 60° F).

To give the plant a dormant period, decrease watering in summer to let the soil dry a bit. But you can also keep plants growing all year-round.

Zones 9–11 for planting outdoors.

Focus on Houseplants

As the outdoor garden begins to wind down in fall, the gardener's focus turns inward. It's time to think about houseplants, and having flowers in bloom indoors during the colder days of autumn and winter.

Moving Houseplants Back Indoors

Spending the summer outdoors is beneficial for many houseplants. The increased light, humidity (depending on where you live), and air circulation can give housebound plants renewed vigor. Autumn is the time to bring them back indoors. Cold-climate gardeners should start to move houseplants back inside in early fall, while in the South and along the West Coast many plants can stay outdoors until later in the season. Here are some tips on making the transition easier for your plants.

If your plants have been in a fairly bright location all summer, set them in the shade for several days before you bring them indoors; this helps them accustom gradually to lower levels of light. To further minimize stress to the plants, make the move indoors on a day when outdoor temperatures are close to the temperature in your house. If the nighttime temperatures outdoors have been dipping down to 50° or 55°F, you can move your plants to an unheated but protected sun porch or next to a window in a shed or garage for a few days before taking them into the house. This two-step process will avoid shocking the plants with the radically different temperatures.

Before carrying the plants indoors, inspect each carefully for signs of disease or insects. If possible, hose off plants, pots, and saucers to dislodge any hitchhikers (including insect eggs). If you find any problems, it's best to attend to them right away to keep them from spreading to other houseplants. Spray insects with insecticidal soap or other pesticide, or wash off aphids with a strong spray of water from a hose. If plants are diseased, you can try treating them with an appropriate fungicide—but it's usually better just to discard them and not bring them indoors.

If your plants appear to be healthy, it's still a good idea to isolate them from your other houseplants for a week or two after the move. This provides extra insurance to make sure no pests escaped your notice during the outdoor inspection.

Repot plants that have outgrown their pots before you bring them indoors. If you are potting up any garden plants to bring indoors, shake off most of the garden soil from their roots and plant them in potting mix (which is less prone to compaction and less likely to harbor pests or pathogens than garden soil).

An Autumn Rest for Indoor Plants

Most plants, whether they're growing indoors or out, go dormant at some time during the year. They stop blooming, stop growing, may look a bit faded, and may even lose a few leaves. Herbaceous (nonwoody) perennials growing outdoors in temperate climates die back to the ground in winter. Annuals die after blooming and setting seed. Bulbs lose their foliage; some bulbs can be lifted from the soil, dried off, and put in storage until new shoots signal the end of dormancy. When their dormant rest period is over, plants begin another cycle of growth.

The time of year a plant goes dormant is related to the native habitat of its ances-

Mealybugs are a common affliction of houseplants. To remove them, dip a cotton swab into rubbing alcohol...

...and then dab the alcohol onto the cottony-looking mealybugs wherever they appear on leaves and stems.

Needing no dormant period, African violets will reward you with flowers year-round.

tors—the place where they grow naturally in the wild. Many garden flowers and houseplants are not North American natives but originally came from different parts of the world. Tuberous begonias, for example, come from Central America, just north of the equator; they go dormant in winter the way our native plants do. But Cape primroses (*Streptocarpus*) are native to Africa where seasons are reversed, so in their original species forms they bloom in winter and rest in spring. Some flowering houseplants have been extensively hybridized to bloom off and on practically year-round. Besides Cape primroses, African violets, and wax begonias are other good examples of ever-blooming plants. However, these are the exception; most houseplants do have definite dormant times.

Some plants' dormant periods can be forced to bring the plants into bloom outside their normal season. Forcing can reward you with amaryllis blossoms at Christmas and with tulips, fragrant narcissus and hyacinths, and other bulbs during the bleakest days of January and February. (See pages 184–185.)

Plants' Needs During Dormancy

Whether plants stayed indoors all summer or spent the season outside, they need the same treatment when they become dormant. When they stop actively growing, they need less food, water, and light.

Most importantly, do not fertilize dormant plants. They need to rest and stop growing actively during dormancy. Also, give your plants less water when they are dormant. It's best to water only when the plants start to wilt, or when the soil feels dry a couple of inches below the surface. Try not to give your dormant plants more water than they really need. Overwatering, especially during dormancy, is a good way to cause root rot.

Northern gardeners don't need to worry about reducing light levels for their dormant houseplants, because reduced light levels will occur naturally as autumn progresses. However, gardeners in the South may need to shift plants from one windowsill to another to make sure the light will be sufficiently reduced.

Flowering plants native to regions outside the tropics are most likely to rest at some time during the year. Except for African violets and their relatives, and non-tuberous begonias, watch your plants for signs that they are going dormant. They will stop blooming and will not put out new growth. They may just generally look "tired." After a rest period, they will respond with renewed vigor and fresh growth. When the plants begin to grow again after several weeks, you can gradually increase the amounts of light, water, and fertilizer.

Needing a dormant period between blooming times, the orchid below left is resting. The orchid to its right is actively growing, having sent out a budding stem.

Early Autumn — Cooler Climates

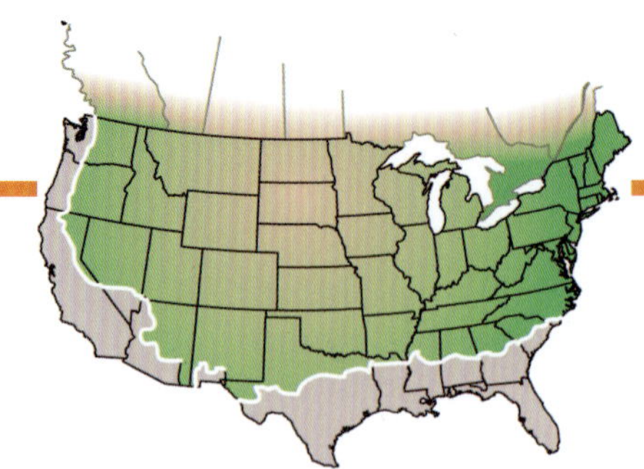

As shown on accompanying maps, if you live where winters are cold—from the mid-latitudes to southern Canada—use the information on the "Cooler Climates" pages as your guide. If you live in the South, Southwest, or mild regions along the West Coast, you'll find the information on the facing "Warmer Climates" pages more useful.

Established plants

As the days grow shorter and the temperatures turn cooler, keep spent flowers picked off mums, dahlias, late-blooming roses, and other fall flowers.

Begin cleaning up the garden, particularly in those beds where spring and summer flowers have finished blooming and no autumn flowers have been planted. Edge and mulch existing beds of perennials and bulbs.

Prepare garden beds for autumn planting of perennials, roses, and bulbs. Dig the soil deeply, work compost or other organic matter into the soil, and rake the beds smooth. In other parts of the garden, pull up and dispose of annuals as they finish blooming or are killed off by frost.

Continue fertilizing outdoor annuals and container plants still in bloom, but only if your first frost is still several weeks away. But stop fertilizing perennials and shrubs now so they will have a month or more to harden (toughen) before the ground freezes. One exception to this rule is peonies. You can fertilize peonies that don't need dividing with rich compost or all-purpose fertilizer. If your garden includes roses, keep watering late roses as they finish blooming, but you should stop fertilizing them.

Continue watering all plants, unless rain waters the garden for you.

Start dividing and transplanting early-blooming perennials. Dig up and divide crowded clumps of daylilies, irises, and other spring and summer flowers. After the first light frost, cut back and dig dahlias, gladiolus, and other tender bulbs for winter storage.

Cut back stems of perennials that have finished blooming.

Start returning houseplants indoors. For a few more weeks, you can leave out plants that may need cool weather to set buds, such as Christmas cactus, and those that bloom in cool weather.

Cut back, after the first frost, all perennials that have finished blooming. Cut to a few inches above the ground.

Planting

Dig up and transplant into pots marigolds and other annuals that will continue to bloom indoors during fall and winter. Take cuttings from begonias, geraniums, and impatiens before the first frost in order to start new plants indoors.

Take cuttings from impatiens and other tender perennials to start new plants.

Transplant seedlings of early bloomers (if they're big enough) to their permanent locations in the garden. Keep smaller seedlings in a cold frame over the winter; move them to the garden when spring arrives.

Plant bulbs that bloom in late winter and spring, such as winter aconite, crocuses, daffodils, scillas, and snowdrops.

Plant peonies, Oriental poppies, and other perennials as soon as they arrive from the nursery. You can plant pansies from a garden center and lily bulbs now, too (or in spring).

Sow seeds outdoors of early-blooming hardy annuals (except in very cold climates of the far North). These annuals include larkspurs and poppies, for bloom next spring.

Planning

As you go about your autumn chores, take time to evaluate the results of this year's garden. In your garden journal, make note of successes and failures, unproductive points in blooming schedules, colors to add next year. Then later in the season you'll be able to refer to your notes in making plans for changes.

Warmer Climates

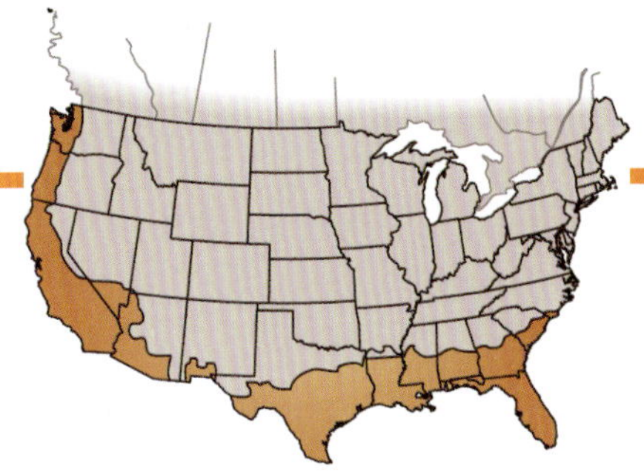

Established Plants

Plenty of plants are still blooming in warmer states, with gardeners busy deadheading annuals and perennials as their flowers fade. If you are growing camellias, you need to disbud them when the flower buds are big enough to distinguish from leaf buds. Thin each flower cluster to one bud, or at least thin the clusters so the buds are not touching.

Transplanting: Foxgloves, shown here at life's end in their second summer, are biennials and can be transplanted in early autumn of their first year.

Water in the warm South and Southwest during hot dry spells.

Fertilize chrysanthemums for the last time when they have set flower buds. Continue to feed annuals and container plants still in bloom.

Start preparing garden beds for planting later in fall. Dig in some compost or other organic matter and rake the soil smooth.

Begin cleaning up by pulling up weeds and annuals that have finished blooming, and then toss them on the compost pile. As long as the plants are not diseased or infested with pests, toss them—along with leaves—on the compost pile. Edge and mulch existing beds of perennials and bulbs where you won't be dividing plants or planting new ones this season. Put leaves and plant debris (as long as the plants are not diseased or infested with pests) on the compost pile.

Begin dividing perennials—such as irises, daylilies, Shasta daisies, and Stokes' asters—that bloom in spring and in early summer.

Planting

When they arrive from the nursery, put new hyacinth and tulip bulbs in the refrigerator until it's time to plant them in late November. If you live in southern California or other of the warmest climates, refrigerate daffodil bulbs as well (unless you select varieties such as tazetta types that are adapted to warm winters).

Plant newly ordered plants when they arrive from the nursery. Mail-order nurseries begin shipping spring-blooming perennials in early fall. Be sure to note on your garden plan where you put them if you haven't already done so. If you don't, you'll likely forget the exact locations by spring, and might unintentionally uproot the plants when working in the garden early next spring before they send up new top growth.

Plant pansies now for winter color. In the warmest climates, you can sow seeds of sweet peas and other annuals for winter flowers.

Transplant biennials (such as foxgloves) and perennials that you started from seed over the summer.

Sow seeds of larkspur, Shirley poppies, and bachelor's buttons for flowers early next spring. Finally, start taking cuttings from garden annuals to pot up for indoor flowers in winter.

To divide perennials, such as this phlox, dig up the root clump and split it into sections with a spade or other tool.

Replant divisions immediately, whether in pots or in the garden so the roots don't start to dry out.

Established Plants

Continue fall cleanup as the season progresses. Weed and cultivate garden beds and borders where frost has killed tender plants. Cultivation helps to get rid of perennial weeds and also aerates the soil. But be careful not to disturb the roots of perennials and bulbs. Hardy bulbs will not be visible above the soil surface now, but your garden plans should remind you where they are planted. Garden plans also come in handy if you want to find bulbs to divide or transplant, which you can also do at this time.

Rake up fallen leaves and put them on the compost pile, or shred them to use as mulch. Pull up annuals as they are killed by frost. Collect garden stakes, and tie them in bundles for storage.

Lift most of your tender bulbs for winter storage as soon as frost occurs. However, dig tuberous begonias and tuberoses before the first frost strikes. Move to a cold frame or cool basement any tender perennials that you want to winter over.

Clean up the garden and prepare it for early spring planting. These raised beds promote good drainage.

Divide crowded bulb plantings, including lilies, crocuses, daffodils, and others. In addition, divide late spring perennials now, plus any others still needing division this season.

Winterize roses after the first frost but before the ground freezes. To do this, there are several methods. You can lightly prune and then tip them on their side before covering with mulch, as shown below. Or you can mound up soil around the base of the plants, and mulch the plants to protect the canes from winter damage.

Bring indoors the rest of your houseplants that spent the summer outside.

Planting

In October you can continue planting early spring bulbs and start planting tulips. If you live where winters are very cold and without much snow cover, wait until the ground freezes before mulching beds of newly planted bulbs. This will minimize soil heaving.

Protect tree-form roses (left) by wrapping the trunks. Protect climbing roses (below) by weighting down the canes and applying a thick insulating layer of mulch.

Warmer Climates

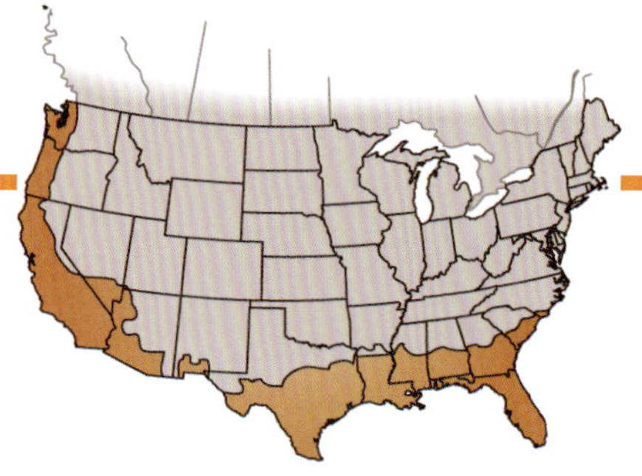

Established Plants

The autumn garden is in full bloom now. To keep plants healthy, continue fertilizing heavy feeders, such as chrysanthemums. Stake tall-growing mums to prevent wind damage.

Divide crowded plantings of bulbs such as crocuses, daffodils, and lilies. Also continue to lift tender bulbs for winter storage. If you live in an area where frost occurs, dig tuberous begonias and tuberoses before the first frost. Dig dahlias, gladiolus and all other tender bulbs after the first frost.

Divide summer-blooming perennials, and continue dividing and transplanting any other perennials that still need to be divided this season.

Mulch perennials you planted this season. Start mulching your roses, too, but wait until mid- or late winter to prune.

Check on any seedlings you sowed or set out in the garden last month. Water them if the weather is dry.

Continue cleaning up by pulling perennial weeds from garden beds and raking and composting leaves. As annuals finish blooming, pull them up and compost them, too.

Planting

If the weather is still mild, continue planting new perennials from the nursery. You can also prepare to plant spring bulbs that have been stored in the refrigerator for six to eight weeks. But wait to plant them out in late autumn when the soil cools.

Begin sowing seeds of cool-weather annuals and biennials for winter and spring flowers. These include sweet alyssum, bachelor's button, larkspur, poppy, snapdragon, sweet pea, and sweet William. In the warmest climates, you can also sow calendulas, nasturtiums, and annual phlox for winter color.

Planning

Plan ahead for winter bloom indoors. If you like the bright blossoms of kalanchoe, now is the time to start their dark treatment to stimulate blooming. You can keep potted plants outdoors in a shady spot in summer and then move them indoors in mid autumn. If you give them 13 hours of darkness every day until buds are set, you'll be rewarded with flowers in winter.

Stake mums and other late bloomers if your garden is in a windy location.

Continue cutting flowers to bring indoors. Chrysanthemums, dahlias, orange cosmos (as shown) and many others keep blooming well into autumn.

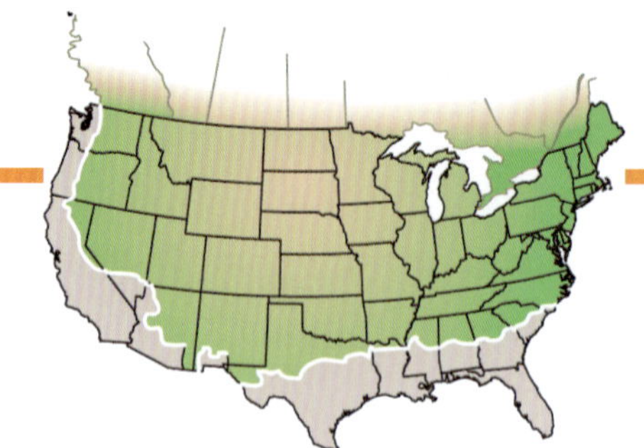

Established Plants

By late autumn, hard frost will have hit many northern and high-altitude gardens. The clear blue skies and crisp temperatures of October are giving way to the gray, blustery days of November, and winter is on the way. If you live where winters are cold, finish cleaning up your garden and start new plots before the ground freezes and the weather becomes too cold to work outdoors.

Cut back perennials to 1 to 2 inches. If you have peonies, cut the stems all the way back to the ground. As your chrysanthemums die, cut them back to the ground as well. Make sure woody perennial vines, such as wisteria, are securely fastened to their supports before winter sets in.

Cover the garden with a good layer of mulch after you've cut back established perennials and placed new plantings in the ground. Once hardy bulbs and perennials go dormant in winter, when the soil freezes, their greatest winter danger comes from soil that freezes and then thaws during mild spells, and then refreezes. Repeated cycles of freezing and thawing can cause the ground to buckle and heave, pushing bulbs and perennial roots right out of the soil. Lying exposed on the soil surface, they can be damaged by frigid air and drying winds. The goal of a winter mulch is to keep the soil frozen all winter, so the plants can rest peacefully in dormancy.

Mulch with shredded leaves, salt hay, compost, or boughs pruned from conifers. (In areas where the ground doesn't freeze until December, discarded Christmas trees are an easy source of boughs.) When the ground freezes, put down a layer of mulch at least 6 inches thick. If you live in a very cold climate where snow cover isn't reliable, in the far North, make the layer a foot thick.

Planting

You can continue planting tulip and lily bulbs until the ground freezes. Gardeners in milder areas, such as the mid-Atlantic from New Jersey south, can sow sweet peas in pots. However, keep them in a cold frame over winter, and then move them to the garden as soon as the soil can be worked in spring.

Planning

Although you probably won't be making most seed and nursery orders until the new spring catalogs arrive in winter, it's wise to order rare or popular varieties now for shipment early next year. If you wait until January or order later, nurseries may be sold out.

Use a garden hose and horticultural lime to lay out irregular beds before the ground freezes. Cool weather is a good digging time.

Winter mulch helps protect plant roots from damage that would otherwise result from freeze-thaw cycles. The mulch keeps the ground frozen. After the soil freezes in fall, cover plants with 6 or more inches of loose mulch. Fallen leaves are a handy source.

Warmer Climates

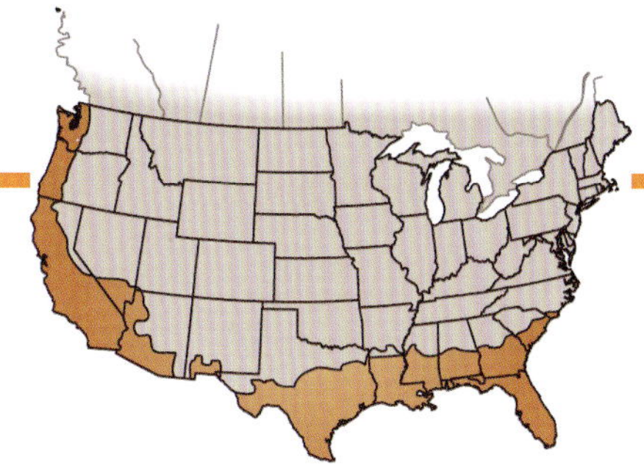

Established Plants

Late autumn weather is delightful in warm climates and is often the most pleasant weather of the year. Now gar-den work can be a real pleasure. Although you don't need to prepare your plants for the extreme conditions northern gardeners face each winter, there are still cleanup chores to finish. Gardens need to be weeded and edged, and in dry climates they need to be mulched, too, to conserve moisture.

An edging of stones or bricks allows you to mow up to the garden's edge without damaging plants.

Cut back annuals still in gardens from summer, to shape them and encourage a new flush of flowers, or pull up the old plants and start over with cuttings or seedlings.

Cut back the plants to 1 to 2 inches oncc thc plants go dormant. If the tops are still green, leave them in place. In the upper South and the Northwest, after chrysanthemums finish blooming, leave the old foliage in place to provide win-ter protection for the crowns.

Dig and store any summer bulbs still remaining in the garden.

Planting

If you started biennials or perennials from seed earlier in the season, the seedlings should be ready to transplant to their permanent garden locations. In the lower South and other of the warmest regions, such as the Deep South, continue to dig and divide perennials.

Plant, after at least six weeks' refrigeration, crocuses, daffodils, hyacinths, tulips, and other spring bulbs.

Continue sowing cool-weather annuals; though these are summer plants elsewhere, they bloom in winter and early spring in warm climates. This is also a good time to start seeds of perennials that bloom in late spring and summer. Also sow outdoors hardy annuals such as larkspurs, poppies, sweet peas, and bachelor's buttons. Start seeds of hardy annuals indoors for planting out in winter or early spring.

Mulch, in a dry climate, any new plantings in beds and borders. Replenish the mulch around your roses, too.

Planning

If you grow rare or popular plant varieties, you may want to order them now for shipment early next year. If you wait until January, suppliers may be out of stock.

Prepared bulbs (prechilled), such as these nar-cis-sus, should be planted before the ground freezes. (See "Bulb Planting Depths" on pages 182–183 for further guidance.)

Indoor Gardens

ALL CLIMATES

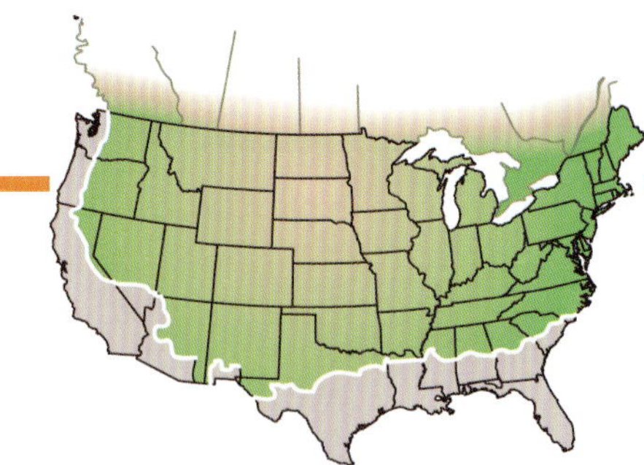

Early Autumn

Although there's plenty to do in outdoor gardens in fall, it's also time to give thought to your indoor garden—especially to plan what you want to have blooming in winter.

Let plants go dormant if it's their time for it. About now, vines such as bougainvillea and jasmine usually stop blooming. When they do, cut back on water and stop fertilizing to prepare the plants for a winter rest. Prune back the bougainvillea. Amaryllis, depending on when you started it growing, may also begin its dormant period now. Remove the leaves as they fade and die back. Then let the bulb rest for at least a month before repotting and starting to water and feed it again.

Pot up tender perennials, such as these wax begonias, as well as cyclamens, impatiens, and geraniums. After being cut back, they will provide flowers indoors in winter.

Planting

If you want to start new poinsettias for Christmas flowers, take cuttings from existing plants by mid-September. Pot up spring bulbs you want to force into bloom indoors in winter. To begin the forcing process, pot crocuses, daffodils, tulips, and other hardy bulbs from now until late autumn and place them in cold storage. For more details, see “Forcing Bulbs Indoors,” pages 184–185.

Mid Autumn

Continue to pot up spring bulbs that you want to force into bloom indoors for winter flowers.

Start planting in late October or early November, paperwhite narcissus bulbs

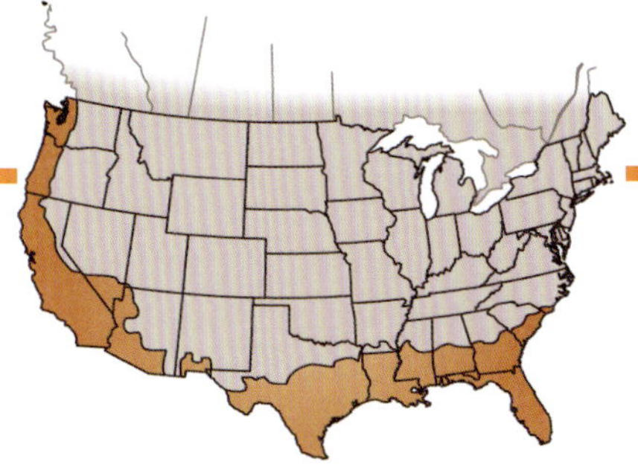

Digging and repotting this cyclamen may provide another year of bloom.

Plant bulbs for forcing close together, but not touching. Label each pot with plant name and planting date.

at two-week intervals for a succession of winter flowers.

Begin giving poinsettia plants long nights (at least 12 hours of darkness per day) if you started them from cuttings. This will help them bloom for Christmas.

Late Autumn

As autumn draws to a close, continue to plant paperwhite narcissus bulbs at two-week intervals to have lots of their fragrant white flowers to perfume your home all winter long.

Pot up hardy bulbs for winter forcing as late as November. If you pot them any later, after their necessary cold storage period, they won't bloom much before normal outdoor blooming in spring.

Check houseplants periodically. Frequently check the houseplants you brought back indoors after their summer vacation outside to make sure they're not carrying any pests with them. As summer-blooming houseplants go into dormancy, reduce watering and stop fertilizing them.

Forcing bulbs is well worth the effort involved in potting and providing a cold period. The results add color to a room in winter when you most need it.

Chapter 8 *Winter*

Whether you live in a colder or warmer climate, winter is no reason to put away the trowel and pruners. Winter is a time of rest and renewal, and a time to consider the results of the past year. Now perennials lie dormant under their blankets of mulch or snow. Summer's annuals have long since finished their life cycle—though warm-climate gardeners can grow new ones.

Yet winter still has flowers to offer. In warmer climates outdoors, there are primroses, pansies, and other cool-weather perennials and annuals, plus flowering shrubs—camellias, heathers, winter jasmine, winter honeysuckle, and witch hazels. In the North, late winter brings the earliest bulbs and shrubs, cheering gardeners' hearts. Though usually thought of as early spring flowers, the flowers that open in February and March in colder climates bloom several weeks before spring weather arrives and so are really late-winter flowers.

Indoors in winter, homes can be full of color and fragrance from the bulbs that began their forcing process in autumn. Other houseplants, too, bloom in winter. So do plants started from cuttings taken from last summer's outdoor annuals. Winter also brings holiday specialties such as poinsettias and holly.

Left to right, opposite: narcissus, tulips, and hyacinths

Winter Gardens

This chapter explores the possibilities for winter flowers, both indoors and out. Here you'll learn about colors that predominate in winter and which flowers provide which colors. You'll also find suggestions for a variety of plant combinations to try in your gardens.

This is the time of year when flowers are especially welcome in most homes. To help you fill your house with flowers, you will find tips on creating winter arrangements and some holiday decorations, too. There's also information on bringing forced bulbs into bloom and forcing early flowers from branches of shrubs you can cut and bring indoors. For the holidays, or simply to share a bit of cheer, there are ideas for gifts to give from your garden.

Winter Colors

For indoor gardeners, a whole palette of colors is available in winter. You can choose and combine in practically any color scheme you like, by growing houseplants, forcing bulbs and branches, or starting annuals from seeds or cuttings.

Outdoors, the choices are more limited. Winter's outdoor colors are mostly cool, clear, and clean—blue, violet, and white—with some yellow to brighten the scene. You won't find the soft pinks and lavenders of spring, the bright golds and roses and purples of summer, or the warm bronzes and russets of autumn. Winter flowers tend to match the feeling of the season, with its cold temperatures, clear air, and sense of purity and cleanness.

Winter's indoor color palette is richer than many people imagine. Year-round bloomers here include salmon-colored begonias and blue African violets. Many orchids, such as these yellow cymbidiums, bloom in winter.

Early Bulbs

Early bulbs are a special delight in the outdoor garden. Plant them in drifts underneath evergreen or deciduous shrubs, among perennials in beds and borders, in woodland gardens, or in patches of lawn that can be left unmowed until the bulb foliage dies back in late spring. One caution is to avoid crocuses in woodland areas, because they need lots of sun to put on their best show; snowdrops (*Galanthus*) or squills (*Scilla*) would be a better choice for a shady spot.

Most of the early bulbs are small and inexpensive, so you can plant lots of them. The hours spent planting the bulbs in fall will prove well worthwhile when the flowers burst forth as winter begins to ease its grip.

Year-Round Bloomers

Some houseplants flower off and on all year. Their blossoms are especially welcome in winter, when flower choices become more limited for most gardeners. Consider adding some of these ever-blooming plants to your collection to make sure you'll have plenty of flowers all winter long.

- *Achimenes* hybrids (monkey-faced pansy). Blooms all year under fluorescent lights.
- *Anthurium scherzerianum* (flamingo flower). Blooms best under lights.
- *Begonia Semperflorens-Cultorum* hybrids (wax begonia). Blooms with as little as two hours of sun a day.
- *Crossandra infundibuliformis* (firecracker flower). Blooms best under lights.
- *Exacum affine* (Persian violet). Blooms best under lights.
- *Impatiens* hybrids (impatiens). Plants grown from cuttings taken in summer will bloom indoors in winter under lights.
- *Lantana* species and hybrids (lantana). Blooms all year under lights.
- *Manettia luteorubra* (Brazilian firecracker). Blooms off and on all year under lights.
- *Oxalis* hybrids (shamrock plant). Bloom off and on all year, though most heavily in summer and fall.
- *Pelargonium × hortorum* (zonal geranium). Plants grown from cuttings taken in summer will bloom indoors in winter under lights or in a sunny window.
- *Pentas lanceolata* (Egyptian star cluster). Blooms best under lights.
- *Saintpaulia* hybrids (African violet). Will bloom happily under lights or on a bright windowsill.
- *Streptocarpus* hybrids (Cape primrose). The newer Cape primrose hybrids bloom practically year-round under full-spectrum fluorescent lights or on a bright, cool window ledge.

Winter Annuals for Warm Climates

Mid and Upper South

Antirrhinum majus (snapdragon)
Browallia speciosa (sapphire flower)
Centaurea cyanus (bachelor's button)
Consolida ambigua (larkspur)

'Carpet of Snow' sweet alyssum

Dianthus species (garden pink)
Eschscholzia californica (California poppy)
Gaillardia pulchella (blanket flower)
Gypsophila elegans (annual baby's breath)
Iberis umbellata (annual candytuft)
Lathyrus odoratus (sweet pea)
Limonium species (statice)
Lobularia maritima (sweet alyssum)
Lupinus species (annual lupine, bluebonnet)
Matthiola incana (stock)
Nicotiana × sanderae (flowering tobacco)
Papaver rhoeas (Shirley poppy)
Phlox drummondii (annual phlox)
Verbena species
Viola × wittrockiana (pansy)

Coastal South

The above, plus the following:
Calendula officinalis (pot marigold)
Petunia × hybrida

Southern California and the Southwest

Antirrhinum majus (snapdragon)
Arctotis stoechadifolia (African daisy)
Bellis perennis (English daisy)
Calendula officinalis (pot marigold)
Eschscholzia californica (California poppy)
Iberis umbellata (annual candytuft)
Lathryus odoratus (sweet pea)
Lobularia maritima (sweet alyssum)
Nemesia strumosa
Nigella damascena (love-in-a-mist)
Pericallis × hybrida (cineraria)
Phlox drummondii (annual phlox)
Primula species (primroses, grown as annuals)
Scabiosa atropurpurea (pincushion flower)
Trachymene coerulea (blue lace flower)
Viola × wittrockiana (pansy)

California poppy

The Winter Palette

Plants noted here in **boldface type** are described in detail in "Flowers for Winter Gardens" on page 214. In all listings in this book, plants are arranged alphabetically by scientific (botanic) name. When scientific and common names are the same in such lists, just one name is mentioned.

RED FLOWERS

Poinsettia

***Abutilon* cultivars (flowering maple)**
Anemone coronaria (poppy anemone)
Antirrhinum majus (snapdragon)
Ardisia crenata (coralberry), red fruits
Begonia species (wax and tuberous begonias)
Callistephus chinensis (China aster)
Capsicum annuum (ornamental pepper), red fruits
Cuphea ignea (cigar plant)
***Cyclamen persicum* (florist's cyclamen)**
Erica carnea (winter heath)
***Euphorbia pulcherrima* (poinsettia)**
Hibiscus rosa-sinensis (Chinese hibiscus)
***Hippeastrum* cultivars (amaryllis)**
Hyacinthus orientalis (hyacinth)
Impatiens cultivars
Kalanchoe blossfeldiana
Lachenalia species (Cape cowslip)
Manettia luteorubra (Brazilian firecracker)
Mimulus × *hybridus* (monkey flower)
Pericallis × *hybrida* (cineraria)
Primula species (primrose)
Rhododendron cultivars (azalea)
Rosa cultivars (miniature rose)
***Schlumbergera* × *buckleyi* (Christmas cactus)**
Solanum pseudocapsicum (Christmas cherry), red fruits
Tropaeolum majus (nasturtium)
Tulipa cultivars (tulip)

PINK FLOWERS

Florist's cyclamen

Abutilon cultivars (flowering maple)
Anemone coronaria (poppy anemone)
Antirrhinum majus (snapdragon)
Begonia species (wax and tuberous begonias)
Callistephus chinensis (China aster)
Camellia cultivars
Clarkia amoena (satin flower)
***Cyclamen persicum* (florist's cyclamen)**
Eranthemum pulchellum (blue sage)
Erica carnea (winter heath)
***Euphorbia pulcherrima* (poinsettia)**
Freesia cultivars
Hibiscus rosa-sinensis (Chinese hibiscus)
***Hippeastrum* cultivars (amaryllis)**
Hyacinthus orientalis (hyacinth)
Impatiens cultivars
***Jasminum polyanthum* (jasmine)**
***Mimulus* hybrids (monkey flower)**
Pentas lanceolata (Egyptian star cluster)
Pericallis × *hybrida* (cineraria)
***Phalaenopsis* cultivars (moth orchid)**
***Primula* species (primrose)**
Rhododendron cultivars (azalea)
Rosa cultivars (miniature rose)
***Saintpaulia* cultivars (African violet)**
***Schlumbergera* × *buckleyi* (Christmas cactus)**
***Streptocarpus* cultivars (Cape primrose)**
Tulipa cultivars (tulip)
Veltheimia bracteata (forest lily)
Zantedeschia species (calla lily)

ORANGE FLOWERS

'Excellent Orange' marigold

Antirrhinum majus (snapdragon)
Calceolaria cultivars (pocketbook plant)
Calendula officinalis (pot marigold)
Celosia argentea (crested cockscomb)
***Clivia* (kaffir lily)**
× *Citrofortunella microcarpa* (Calamondin orange)
Hippeastrum cultivars (amaryllis)
Impatiens cultivars
Kalanchoe blossfeldiana
Tagetes species (marigolds)
Thunbergia alata (black-eyed Susan vine)
Tropaeolum majus (nasturtium)
Tulipa species (tulip)

YELLOW FLOWERS

Pot marigold (Calendula)

Antirrhinum majus (snapdragon)

Calceolaria cultivars (pocketbook plant)
Calendula officinalis (pot marigold)
Celosia argentea (crested cockscomb)
Chimonanthus praecox (wintersweet)
Crocus species and cultivars
***Eranthis hyemalis* (winter aconite)**
Forsythia species
Freesia cultivars
***Hamamelis* (witch hazel)**
Iris danfordiae
***Jasminum nudiflorum* (winter jasmine)**
Lantana camara
Mimulus × hybridus (monkey flower)
Narcissus species and cultivars
***Paphiopedilum cultivars* (lady slipper orchid)**
***Primula species* (primroses)**
Tagetes species (marigolds)
Thunbergia alata (black-eyed Susan vine)
Tropaeolum majus (nasturtium)
Tulipa cultivars (tulips)
Zantedeschia species (calla lily)

BLUE & VIOLET FLOWERS

Polyanthus primrose

Anemone coronaria (poppy anemone)
Browallia speciosa (sapphire flower)
Callistephus chinensis (China aster)
***Chionodoxa luciliae* (glory-of-the-snow)**
Crocus species and cultivars
Eranthemum pulchellum (blue sage)
Exacum affine (Persian violet)
Hyacinthus orientalis (hyacinth)
Iris reticulata
Muscari species (grape hyacinth)
***Primula species* (primroses)**
***Saintpaulia cultivars* (African violet)**
***Scilla mischtschenkoana* (Persian squill)**
***Streptocarpus cultivars* (Cape primrose)**
Torenia fournieri (wishbone flower)

PURPLE FLOWERS

Martha Washington geranium

Anemone coronaria (poppy anemone)
Antirrhinum majus (snapdragon)
Brunfelsia pauciflora (yesterday-today-and-tomorrow)
Bulbocodium vernum (meadow saffron)
Clarkia unguiculata (satin flower)
Crocus species and cultivars
Daphne mezereum (February daphne)
Daphne odora (winter daphne)
Eranthemum pulchellum (blue sage)
Freesia cultivars
Geranium
Impatiens cultivars
Mimulus × hybridus (monkey flower)
Pentas lanceolata (Egyptian star cluster)
Pericallis × hybrida (cineraria)
***Saintpaulia cultivars* (African violet)**
***Streptocarpus cultivars* (Cape primrose)**
Tulipa cultivars (tulips)
Veltheimia bracteata (forest lily)

WHITE FLOWERS

Calla lily

Abeliophyllum distichum (white forsythia)
Anemone coronaria (poppy anemone)
Begonia species (wax and tuberous begonias)
Callistephus chinensis (China aster)
Camellia cultivars
Carissa macrocarpa (natal plum)
Coffea arabica (Arabian coffee plant)
Crocus species and cultivars
***Cyclamen persicum* (florist's cyclamen)**
***Euphorbia pulcherrima* (poinsettia)**
Freesia cultivars
***Galanthus nivalis* (snowdrop)**
***Helleborus niger* (Christmas rose)**
Hibiscus rosa-sinensis (Chinese hibiscus)
***Hippeastrum cultivars* (amaryllis)**
Hyacinthus orientalis (hyacinth)
Iberis umbellata (annual candytuft)
Impatiens cultivars
***Jasminum sambac* (Arabian jasmine)**
Lonicera fragrantissima
Narcissus species and cultivars
Ornithogalum species (star-of-Bethlehem)
Pericallis × hybrida (cineraria)
***Phalaenopsis cultivars* (moth orchid)**
***Primula* (primrose)**
Rhododendron cultivars (azalea)
Rosa cultivars (miniature rose)
***Saintpaulia cultivars* (African violet)**
Salix discolor (pussy willow)
***Schlumbergera × buckleyi* (Christmas cactus)**
***Streptocarpus cultivars* (Cape primrose)**
Thunbergia alata (black-eyed Susan vine)
Tulipa cultivars (tulip)
Viburnum species
Zantedeschia aethiopica (calla lily)

Christmas rose

Brighten a winter windowsill by pairing pink Reiger begonias (front) with something rosy red, such as these cyclamens.

Combining Winter Flowers Indoors & Out

Here are some plant combinations to experiment with in your winter gardens, indoors and out. For indoors, you'll find plant combinations to be used in a variety of color schemes that will work with a variety of decors. Use the ideas on these pages to help you experiment with some of your favorite plants to create a range of effects. Most outdoor gardens in this season are based on shrubs and bulbs that bloom in late winter.

Indoor Gardens

If you started annuals from seeds or cuttings in summer or fall to bloom in your indoor garden in winter, there are lots of color combinations possible. For example, group China asters in pink and rosy red with pink impatiens and purple browallia. Another red-and-pink combination is red hibiscus with pink geraniums. For a variation, display pink camellias with cyclamen in deep rose and soft lavender. Pink geraniums and purple Persian violets (*Exacum*) are another unusual—and quite handsome—pair.

African violets in shades of purple, red-violet, pink, and white offer a colorful but simple combination. You can add even more variety by growing cultivars with different flower forms: mix single- and double-flowered types, ruffled flowers, and picotee flowers (those whose petals are edged in a different color). In a room that's too cool for African violets, Cape primroses (*Streptocarpus*) can make their own show in a similar range of rosy red, pink, and purple hues.

Amaryllis is a classic winter flower. Try a few in soft shades of pink and salmon, with the small, fragrant trumpets of freesias in purple and creamy white. Red and pink amaryllis, white cyclamens, and hanging pots of trailing, white-flowered jasmine can fill an entire window.

Because of their similar tall stature and bold form, calla lilies can substitute for amaryllis in plant groupings. Tall white calla lilies look lovely behind rose and white cyclamens. If you prefer bright red to rosy pinks, try grouping coralberry (*Ardisia crenata*) with red kalanchoes and white fairy primroses for a red-and-white theme.

Forcing bulbs allows you to work with all of the colors of spring. If you are forcing bulbs, try showing off blue, violet, and pink hyacinths with cream-colored daffodils and paperwhite narcissus. This combination is as fragrant as it is beautiful. For a real taste of spring, group forced daffodils in golden yellow, some with orange centers, and crocuses in white, gold, and vibrant purple. A dish garden of blue-violet *Iris reticulata* and dwarf narcissus forced into bloom at the same time can dress up a table or countertop.

If you love fragrant flowers, you'll enjoy heavenly scented paperwhite narcissus placed near other forced narcissus and daffodils, or a grouping of lavender, yellow, and white freesia. Or

Forced bulbs, like these narcissus, burst into bloom, transforming a winter windowsill into a spring garden.

Outdoor color is harder to have in winter, but one of the plants that obliges—and with fragrance—is Chinese witch hazel (**Hamamelis mollis** 'Brevipetala').

you can pair sweet olive (*Osmanthus*) with the similarly scented jasmine (*Jasminum polyanthum*).

For the holidays, red amaryllis makes a fine display with red, pink, and white poinsettias. Or combine Christmas cactuses in shades of magenta, rose, pink, and white.

For a blue-and-white scheme, the traditional colors of Hanukkah, try blue and white poppy anemones with white China asters. You can easily substitute camellias, or chrysanthemums from the florist, for the asters.

Outdoor Gardens

At this time of year outdoor flowers are especially valuable. Most of them are supplied by bulbs and shrubs. Most of the winter-blooming shrubs have flowers in yellow or pinkish mauve. These shrubs can be beautifully complemented by bulbs that bloom in white, such as snowdrops, or in shades of blue and deep violet, such as *Iris reticulata*.

Yellow is also a dominant color for early bulbs. Consider the numerous color schemes available with yellow-flowered bulbs and shrubs. You can create a gold-and-white garden by planting snowdrops, winter aconite, and early white crocuses; set these in front of and among dwarf conifers or other evergreens to accentuate the colors. Early blooming shrubs such as fragrant witch hazels or winter hazels can be underplanted with snowdrops or early white crocuses.

If you'd like to add blue or purple to a yellow-and-white garden, you could try a combination such as Chinese witch hazel underplanted with snowdrops and blue Siberian squills. Simple bulb gardens can be created with snowdrops, yellow winter aconite, and blue glory-of-the-snow. Or substitute purple, white, and yellow crocuses for glory-of-the-snow.

If you prefer yellow-and-blue or yellow-and-purple gardens, you might enjoy an early iris bed of *Iris reticulata* in deep blue and purple with yellow *Iris danfordiae*. Yellow amur adonis or winter aconite will harmonize nicely with blue Persian or Siberian squills. Glory-of-the-snow can provide a carpet of starlike blue flowers under the branches of yellow forsythias. Evergreen vinca, which begins producing its purple flowers in late winter in warmer climates and early spring farther north, is beautiful when planted around and among yellow and cream-colored daffodils.

A bed of early-blooming species crocuses, such as *Crocus chrysanthus*, in assorted shades of purple, lavender, golden yellow, and white makes a fine show on its own, especially when the flowers are backed by deep green conifers or other evergreen shrubs. Lavender or yellow crocuses also look lovely in concert with ornamental grasses, which in many gardens retain their tawny, graceful dry seed plumes all winter. Try maiden grass (*Miscanthus* species) or switch grass (*Panicum virgatum*), for example.

Though the classic colors of crocuses look good together and with evergreens or tawny grasses, these colors do not necessarily harmonize well with the colors of many of the early shrubs. Avoid a mixture of bright yellow and cool lilac or purple. Don't plant your lilac crocuses with common forsythia or witch hazel, or gold crocuses with purple *Rhododendron mucronulatum*. However, there is one forsythia hybrid, *F.* × *intermedia* 'Spring Glory', whose soft, light yellow flowers mix nicely with lilac crocuses.

This early-blooming bulb, Iris reticulata, will flower in late winter and early spring even if snow remains.

Making Winter Flower Arrangements

Winter is the time when flowers—both fresh and dried—are most appreciated. The forced bulbs and houseplants described on page 203 provide a supply of flowers for cutting as well as display. If you're reluctant to pilfer from potted plants, you can set up a light garden—an indoor growing area under a couple of fluorescent light fixtures—to grow annuals and potted plants just for cutting. The holiday season brings classics, such as wreaths and arrangements of evergreen branches and leaves. Incorporating flowers, using techniques described here, adds interest and beauty to these traditional decorations.

Winter flower arrangements call for creativity. To get the greatest variety, use outdoor flowers if you have them, forced bulbs and branches, and flowers and leaves from houseplants. You can also supplement homegrown flowers with blossoms from the florist. And don't overlook broad-leaved evergreens as a source of foliage for winter arrangements. The glossy leaves of magnolia, boxwood, and other broad-leaved evergreens are lovely with poinsettias and other flowers.

Poinsettias are probably the most popular Christmas plants, now available in red, pink, white, or white flushed with pink. The flowers themselves are the tiny yellowish centers. The big petallike parts are actually showy bracts. Although most people display them only as potted plants, poinsettias also make dramatic additions to flower arrangements. Poinsettias combine well with evergreens, boxwood, holly, or dried baby's breath.

Traditionally poinsettias haven't been successful as cut flowers because their cut stems bleed a thick, milky sap (typical of all plants in the genus *Euphorbia*). This sap prevents the stems from taking up water. Photographs below show how to keep cut poinsettias looking good for eight to 10 days.

When specially treated, as below, poinsettias can be used as cut flowers and combined with seasonal greens for colorful Christmas arrangements.

How to Succeed with Poinsettia Cut Flowers

Caution: Some people's skin is sensitive to the milky sap of poinsettias and other plants in the genus *Euphorbia*. As a precaution, avoid touching the sap, or wear protective latex gloves.

Tools & Materials: Pruning shears or knife, candle **Difficulty:** Easy

1 Sear poinsettia stem ends over a flame or dip them quickly in boiling water. This trick stops the flow of milky sap that would otherwise keep the stems from taking up needed water.

2 Insert treated stems into florist's water tubes, which have a rubberized cap and small hole that makes a watertight seal around the stem. Then hide the tubes inside your arrangements.

This garland of greens, roses, and mums was photographed in England in autumn—a concept easily adapted in winter by substituting dried flowers.

How to Decorate Holiday Wreaths & Garlands

At Christmas many homes are full of evergreens—garlands, ropes, wreaths, and swags grace front doors, mantelpieces, tables, and sideboards. They also festoon stair rails and surround doorways. When collecting or buying greens for decorations, don't just limit yourself to pine. Although long-needled pines are lovely, also consider fir, hemlock, cypress, yew, cedar, and even arborvitae. For texture contrast, mix in some aromatic boxwood or glossy green bay, magnolia, or camellia leaves.

In addition to traditional evergreens, wreaths can also be fashioned from ivy, dried grapevines, or Virginia creeper vines. You can decorate wreaths, swags, and garlands with bayberries, mistletoe, and bright orange bittersweet berries. Holly makes another attractive addition; besides the familiar green kind, there are also hollies with green-and-

How to Make Conifer Wreaths & Garlands

To make a wire-based wreath, follow instructions in accompanying photos. Buy a wire hoop at a garden center, or shape your own hoop from a sturdy coat hanger. (Or buy a foam wreath base at a craft store. If you use a foam base, you can attach greenery with wire, florist's picks, greening pins, or glue. With a foam base, overlap the greens to hide the fasteners and achieve a nice, full look.)

To make a rope-based garland, the techniques for tying branches in place are virtually the same as shown for a wreath, except that you may wish to include flowers or berries as you wrap the branches.

Tools & Materials: For a hoop wreath, pruning shears, green florist's wire, pliers to cut the wire, plastic sheeting, fresh-cut conifer boughs. For a garland, same tools and materials, plus rope or twisted and tied pantyhose or strips of fabric. **Difficulty:** Easy

1 Cut and assemble small bunches of conifer branches, as well as 20 or so 6-in. lengths of florist's wire to fasten each bunch to the hoop.

2 Hold each bunch to the hoop as you tightly wrap and tie the wire. Then fit the next bunch over the first, somewhat like fitting one funnel over another.

3 Use roughly 3-ft. lengths of wire to secure the bunch positions along the circumference of the wreath, positioning branches to best effect as you wrap.

4 Use your favorite cold-hardy decorations, whether they be gold-sprayed walnuts and imitation apples shown here or dried fruits and flowers.

Use dried flowers from your garden to dress up holiday wreaths of all types.

Dried yellow statice decorates this home-made twig wreath.

white variegated leaves, and some with yellow berries.

Poinsettias, camellias, amaryllis, and other cut flowers can be cut with short stems and placed in individual plastic water vials (available at most florist shops), which are fastened to the greens and easily camouflaged amid the foliage. You can also decorate wreaths and swags with bunches of dried flowers. Possibilities include small clusters of baby's breath, purple statice, golden yarrow, pink strawflowers, red or pink rosebuds, or magenta globe amaranth. For a different look, decorate wreaths and garlands with pine cones, nuts (sprayed gold or silver if you like), ornamental peppers, and colorful fruits, including apples, kumquats, lemons, and pears.

How to Make a Grapevine Wreath

If you collect grapevines in winter, soak them in water for a few hours to make them more pliable. (Vines collected and woven in summer will be pliable enough.) Note: Because wild vines may extend high into trees, you may need a pole pruner to free them high up. Also, vine tendrils cling to their supporting structure, so you may need to tug on them vigorously to bring them down.

Tools & Materials: Pruning shears for thin vines and a pole pruner for high-climbing vines. Several vines totalling at lease 50 feet in length. **Difficulty:** Moderate

1 Use the base end of your thickest vine to form a circle, securing it in your gripping hand (left hand shown here). The starter vine here measured about 15 ft. long. Because the vine is rough, wear protective gloves.

2 Pull the remaining full length of the vine completely through the inside of circle, then outside and inside again repeatedly wrapping the vine along the circle. Continue this procedure with subsequent vines until your wreath is as thick as you want it.

3 Tidy up by pruning branches that won't tuck neatly into the wreath without breaking. Spare the attractive tendrils.

4 You can decorate grapevine wreaths with dried flowers or berries, or simply leave the wreaths plain.

Forcing Bulbs into Bloom

The bulbs you potted up for forcing in autumn will be ready to bring into bloom at various times during the winter. After bulbs have been in cold storage for the required length of time, bring them from their dark, cold storage place into bright light, but not direct sun. Clean any dirt from the outside of the pot.

When the shoots are 2 to 3 inches tall and bright green, put the pot on a sunny but cool windowsill. A cool environment is important. If the temperature is too warm, the bulbs will only send up leaves and may not bloom. Give the plants as much light as possible to get the sturdiest growth. Dim light will cause the stems to grow lanky and floppy.

Water your bulbs when the soil (or other potting medium) dries out. You can judge this by the weight of the pot—dry soil is significantly lighter than wet soil. Another way to test for dryness is to tap the outside of the pot: a hollow sound means the soil

Forced bulbs can fill your home with color. They'll last the longest on a sunny, but cool, windowsill.

Paperwhite narcissus grow fast in water or in soil. They reach this stage of growth in one week and bloom in a few weeks.

When growing narcissus in soil, cover the soil surface with sphagnum moss, both for appearance and to help retain moisture.

As narcissus grow, turn their pot or glass jar daily so the plants don't start leaning strongly toward the light.

is dry; a dull sound means it's moist. When it's time to water, use room temperature water, because cold water will shock the plants and slow their growth.

As the plants grow, turn the pots often so the stems grow straight. Stake tall or floppy plants to keep their stems from bending over. Keep the soil loose and aerated by gently stirring the surface occasionally. To get the longest life from the flowers once they open, put the plants in a cool, but not cold, place at night and keep them away from drafts. When the flowers fade, clip them off.

The 'Apple Blossom' amaryllis, left, sent up its shoot quickly after planting and receiving regular watering.

At right are the same 'Apple Blossom' and 'White Christmas' amaylis 10 days after the photo above.

Saving Forced Bulbs

Unless you plan to discard the bulbs after they bloom, don't stop watering the plants when the flowers fade. If you didn't mix bulb fertilizer into the soil at planting time, start fertilizing every couple of weeks with half-strength liquid plant food. Continue watering for a month or two more to let the foliage grow and nourish the bulb. Then gradually taper off watering and let the foliage die back. You can then store the bulbs until it's time to plant them outdoors or, for amaryllis, until it's time to begin to force them again.

Bulbs forced indoors usually cannot be forced a second time (except for amaryllis), but they can be planted outdoors if they are hardy in your area. They may not bloom for a year or two. During this period they regain their strength, so any flowers will most likely be smaller than those you forced indoors. To replant forced bulbs outdoors, wait until the foliage has died back. Then take the bulbs out of their pots, brush off the soil, and inspect them for signs of mildew, rot, or disease. When the bulbs are clean and dry, store them in a cool, dry place until planting time in fall.

Gifts from the Garden

Flower gardeners are never without homegrown gifts to give friends and family for Christmas and other special occasions. A blooming plant presented in a pretty bowl or basket makes a gift the recipient can enjoy for a long time. Such a plant can be a winter-flowering houseplant, a pot of forced bulbs, or, for a reminder of summer, a flowering annual that you started from seed or a cutting in summer or fall.

Kalanchoes in a basket

If you have blooming flowers that are suitable for cutting, you can hand-tie a bunch of flowers for a special gift. Cut the flowers; arrange them to form a pleasing display; and wrap the stems together with florist's wire right before you present them. Cover the wire with a decorative ribbon, and tie a nice bow. Dried flowers can also be presented in a hand-tied bunch, providing a charming instant arrangement to put in a vase or basket. Another cut-flower option is a small bouquet of winter flowers arranged in a vase or bowl.

If you plan to save bulbs after forcing, remove spent flower stems and let the leaves mature. This paperwhite narcissus wouldn't survive transplanting outdoors north of Zone 8.

Branches can be cut from spring-flowering trees and shrubs and forced into early bloom indoors. These forsythias, pussy willow, and dogwood are classic examples, but many other kinds of branches can be forced as well.

How to Force Branches

Cut the branches with a sharp knife or pruning shears to ensure a clean cut. To increase their capacity to absorb water, slit the cut ends and scrape off the outer bark to about 3 inches. Or split the cut ends with a hammer without smashing them as shown on page 127. After cutting, soak the branches—the entire branches, not just the ends—in lukewarm water for 24 hours in a warm room, if possible, where the temperature is 70° to 75°F. An unused bathtub works well for this. Then place the stem ends in a container of cool water in a cool, dim place (a basement or attached garage, perhaps) where the temperature is 60° to 65°F.

After a few days move the branches to a brighter, warmer spot. But don't put them in a sunny window. A north-facing windowsill is a good location.

Forcing Branches into Bloom

You can enjoy blossoms from flowering shrubs and trees a month or two ahead of their normal outdoor blooming time by cutting branches and forcing them to bloom indoors. Forcing can begin during the bleakest part of winter, when it seems that spring will never come. Pussy willow (the easiest of all branches to force) and witch hazel can be cut in January in many places. A month later it's time to cut forsythia and cornelian cherry, and about a month after that you can cut branches from flowering crabapple trees. Peach blossoms, too, can be forced, as well as those of other fruit trees. If you prune your fruit trees after their buds begin to swell, you can force the branches.

Cut the branches you want to force after the buds begin to swell in late winter or early spring. Timing is important. If you cut the branches too early, the buds will drop off or shrivel. If you cut the branches too late, their buds won't bloom any earlier than the plant's normal outdoor flowering time. Watch for that first fattening of buds. It's best to cut the branches on a mild day or during a thaw, around noon; the branches will be filled with sap and yield better flowers

To get the longest life from your forced branches, change the water and cut another inch off the stems approximately once a week. You can add some cut-flower conditioner to the water if you like, or some charcoal (the type used for aquariums, not barbecue briquettes). Add fresh charcoal or conditioner whenever you change the water. Once a day, or at least three times a week, mist the branches with lukewarm water to mimic the effect of a gentle, soaking spring rain. Mist thoroughly, until the branches are dripping.

As the flowers begin to open, arrange the branches in a vase and move them into bright sunshine. The sunlight will intensify the color in mature buds. Flowers that open in the shade will be paler.

If you are forcing the flowers for a special event and you find that they are opening before you want them to, you can slow down the process by moving the branches to a cool, shaded location where the temperature is between 50° and 65°F. If your flowers are opening too slowly, you can speed them up by setting the branches in warm water (about 110°F) each morning. Let the water cool during the day, and replace it with fresh water the next morning. Misting the branches with warm water will also help hasten blooming.

Forcing Hints

When deciding which of the flowering shrubs and trees on your property are the best candidates for early forcing, remember that plants that produce flowers before leaves (like forsythia) are easier to force than plants that produce leaves first (such as deutzia and weigela). Consider, too, that the later a plant blooms outdoors, the longer it will take to force. The closer to their natural flowering time branches are cut, the less time it will take to force blooms.

Flowers for Winter Gardens

The flowers you can grow outdoors in winter depend on where you live. Warm- climate gardeners have many more choices than those in colder regions. But no matter where you live, there are winter flowers you can grow. This chapter contains basic information on growing a variety of winter plants; to accommodate cool-climate gardeners, a number of indoor plants are included here.

The following winter-flowering plants are listed alphabetically by their scientific (botanical) names. These plants are readily available at local nurseries and from mail-order catalogs. They are also reliable and easy to grow if you provide the recommended conditions. For each plant you'll find descriptive information, suggestions for using the plant in the garden, and basic guidance on planting and care. Most plants adapt to a range of soil pH (acidity or alkalinity); for plants with a special need, the preference is noted. For an explanation of the plant naming system, see page 31.

Abutilon / Flowering Maple

Flowering maple

The large bell-shaped blossoms of flowering maples are quite beautiful in pots indoors or, during warm weather, outdoors on patios. Blooming in a range of shades of red, pink, orange, yellow, and white, they make good cut flowers as well. Flowering maples were popular in Victorian parlors, so popular that they were sometimes called parlor maples. Today there are numerous species and improved hybrids to choose from. And many of today's selections are ever-blooming.

Flowering maples get their common name from the shape of their leaves, which resemble maple leaves to varying degrees. They are big plants. Older species and cultivars can grow large—to 4 feet or more. But many cultivars sold today are dwarf forms that grow a foot or so tall. Some are cascading and good in hanging baskets. Give them plenty of pot space, and prune them in spring to keep them bushy. Some of them grow upright, and others are better suited to hanging baskets. While a few kinds of flowering maple are hardy to Zone 8, most can only be grown outdoors in Zones 9 and 10.

Flowering maples thrive in an all-purpose potting mix. (See page 116 for information.) Give these tender plants warm daytime temperatures around 70°F, with a 10° drop at night. Keep the soil evenly moist, and mist the plants every day to increase humidity levels.

In winter these plants need full sun, which means a south-facing window where light isn't blocked by branches or buildings. In summer they can be moved to a partly shaded spot outdoors, ideally where they receive four hours of morning sun.

As the plants grow, pinch back the new shoots to encourage a bushy shape. Flowering maples do not go into dormancy but grow year-round. To keep them vigorous, in spring cut back the main stems by half and prune the lateral stems back to 3 or 4 inches. Flowering maples don't need much fertilizer. An occasional dose of a houseplant fertilizer that is low in nitrogen (such as a 15-30-15 formula) should do the job.

Ever-blooming hybrid cultivars include 'Crimson Belle' (rich red), 'Satin Pink Belle' (pink), 'Huntington Pink' (pink), and 'Moonchimes' (yellow). *Abutilon megapotamicum* 'Variegatum' and *A. pictum* 'Thompsonii' have gold-mottled leaves.

Chionodoxa / Glory-of-the-Snow

These delightful little plants start producing their star-shaped flowers of blue, white, or pink in late winter or early spring, depending upon where you live. The two common species, *Chionodoxa luciliae* and *C. sardensis*, both grow 3 to 6 inches and share the common name glory-of-the-snow. They can be used in rock gardens, borders, and beds or naturalized beneath shrubs and trees. The plants will spread from self-sown seeds and will eventually carpet the area with their flowers. You can speed up their spread by dividing clumps regularly.

If you live in a cool climate where summers are mild, plant glory-of-the-snow in full sun. If your summers are hot, pick a site that receives partial shade during late

Glory-of-the-snow

spring and summer. *Chionodoxa luciliae* is hardy in Zones 3–9 and *C. sardensis* in Zones 5–9. They need some below-freezing temperatures in winter in order to bloom.

Plant the bulbs in autumn, 2 to 3 inches deep and 3 inches apart, in well-drained soil that contains plenty of organic matter. Water regularly during the growing and blooming seasons if rains are sporadic in your area. Taper off the watering when the foliage begins to die back.

Glory-of-the-snow multiplies quickly. Bulbs should be dug up, separated, and replanted in early autumn every few years, when the plants noticeably lose vigor and the flower quality and quantity decline.

Clivia / **Kaffir Lily**

This beautiful winter-blooming houseplant is closely related to the amaryllis, which it resembles. The plant has long, broad, straplike leaves of deep glossy green and reaches a height of 18 to 24 inches. Its fragrant trumpet-shaped flowers are orange with yellow centers and come in clusters in the center of the plant. Yellow cultivars are also available, though generally expensive. There are several species of kaffir lily, but Clivia miniata is the one that blooms in winter to spring indoors.

Growing kaffir lilies is quite similar to that of amaryllis, which also grow from bulbs. Plant the bulb in an all-purpose potting mix. (See page 116.) Keep the newly planted bulb in partial shade until the first shoots appear; then move it to a spot on an east-facing windowsill where it will get bright light but no direct sun.

These plants are tender; they like warm temperatures of 65° to 70°F during the day and 5° to 10°F cooler at night. Keep the soil evenly moist as the plants grow. Feed them every two weeks during their growing season with a half-strength liquid all-purpose fertilizer.

Cut back the flower stalks when the plants finish blooming. Continue to water and fertilize the plants so the leaves have a chance to nourish the bulbs.

To stimulate new blooms, stop fertilizing in late fall or early winter, and let the soil dry out somewhat between waterings. Also at this time, give the plant cool nighttime temperatures around 50°F.

Kaffir lily

Kaffir lilies bloom best when potbound, so repot them into larger pots only when you find roots pushing through the surface of the soil. This will happen every three to five years.

Crocus / **Early Crocuses**

'Dutch Yellow' crocus

The first crocuses to bloom are the species types, which begin poking their heads above the ground as early as January, depending on where you live. These early-blooming plants, with their familiar chalice-shaped flowers, grow cheerfully in pots, beds and borders, and rock gardens. They can also be naturalized in lawns that can be left unmowed until the bulbs' foliage dies. The flowers come in shades of yellow, white, and purple; striped and bicolored types are available as well. Their slender, grassy leaves are usually striped with white.

Early-blooming crocus species include angora crocus (*C. ancyrensis*), lilac tommies (*C. tommasinianus*), white or lilac Scotch crocus (*C. biflorus*), snow crocus (*C. chrysanthus hybrids*) in a range of colors, and orange-yellow cloth-of-gold crocus (*C. angustifolius*). Hardiness varies with species; those listed here are suited to Zones 3–8.

Plant corms of early-blooming crocuses in early fall, 3 to 4 inches deep and 3 to 4 inches apart, in full sun. You can also plant them under deciduous trees if the trees don't leaf out until after the plants finish blooming. In areas where the summer sun is very strong, crocuses need some filtered shade in summer. Plant the corms in well-drained soil, and water regularly during the growing season if the weather is dry. Taper off watering when the leaves start to die back in summer. Crocuses like a dry dormant period but can tolerate regular rainfall if they are planted in a soil that drains quickly. They spread rapidly and need to be divided every three or four years.

Crocuses can be grown in pots for one season, but they must be planted out in the garden afterward if they are ever to bloom again. To grow them in containers, pot the corms in an all-purpose potting mix of equal parts of peat moss, builder's sand, and organic matter (compost or leaf mold), as described on page 116. A small amount of a high-phosphorus fertilizer can be added to the potting mix if you intend to transplant them outdoors. A 5-inch pot will hold ten corms.

Florist's cyclamen

Cyclamen / Florist's Cyclamen

This classic winter houseplant has lovely waxy flowers, whose curved-back petals give them a form reminiscent of shooting stars. In fact, shooting star is another nickname for the plant. Cyclamen flowers come in many lovely shades of pink, rose, magenta, and red, as well as white; cultivars generally grow to about 8 inches.

Tender Cyclamen persicum is the species from which most of today's indoor cultivars have been bred. The plants grow from tubers and bloom in late autumn and winter. When they stop flowering in spring, move the plants to a cool, dark place and gradually withhold water to let the leaves die back. Remove all the dead flowers and leaves and allow the tubers to rest over the summer. Keep the soil barely moist; don't let it dry out completely. In late summer when new shoots appear, you can repot the tuber and start watering and fertilizing regularly.

Cyclamens hold up best in cool temperatures of 55° to 60°F, especially when they are in bloom. Give them bright light, but no direct sun, from an eastern exposure. Feed the plants every two weeks with half-strength liquid all-purpose fertilizer when they are growing and blooming. Keep the soil evenly moist; these plants usually need more frequent watering than most houseplants. Set the plants on pebble trays to increase humidity levels in their immediate vicinity.

Eranthis / Winter Aconite

The buttercup yellow flowers of winter aconite (*Eranthis hyemalis*) bloom in late winter along with snowdrops and early crocuses, which all make nice companions in the garden. Winter aconites grow just a few inches tall, and their large flowers have flat, broad petals that are pointed at the tips. The flower stalks arise from a low mat of divided (segmented) leaves.

Winter aconite is hardy in Zones 4–9. It's not demanding in terms of its care. The plants do fine in any reasonably fertile, well-drained soil. Winter aconite grows well in shade, a characteristic that increases its versatility. Even better, the plants can be left undisturbed for years as they spread; you don't ever have to divide winter aconite unless you want to propagate new plants. They do self-sow and can spread into other parts of the garden or a nearby lawn. But their spreading habit makes them good choices for naturalizing under trees and shrubs.

Plant the bulbs in late summer or very

Winter aconite

early autumn, 3 inches deep and about 3 inches apart. Be careful to purchase winter aconite from a reliable nursery that sells only propagated stock, not bulbs collected from the wild. Winter aconite is endangered in its native Eurasia as a result of overcollection.

Euphorbia / **Poinsettia**

Poinsettia

Although we don't think of the poinsettia (*Euphorbia pulcherrima*) as a shrub, in its native Mexico it is indeed a shrubby perennial. Where it survives outdoors (Zone 11, warmer parts of Zone 10), a poinsettia can grow taller than the normal 24 to 36 inches of an indoor plant. What we recognize as the poinsettia's flower is actually made up of colorful bracts, petallike structures surrounding the true flowers, which are tiny and inconspicuous. In addition to the traditional red poinsettia, cultivars are now available in pink, white, and white flushed with pink.

When the plants are growing and blooming, give them warm temperatures of 65° to 70°F during the day, with a 10° drop at night. A bright southern window covered with sheer curtains that filter the sun is a perfect spot. Keep the soil evenly moist but not soggy; do not overwater. Use an all-purpose potting mix. (See page 116.) A good potting mix is two parts potting soil, one part milled sphagnum moss, and one part vermiculite.

Poinsettias bought at Christmastime can be brought into bloom again in subsequent years if you know how to treat them. The plants go into dormancy when they finish blooming. When their color fades, move them to a cool place with filtered light, stop fertilizing, and water them just enough to keep the soil from completely drying out. When new growth starts in spring, cut back the stems, repot the plants, bring them back to a bright spot, and resume regular watering. Feed the plants once a week in summer and fall with a half-strength liquid houseplant fertilizer. Poinsettias enjoy spending the summer outdoors; they are tender, so bring them back inside well before nighttime temperatures turn cold.

To bring indoor plants into bloom for the holidays, you must artificially regulate the day length. Beginning in autumn, give the plants 12 to 14 hours of complete darkness daily, to simulate the long nights of winter. The plants need two months of this dark treatment for the bracts to change color.

To provide the necessary dark period, set the plants in a closet or cover them with dark cloth at night to exclude light, for even electric lights in a room could prevent blooming.

Galanthus / **Snowdrop**

Snowdrop

Among the earliest and most welcome heralds of spring in cold climates, snowdrops (*Galanthus nivalis*) can be seen blooming in woodlands before the last snow has melted. The dainty white flowers grow 6 to 10 inches tall; most have tiny green spots at the petal tips. Snowdrops can be planted in beds or borders but are best used in rock gardens, under deciduous trees and shrubs, or naturalized in unmowed grassy areas. They bloom at the same time as winter aconite, and the two plants make an attractive combination in the garden.

Snowdrops like lots of sun when they are growing and blooming, but they need to be shaded from the hot summer sun. Under deciduous trees and shrubs is a perfect location for snowdrops; their leaves will provide filtered shade for the plants during the time of year when they need it. Snowdrops are hardy in Zones 3–9 and need some subfreezing winter temperatures to bloom.

Galanthus / Snowdrop (continued)

Plant the bulbs in autumn, 3 to 4 inches deep and 3 inches apart, in well-drained soil enriched with compost or leaf mold. Snowdrops like heavier soil than most bulbs do, and they also like moisture, so water them when rainfall is sparse. The bulbs don't need to be divided very often. When clumps appear overcrowded, dig and divide them right after the flowers fade in spring. Transplant the bulbs carefully, and give them plenty of water after you replant them.

Hamamelis / Witch Hazel

Although shrubs are not the real focus of this book, some play such valuable roles in the garden that they can't be left out. One of these is hybrid witch hazel (*H.* × *intermedia*), whose fragrant yellow or reddish flowers are so welcome in late winter.

The shrubs vary in height from 6 to 20 feet, depending upon cultivar. The flowers' narrow, strap-shaped petals look like little bunches of wavy ribbons. Witch hazels are hardy in Zones 5–9 and are easy to grow. They tolerate any average garden soil but seem to prefer soil that is moist and well drained. You can grow them in either full sun or partial shade.

Witch hazel flowers

When the plants open their bright flowers in February, cut a few branches and bring them indoors to force, so you can enjoy the pleasant flower scent as well as the outdoor color.

Witch hazel

Helleborus / Christmas Rose

Christmas rose

This lovely perennial (Helleborus niger) sends out its flowers in winter in mild climates and in early spring where the soil freezes. It is hardy in Zones 4–8. The plant takes a couple of years to establish itself in the garden, and it is fairly demanding in terms of its environmental conditions, but the rewards are worth the extra effort. The unusual flowers are white and develop a pinkish or greenish tint as they mature. They are long-lasting in the garden and make good cut flowers.

Christmas roses need a shady spot where the soil is cool, moist but well drained, and rich in organic matter. Dig in lots of compost, well-rotted manure, and leaf mold when you prepare the planting area, and topdress liberally once a year to keep the soil in good condition. The plants spread very slowly, so you won't need to divide or move them. The leaves are evergreen and may dry out in harsh winter winds. If wind is a problem in your garden, you can protect the foliage from its drying effects by spraying with an antitranspirant (usually available at garden centers).

Amaryllis (center)

Hippeastrum / Amaryllis

Although winter is not the only time of year amaryllis bulbs can be brought into bloom, they are most often seen in this season, especially around the holidays. Their enormous trumpet-shaped flowers (up to 8 inches across), clustered atop straight 2-foot stems, are flashy and hard to miss. Each bulb sends up one, or sometimes two, flower stalks, each of which is topped by a cluster of three to six huge, trumpet-shaped flowers. Many hybrid cultivars are available in a range of warm colors, along with white and white brushed or edged with red or pink.

In frost-free areas amaryllis can be planted outdoors. Since most people grow amaryllis as a houseplant, indoor culture is discussed here.

Most mail-order nurseries ship amaryllis bulbs in autumn. If you want to have flowers for Christmas, order your bulbs so you have them by the middle of October. You can also purchase prepotted bulbs at nurseries or from catalogs at this time. New bulbs usually bloom about six weeks after you start to water them.

Plant each bulb in an 8-inch pot, in a good all-purpose potting mix. (See page 116.) Set the bulb so the top third of it is above the soil level. Water sparingly until shoots appear, then water regularly to keep the soil evenly moist. The bulb doesn't need any fertilizer to produce its first flowers. Keep the plant in a bright window where it will get some sun, and turn the pot every couple of days so the stem grows straight. Flower stems are very thick and usually don't need staking.

The flowers usually last a month to six weeks. When they fade, cut off the big stalk and let the leaves grow to nourish the bulb. Feed every two weeks during the growing season with half-strength liquid all-purpose plant food. You can move the plant outdoors for the summer if you like, but in any case you should continue to water it. At the end of summer, start cutting back on water to encourage the foliage to die back. When leaves turn yellow, remove them, stop watering entirely, and set the pot in a cool, dark basement or closet. In two or three months when new shoots appear, move the plant back into the light and resume watering.

Amaryllis bulbs usually last for several years. The plants bloom best when potbound, so you only need to repot them every two or three years. If you mix in time-release fertilizer when you repot, you won't need to fertilize for a year or so.

Jasminum / Jasmine

Outdoor jasmines are usually associated with southern gardens, but the winter jasmine (Jasminum nudiflorum) grows in Zones 6–9. Better still, it flowers in late winter in cool climates and practically all winter long in warmer areas. The plant is a shrub with scandent (climbing) stems. It grows to 10 feet and is quite effective planted in front of a stone wall, along a bank, or massed into an informal hedge. It has fragrant, clear yellow flowers.

Winter jasmine sends out its flowers before its leaves. The flowers bloom on wood produced the previous year, which means it's important to wait until just after bloom to prune the plant. The shrubs need full sun in order to bloom well. But they're not fussy about soil, growing happily in just about any reasonably fertile, well-drained garden soil.

In addition to winter jasmine, there are several other jasmines (such as Jasminum polyanthum) that make heavenly scented winter houseplants. Indoor jasmines need bright light, preferably with direct sun in the morning. A southern or eastern exposure is best for these plants. Pot them in an all-purpose growing medium. (See page 116.) Keep the soil moist, and mist the plants once or even twice a day to boost humidity levels. These tender jasmines like cool temperatures of 50° to 60°F indoors. Feed the plants once a month when they are growing actively, with an all-purpose houseplant fertilizer.

Indoor jasmines are lovely in hanging baskets. Their stems arch over the sides of the pot, and the graceful clouds of sweetly fragrant flowers float airily above the foliage. When the flowers fade, cut back the flowering stems by several inches.

Winter jasmine

Kalanchoe

Kalanchoe / Kalanchoe

This delightful little houseplant (Kalanchoe blossfeldiana) fires up its bright blossoms just when people need them most—in the depths of winter. The succulent plants grow to 12 inches; they bear loose clusters of small tubular flowers in shades of red, orange, and yellow above broadly oval, glossy green leaves with scalloped edges. Kalanchoe often continues blooming well into spring.

Give tender kalanchoe average household temperatures, ideally with a 5° to 10°F dip at night. A light, loose all-purpose potting mix, or one suited for cacti and succulents (such as a blend of equal parts potting soil, compost, and sharp sand or perlite) is best. A bright southern window is the best location for the plant. Allow the soil to dry a bit between waterings—it should feel dry an inch below the soil surface before you water again. While plants are blooming, feed every two weeks with a liquid flowering houseplant fertilizer.

These plants can be difficult to rebloom at home. If you want to try for another year of bloom, cut back on watering in early to midfall to give the plant a dormant period for a few weeks. While the plant rests, water just enough to keep the leaves from shriveling. After the dormant period, resume normal watering and cover the plant or place it in a closet each night so it's in the dark for 14 hours a day. Continue for at least four weeks. Then return the plant to its bright window to set buds. An easier approach is to start new plants for next season's flowers by taking cuttings when the plant finishes blooming.

Paphiopedilum / Lady Slipper Orchid

Lady slippers are among the most widely grown orchids. Many are easy to grow and bring into bloom indoors. Many of the hybrids bloom twice a year, often in winter. Their waxy flowers are characterized by a rounded lip, which is called a pouch. Hybrids bloom in unusual shades of purple, maroon, deep red, pink, or white—often striped, streaked, flushed, veined, or mottled on the petals or sepals. Flowers grow on stems about 10 inches long and last a very long time on the plant, sometimes two months.

The critical factors for lady slippers (as for other orchids) are light, temperature, and humidity. They grow well in a north or east window or under fluorescent lights (set to provide 12 hours of light a day). Plants with solid green leaves need temperatures of 60° to 75°F during the day, with a 15° drop at night. Plants with mottled leaves need to be a bit warmer, 70° to 80°F during the day and 15° cooler at night. The nighttime drop is crucial; you may find it easiest to grow the plants in an unused bedroom or a separate plant room where you can regulate the temperature without making your living quarters uncomfortable. Tender lady slippers enjoy spending the summer outdoors in a shady, protected spot. A lath house, if you have one, is ideal.

Plant lady slippers in a growing medium that holds moisture but still drains well, such as osmunda fiber or finely chopped fir bark, or a packaged orchid medium (available at garden centers or from specialty orchid nurseries). It's important to keep the medium evenly moist. Once or twice a month, feed the plants with an orchid fertilizer or half-strength fish emulsion. To give the plants the high humidity they need, keep them on a pebble tray and mist them daily. It's better to mist the plants in the morning rather than in the afternoon, for moisture sitting on the leaves at night can cause disease problems.

The plants rest briefly when their new growth has matured. Cut back on watering and stop fertilizing the plants during this time. Resume normal watering and fertilizing after a few weeks. When the first flower bud forms, stake the plant to help the slender flower stems support the weight of the heavy flowers.

Phalaenopsis / Moth Orchid

Moth orchid

The flowers of moth orchids really do resemble moths, with their broad, flat, widespread petals and sepals. The glorious flowers bloom in long, arching sprays on 12- to 36-inch stems, opening in a succession that can continue for an incredible five months. Hybrids can be pure white, shades of pink, greenish yellow, apricot, orange, tan, or beige. There are also white flowers with a colored lip, white flowers striped with pink or red, and a host of other spotted, barred, and flushed patterns. Most species bloom in spring, but some hybrid moth orchids are ever-blooming, and most others bloom anytime during the year, often during the winter. Moth orchids are among the easiest orchids to grow indoors.

Tender moth orchids like warm, humid conditions quite similar to those enjoyed by African violets. The plants are epiphytic, meaning that in nature they grow above the ground (often perching in trees) and take moisture and nutrients from the surrounding atmosphere rather than from the soil. What this means for gardeners is that the plants need a looser, coarser potting medium than lady slippers, which are terrestrial plants. You can grow moth orchids in baskets of fir bark mixed with chopped tree fern fiber, or you can attach the plant to a slab of tree fern fiber, not putting it in a pot at all. Give moth orchids a bright north or east window where they won't be exposed to direct noontime sun. Or you can provide 12 to 16 hours of fluorescent light a day. Moth orchids, like lady slipper orchids, enjoy spending the summer outdoors in a shady, protected place.

Good air circulation is important for moth orchids, as is moisture. Keep the potting medium evenly moist; if you're growing the plant on a piece of tree fern fiber, mist the roots often. During the day, moth orchids need temperatures of 70° to 85°F, with a drop to 60° or 65°F at night. Feed the plants with half-strength orchid fertilizer or dilute half-strength fish emulsion every other time you water, year-round.

Primula / Primrose

Primroses are favorite spring garden flowers. But some of the tender species, such as fairy primrose (*Primula malacoides*), poison primrose (*P. obconica*), and Chinese primrose (*P. sinensis*), bloom indoors in winter, adding their cheerful colors to houseplant displays. Colors range from reds and pinks through mauve, lilac, purple, and white, depending on species. All are characterized by flowers growing singly or in clusters on top of tall stems (12 inches or taller) that arise from a basal rosette of slightly fuzzy, oval-shaped leaves.

Grow primroses in a humusy soil mix. A blend of one part potting soil, two parts leaf mold or peat moss, and one part perlite or builder's sand makes a good medium. The plants need cool temperatures: 55° to 60°F during the day, with a 10° drop at night. You can grow them in a bright north or east window, or under fluorescent lights turned on for 12 to 14 hours a day. Keep the soil evenly moist, and feed the plants twice a month while they're blooming, with a half-strength all-purpose fertilizer or dilute fish emulsion or seaweed extract. Primroses won't bloom well if potbound, so you will need to repot them each year after they finish blooming.

Fairy primrose

Saintpaulia / **African Violet**

African violet

The African violet is the most popular houseplant in America, and with good reason. It adapts well to indoor conditions, blooms year-round, and comes in a staggering array of flower forms, an assortment of pretty colors, and a range of plant sizes, too. The flowers can be single or double, ruffled or fringed, white-edged or bicolored. The color range is limited to purple, pink, and white, but there are so many shades and variations that you won't run out of choices. While most African violets grow in neat, low rosettes, there are also trailing and creeping types. They range in height from less than 3 inches to about 16 inches.

African violets grow well in a soilless potting mix of equal parts of shredded sphagnum peat moss, perlite, and vermiculite—a medium that holds moisture but drains well. The plants grow well in bright east or north windows. Or grow them under fluorescent lights kept on for 12 to 18 hours a day; place plants about 10 inches below the lights.

The plants will tell you if they are getting the right amount of light. If the light is insufficient, the plants will bloom poorly, and the leaves will be dark green in color and ascending toward the light. Variegated leaves may turn solid green. African violets that are getting too much light develop droopy yellow leaves that look burned around their edges. To keep the plants symmetrical, give the pots a quarter turn every couple of days.

African violets are tender and like warm temperatures of 65° to 75°F. They like high humidity, too, although they can adapt to the dry atmosphere present in so many homes in winter. Contrary to a common misconception, however, the plants do not need a lot of water. Water them only when the soil surface is dry, and avoid getting water on the leaves and crowns. You may find it easier to water the plants from the bottom, by setting the pots in a tray of water. Feed the plants every week or two with quarter-strength liquid all-purpose fertilizer.

African violets tend to develop long necks below the leaves as they get older, which ruins the look of the plant. To rejuvenate a necky plant, cut through the stem with a sharp knife, about an inch below the bottom leaves. Scrape off the tough outer layer of stem to expose the green tissue below, then place the whole top of the plant in a soilless propagating medium to root. When roots form, pot up the new plant. The topless stem of the original plant can be left in its pot and cut back to 1 inch in length. Give the stub a dose of half-strength fertilizer, and the plant should begin to send out new leaves in a couple of weeks.

Schlumbergera / **Christmas Cactus**

Christmas cactus

Christmas cactus (Schlumbergera × buckleyi) is as easy to grow as its Thanksgiving-flowering relative and requires the same kind of care. Both plants are dependable bloomers. Christmas cactus blooms from early to midwinter in shades of pink, fuchsia, red, rose, and white, including many lovely pastels.

The plant is distinguished from other members of the genus by the scalloped edges of its flat, segmented stems. These stems grow upright at first, but as they elongate they arch gracefully. The plants grow slowly.

Like the rest of the holiday cactuses, the Christmas cactus is an epiphytic plant. It grows best in a light, well-drained potting mix. A blend of one part potting soil, two parts peat moss, and one part perlite or builder's sand suits it well, or use an all-purpose fertilizer.

The tender plant thrives in a warm room, with a temperature around 65° to 70°F. Give it an east or west window with bright light. The plants are said to need long nights and cool temperatures in order to set buds, and to be safe, it is best to give them those conditions. However, some people find their plants bloom just fine if left indoors all year on a natural daylight schedule.

Individual flowers last only a few days, but the plant sets many buds and continues to set more after the first flowers wilt. Keep faded flowers picked off. After the plant finishes blooming it produces new leaves. Throughout this time it appreciates a weekly or biweekly watering and an occasional dose of all-purpose plant fertilizer. Sometime in late spring, growth stops and the plant rests. At this time, water it only when the leaves start to look a little shriveled.

In late summer or early autumn, start to water more often. Also fertilize the plant as it begins to set buds.

Scilla / Squill

Squills are among the most productive and charming of bulbs. They bloom lavishly and spread quickly, carpeting the ground with their little blue flowers. The most familiar kind, brilliant blue Siberian squill (*Scilla siberica*), blooms in early spring in most gardens. But Persian squill (*S. mischtschenkoana*) blooms in late winter, when it adds a dash of cool, clear color to gardens. Its pale blue flowers have a darker stripe down each petal; they grow on 4- to 5-inch stems. Persian squill is hardy in Zones 6–9.

Because they spread so rapidly, squills are excellent plants to naturalize in lawns, especially beneath the branches of deciduous trees. Their inconspicuous grassy leaves die back before the lawn needs to be mowed in spring. You can also plant scillas in beds and borders or in rock gardens.

Squills are extremely easy to grow. They make themselves at home in any well-drained, loamy soil, especially if it tends to be sandy. An annual topdressing of compost or leaf mold in fall will ensure that the soil stays rich in organic matter and contains plenty of nourishment for the bulbs. Plant squills in partial shade, about 3 inches deep and 3 to 4 inches apart, in the fall. They need very little care after planting.

You can divide the bulbs every four years or so or just leave them alone to naturalize. In addition to spreading by means of bulblets formed on the bulbs, the plants also self-seed, and the seeds grow into blooming-size bulbs in just a few years.

Persian squill

Streptocarpus / Cape Primrose

Streptocarpella Cape primrose

This close relative of the African violet is becoming increasingly popular among indoor gardeners. Its tubular flowers bloom in shades of crimson, pink, violet, blue, or white. The newer hybrids flower practically year-round, and they are especially welcome in winter. The flowers are carried on 6- to 10-inch stems above a low rosette of long, broad leaves. Among the available cultivars, those with blue and purple flowers are considered generally easier to grow than those blooming in red or pink hues.

Cape primrose is easy to grow as long as you can supply its four basic needs: lots of light but no direct sun, cool (55°–65°F) temperatures, excellent drainage, and plenty of moisture. These tender plants thrive in the same peat-perlite-vermiculite potting mix that suits African violets. You can grow Cape primroses in an east window, or in a fluorescent light garden with 12 to 14 hours of light a day.

Group the plants on pebble trays to keep the humidity high. Let the soil dry somewhat between waterings. When the plants are growing actively, feed them with half-strength liquid fertilizer every time you water.

You can propagate many houseplants by division. Simply remove the rootball from the pot, and pry or cut it apart before repotting new plants in fresh potting mix.

Winter Activities

In December, seed and garden catalogs arrive, providing hours of enjoyment and inspiring planning for the coming year. As you update your garden plans and order seeds and plants, a new gardening year begins.

In cooler climates, winter activities center around the indoor garden. Although outdoor beds and borders lie frozen and resting, indoors there are bulbs, houseplants, and annuals to enjoy and maintain. Then in February, the earliest outdoor bulbs break through the earth to begin blooming, and the gardening cycle begins anew.

In warmer climates, the outdoor gardening season never really ends. Winter flowers must be cared for, both indoors and out. And outdoor planting begins in February, or even January in the warmest locations.

The Indoor Environment

Central heating changes the indoor environment for plants. Temperatures may vary widely within a room. It may be hot directly above a radiator, cool next to a window, and cold and drafty near a door. A windowsill can become quite hot on a sunny day and quite cold at night, even when the thermostat in the room records a fairly even temperature. A windowpane—even a storm window—may be cold enough to damage plant leaves that come in contact with the glass.

In many rooms, heat sources are located beneath windows, which creates even wider temperature fluctuations there. To avoid shocking houseplants with extreme temperature swings, never put them on windowsills directly above a heat source.

The more aware you are of the environment in your home in winter, the better you will be able to choose suitable places for plants. Following are some tips.

Temperature

Place thermometers on windowsills and other plant-growing places to monitor day- and nighttime temperatures. Then match cool-loving plants to cool places and heat lovers to warm places, as specified in the table "Temperature Needs of Winter Houseplants" on page 226.

Humidity

Take measures to increase the humidity level around your plants. In many northern homes in winter, the relative humidity can get as low as 20 percent (that's drier than a desert). Although that's fine for cacti, most popular houseplants need 40 to 60 percent humidity. Plants growing in air that is too dry begin to look pale, their leaves curl under, and they may turn brown at the tips and along the edges. They also become much more susceptible to spider mites, troublesome pests that can be difficult to eradicate. Giving these plants more water won't help. You need to put water vapor into the air around them. Fortunately, increased winter humidity makes the indoor environment healthier for humans as well as plants.

Here are some ways to increase humidity for your plants.

Furnace Humidifier. If you have a hot-air furnace and it doesn't have a humidifier in its air-conditioning system, you can have one installed or install one from a kit.

Room Humidifier. Another option is placing an electric humidifier in each room where you have plants. These units can significantly increase humidity. Because the mist feels cool, don't position the humidifier where it will blow directly onto tropical houseplants that need warm conditions.

Keep plants back from windowsills in winter, where the leaves could be damaged if they touch the cold glass. Also, avoid placing plants over radiators.

Wilted Plants

If the air is so dry that your plants actually wilt, you may be able to save them by enclosing them individually in clear plastic bags. Support each bag with three or four stakes pushed into the pot. Water normally and let the water drain before enclosing the plant. Then blow up the bag, place it upside down over the stakes, and fasten it under the saucer. Move the plant out of direct sun. Tweak the plastic so that it doesn't touch the plant. Leave the plant in the bag until the foliage revives.

Moisture tent for wilted plant

Low-Tech Strategies. Inexpensive strategies include the following:

- Group plants together on pebble trays, shallow plastic trays of pebbles kept filled with water. Simply place flower pots, saucers and all, on top of the pebbles, thereby increasing humidity around the plants as water evaporates from the tray.
- Mist plants regularly with tepid water. Smooth-leaved plants benefit most from this treatment. Do not drench plants so that water sits in the leaf axils, where it could encourage disease.
- Place open containers of water near heat sources, such as on top of wood stoves and radiators, and elsewhere around the room to simply evaporate.

Winter Vacation Care

Before you leave on a winter vacation, make arrangements to help your houseplants survive in your absence. The best option is to have a skilled, plant-loving friend stop by every few days to take care of your plants.

If that's not possible, and you need to leave your plants on their own, the following tricks will help. With the right preparation, your plants should be able to survive two, even three, weeks without you.

Moisture & Humidity

The basic strategy is to water the plants normally before you leave, and then slow down their respiration rates until you come back. One way to slow respiration is to enclose large plants in clear plastic moisture tents. In effect, you will be creating a miniature greenhouse that will maintain enough humidity around each plant to keep it from wilting. To do this, place three or four stakes in each pot and drape a plastic bag over them, ensuring that the plastic does not touch the foliage. In addition, move the plants away from windows so they don't receive any direct sunlight; otherwise, the air inside the bag will heat up and literally cook the plant.

If you have a number of smaller plants, you can group them together and cover them with clear plastic sheeting, a large plastic bag, or even an old aquarium. Or you can construct a greenhouse-like box, as shown on the opposite page. Simply place the plants on a pebble tray, and cover them with the tent assembly.

As important as moisture will be while you are away, don't overwater plants and then enclose them in plastic. The combination of standing water around roots and lack of ventilation could cause root rot. Instead, let the excess water drain from the pots as you normally do before enclosing them in plastic.

Plants that grow well in constantly moist soil can be handled with a system of wicking, as shown at right. If you use a

Temperature Needs of Winter Houseplants

Some flowering plants must have warm or cool temperatures indoors. Below is a listing of the temperature preferences of various houseplants. Cool temperatures mean approximately 50° to 60°F during the day, with a 5° drop at night. Warm temperatures mean 70° to 80°F during the day, with a 10° drop at night.

Plants That Like It Cool

Ardisia crenata (coralberry)
Camellia cultivars
Chrysanthemum (florist's mum)
Cyclamen (florist's cyclamen)
Freesia cultivars
Hyacinthus orientalis (Dutch hyacinth)
Hydrangea macrophylla (hydrangea)
Jasminum species (jasmine)
Narcissus species and cultivars (daffodil)
Pericallis × hybrida (cineraria)
Primula species (primrose)
Rhododendron cultivars (azalea)
Rosa cultivars (miniature rose)
Solanum pseudocapsicum (Christmas cherry)
Streptocarpus cultivars (Cape primrose)
Tulipa cultivars (tulip)
Zantedeschia cultivars (calla lily, white varieties)

Plants That Like It Warm

Achimenes cultivars (monkey-facedpansy)
Aechmea species (vase plant)
Episcia cupreata (flame violet)
Euphorbia milii (crown-of-thorns)
Saintpaulia cultivars (African violet)
Acalypha hispida (chenille plant)

Plants That Like It In Between

Abutilon cultivars (flowering maple)
Begonia Semperflorens-Cultorum hybrids (wax begonia)
Browallia speciosa (sapphire flower)
Calceolaria cultivars (pocketbook plant)
Euphorbia pulcherrima (poinsettia)
Fuchsia cultivars
Gardenia augusta
Hibiscus rosa-sinensis (Chinese hibiscus)
Hoya carnosa (wax plant)
Kalanchoe species
Oxalis species (shamrock plant)

A homemade wick system can keep a plant moist. Place one end of a cotton rope in a bucket of water and insert the other end into the pot, either through the top or up the drainage hole. The wick will draw water from the bucket for the plants.

A water reservoir and capillary matting allow you to keep soil of multiple plants moist for more than a week. The soil draws moisture upward, demonstrating a physics principle called **capillary action**, which is the basis for bottom-watering techniques.

wicking system, you don't need to enclose the plants in plastic bags.

Light

Also consider your plants' need for light. Don't leave your plants in the dark while you're gone. Houseplants grown with insufficient light are more likely to have aphid problems. If you can leave curtains or blinds open and the plants are reasonably close to the windows, they should receive sufficient light. Just remember to keep them out of direct sunlight if you've covered them with plastic. An alternative is supplemental fluorescent light, regulated by a timer.

Homecoming

Once you're back from your trip, inspect all the plants and water those that are dry. (If the soil in the pot feels dry an inch below the surface, water the plant.) Leave the plastic bags on the plants for a few days, partially lifting them off for a little longer each day. This allows the plants to become reacclimated to the environment in the room.

Supplement room lighting with flourescent lights regulated by a timer. To grow well, many plants need up to 16 hours of fluorescent light per day.

Dormant Pruning

Prune outdoor flowering shrubs that bloom on new wood (such as crape myrtle, butterfly bush, abelia, and hydrangea) while they are still dormant. Gardeners in cool climates should prune in late winter or early spring. Gardeners in warm climates can prune anytime in winter before new growth appears.

Prune to remove dead or damaged wood, to eliminate some of the oldest branches and thereby promote new growth, and to improve the plant's shape. Finish pruning before new leaves sprout.

Create a Vacation Moisture Tent

Inexpensive and easy-to-cut ½-inch polyvinyl tubing lets you create moisture tents of any size and shape. The method shown allows either a long, rectangular frame for multiple plants or a tall one for a single plant. After use, the frame quickly disassembles for compact storage.

Tools & Materials: Hacksaw, electrician's tape, ½-inch plastic CPVC tubing with 4 elbows and 2 tees; clear polyethylene sheeting; enough pebble trays to allow placement of plants so they don't touch. **Difficulty:** Easy

1 Cut the two "ceiling" tubes about an inch shorter than the diagonal of the "floor space" to be covered. Brace the held portion on a sturdy support.

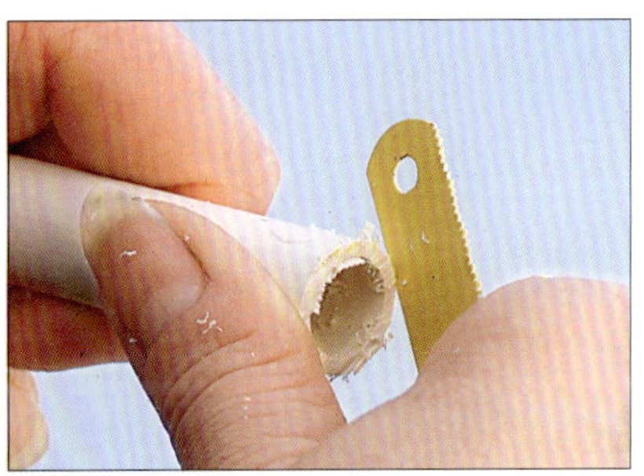

2 Ream rough edges of the cuts with the back of the saw blade. The blade shown had 24 teeth per inch; 32 teeth would have provided a smoother cut.

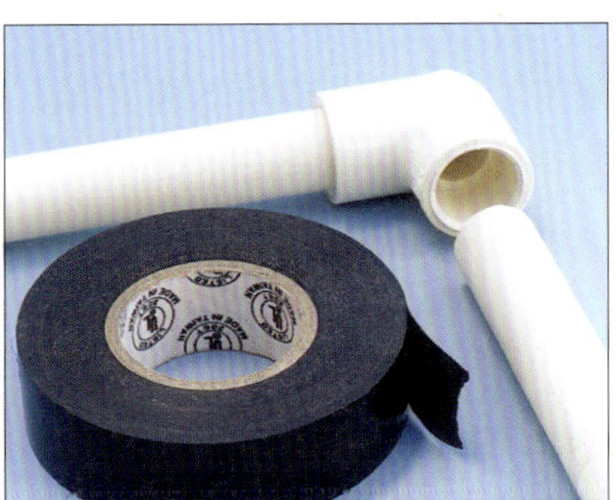

3 Slip cut ends into the elbows; friction will hold them strongly enough. Fasten the "ceiling joists" with electrician's tape.

4 Before fitting the assembly over the plants, water them normally. Excess moisture will drain into the pebble tray.

Early Winter — Cooler Climates

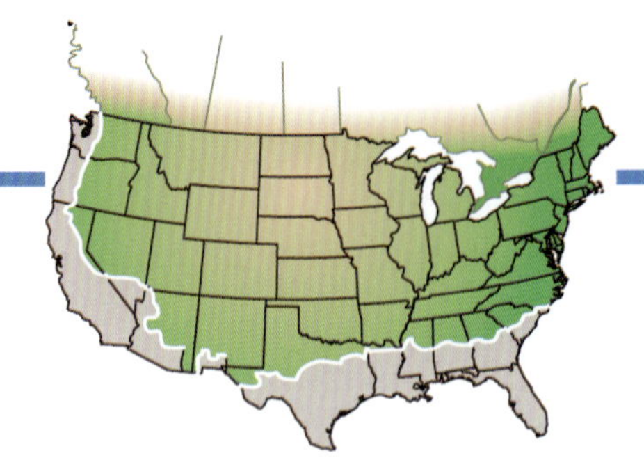

As shown on accompanying maps, if you live where winters are cold—from the mid latitudes to southern Canada—use the information on the "Cooler Climates" pages as your guide. If you live in the South, Southwest, or mild regions along the West Coast, you'll find the information on the facing "Warmer Climates" pages more useful.

Established Plants

Where winters are cold, most flower-growing activities occur indoors now. See page 233 for indoor gardening tasks.

Check pots of bulbs you are forcing weekly to make sure the soil doesn't dry out. Although most types of bulbs being forced are still in cold storage (buried outdoors or set in a covered cold frame or unheated shed or garage), as described on page 184, they do need some attention.

Water outdoor perennials, roses, and shrubs a final time before the ground freezes. They'll have a better chance of surviving winter if they start out well hydrated.

Mulch beds and new fall plantings once the ground has frozen. This is especially important where plants aren't protected by a blanket of snow all winter. Both mulch and snow protect dormant plants from temperature swings and keep them from being heaved out of the ground.

Planning

This is a good time to finish revising your garden plans and making changes for next season. Note any alterations you want to make in bed and border layouts, color schemes, and plants (as shown below). Decide which new plants you want to try, which ones you want to grow again, and which you will eliminate.

Study seed and garden catalogs and begin making up orders. Order unusual plants and new varieties as early as you can, because suppliers may run out of stock later on.

The author's own garden plan, below, shows part of a sunny border for summer. Plans can be as simple or elaborate as you want and can greatly help you avoid mistakes when ordering seed and plants.

Warmer Climates

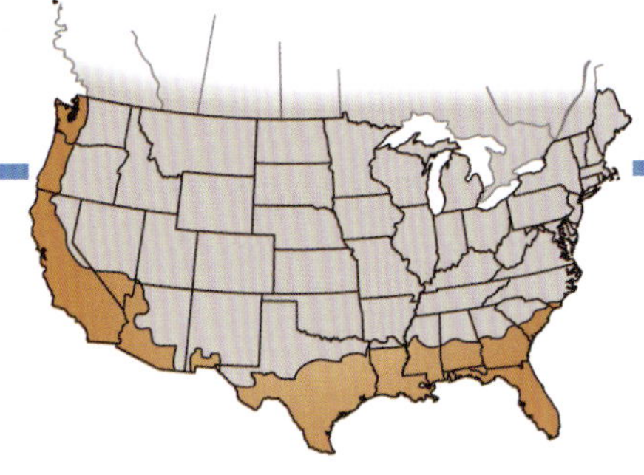

Established Plants

Gardeners in warm climates have more to do outdoors in winter than cold-climate gardeners, while also tending indoor plants. If you are forcing bulbs, they will now be in a refrigerator or other cold storage area. (See pages 184–185.) Check the pots once a week to make sure the soil does not dry out.

Water all outdoor plantings thoroughly before winter really sets in. While you are outside, pull any weeds that you find remaining in flower beds and borders.

Feed early-blooming perennials with rock phosphate and compost or with an all-purpose fertilizer. Fertilize the roses that will begin to grow in winter.

Finish planting out bulbs once they have chilled in your refrigerator for six to eight weeks.

Sow seeds of slow-growing hardy plants indoors, so you'll have seedlings ready to plant outdoors in late winter or early spring. These plants include pansies, snapdragons, beebalm, and others.

Sow seeds of cool-weather annuals outdoors. These plants include sweet alyssum, forget-me-nots, and sweet peas.

Planning

Early winter is also the time to finish revising your garden plans to make changes for next season. Note any alterations you want to make in bed and border layouts, color schemes, and plants. Decide which new plants you want to try, which ones you want to grow again, and which you will discard. When your plans are complete, you can start making up seed and plant orders. It's a good idea to order unusual varieties as early as you can, because suppliers may run out of stock later on.

Irises grow from rhizomes (bearded iris, top) and from bulbs (Iris reticulata, above left). The rhizomatous type should be planted shallowly, barely covered with soil. The bulb type should be planted 6 inches deep.

When planning your gardens**,** also consider mulch texture and color. ***Inorganic mulches*** *include **1** granite, **2** beach pebbles, **3** crushed brick, **4** crushed marble, **5** brown lava, **6** red lava, and **7** beach stones.* ***Organic mulches*** *include **8** aged hardwood chips, **9** fresh hardwood chips, **10** red-dyed cedar, **11** shredded cedar, **12** pine-bark nuggets, **13** shredded pine bark, **14** shredded hemlock, **15** pine needles, and **16** shredded cypress.*

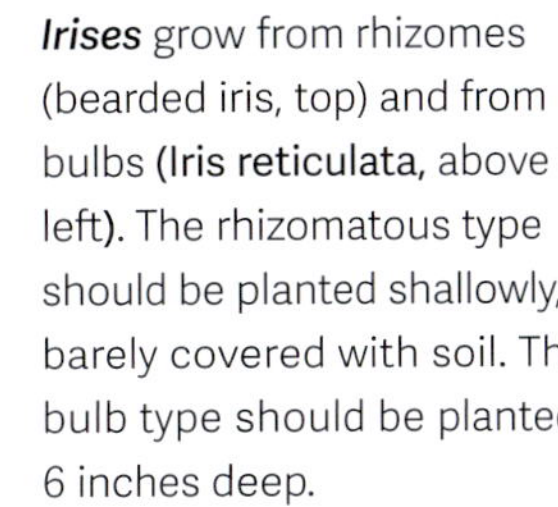

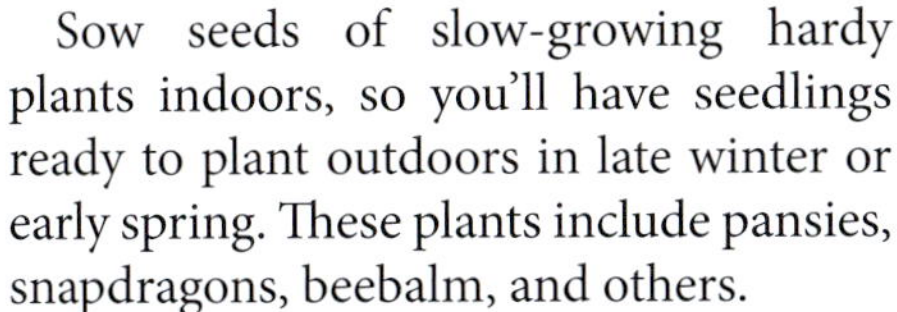

Midwinter

Cooler Climates

Established Plants

Check the outdoor garden for signs of soil heaving, caused by freezing and thawing. If you notice any roots or crowns that have become exposed, cover them with soil or compost. If you haven't mulched your perennials for winter, you should now mulch any beds where heaving is occurring. If strong winds blow the snow cover off your perennial beds—especially if they are located next to the house where warmth from the house might thaw the ground, shovel snow onto the beds to insulate them and help keep the soil frozen.

Periodically check tender bulbs you are storing over winter to be sure they are not rotting, drying out, or sprouting. If any bulbs are shriveling, mist them lightly. Discard any mildewed, rotting, or damaged bulbs.

Planting

Start slow-growing annuals from seed indoors in January or February to make sure they will bloom by summer. Slow growers include begonias, datura, geraniums, heliotrope, lantana, salpiglossis, salvia, schizanthus, snapdragons, statice, stocks, torenia, and verbena.

Planning

Complete any remaining seed and plant orders, and place them.

Clean and sharpen garden tools in need of maintenance. Keeping your tools in good working order will improve their effectiveness and extend their life. Use a steel brush, as shown at right, to remove dirt from spades, shovels, and trowels. Sharpen dull blades with a file. Wipe down the blades and wooden tool handles with an oily rag, or dip blades into a bucket of oiled sand.

Sharpen pruning shears professionally for best results. Dull shears are difficult to use, and they are likely to crush and mangle stems and branches instead of cutting them cleanly.

Use a wire brush to clean dried soil and rust from tools. If the storage area is damp, protect the metal as shown in the photo below.

Start seeds of slow-growing annuals to ensure that you'll have summer blooms.

A bucket of sand filled with used motor oil can further clean wire-brushed tools and supply a rust-inhibiting coating.

Warmer Climates

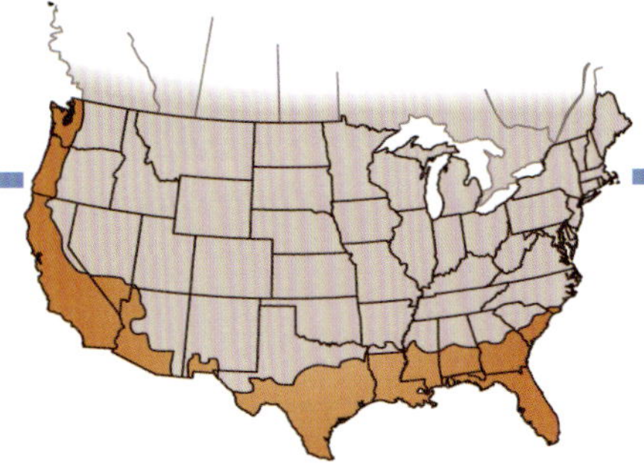

Established Plants

Prune shrubs that bloom on new wood, including crape myrtle, to encourage the growth of new wood, resulting in more flowers in spring. (This is described under "Dormant Pruning" on page 181.)

Fertilize camellias using a product formulated for acid-loving plants.

Begin checking your spring bulb beds for emerging leaves. Pull the mulch away when you see the first shoots.

Planting

Outdoors, sow seeds of pansies, sweet peas, stocks, and other hardy annuals by early January. Late in January you can plant seeds of bachelor's buttons, calendulas, columbines, larkspur, petunias, phlox, poppies, and snapdragons.

Set out, in cooler parts of the West, seedlings of calendula, nemesia, pansy, primrose, schizanthus, and sweet William. In warmer areas, you can also plant out annual candytuft, delphiniums, four o'clocks, larkspur, petunias, pinks, poppies, salvia, and snapdragons.

Take cuttings from woody perennial vines and shrubs to root for new plants. Cut the bottom at an angle, so you will remember which end goes into the rooting medium.

Planning

Finish your seed and plant orders if you haven't yet done so.

Check your garden tools to see if they are in need of maintenance. Keeping your tools in good working order will improve their effectiveness and extend their life. Use a steel brush to remove dirt from spades, shovels, and trowels. Sharpen dull blades with a file. Wipe down the blades and wooden tool handles with an oily rag, or dip blades into a bucket of oiled sand.

Sharpen pruning shears yourself or take them to a professional. Dull shears are difficult to use, and they are likely to crush and mangle stems and branches instead of cutting them cleanly.

Keep pruners sharp. Bypass pruners (left) sever more cleanly than anvil types, which tend to squash capillaries of soft-stemmed plants and damage bark of woody plants. Because anvil pruners are efficient to use, requiring less travel of the handles, they are often preferred for rough work.

Sharpen tools with a mill file (as shown) or a sharpening stone.

When pruning woody plants, place the sharp blade nearer the wood you'll save.

Late Winter

Cooler Climates

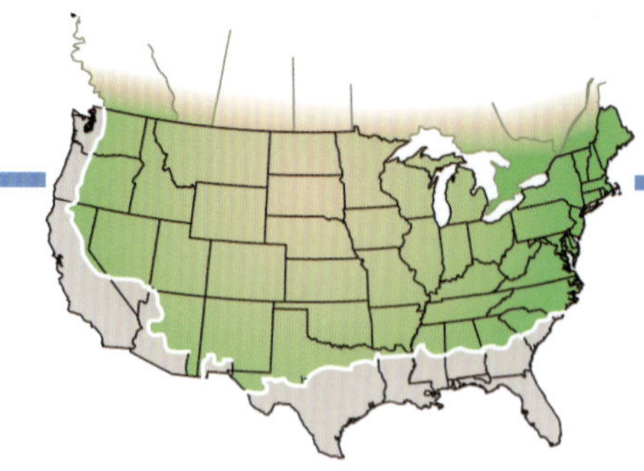

Established Plants

Remove winter mulch from outdoor beds of crocuses, snowdrops, and other early bulbs as the first shoots appear. Leave the mulch in place around daffodils, hyacinths, and tulips because their shoots won't be up until later.

Check perennial beds for signs of soil heaving. Press any exposed plant crowns back into the ground, if the ground is soft enough to do so. If the ground is still frozen, cover exposed roots with compost or soil. Where the ground is still somewhat frozen, pile more mulch onto any beds where heaving is occurring.

Cut branches of early spring-blooming trees and shrubs, such as forsythias, for forcing indoors. Check plants periodically; when the buds start to swell, the branches are ready for cutting. See "Forcing Branches into Bloom" on page 213 for more information.

Planting

Indoors, February is the time to start perennials and slower-growing annuals from seed. These include begonias, columbines, dahlias, delphiniums, dianthus, geraniums, gaillardia, impatiens, lisianthus, lupines, marigolds, penstemon, petunias, Iceland and Oriental poppies, primroses, rudbeckia, salvia, snapdragons, strawflowers, and sweet alyssum. Most of these seeds germinate best in temperatures of 65° to 75°F. For sturdy, compact plants, give the seedlings full-spectrum fluorescent lights. Position the lights just 2 to 4 inches above the tops of the seedlings and keep them on 16 hours a day. If you can't set up a light garden, the next best option is to grow seedlings in a sunny window; turn the pots daily to encourage even growth.

Sow seeds of flowering vines such as cup-and-saucer vine (*Cobaea scandens*) and black-eyed Susan vine (*Thunbergia alata*) so they will be ready to set outdoors when the weather turns warm. Where the growing season is short, you can start tuberous begonias under lights to have flowers earlier in summer.

Warmer Climates

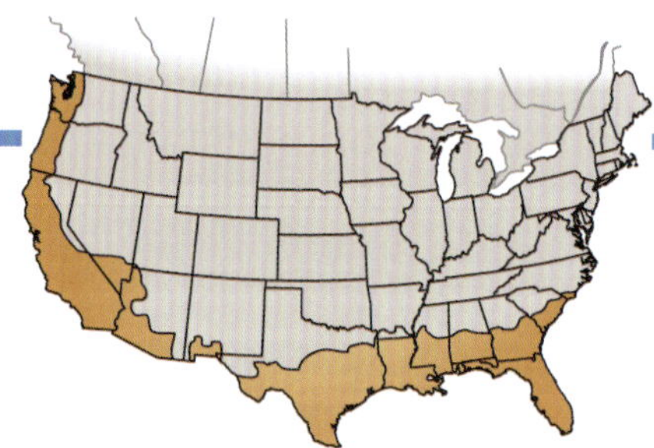

Plant gladiolus corms every two weeks until April in the warmest of climates. Check to ensure that they are healthy and undamaged.

Established Plants

Start removing winter mulches from outdoor flower gardens after the danger of hard frost has passed.

Start weeding and fertilizing beds of perennials and biennials. Irises, lilies, and other summer-blooming bulbs can be fertilized, too, and topdressed with compost.

Prune perennials that need shaping. Fuchsias, marguerites, and geraniums are three plants that may have become ungainly by late winter.

Prune rosebushes, fertilize them, and put fresh mulch over the root zone.

Planting

Sow sweet pea seeds outdoors, if you haven't already done so, as soon as the soil can be worked. Gardeners in the warmest climates can set out plants of dianthus, larkspur, pansies, petunias, phlox, stocks, snapdragons, sweet alyssum, and sweet William around the middle of February, or after the last expected hard frost.

Sow seeds of coreopsis, gloriosa daisies, impatiens, petunias, and sweet alyssum in flats to transplant later.

Sow seeds of California poppies, cosmos, forget-me-nots, and nasturtiums directly into the garden.

Plant gladiolus corms (only in very mild climates) every two weeks during February and March for a succession of flowers later on. Gardeners in the warmest areas can also plant bulbs, corms, and tubers of hardy amaryllis, tuberous begonia, canna, and dahlia. Fertilize with compost and rock phosphate or bulb fertilizer after planting.

Take a cutting by severing the tip of the stem above a node (dormant bud).

Take cuttings from wax begonias and impatiens (growing indoors) to root them for planting outdoors later in containers or in garden beds.

Early Winter

If you are again forcing last year's amaryllis bulbs, remove the top inch of soil from the pot and replace it with compost or fresh potting soil. If you aren't adding compost, feed the plant with a slow-release houseplant fertilizer.

After Christmas, move poinsettias to a bright window to help them last longer. Also keep the soil moist, and maintain a nighttime temperature of about 60°F.

Check houseplants regularly for signs of pests or diseases. If you notice that the foliage of smooth-leaved plants has collected dust, clean the leaves by wiping smooth leaves with a damp sponge or cloth, or brushing textured leaves with a clean paintbrush or other soft brush. If you do spot pests, try washing them off in the kitchen sink. If that doesn't control them, spray the plants with insecticidal soap. Isolate the affected plants to prevent the problem from spreading.

Clean dust from smooth-leaved plants with a damp sponge or cloth.

Midwinter

As winter progresses, continue to monitor houseplants for pests, and keep their leaves clean. Be sure to clean both upper and lower leaf surfaces when you wash foliage.

Place tropical houseplants in the shower for a midwinter treat, gently running lukewarm water on them. After a couple of minutes, turn off the water, close the shower curtain, and let the plants bask in the humid atmosphere for an hour or two.

Keep azaleas and other holiday gift plants moist and cool so they hold their flowers longer. Azaleas in particular may need to be watered every day if the air in your home is very dry in winter.

Begin withholding water from poinsettias when they start to lose their color, thereby letting them go into their natural period of dormancy.

Water azaleas almost daily if the room air is dry, and keep them cool. This will keep the flowers blooming longer.

Commercially made moisture tents can help plants retain water in dry rooms and when you are on vacation.

Late Winter

If you have forced paperwhite narcissus into bloom indoors, throw out the bulbs once they have finished blooming. In Zones 8–10, you can safely transplant these outside for blooms in future years.

Save bulbs of forced crocuses, daffodils, and other hardy bulbs for replanting outdoors, as described on pages 181–182.

Continue checking houseplants on a regular basis. Look for pests and diseases, and watch for pale leaves or brown edges that might indicate that plants need more humidity. Also keep them clean.

Check tender bulbs in winter storage periodically to make sure they aren't drying out, rotting, or sprouting. Mist any dry bulbs, and immediately throw out any with signs of rot or disease. If some bulbs sprout and start to grow, you can try planting them in pots until outdoor planting time in spring.

Other Gardening Pursuits SECTION 3

CHAPTER 9 *Herb Gardens*

Herbs are a fascinating group of plants with a history of cultivation stretching back to the dawn of civilization. Once the herb garden was a practical project, necessary for supplying flavorings for the kitchen and medicines for the family. Today, gardeners are less likely to grow herbs for medicinal purposes than for their attractive looks, pleasing fragrances, and tasty flavors. Whether your interest is kindled by taste, aroma, beauty, or history, you'll find herbs a satisfying addition to your garden.

What is an Herb?

Traditionally, herbs have been defined as plants that are useful to people. The oregano and thyme on your pizza are herbs just as the ornamental foxglove, from which we once extracted the medicine digitalis, is an herb. The insecticide pyrethrin is derived from the painted daisy, making it an herb as well. The list goes on and on; we use herbs and herb products every day.

Ordinarily, gardeners consider herbs to be the plants used as food seasonings, teas or home remedies, those with note-worthy fragrances, and—increasingly—those that please the eye. We grow basil, chives, marjoram, rosemary, tarragon, and thyme for their flavorful leaves. Coriander and dill provide tasty leaves and seeds. For fragrance, we plant scented geraniums, mints, sages, and sweet woodruff. And we grow lamb's ears for its soft silver leaves; bee balm for its fiery flowers; and germander for its compact form, ideal for an herbal hedge.

Choosing Herbs

In addition to an herb's taste, aroma, and appearance, consider its preferred growing conditions when choosing what to grow. Herbs are such a diverse group of plants that broad generalizations are often misleading. Most herbs thrive in moderately fertile, well-drained soil in a sunny location; some do well in poor soil or partial shade, and a few tolerate soggy soil. Despite a reputation as carefree plants, some herbs may be affected by insects and diseases just as other plants are. A few herbs, such as dill and basil, are annuals. Most, though, are perennials; these must be able to tolerate the extremes of winter cold and

Herbs are so easy to grow and maintain that you can create a magnificent herb garden in only a year or two, opposite.

Herbs include plants that are used for seasoning, fragrance, medicinal qualities, and appearance.

summer heat in your climate. If you live in a cold-winter climate and want to grow an herb that's too tender for your winters—rosemary, for instance—you can grow it in a pot and overwinter it indoors. Plants adapted to the conditions of your area (soil, temperatures, rainfall, and so on) are more likely to succeed for you and to require less regular care. The table at right and the Herb Gallery at the end of this chapter will help you choose plants for various uses and growing conditions.

Herbs in the Home Landscape

With such a wide variety of flowers, foliage, and forms to choose from, you can consider an herb for a spot in a flower bed or border just as you would any other annual, perennial, or shrub. Take advantage of aromatic herbs such as lavender, clary sage, and dianthus, which have scents that waft through the air, by placing them near seating or upwind of open windows. Place herbs with leaves or flowers that must be crushed to release their fragrance, such as mints and sage, within easy reach. If herbs can withstand light foot traffic, as do chamomile, pennyroyal, and oregano, plant them between flagstones on a path or patio. Plant herbs such as creeping thyme in soil that fills the spaces between stones in a wall or rocky outcrop. Use santolina or creeping thyme as a sunny ground cover. The small stature, leaves, and flowers of a number of herbs fit nicely with the diminutive alpine plants traditional in rock gardens.

Some Favorite Herbs

For Cooking

Anise	Dill	Mustard
Basil	Fennel	Oregano
Bay	Garlic	Parsley
Caraway	Lemon balm	Rosemary
Chervil	Lemon grass	Sage (various)
Chives	Lovage	Sorrel
Coriander	Marjoram	Tarragon
Cumin	Mint (various)	Thymes (various)

For Edible Flowers

Borage	Nasturtium	Violet
Calendula	Rosemary	Sage (garden)
Chives	Viola	Sage (pineapple)

For Fragrance

Note: * indicates herbs with fragrant flowers

Basil	Lemon thyme	Scented geranium
Bee balm	Lemon verbena	Sweet marjoram
Chamomile	Mint	Sweet woodruff
Catnip	Oregano	Tansy
*Dianthus (some)	*Rose (some)	Tarragon
Lavender	Rosemary	Thyme
Lemon balm	Santolina	Southernwood

For Beauty

Artemisia	Hyssop	Rose
Bee balm	Lady's Mantle	Rue
Calendula	Lamb's Ears	Sage (various)
Chives	Lavender	Santolina
Feverfew	Nasturtium	Sweet woodruff
Foxglove	Purple Basil	Thyme (various)
Germander	Purple Coneflower	Violet

Herbs can make home landscapes varied and interesting. As pictured at left, foxglove, valarian, lamb's ears, and poppies complement a bed of ornamentals.

Kitchen Herb Garden

If your interests are culinary, grow herbs used for food and flavoring where they'll be handy—near the kitchen door. Such gardens are often small and laid out geometrically, but they can also be planted as a border along the back walk or around a patio. Divide the plantings into beds with narrow paths of wood chips or brick to emphasize the geometry and provide easy access.

Kitchen herb gardens can grow on a windowsill as easily as in a backyard.

Suggested Plants. You'll undoubtedly have favorite herbs you'll want to plant, but consider including oregano, sage, chives, thyme, and tarragon. These perennials can form the foundation of the garden. Plan spaces for them first because they will remain in the garden for years and will spread considerably while they're there. When they're young, fill in spaces between them with annuals. (Place tall annuals where they won't shade or crowd the young perennials.) Chives and oregano will self-sow everywhere if you let the flowers go to seed; instead, cut the flower stems when blooms are half-open, and hang them upside down to dry for use in indoor bouquets.

Small herbs grow well in the tight quarters that this wagon-wheel plant-er provides.

Must-have annuals for any herb garden are green-or purple-leaved basil, fern-like parsley, tall and airy dill, and leafy coriander, which is known as cilantro when grown for its leaves. Plant the annuals where you can clean them up in the fall without disturbing your perennials.

Several indispensable herbs are woody. Rosemary and lemon verbena are shrubs, though they're usually referred to as tender perennials. Sweet bay grows slowly into a tree. With the exception of a hardy rosemary named 'Arp', which survives in sheltered sites in Zones 7 or 6, none of the three overwinters in areas colder than Zone 8. If you live in a cold-winter region, plant these tender herbs in containers, or pot them up at the end of the season. Bring them indoors for the winter months. You'll need to repot both rosemary and sweet bay every two to three years because they get quite large as they mature.

Knot Garden

If you're ambitious, consider an herbal knot garden. Knot gardens can be spectacular additions to your landscape, but they are time-consuming to make and can be tedious to maintain. If you're interested in creating a knot garden, it's worthwhile to visit one and talk with the gardener to find out what's involved. A local nursery or garden club may be able to refer you to someone in your town who has a knot garden.

Knot refers to the intertwining pattern of low-growing, neatly trimmed hedges that form interlocking geometic shapes—circles or diamonds, for example. The hedges appear to twine together, one over or under the other, like the strands in a knot. This is an illusion enhanced by careful planting and clipping

Knot gardens are traditionally formed by low-growing hedges. Plants can fill interior spaces or, as shown here, colored stones and other mulches can be used.

where one hedge intersects another. In an herbal knot garden, the outline is usually made with low-growing evergreen herbs, such as germander or santolina. The spaces they create are filled with other herbs, often with foliage or flowers in contrasting colors. You can make an herbal knot garden for purely decorative purposes or get double duty from it, planting the interior spaces with culinary or fragrant herbs. Remember that the appearance may suffer when leaves, flowers, or whole plants are harvested for use. Instead of herbs, you can also plant spring bulbs followed by annual flowers as fillers.

Making a Knot Garden. First prepare the soil as you would for a new garden bed. (See Chapter 2, pages 34–43.) Lay out the lines of the hedges using garden lime as "chalk" to draw the pattern on the soil surface. Create circles or arcs with string and a stake (the stake at the center, the string forming the radius). Use straight pieces of wood or flexible garden hose to lay out other shapes. Plant the hedge plants first; then fill in the centers. The hedge plants may take a season or two to grow together. Prune by cutting back the stem tips to encourage bushy growth. Pruning time and amount depends on the plants. A knowledgeable nursery staff member or herb gardener can help you select appropriate herbs for the hedges in your knot garden, as well as teach you the best pruning times and techniques.

Container Gardens

Many herbs make excellent container plants. If your gardening is restricted to a patio or balcony, you can easily grow mints, chives, basil, parsley, and many other herbs in pots. Container planting also allows gardeners in cold-winter climates to move tender herbs such as sweet bay and rosemary inside for the winter. You can have fun combining plants in single pots, arranging groups of containers for best effect, and placing potted herbs in garden settings to provide added interest. As long as they have the same sun and moisture requirements, you can combine different herbs (as well as other plants) in the same container. Try creeping thyme or chamomile as a ground cover for a sweet bay tree. Edge a pot of geraniums with curly-leaved parsley. Combine chives, parsley, and thyme in a window box or deck-railing box.

Annual and tender perennial herbs are grown the same way as other container plants. (See Chapter 4, pages 63–64.) Remember that containers must have drainage holes, the soil must drain well, the plants will need periodic fertilizing, and the containers may need watering as often as twice a day.

Perennial herbs and those that are shrubs or trees can be grown in pots, too. These plants need special care to keep them healthy from year to year. Overwintering herbs indoors in pots or growing them indoors year-round is problematic because light levels, even in south-facing windows, are seldom sufficient. Plants may survive, but growth and flavor will be weak and shoots and stems will be "leggy" (elongated with leaves spaced too far apart).

Container gardens of herbs make practical and decorative additions to any space, indoors or out.

To ensure robust health in overwintered herbs, grow them under fluorescent lights. Place them so that their top leaves are a few inches below the tubes, and keep the lights on for 16 to 18 hours a day. Make sure the soil doesn't dry out. Fertilize plants that continue growing every month, but don't fertilize plants that normally go dormant during the winter. As the plants grow, they'll need to be pruned and repotted in the same or larger pots.

Getting Started with Herbs

Herbs comprise annuals, perennials, shrubs, and trees, and are grown and cared for like other members of their respective groups. You can buy plants from a nursery, or you can start many annual and perennial herbs from seeds, as described in Chapter 4, pages 64–67. Nursery-bought plants are your only option for true French tarragon, particular mints, and oregano, which need to be grown from cuttings or divisions to produce the desired characteristics. Depending on the herb, you can increase your supply of plants by dividing clumps in your garden or rooting cuttings. Planted in moderately fertile, well-drained soil, many herbs require little routine care after they've become established. Poor drainage is the bane of many herbs because soggy soil readily rots their roots (especially over winter) or harbors fungal diseases. If your soil doesn't drain well, consider growing herbs in raised beds or containers.

Combining raised beds and containers makes it possible to grow a wide variety of herbs in a small area.

Harvesting Herbs

Herb leaves can be harvested throughout the growing season. Depending on the plant and your needs, you may gather just a few leaves or cut away half or more of its foliage. For some herbs, picking stimulates new growth and provides a long season of harvest. Harvest in the morning, when the dew has dried off the leaves but before the heat of the day has driven off some of the plant's flavorful oils. Descriptions in the Herb Gallery offer specific information on harvesting certain herbs.

Herbs that you wish to use fresh will keep for a short time in a vase of water. Leaves can also be dried and stored for long periods. Bind small bundles of stems together with rubber bands, and place the bundles in a dry, well-ventilated place, out of direct sun. You can hang the bundles or place them on screens (for air movement). Turn the bundles regularly to ensure uniform drying (and to check for mildew and mold). When the leaves are brittle, strip them off the stems, and put them in lidded jars. Don't crush the leaves until you use them; crushing releases their oils.

To collect herb seeds, harvest when the seeds begin to turn brown. Band seed stalks together in small bundles, and put the bundles inside a paper bag tied around the stem. As they dry, the seeds will drop into the bag.

For other methods of preserving herbs, including oven drying, microwave drying, and freezing, contact your Cooperative Extension Service or consult one of the many books devoted to herbs.

Dried seeds drop from the plant. To keep them, enclose the seedheads in paper bags before they are completely brown.

Getting Started with Herbs

Buy Plants

French tarragon, Germander, Lemon thyme, Lemon verbena, Lavender, Mints, Oregano, Parsley, Rosemary, Sage, Sweet bay, Thyme, Winter savory

Direct Seed Outside in Spring

Coriander, Chamomile, Chervil, Chives, Dill, Lemon balm, Summer savory

Start Early Indoors

Basil, Parsley, Sweet marjoram

Herb Gallery

Unless otherwise stated, plants all grow best in fertile, well-drained garden soil in full sun or light shade.

Annuals

Basil *(Ocimum basilicum)*
Prized as a flavoring for pesto and as a tasty companion to tomato in all its forms, basil also has a long medicinal history. It was once a folk remedy for fever and snakebite but was also used for more mundane purposes of settling the stomach and aiding digestion. Basil is an attractive plant. Lustrous, deliciously fragrant leaves grow on a sturdy, many-branched plant that can reach 2 or 3 feet tall. Sweet basil is the most common culinary basil, but a variety of cultivars provide different leaf sizes, colors, flavors, and fragrances. Purple-leaved forms, such as 'Purple Ruffles' and 'Opal', are attractive in combination with other plants in the garden or in groups of containers. You can direct-seed basil into the garden after the frost-free date, but for earlier harvest, buy plants or start seeds indoors. Plant seeds indoors about 6 to 8 weeks before the last frost. Plants remain productive for months if you pinch off the flower spikes before the tiny white flowers open and harvest leaves and branches rather than the whole plant.

Genovese basil

Chervil *(Anthriscus cerifolium)*
Chervil's ferny, finely cut leaves resemble and are used like parsley, though their flavor is more like lemony licorice. It is a common seasoning for salads and fish and is one of the ingredients of the French *fines herbes* seasoning. Plants grow 1 to 2 feet high and bear umbels of white flowers in midsummer. They bolt to seed quite quickly and do not tolerate hot weather, so plant seeds in early spring and late summer.

Chervil

Coriander
(Coriandrum sativum)
A must for the kitchen garden, coriander, also called cilantro, quickly produces a crop of ferny leaves, followed by clusters of pale flowers on 1- to 3-foot stalks. Use fresh-cut leaves to flavor salads and soups or in Mexican and Oriental dishes. The scented seeds are crushed and used to season a variety of foods. Direct-seed in early spring, adding small patches at 2- to 4-week intervals until late summer to ensure a continual supply. Thin seedlings to 6 inches apart. Because the plant grows and is harvested so quickly, it's not a good candidate for ornamental plantings.

Cilantro

Dill *(Anethum graveolens)*
Well known to many as a seasoning in pickles and vinegar, dill seeds are also used in some breads. The ferny leaves are used to flavor fish, lamb, and salads. Fragrant, finely divided leaves form quickly, followed in midsummer by 3- to 4-foot-tall branching stalks topped with umbels of small yellow flowers. Freshly cut flowering stalks and dried seed heads make attractive fillers in flower arrangements. Sow seeds in the garden in early spring and, for a fall crop, in midsummer. Thin to 18 inches apart if you want seeds, 4 inches apart if you want only leaves. Dill self-seeds readily.

Dill

Parsley *(Petroselinum crispum)*
Two kinds of parsley are commonly grown. Both form foot-tall rosettes of finely cut leaves. Italian parsley has flat leaves and a stronger flavor than the curly leaf types that are familiar as a garnish. Both are rich in vitamins A and C. Plants are biennial, forming a tall flowering stalk in the second year, but most people grow them as annuals. Buy plants, or start seeds indoors, 8 to 10 weeks before the last frost. Plant seedlings 8 to 12 inches apart. Keep the transplants moist. Harvest stems on the outside edges of the plant, and new growth in the center will provide a long-lasting supply of leaves.

Curly leaf parsley

Italian parsley

Sweet Marjoram *(Origanum majorana)*
The tiny gray-green leaves of this bushy little plant are used fresh or dried to flavor meats and vinegars and as a scent in perfumes. It bears inconspicuous white flowers for much of the summer. Sweet marjoram is perennial in Zone 9. In colder climates, grow as an annual in pots or garden beds, where it makes a fine edging. Start indoors from seed sown 8 weeks before the last frost, or buy plants. A slightly alkaline to neutral pH gives the best results.

Sweet marjoram

Scented geranium *(Pelargonium species and hybrids)*
Tender perennials grown as annuals, the many types of scented geraniums all have strongly scented leaves and form mounds 1 to 3 feet high. Most have sparse but attractive little flowers in white, pink, or lavender. Leaves are used for flavoring and in sachets and potpourris. The range of scents includes lemon, lime, apple, rose, nutmeg, coconut, ginger, and peppermint. Your local nursery probably won't carry them all, but they might order plants for you. Buy plants for use in the garden or in containers. Wait until after the last frost to move them outside. Pinch back the growing tips to keep the plants bushy. They become extremely leggy in shady conditions. Container plants overwinter well indoors. Put them in a bright window or under lights, and don't give them as much water as they had outdoors.

Rose-scented geranium

Perennials

Bee Balm *(Monarda didyma)*
Bee balm is grown today chiefly for its ornamental qualities, but its minty leaves also make fine tea and have been used for relieving fevers, colds, and intestinal gas. In early summer, slender, straight, leafy stems from 2 to 4 feet tall are topped for weeks with shaggy clusters of small tubular flowers in shades of red, pink, purple, or white. Bee balm is a good plant for a perennial border, and bird lovers grow it to attract hummingbirds. Bee balm thrives in full sun, except in hot climates where it does best with some afternoon shade. Buy plants to be assured of getting particular flower colors. Bee balm tolerates heat if grown in fertile, moist soil, but never tolerates dry conditions. Plants spread to form large patches. The center tends to die out once a plant reaches four to five years old; divide and replant the young vigorous growth to keep the planting looking good. Older cultivars are susceptible to powdery mildew. This fungus destroys the leaves and looks terrible, but it seldom kills the plant. Zone 4.

Bee balm

Chamomile, Roman *(Chamaemelum nobile)*
Known to children as Peter Rabbit's favorite tea, Roman (or English) chamomile is also used as an herbal ground cover. It tolerates light foot traffic and releases a pungent aroma when stepped on or mowed. Branches of finely dissected leaves form a low spreading mat about 6 inches tall. Chamomile requires full sun, tolerates heat, and grows best in slightly dry soil. Zone 4. German chamomile (*Matricaria recutita*) has similar leaves and flowers but is an annual that grows up to 30 inches high. This is the chamomile of choice for making tea. Sow seeds directly in the garden. Give it more moisture than its perennial cousin.

German chamomile

Chives *(Allium schoenoprasum)*
Enjoy the scent of this little onion's lavender flowers in late spring, and snip the mildly onion-flavored leaves for salads and soups from spring until hard frost. Slender, hollow leaves grow 1 to 1½ foot long. Garlic chives (*A. tuberosum*) have solid, flat, garlic-flavored leaves and edible white flowers on 2- to 3-foot stalks in late summer. Chives are vigorous self seeders; prevent invasive growth by snipping flowers before they form seeds. Chives are easy to grow from seed sown in the garden or started indoors, but it's faster to divide a clump from a friend's garden. Zone 3.

Chives, standard

Garlic chives

English lavender *(Lavandula angustifolia)*
Few plants are as striking in the landscape as a hedge of lavender in full early-summer bloom. And lavender smells as good as it looks. When not in flower, the neat, rounded 2-foot-tall mounds of narrow gray leaves are also attractive. Cultivars offer a range of heights and flowers in pink, white, or lavender-blue, as well as the purple of the species. Lavender is used as a flavoring and in perfume and cosmetics; it has been used as an antiseptic treatment for fever, burns, and eczema. Home gardeners can easily dry lavender flowers for use in sachets and potpourri—pick the flower stalks as soon as the flowers open, and hang them upside down in a cool, shady, well-ventilated room to dry. Buy plants unless you're growing the new annual, 'Lavender Lady', which can be started from seed early indoors and transplanted to the garden. Lavender needs well-drained soil and will tolerate drought once established. It usually does poorly in hot, humid climates. Lavender is evergreen in mildwinter climates (Zone 8). In cold-winter areas, prune winter-damaged shoots back to healthy growth in late spring. Zone 5.

English lavender

French tarragon *(Artemisia dracunculus var. sativa)*
Tarragon is grown for its deliciously flavor-ed leaves rather than its nondescript appearance. The plant is a mass of stems 2 feet or more in length, covered with shiny, narrow, dark green and strongly aromatic leaves. A single plant slowly spreads by creeping rhizomes to form a patch. The anise-flavored leaves are used in salad dressings, vinegar, and in egg, fish, and chicken dishes. Tarragon tolerates poor soil but not drought. True French tarragon seldom flowers and is sterile, so you'll need to buy plants or get divisions from a friend. Cut the plant back to maintain the size you want. Avoid Russian tarragon, which lacks flavor and good looks and is commonly sold as "tarragon." Zone 3.

French tarragon

Germander *(Teucrium chamaedrys)*
Once used as a tea to treat throat ailments and fevers (a practice not recommended due to its ability to cause liver damage if ingested), germander is a shrubby perennial that's grown for its attractive flowers and evergreen or semievergreen foliage. Plants form neat bushy clumps about 1 foot tall and wide. The upright stems bear small, shiny, aromatic leaves. Germander makes a tidy edging or hedge that can be sheared for a more formal look. Clusters of small purple flowers line the stems in midsummer and attract bees. There is also a white-flowered form. 'Prostratum' grows just 4 to 6 inches high and spreads over several feet; 'Variegatum' offers leaves with white, cream, or yellow markings. Germander tolerates heat, poor soil, and drought, but needs good drainage. Buy plants. Shear plants in spring to create a full, dense bush, and shear again after flowering to maintain a tidy form. Zone 5.

Germander

Greek oregano *(Origanum vulgare subsp. hirtum)*
If you're fond of Mediterranean cookery, grow Greek oregano—a particularly pungent form of this popular herb that makes a patch of leafy stems about 2 feet tall. If you grow this plant from seed, select only the white-flowered plants. But even among the white-flowered selections, you'll find that both fragrance and flavor will vary from plant to plant. To guarantee good flavor, choose plants in person. The subspecies, 'Aureum', reaches just 12 inches tall; its leaves are bland tasting but are a lovely yellow-green color that looks good as a ground cover in beds or containers. Oregano tolerates heat and dry soil. Zone 5.

Greek oregano

Lamb's ears *(Stachys byzantina)*
Once used to stop bleeding in minor wounds, lamb's ears' only therapeutic value today comes from the pleasure of stroking the soft woolly surfaces of its thick, silver gray leaves. The plant's low mound of foliage makes it ideal as an informal edging for flower beds, paths, and patios, and the woolly leaves make lamb's ears indispensable for children's gardens. In late spring or early summer, most cultivars produce foot-tall stalks of small leaves and pink or purple flowers. Some people find the flowers attractive; others cut off the stalks. 'Silver Carpet' is a nonflowering cultivar. All cultivars tolerate heat but not high humidity, which rots the leaves. Buy plants, and set them 12 to 18 inches apart as an edging. Increase your supply by dividing mature plants in spring or fall. Zone 5.

Lamb's ears

Lemon balm *(Melissa officinalis)*
The heavily veined leaves of this herb have a delicious, lemony flavor and aroma. They're used fresh to flavor drinks, salads, and fish dishes. Sheared regularly, the upright stems will form a bushy mound about 2 feet high. Shearing also removes the insignificant flowers and keeps the plant from invasive self-seeding. Although it is a mint, its rootstock spreads slowly, so lemon balm can be used in mixed plantings. Buy plants, or grow them from seed; you can sow lemon balm directly in the garden. Zone 5.

Lemon balm

Lemon verbena *(Aloysia triphylla)*
Grown for the lemon fragrance of its leaves, this tender shrub bears clusters of tiny lilac or white flowers in summer. Grown in the ground in mildwinter climates, it will reach 10 feet tall. Pinch off the growing tips of the stems to encourage a bushier habit. Gardeners in cold-winter areas grow lemon verbena as an annual in the garden or in containers, where the plant's growth is stunted

Lemon verbena

and it usually doesn't flower. Use fresh or dried; it adds a lemony scent to sachets and potpourri. Buy plants, and grow them in well-drained soil. Overwinter container plants under lights in a cool, dry spot. Zone 8.

Mint *(Mentha species)*

Gardeners can choose among numerous types of mints, each with a different fragrance and flavor. In addition to the familiar spearmint and peppermint, there are chocolate, orange, apple, and pineapple-scented mints. If you're willing to police the groups' invasive tendencies, you can have fun growing and comparing different types. Spearmint (*M. spicata*) has dark green leaves and grows to 3 feet tall. It forms whorls of tiny pink, lilac, or white flowers in summer. The leaves of peppermint (*M.* × *peperita*) can be green, purple, or green marked with white. Both species are very invasive. Pineapple mint (*M. suaveolens* 'Variegata') is less invasive and offers lovely, variegated bright green and white leaves. Buy all mints as plants; they don't come true from seed. Plant them in an out-of-the-way place where it's okay if they spread, or be prepared to monitor their growth and uproot shoots that stray too far. You can also plant mints in pots and sink the pots into garden beds. To eliminate control problems completely, grow them in containers.

Spearmint

Peppermint

Rosemary *(Rosmarinus officinalis)*

Used as a flavoring, infused as tea, and dried for aromatic sachets, rosemary is a handsome addition to the landscape in warm-winter climates or, where winters are cold, to a container garden. Upright forms grow from 4 to 6 feet tall and can be grown as hedges or specimen plants, either trained and sheared or left "natural." Low, spreading forms make fine ground covers or look good trailing over a wall. All rosemary plants have aromatic, needlelike leaves and bear small flowers for weeks in winter and spring. Flowers can be blue, lavender-pink, or white. Buy plants because this herb grows so slowly. Rosemary requires well-drained soil and does well in hot, dry conditions. Prune in spring to control size and shape of the plants. Cold-climate gardeners grow rosemary in containers, overwintering it in a cool but sunny room or under lights. Most rosemaries are hardy to Zone 8; 'Arp' survives in Zone 6 on well-drained sites protected from cold winter winds.

Rosemary

Sage *(Salvia species)*

There are numerous sages for the landscape and kitchen garden. Annual sages are popular plants for flower beds and containers, but perennial sages outnumber the annual types. Perennial sages include both herbaceous and shrubby types. Sages have long been used for culinary and medicinal purposes, although modern gardeners are often more attracted to their ornamental qualities.

Garden sage

(*S. officinalis*, Zone 5) is a bushy perennial growing about 2 feet high and wide with woody growth at its base. The small, elongated, fragrant, gray-green leaves are used in seasonings and in teas. In early summer, the plant bears eye-catching spikes of small, blue-purple flowers. The plant is evergreen in warm-winter climates, but the foliage dies back to the base in colder areas. Grow sage in containers, as a specimen, or in massed plantings in well-drained garden soil. Cultivars offer gold, purple, or variegated leaves. Several other sages are cold hardy. Meadow sage (*S. pratensis*, Zone 3) is a smaller bush that forms a rosette of fragrant dark green leaves and bears blue, violet, rosy, or white flowers. Clary sage (*S. sclarea*, Zone 4) is a biennial. It produces a clump of large gray-green leaves the first year and branching flower stalks the second. The flowers are small and white, but the colorful bracts are ornamental. You can maintain clary sage in your garden by transplanting the self-sown seedlings in midsummer.

Culinary sages

Many sages are tender perennials or shrubs that are evergreen within their zones and are grown in pots elsewhere. Cleveland sage (*S. clevelandii*, Zone 8 or 9) forms a roundedmass of gray-green foliage with tall spires of fragrant lavender flowers from spring to summer. Pineapple sage (*S. elegans*, Zone 9) is a fast-growing perennial with deep green leaves that smell and taste like pineapple. Hummingbirds are attracted to the red flowers that bloom from late summer to frost.

Savory *(Satureja species)*
Two savories, one perennial and the other annual, are grown as flavorings for vegetables and soups and for use in medicinal teas. Winter savory (*S. montana*, Zone 5) is a shrubby perennial with small flowers in late summer. Forming a mound of glossy evergreen leaves about 1 foot tall and 2 feet wide, it makes an attractive low hedge for an herb garden. Grow in well-drained soil. Winter savory tolerates some drought. Harvest leaves before bloom.

Summer savory

Summer savory (*S. hortensis*) is an annual that's not much to look at—a loose collection of slender, gray-green leaves on 18-inch stalks, topped by a smattering of tiny flowers. But because its leaves and stems are milder in taste and aroma than those of its perennial relative, this plant is often grown in pots for kitchen use.

Sweet bay *(Laurus nobilis)*
This small tree provides the bay leaves widely used in cooking. It is also a versatile landscape and container plant. In warm-winter climates, sweet bay's dense, dark evergreen foliage makes an excellent backdrop for other plants. It can be trained and clipped as a formal hedge or shaped into topiary forms. Left on its own, sweet bay grows slowly to form a roughly conical tree, 10 to 40 feet tall. Sweet bay is an excellent container plant, and can be cut back to control its size. Grown in the ground, sweet bay needs good drainage but, once established, tolerates a range of soil conditions, including drought. In cold-winter areas, container-grown sweet bays must be moved into a cool, well-lighted room before temperatures drop below 20°F. Zone 8.

Sweet bay

Sweet woodruff *(Galium odoratum)*
Known today primarily as a tough perennial ground cover for shady areas, sweet woodruff has a history of use as a flavoring. Traditionally, May Day revelers in Europe added fresh shoots to their white wine, but today we know that an excess of this herb can be mildly toxic. The dried leaves bring a clean, fresh scent to potpourri and sachets. Plants grow 6 inches high, spreading to form a thick mat of aromatic deep green leaves topped in late spring with clusters of small white flowers. Sweet woodruff can be evergreen in warm-winter areas. Grow this herb in partial or full shade. Plants spaced 1 foot apart will soon fill in, spreading by runners and self-seeding. In rich moist soil, it can be invasive. Zone 4.

Sweet woodruff

Thyme *(Thymus species)*
A variety of thymes are grown as culinary or landscape plants. All are low-growing perennials. Common thyme (*T. vulgaris*) forms a foot-tall, upright clump of wiry stems and narrow gray-green leaves. In summer, it's covered with tiny lilac flowers. Lemon thyme (*T.* × *citriodorus*) has lemon-scented leaves and a spreading habit. Woolly thyme (*T. pseudolanuginosus*) and mother-of-thyme (*T. serpyllum*) make excellent ground covers. Fragrance varies among seedlings, so choose the most aromatic plants at the nursery. You can also grow thymes from seed started indoors about six to eight weeks before the last frost. Thyme tolerates drought once established, but soggy soil readily kills it. In cold-winter areas, drying winds kill shoots. If you lack a consistent snow cover, cover plants with pine boughs or straw mulch over the winter. Zone 4.

Lemon thyme

Chapter 10 *Ground Covers*

Ground covers—plants that produce stems, branches, and foliage in sufficient density to cover the ground and prevent other plants from growing beneath them—are expanding their place in American home landscapes. For many people, a flawless carpet of rich green lawn continues to be the symbol of a well-maintained property. But increasing numbers of homeowners are discovering the useful and attractive qualities of other ground covers. In areas where lawn grasses struggle to survive because of heavy shade, steep slopes, or a dry climate, a variety of other ground-covering plants will thrive. Because they often need less water, fewer nutrients, and minimal care, these alternatives to grass can save you time and money. Homeowners are also using alternative ground covers to add variety and interest to the landscape. With attractive colors and textures of their own, ground covers are effective as complements to the house, patio, deck, and entryway, and as living carpets beneath plantings of trees and shrubs or woven through flower beds and borders.

Introducing Ground Covers

A wide range of perennials and shrubs grow densely enough to make good ground covers. Some initially require large numbers of small plants, but these often multiply rapidly. Others, including larger perennials and low shrubs, cover the ground with fewer plants but wider-spreading leaves and branches.

Ground covers can be less than an inch to several feet tall and are valued primarily for their foliage, which can be as thin as a blade of grass or as broad as a dinner plate. They come in every green imaginable as well as in silvers, grays, bronzes, yellows, and more. Many ground covers offer lovely blooms as well, from the blizzard of tiny white blossoms that cover snow-in-summer to

Ground covers can add unexpected beauty to a landscape, opposite. Here, they supply color and a textured background.

Perennial evergreen ground covers, such as these heathers, look good through the year with their variously colored foliage.

the elegant flowers of daylilies. Evergreen ground covers supply a welcome dose of color in the winter landscape. Other perennial ground covers are deciduous, meaning they drop their leaves or die back to the ground in the fall. But even these may continue to please the eye with attractive bark or branching patterns or by providing shelter for overwintering birds or other wildlife.

The discussions that follow provide suggestions for taking advantage of the diversity of ground cover plants to deal with difficult sites—shady, sloped, or dry. But choosing a ground cover depends on more than matching plants to growing conditions. Think about how you use the site.

Does your yard cater to games such as touch football, volleyball, badminton, or croquet, or to overspill from parties on the deck or patio? Few ground covers are as well suited to sports and other active entertainments as lawn grass, so you'll want to maintain enough turf for them.

But there may be substantial portions of the yard that don't require the durability of grass. For places that are adjacent to areas of activity or high traffic, such as patios and entrances, consider ground covers that will withstand occasional forays by ball-chasing children or wandering visitors. For more out-of-the-way spots, select a ground cover for its looks or its easy maintenance.

Shade-tolerant ground covers, such as this periwinkle, or myrtle, provide a wonderful carpet under trees.

Year-Round Considerations. Imagine how a ground cover will look and function throughout the year, particularly in winter. Evergreen ground covers are preferred by many because of their year-round foliage. The bare branches of deciduous shrubs and the dried leaves and stems of ornamental grasses and other deciduous perennials can also be striking through the winter. But you might appreciate these qualities more at a distance than up close. Deciduous shrub and perennial ground covers don't cover the soil as well when dormant as they do when in full growth, and some perennials disappear altogether for at least part of the year. Deciduous ground covers can be effective in beds and borders, but their appearance (and disappearance) may be less practical or satisfying in other areas. Vines can be effective ground covers, but establishing a dense, weed-suppressing cover can take time as well as persistent weeding and pruning. Once established, the aggressive growth of the vines may overpower the space allotted to them. Annuals last only part of the year, so they are primarily used as temporary cover between slow-growing perennials and shrubs.

Ground Covers for Shady Places

Most lawn grasses suffer in dense shade. If they're growing under trees, this difficulty is usually compounded by the tree's competition for water and nutrients. Many favorite flowering plants also suffer in shade. In these situations, shade-loving ground covers provide attractive substitutes.

Common shade-loving, evergreen vining or creeping ground covers include creeping Jenny, English ivy, lamium, pachysandra, vinca, and winter creeper. For a grassy look, there's lilyturf, which tolerates root competition. Taller deciduous plants include a wide range of hostas and some ferns. Hostas with variegated or light-colored leaves can brighten a shade garden. Ajuga, astilbe, lily-of-the-valley, and sweet woodruff provide colorful flowers, and astilbe has attractive seed heads in late summer and fall. Ground covers that can become a nuisance in a sunny spot (for example, variegated goutweed) grow more slowly and are less problematic in the shade.

Ground Covers for Slopes

Slopes often pose difficult growing conditions, including poor soil, hot sun, and drying winds. Steep slopes also can be a chore to mow. Instead of struggling to grow or mow grass on a slope greater than about 20 degrees, plant a ground cover more suitable to the site's conditions.

Valued ground covers for slopes include Asian jasmine (*Trachelospermum calycinum*), ivies, winter creeper, and pachysandra, all of which are evergreen. Junipers and cotoneasters are useful shrubs, as are several forms of bearberry (also called kinnikinick). Various ice plants, which flower in blazing colors, are widely used in California and mild-winter areas of the Southwest. The prostrate form of rosemary also makes an attractive cover in mild-winter areas, with evergreen leaves and pale lavender flowers in winter and spring. Other possibilities include verbena, vinca, honeysuckle, daylily, evening primrose, mahonia, crown vetch, various sedums, and Aaron's-beard (*Hypericum calycinum*). Once established, these ground covers check erosion

Groundcovers for slopes, such as this creeping juniper, must often tolerate thin soils, hot sun, and drying winds.

Groundcovers for dry soils, such as this gazania, can add a spot of bright color to the landscape for a portion of the year.

by creating a network of soil-retaining roots and protect soil from driving rain and wind.

Ground Covers for Dry Soils

Americans are increasingly conscious of the amount of water required to maintain residential plantings, particularly the lawn. Drought-tolerant ground covers can help reduce water use while adding variety to the landscape. Plants tolerant of dry conditions are particularly valuable for slopes, which are likely to be drier than nearby areas and more difficult to water artificially.

Good plants for dry sites include blue fescue, fragrant sumac, kinnikinick, cotoneaster, and junipers. Candytuft, evening primrose, and verbena provide colorful flowers, as do many of the low-growing sedums, which have distinctive fleshy leaves that show to advantage after the flowers have gone. Ceanothus, lantana, and African daisy are useful for warm areas. In the north, the vining stems of winter creeper and vinca cover dry sites quickly.

Ground Covers to Walk On

Few ground covers are as durable as lawn grass, but some can stand up to occasional or light foot traffic. Grow these sturdy plants in low-traffic areas, as outdoor "area rugs," or insert them between flagstones, bricks, or other pavers in paths and patios.

Thyme forms a low woody mat covered with tiny, fragrant leaves. The strawberry-like foliage of spring cinquefoil (*Potentilla tabernaemontani*) is perhaps a bit more durable and is covered with numerous yellow flowers in spring and summer. Try either between the flagstones of a path or patio. Other ground covers that take some foot-traffic include ajuga, chamomile, common thrift, Himalayan fleece flower (or knotweed), moss pink, sweet alyssum, and sweet woodruff.

Groundcovers to walk on include baby's tears (Soleirolia soleirolii). Most tolerate light foot traffic but aren't as sturdy as lawn grass.

Eye-Catching Ground Covers

Planted in broad swaths, as free-form islands, or as an edging to a walkway or a drive, ground covers can be primarily decorative elements, adding color and texture to the scene. A massed planting of low shrubs, such as prostrate juniper, or ornamental grasses, such as blue fescue, creates an attractive, undulating contrast to a nearby lawn. Large patches of hostas, astilbes, violets, or ferns provide a transition to a woodland garden. A meadow-like planting of grasses and wildflowers can brighten even a small backyard. Annuals such as creeping zinnia, gazania, and nasturtium can be used as fillers while slow-growing plants mature, and will burst with colorful flowers or foliage for a season—or longer in mild-winter areas. Perennials that you usually think of planting in a garden border—but form lovely, carefree ground covers on their own—include daylilies, hardy geraniums, and sundrops.

Eye-catching ground covers, such as these coleus and impatiens, can add color and texture to a landscape.

Ornamental Grasses

Many ornamental grasses make fine ground covers, but the larger species require considerable space to fulfill that function. On a residential lot, a few large grasses planted together will take up a lot of space, but they're more likely to function as accents or focal points, not ground covers. Smaller ornamental grasses make practical ground covers for modest home landscapes. The two grasses covered in the Ground Cover Gallery, pages 254–259, are widely available and tolerate a range of growing conditions.

Planting on a slope gives better results if you terrace.

Growing Ground Covers

Growing healthy ground covers depends to a large extent on plant selection. As always, plants adapted to conditions in your area require less site preparation and less long-term care than plants that are marginal in your area. Ground covers are usually planted in large areas. Rather than attempting to correct soil that is too moist or dry with amendments, choose plants that tolerate your soil conditions. That said, prepare the soil as well as possible—good soil benefits any plant. Keep in mind that ground-cover plantings can be difficult to weed, so be thorough when eradicating weeds prior to planting.

Where many small plants are needed, prepare the site as you would for a garden bed. (See Chapter 2, pages 34–43.) For large, ground-covering shrubs, it is more efficient to prepare individual planting holes. Make the holes slightly larger than the plants' root balls. If you're planting in native soil or around a new house, dig wide, shallow holes and loosen the remaining soil. Work compost, dried manure, or other amendments into the bottom and sides to encourage plant roots to extend both out and down.

Planting under shallow-rooted trees requires some care. Do not excavate the entire area. If you are starting small ground-cover plants such as pachysandra, spread a 4- to 6-inch layer of topsoil over the area, and transplant into that. This depth will give the plants a good start. Do not add more than 6 inches of topsoil, because you'll run the risk of suffocating the tree's roots. For larger plants such as hostas, dig individual holes, avoiding the trees' roots as much as possible. Because the new plants will be competing with the trees for nutrients, mix in extra compost, dried manure, or other amendments to give the plants a sure start.

Start ground covers with plants rather than seeds. The larger and more sturdy the plants, the faster they will cover the area.

Start with Plants

Ground covers are really no different from other plants—you just plant more of them over larger areas, so the discussions of planting and care on pages 44–59 apply. The summary here highlights the more important points.

Purchase your ground covers as plants. There are few perennial ground covers that an average homeowner can easily grow indoors from seed and few, if any, that are easily established by direct seeding. The number of plants you'll need depends on the type of ground cover you are using as well as the size of the area you're planting. Take a site plan, drawn to a measured scale, to your nursery or garden center, and they can calculate how many plants will be required for the ground cover you've chosen.

Planting Ground Covers. Transplant young plants in staggered rows, spaced according to their mature size. Even though plants that are more closely spaced will fill in more quickly, crowded conditions as they mature can make them unhealthy or ungainly. Be sure to water young plants—even drought-tolerant ones—regularly during the first season. Mulch with compost, bark chips, or grass clippings to conserve moisture and keep weeds down. When planting large numbers of plants, spread the mulch first and dig through it to place each plant. Pull the mulch away from the plant's crown to avoid disease problems. If you're using large, slow-growing ground covers, consider planting annual ground covers between them for several seasons. Use annuals that won't shade the young ground-cover plants by growing taller than they are.

Transplant ground covers in staggered rows to guarantee more even coverage when the plants mature.

Planting on a Slope. Slopes pose special problems of erosion from wind or rain. On mildly sloped sites, you can construct small "terraces" by mounding earth on the downhill side to hold young plants in place until their roots are anchored. On steeper sites, you can push a wooden shingle into the ground below each plant or pile up a few rocks. Planting in staggered rows helps avoid erosion by keeping water from running off in a straight line. Heavy mulch also breaks the force of driving rain or wind on a slope. If the site is particularly steep and conditions are windy or rainy, consider covering the soil with water-permeable landscape fabric or netting. Spread the fabric or netting, and cut an "X" through the material to set each plant in place. Landscape netting and fabric are available at nurseries and garden centers.

Expanding Ground Covers

Once you've gotten a ground cover started, you can expand your patch or start a new one from the plants already there.

Some plants reproduce from aboveground stems, called runners, or stolons. To aid this process, pin several stems to the ground at a node—a swelling on the stem where a leaf or branch can develop—but don't sever them from the parent plant. Regularly moisten the surrounding soil. Roots will form at the nodes. When the stems offer some resistance to a gentle tug on the node, sever these new plants from the parent, dig them up, and transplant them.

Some ground covers spread by underground runners called rhizomes. Dig up the offspring of these plants with some roots attached, cut the connection to the parent plant, and transplant. Clump-forming plants, such as daylilies and hostas, can be divided as shown in Chapter 4 (on page 69), and the divisions set out to enlarge the patch.

Expand your ground covers by dividing the plants you have.

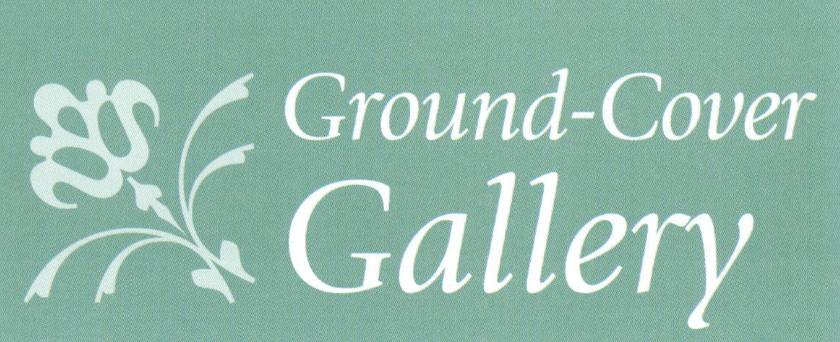

Ground-Cover Gallery

Following is a select list of easy-to-grow ground-cover plants.

Ajuga *(Ajuga reptans)*
A low-growing, mat-forming perennial, ajuga has glossy leaves that are evergreen in mild winters. Erect, 6-inch spikes densely packed with small flowers are very showy for a few weeks in May. 'Alba' has green foliage and white flowers; 'Bronze Beauty' has dark, purplish bronze foliage and blue flowers. Grows in sun or shade. Plant 8 to 12 inches apart. Shear off the flowers after they fade (in a large planting, a mower works well). Ajuga spreads quickly and can invade your lawn unless you keep cutting along the edge or install an edging. It's easy to start new plants from rooted runners. Zone 3.

Ajuga

Bergenia *(Bergenia cordifolia)*
A perennial used as a specimen plant or ground cover, bergenia forms a clump up to 18 inches tall and 2 feet wide of large, glossy, tropical-looking leaves. Summer foliage is green but turns bright red in the fall. In mild-winter areas, the foliage looks good through the winter. Clusters of white or rosy red flowers are held just above the foliage in late spring. Cultivars include 'Bressingham White', with white flowers, and 'Bressingham Ruby', with reddish flowers and leaves that are maroon on the undersides. Berginia prefers partial shade or, in cool-summer areas, full sun. Water during dry spells. Plant rhizomes about 15 inches apart and increase by dividing crowded clumps. Zone 3.

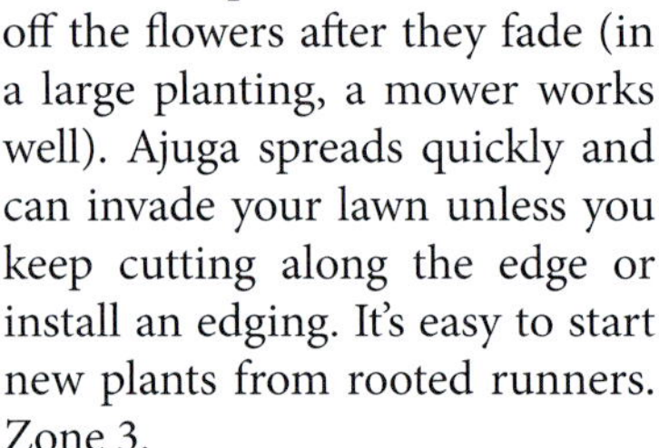

Bergenia

Blue fescue *(Festuca glauca,* also sold as *F. ovina* and *F. ovina var. glauca)*
A neat, compact perennial grass, blue fescue forms a dense tuft of thin, blue-green leaves about a foot tall and a foot wide. It presents an undulating expanse of small mounds when massed as a ground cover. Slender flower spikes appear in early summer and soon turn tan. 'Sea Urchin' is a popular cultivar with especially blue foliage. Blue fescue requires full sun and well-drained soil. It tolerates dry conditions. Plant 12 inches apart. Cut old foliage to the ground in late winter. Divide clumps only when plants become crowded. Zone 4.

Blue fescue

Common thrift *(Armeria maritima)*
An evergreen perennial, thrift forms cushions of narrow, grasslike foliage. In spring, small ball-shaped, rosy pink flowers rise above the foliage on long wiry stems. Plants grow about 6 inches tall and spread slowly to about 1½ feet. This plant requires full sun and good drainage but little fertilizing or watering. Space individual plants about 1 foot apart. Thrift is also called sea pink, so it's no surprise that it grows wonderfully at the shore. When the center of a clump begins to die, divide plants in either spring or fall. Zone 3.

Common thrift

Cotoneaster *(Cotoneaster species and cultivars)* Several of the following shrubs make effective and attractive ground covers. Bearbeary cotoneaster (*C. dammeri*) grows less than a foot tall but spreads rapidly to cover an area up to 10 feet wide. It sports bright, glossy evergreen leaves that turn purple in cold weather, white flowers in spring, and red berries in fall. Cotoneaster does well in full or partial sun and tolerates dry conditions. It's excellent for slopes. Space plants 3 to 4 feet apart, and prune as necessary to restrict spread. Zone 5.

Cotoneaster

Two deciduous relatives, cranberry cotoneaster (C. apiculatus), hardy to Zone 4, and rockspray cotoneaster (C. horizontalis), hardy to Zone 5, are taller (1 to 3 feet) and bear striking red foliage in fall. Several compact cultivars of the evergreen willowleaf cotoneaster (C. salicifolius) are planted as ground covers in Zone 6 and warmer areas. These include 'Emerald Carpet', 'Repens', and 'Scarlet Leader', all of which are less than 2 feet tall and spread up to 8 feet wide.

Creeping Jenny, or moneywort *(Lysimachia nummularia)* This creeping perennial forms a carpet of round, green leaves. Cheerful yellow flowers last for a month or so in early summer. 'Aurea' has yellow leaves. This plant grows well in full or partial shade. Space about 8 inches apart. Creeping Jenny prefers moist soil that is well-drained. It spreads rapidly by stems that root where they touch the soil. Zone 3.

Creeping Jenny

English ivy *(Hedera helix selected cultivars)* This evergreen vine is an excellent ground cover if you're willing to control its aggressive growth. There are many ivies, so be sure to buy cultivars recommended as ground covers. Some ivies, such as 'Thorndale', have large leaves, 2 to 4 inches long. 'Baltica' and others have smaller leaves. Some ivies with small or miniature leaves grow more slowly and are more suitable for smaller areas. Ivies grow in full sun in cool-summer areas and full to partial shade in hot climates. Plant 8 to 12 inches apart and water regularly during the first year. You'll need to trim back established plantings several times a year to keep them in bounds. With some cultivars, you can mow large areas. Zone 4 or 5 (depending on cultivar). Algerian ivy (H. algeriensis, Zone 9) and Persian ivy (H. colchica, Zone 7) are used as ground covers in warmer climates.

English ivy

Evening primrose, Sundrops *(Oenothera speciosa and O. fruticosa)* These fast-spreading plants form a dense patch of thin leafy stems topped by cheerful flowers all summer. Stems die back after bloom, and plants form a new mat of low-growing red-tinged leaves in fall. O. fruticosa is taller (to 2 feet), and hardier (Zone 4), and it has yellow flowers. O. speciosa reaches about 1 foot, is hardy to Zone 5, and has white or pink flowers. Both bloom during the day and require full sun. Space 1 to 2 feet apart. They tolerate heat and dry soil. To prevent either of these plants from taking over a flower bed, particularly one with rich, moist soil, surround them with a barrier that reaches 8 inches below the soil surface. Zone 4.

Sundrops

Candytuft

Candytuft *(Iberis sempervirens)*
This bushy perennial forms a mound of slender, glossy evergreen foliage, topped for several weeks in spring with clusters of bright white flowers. Cultivars range in height from 4 to 12 inches, and they can spread up to 3 feet. Several cultivars rebloom in the fall. Candytuft requires full or partial sun and also well-drained soil. Plant 2 feet apart. Shear off the top half of the plants after they bloom. They need no other care. Zone 3 or 4.

Ferns *(Various genera)*
These carefree, long-lived perennials are excellent ground covers for shady sites. They form broad patches of distinctive, finely cut fronds in one or another of an attractive range of greens. Evergreen ferns include Christmas fern (Polystichum acrostichoides, Zone 3) and marginal shield fern (Dryopteris marginalis, Zone 3), both with glossy fronds about 2 feet tall. Deciduous ferns include maidenhair fern (Adiantum pedatum, Zone 3), and New York fern (Thelypteris noveboracensis, Zone 4), which reach 2 feet tall, and hay-scented fern (Dennstaedtia punctilobula, Zone 4), a vigorous spreader that grows 2 feet tall with fronds that give off a vanilla-like fragrance when mowed. Ferns require shade and prefer soil with lots of organic matter. Consult knowledgeable gardeners or your local garden center to learn which other ferns do well in your area.

Maidenhair fern

Fountain grass, dwarf *(Pennisetum alopecuroides dwarf cultivars)*
This perennial grass forms a hassocklike clump of arching leaves that are green in summer and gold or reddish tan in fall. Fluffy pink, white, black, or cream-colored flower spikes bloom on arching stems from mid-summer to fall. They turn tan or golden in fall. The foliage of dwarf cultivars such as 'Hameln' and 'Cassian' is 1 to 2 feet high and about as wide, and the flower stalks rise 3 feet. 'Little Bunny' forms a clump less than a foot tall. Fountain grass requires full sun, or partial shade in hot climates, and good garden soil. Space 18 to 24 inches apart. It tolerates dry soil. Foliage and seed heads look good through the winter. Cut the clumps to the ground in late winter. Zone 5.

Fountain grass

Junipers *(Juniperus selected species and cultivars)*
The low-growing forms of these tough shrubs make excellent ground covers. The dozens of species range from 4 inches to about 3 feet tall. Many spread 6 to 10 feet wide or creep indefinitely, putting down roots where shoots touch the ground. Prickly needlelike or scaly foliage clings to the twigs. Colors range from bright green to blue to silvery gray; some are almost gold. Most junipers need full sun; a few tolerate partial sun. Many low-growing junipers tolerate heat, drought, and poor soil, but they vary in

Creeping juniper 'Blue Rug'

their tolerance as well as in rate of growth and hardiness. Both shore juniper (J. conferta) and cultivars of creeping juniper (J. horizontalis) such as 'Bar Harbour' and 'Wiltonii' are particularly versatile, but check plant labels, or consult with staff at your local nursery to determine which junipers perform best in your area. Zones 2–6 (depending on species).

Lamium

Lamium, or spotted dead nettle *(Lamium maculatum cultivars)*
Despite its forbidding common name, this perennial makes an attractive ground cover from early spring until late fall. 'Beacon Silver' forms low mats of heart-shaped silver leaves edged with green. Clusters of lilac-pink flowers bloom in early summer. 'White Nancy' has similar leaves and white flowers. 'Chequers' offers pink flowers and green leaves with a white stripe down the center. All grow under 1 foot tall and spread by rhizomes, or runners, to form a patch. Provide partial shade and moist soil. Space 8 to 12 inches apart. If the plants become shabby, cut the foliage back, and new leaves will appear. Zone 4.

Lily-of-the-valley
(Convallaria majalis)
An old-fashioned favorite, lily-of-the-valley produces sprays of wonderfully fragrant, bell-shaped white or pale pink flowers for several weeks in midspring. Foliage grows about 8 inches tall and looks good all summer. Red berries appear in fall. Lily-of-the-valley is a fine ground cover under shrubs and trees. Though the flowers are small, their scent makes them worth clipping and bringing inside; cut blooms when a quarter of the spray has opened.

Lily-of-the-valley

C. majalis 'Rosea' has pink flowers. Lily-of-the-valley thrives in partial sun or shade and grows in ordinary unamended soils. It tolerates dry conditions, but if the site is too dry plants may go dormant early, dying down as soon as midsummer. Plant the small rhizomes, called pips, in the fall. It spreads readily, and you can lift and transplant clumps easily. Lily-of-the-valley can be invasive in colder climates; hot or dry conditions check its invasiveness. All parts of the plant are poisonous. Zone 2.

Lilyturf

Lilyturf *(Liriope muscari)*
Lilyturf forms clumps or mats of grasslike, evergreen leaves and bears spikes of small flowers in late summer. Foliage grows 1 to 2 feet tall. 'Big Blue' (blue flowers) and 'Majestic' (purple flowers) both reach 2 feet and have dark green foliage. 'Variegata' has lilac flowers and leaves edged with narrow stripes that start out golden yellow and fade to creamy white. Lilyturf grows best in partial sun but tolerates full shade. Plant sprigs 4 to 6 inches apart; set container-grown plants about 1 foot apart. Plants tolerate dry soil for short periods. Mow or shear off the old foliage in early spring. Zone 6.

Creeping lilyturf (L. spicata) is smaller, to 18 inches, with less conspicuous flowers. It spreads by runners to form a dense mat of foliage. An invasive plant, it isn't ideal for use in beds, but it works well under trees where lawn grass struggles. Zone 5.

Moss phlox *(Phlox subulata)*
A delightful, spreading perennial with evergreen needlelike foliage, moss phlox is covered in spring with tiny blooms in pink, white, or lavender blue. It forms a dense mat about 6 inches high. It tolerates some foot traffic and spreads slowly around stones in a patio or walk. This plant is also good for a slope or hillside, or where it can spill over rocks, displaying the dazzling color of its flowers to full advantage. Moss phlox requires full sun and sandy or other well-drained soil. Space about 1 foot apart. It's easy to divide and transplant, so you can expand the area that it covers. Zone 3.

Two other phlox make fine ground covers under the light shade of deciduous trees. Wild sweet William (P. divaricata) grows 8 to 12 inches high and bears pale blue to white flowers for several weeks in spring. Creeping phlox (P. stolonifera) has narrower leaves and flowers in blue, pink, or white, depending on cultivar. Both prefer light shade and moist soil. Zone 3.

Moss phlox

Pachysandra *(Pachysandra terminalis)*
This classic ground cover has glossy evergreen leaves and creeps slowly to form dense patches about 8 inches tall. In spring, small white flowers provide a brief dash of color. Plants do well under and around trees and shrubs. 'Silver Edge' is a lovely cultivar with light green leaves edged in silver-white; it requires full or partial shade and well-drained soil. Plant in spring or fall. Prepare the soil and then spread 2 inches of mulch over the area. Plant four plants per square foot through the mulch. Handweed for the first year or two. After that, you'll never have to tend it again. Zone 5. (It survives on sites sheltered from winter sun and winds in Zone 4.)

Pachysandra terminalis 'Variegata'

Sedum *(Sedum, selected species and cultivars)*
Low-growing sprawling or spreading forms of these perennials make fine ground covers. Sedums have distinctive fleshy leaves that are often evergreen, pretty little flowers, and sometimes attractive seed heads. Leaf colors range from light greenish yellow to purple or bronze. Some evergreen sedum leaves turn color in winter. Popular S. spurium (Zone 3) spreads by creeping stems to form a patch of 6-inch tall, semievergreen foliage, and several cultivars offer different-colored leaves. 'Dragon's Blood' has purple leaves and pink flowers. S. kamtschaticum (Zone 3) has yellow 1- to 2-inch-wide flower clusters in late summer. Growing conditions and spacing vary according to species and cultivar; check plant labels. Ground-cover types are generally easy to grow and trouble free.

Sedum

Sweet violet *(Viola odorata)*
A long-time garden favorite for its lovely fragrance, sweet violet spreads by runners and seeds to make a patch or ground cover about 4 inches high. Dark green, heart-shaped leaves are evergreen in mild winters. Flowers are white, deep violet, or blue, and they bloom in early spring and, often, again in fall. Provide full sun or shade where summers are hot. Violets adapt to most soils. In mild climates, sweet violets can be an invasive nuisance. Zone 4.

Sweet violet

Verbena

Verbena *(Verbena species and cultivars)*
Evergreen and deciduous forms of verbena make excellent ground covers, particularly in hot, dry areas where they grow wild. Their sprawling stems are covered with clusters of lavender, purple, or red flowers from early summer to frost. V. canadensis (Zone 6) reaches 1½ feet tall, has rosy pink flowers and is a good choice for dry sunny slopes. The hybrid cultivar 'Homestead Purple' stays under 1 foot tall and does well in hot, humid climates. Check at your nursery or garden center for new hybrid verbenas that make good ground covers for Zones 6 and warmer. Garden verbena (V. hybrida) is grown everywhere as an annual and can be used as a temporary ground cover. Reaching less than a foot tall, it's available with flowers in a range of bright colors. All verbenas require full sun and well-drained soil.

Vinca *(Vinca minor)*
One of the most versatile ground covers, vinca (also called common or dwarf periwinkle) grows well in shade or partial shade, in hot climates and dry soil, and is excellent for slopes. Its leathery, evergreen leaves are small and glossy and reach about 6 inches tall. Lilac flowers appear for several weeks in late spring. A range of cultivars offers variations in flower and leaf color. Once established, it needs absolutely no care, only control. Vinca can spread 2 to 3 feet per year. Greater periwinkle (Vinca major) is hardy only to Zone 7, is taller with larger leaves and flowers, prefers moist soil, and is even more invasive. Plant both types about 6 inches apart. Both are easy to expand by division. Zone 4.

Vinca minor

Wild ginger *(Asarum species)*
Two wild ginger species make good ground covers for full or partial shade. Eastern wild ginger (A. canadense, Zone 2) is deciduous; its wide heart-shaped leaves seem to float about 6 inches above the ground at the end of long thin stems. European wild ginger (A. europaeum, Zone 4) is evergreen, with smaller glossy green leaves. Both have inconspicuous flowers (hidden beneath the leaves), and both spread slowly—years will pass before they fill in, so be prepared to police for weeds in the planting. They require constantly moist but well-drained soil. Space 12 inches apart. After they're established, they require no routine care.

Wild ginger

Winter creeper *(Euonymus fortunei cultivars)*
In both its shrub and vine forms, winter creeper has many cultivars that make fine ground covers. Its glossy evergreen leaves come in a variety of colors. Some notable choices include: 'Canadale Gold', with compact growth and green leaves edged with a broad yellow stripe; 'Coloratus', a sprawling plant with dark purple leaves in fall and winter; and 'Ivory Jade', which is low and spreading and has leaves trimmed with white edges that shade to pink in winter. Common winter creeper (E. f. var. radicans) has a remarkably varied growth habit—it can sprawl, climb walls, or grow as a bushy shrub and can be invasive. Winter creeper isn't fussy about conditions. It will grow in full sun and shade, tolerates dry spells, and does well on slopes. It does require well-drained soil. Scale insects can cause damage or death; control them with horticultural oil sprays. In cold-winter areas, leaves and stems may freeze. In this case, trim off any damaged shoots in spring, and new growth will follow. Shear as needed to maintain desired form. Zone 5.

Winter creeper

CHAPTER II *Trees & Shrubs*

Trees and shrubs have a special place in the home landscape. They are useful plants. They shelter us from wind, rain, and snow, create privacy, obscure nearby eyesores, and provide food and protection for birds and other wildlife. But they are also something more. As children, we create secret hideaways in a mass of forsythia and swing on ropes suspended from a towering oak. Later in life, we anticipate the first blossoms of azaleas in spring and enjoy the fiery leaves of burning bush in fall. We welcome the cool shade beneath a maple on a sweltering summer's day. In winter, the vivid evergreen foliage of spruce, arborvitae, and yew provide relief from the snowy monotony in northern climes. Spring is signaled in many areas by the fragrant blooms of flowering trees. Trees and shrubs often become life-long companions—all the more reason to choose them carefully.

Deciduous or Evergreen?

The most common—and useful—categories into which trees and shrubs are grouped concern their foliage. Plants that shed all of their leaves at the end of a growing season are called deciduous. Maple, ash, birch, horse chestnut, oak, and crab apple are a few of the many common deciduous trees. Lilac, forsythia, hydrangea, mock orange, sumac, flowering quince, and spirea are among the many handsome deciduous shrubs.

Plants that retain their leaves year-round are called evergreens. These plants drop and replace leaves, but usually a few at a time. When Northerners say "evergreen," they're probably thinking of plants such as pines and spruces, which are conifers—plants with evergreen leaves that are thin, like needles, or tiny and layered like scales on a fish. Some conifers produce seeds in woody cones; others such as yews and gingkos make fleshy fruit, while junipers produce waxy berries. There are also many broad-leaved evergreens, which are especially popular where winters are mild. Their leaves come in a great variety of sizes and shapes. Broad-leaved evergreens include

Trees and shrubs, opposite, create beauty in the home landscape while providing practical benefits, such as privacy, food, and habitat for wildlife, and relief from summer sun and winter wind.

Deciduous trees, such as this sugar maple, drop all their leaves in autumn.

rhododendrons, most hollies, some oaks, citrus, and camellias.

The distinction between evergreen and deciduous, although helpful, isn't clear-cut. In many groups of shrubs and trees, there are both deciduous and evergreen species. Also, many shrubs that are evergreen in mild climates lose some or all of their leaves where winters are cold; these are called semievergreen.

Tree or Shrub?

There is no hard-and-fast dividing line between trees and shrubs. In general, trees have a single stem, or trunk, and grow taller than about 15 feet, while shrubs are shorter and have multiple stems. But there are exceptions. Yaupon holly, a small evergreen tree, can have numerous stems, while a low-growing "shrubby" juniper may have only one; a rhododendron can outgrow many small trees, while a shrub border of lilacs can tower over a diminutive flowering cherry tree. Some plants can serve either as trees or shrubs, depending on how they're trained and pruned. Fortunately, most of us "know" a shrub or a tree when we see one, based on a common-sense judgment involving height, growth habit, and landscape use.

Uses in the Landscape

Both evergreen and deciduous trees and shrubs are versatile plants. They often define the boundaries of our property and delineate spaces for recreation, entertaining, and other activities within those boundaries. And with a vast and delightful variety of foliage, flower, and form, trees and shrubs are grown for their beauty as well as their utility.

Shade trees help to cool the house during summer, and once their leaves drop in fall, allow it to warm in the winter.

Creating Shade

Of all the practical services trees render, none is more appreciated than shading us from the sun. A leafy canopy can lower temperatures beneath it by 15°F. Properly placed in relation to morning, midday, or afternoon sun, a tree can make your patio or deck a welcome haven even in the heat of summer. Morning and early afternoon shade can prevent the buildup of heat inside your house too, saving you money on air conditioning. In cold-winter areas, deciduous trees are ideal—after shading your house in summer, they drop their leaves and allow the sun to warm the house in winter. You can also plant trees and shrubs to shelter favorite shade-loving plants.

Consider the kind of shade you desire when selecting trees. Spreading trees with low branches and lots of leaves—such as the deciduous beech and Norway maple and the evergreen Southern magnolia—cast a deep shade conducive to solitary musings, but few plants will grow in their dense shade. The smaller leaves, upright forms, and deep roots found in red oak, honey locust, Kentucky coffee tree, green ash, and some acacias and eucalyptuses provide a more cheerful atmosphere. The dappled sunlight they create encourages convivial gatherings and allows a wider range of plants to grow under them.

We don't usually think of conifers as shade trees. Many lack a spreading crown and (with the exception of some mature pines) adequate headroom beneath for lounging. Their dense foliage often casts deep shade that is inhospitable to many understory plants. However, by making use of the shade cast beside these plants, rather than under them, you can effectively cool a patio

Trees for Shade

Large Deciduous Trees
Green ash
Lacebark elm
Honey locust
Red maple
Gingko
Scarlet oak

Smaller Deciduous Trees
Dogwood
Redbud
Silverbell
Crab apple
Bradford pear

Large Broad-Leaved Evergreen Trees
Blue gum
American holly
Live oak
Southern magnolia

Smaller Broad-Leaved Evergreen Trees
Silver wattle
Olive
Evergreen ash
Yaupon holly

Planting Under Trees

Homeowners with large shade trees or wooded stands on their property often find it difficult to grow grass in these areas. However, these spots are perfect for small woodland or wild gardens. With the addition of a comfortable bench, they can become a "secret" garden. If the shade is created by deciduous trees, you can turn the area into a special spring garden. Grow spring-flowering bulbs and early-blooming perennials, which will thrive in the early-season warmth and sun under the bare branches and will finish flowering before the trees fully leaf out. In areas that are shady throughout much or all of the growing season, plant shade-tolerant shrubs, perennials, and ground covers. Shade-tolerant annuals such as impatiens and begonias can brighten a shady spot, but it is best to plant them in containers rather than disturb the tree's surface roots with yearly digging.

When you plan a shade garden:

- Observe the area over a growing season, and note the extent of the shade and how long it lasts. Note also the quality of the shade—light, deep, or dappled.
- Remember that practically nothing will grow without some sun, whether it's dappled throughout the day or occurs seasonally (under the bare branches of deciduous trees in spring, for instance).
- To lighten deep shade, prune off the lowest limbs, and thin the upper limbs of deciduous or evergreen trees.
- Choose plants that need less than six hours of direct sun for healthy growth.
- Check with a knowledgeable gardener or nursery staff member to make sure that the tree beneath which you wish to plant is one that won't be damaged if you disturb surface roots. Also determine whether your tree has shallow roots, as maples and birches do, that make it difficult for understory plants to compete for water and nutrients. Dig carefully around tree roots when planting a large plant.
- If you're planting lots of smaller perennials or annuals, you can add up to 6 inches of topsoil under a shallow-rooted tree. If your plans call for substantial grade changes beneath an established tree, consult a certified arborist before proceeding. Adding or removing large volumes of soil under an established tree can severely damage or kill it.
- Some established native trees, such as madrone and certain oaks in California, are sensitive to the root disturbance and watering that often accompany new plantings under their canopies. Consult with an arborist before planting beneath such trees.
- Provide extra fertilizer and water to help the plants compete with the roots of established trees and shrubs.

Planting under trees allows you to grow lovely shade-loving plants such as hostas, ferns, and pachysandras.

or decrease heat buildup in parts of the house with eastern or southern exposures.

Screening & Privacy

Trees and shrubs can provide privacy, block unwanted views, frame a desirable vista, create "outdoor rooms" on your property, or form a backdrop or enclosure for flower gardens. With their dense year-round foliage and regular forms, conifers are ideal for many of these purposes, as are broad-leaved evergreen shrubs. While more limited for these uses, deciduous screens are common; they can offer more color with their flowers and autumn foliage than many evergreens can.

Screening and privacy are easy to achieve with conifers such as these American arborvitae.

Hedges are uniform plantings of trees or shrubs that have been selected for dense branching and foliage. They are frequently used for screens and living fences as well as for delineating "outdoor rooms." Formal hedges are trained and shaped or sheared into geometric shapes; they range in height from less than a foot to over 20 feet. Plants for formal, sheared hedges should retain leaf-covered branches near the ground and have leaves that are small and closely spaced on the stem. Good plants for formal hedges include deciduous shrubs such as burning bush, coniferous trees and shrubs such as hemlock and yew, and broad-leaved evergreens such as boxwood. Avoid cypresses and pines, which don't sprout new growth on old wood; you won't be able to prune them back hard if they get out of hand.

Formal hedges are composed of small-leaved shrubs that retain branches close to the ground, such as this California privet.

Informal hedges are more natural-looking barriers that are pruned lightly, if at all. A natural hedge of plants with a uniform growth habit, such as Japanese holly or Japanese spirea, can present a neat, tidy appearance. More unruly plants make wilder looking but no less effective hedges. Taller plants, such as those listed in "Shrub Choices," opposite, make effective natural screens.

Singly or in groups, trees and shrubs can screen unwanted views or protect you from wind and driving rain and snow. In an informal massed planting, they can do double duty, providing a screen as well as a pleasing composition on their own. A row of columnar trees, such as Japanese privet or incense cedars, will effectively camouflage nearby objects that are tall or large, such as a neighbor's house. By placing a single tree in the line of sight, you can block a view of a distant object from a picture window, patio, or other specific vantage point. Wind can be annoying to people and damaging to plants. Carefully placed trees and shrubs planted singly, in groups, or as hedges, can break the force of prevailing winds.

Planting for Pleasure

Homeowners often plant trees and shrubs simply for the pleasure they will give. Flowers can be prominent among those pleasures. They can be exotic, such as those of the star magnolia or deciduous azalea; simple, such as pussy willow or winter jasmine flowers; or fragrant, such as viburnums, sweet pepperbush, or winter honeysuckle blooms. Broad-leaved evergreens, including rhododendrons, gardenias, and citrus, can provide spectacular, sometimes fragrant, floral displays.

But flowers are so fleeting that you should consider other qualities, too. The leaves of deciduous trees and shrubs provide color for months. They offer greens of every hue as well as the shimmering two-tone foliage of aspens, the deep purple of copper beech, and the reddish new growth of Japanese pieris. Maples, birches, tupelo (*Nyssa sylvatica*), ashes, and others earn their place with spectacular fall foliage colors. Fruits, nuts, and seedpods—both edible and ornamental—recommend deciduous trees and bushes such as crab apples and plums to both humans and wildlife. In winter the striking bark of sycamores and crape myrtle catch the eye, as do the wispy shoots of weeping cherries or willows.

Choosing for Form. Deciduous trees and shrubs come in a wide variety of shapes and sizes, from ground-hugging to towering.

Trees and shrubs add a pleasurable dimension to any garden. Though their flowers fade, and the foliage of some drops in winter, their architectural forms stand out in every season.

Some trees have a spreading shape; others form rounded crowns or rise in a pyramid. Unusual forms, often specially selected and propagated, are popular—there are columnar English oaks and gingkos, or weeping cherries, beeches, and willows. Deciduous shrubs provide virtually any shape you wish, either by growing that way naturally or by being trained to do so.

Trees and shrubs have long been used to complement, accent, or mask architecture. Most common of these uses is the foundation planting, traditionally an arrangement of sheared shrubs at both sides of the front door. Today's foundation plantings are often more imaginative, incorporating trees and shrubs that provide flowers, a range of foliage colors and textures, and interesting natural forms.

Shrub Choices

Shrubs for Shaped, or Formal, Hedges

- Barberry
- Boxwood
- Cherry laurel
- Flowering quince
- Hollies
- Willowleaf cotoneaster
- Pittosporum
- Privet
- Sweet olive

Shrubs for Natural Screens

- Abelia
- Barberry
- Burning bush
- Camellia
- Euonymus
- Highbush blueberry
- Nandina
- Mahonia
- Red-twig dogwood
- Rugosa rose
- Sweet olive
- Sweet pepperbush
- Wax myrtle
- Lilac

Choosing for Beauty. While many evergreens, and conifers in particular, are generally less flamboyant than deciduous trees and shrubs, they are no less beautiful. Evergreen foliage ranges across yellow, blue, and reddish hues as well as greens. Some provide striking cones or colorful berries; Scotch pine and lacebark pine have attractive bark. Evergreens also exhibit a variety of shapes and sizes. Sprawling junipers are ideal for ground covers, whereas a majestic spruce can anchor a large-scale composition. Coniferous trees tend to be conical when young, but with age a number become strikingly picturesque, their branches gnarled, their profiles irregular. There are also conifers with weeping forms. Both broad-leaved and coniferous evergreen shrubs can be trained to almost any shape. Yew, for example, can be a dense, closely cropped hedge or a 40-foot tree.

Shrubs and smaller trees are valuable elements in beds and borders. Mix them among perennials with an eye to combining shapes, colors, and textures for greatest effect. Use one or more as focal points in a bed. A group of taller shrubs or small trees can provide an excellent backdrop and foil for other plants in a bed. Dwarf forms allow you to manipulate the perception of scale in a garden bed or to produce a diminutive grove of container-grown shrubs and trees on a patio.

The vivid color of new leaves makes Japanese pieris, or lily-of-the-valley bush, stand out in any environment.

Textured bark adds to the beauty of the London plane tree.

The Right Plant for the Site

Because trees and shrubs are long-lived and often expensive, make sure your choices are well-suited for the site conditions. Consider their preferences for temperature, sunlight, water, and soil. If you live with sweltering summers, cold winters, drying winds, high humidity, or drought, take those conditions into account. If you choose well, your plants will be more likely to succeed and will require less attention. Your Cooperative Extension Service or local arborist can be a good source of information about which trees and shrubs are proven performers in your area.

Given the large amounts of water required by many trees and shrubs, it makes sense to select those that thrive with the normal rainfall in your area. It is difficult, if not impossible, to alter large areas of soil for the extensive root systems of many trees and shrubs. Similarly, it's best to match soil pH to the plant's requirements. If you have alkaline conditions, for example, trying to grow acid-loving rhododendrons or azaleas will be disappointing unless you create raised beds with specially prepared acid soil for them.

Also consider the mature size of the plant. A full-grown sugar maple, Norway spruce, or eucalyptus can overwhelm a small lot. Shrubs such as junipers that tuck in nicely beneath a picture window when young can block the view in a few years. Mature size is especially important when considering a tree or shrub for inclusion in a bed with perennials. Rather than devote yourself to years of regular pruning, choose plants whose mature size will suit their place in your landscape.

Planting

Trees and shrubs are sold in several ways. Deciduous trees are sometimes sold bare-root; the plants are dormant, with leafless branches and roots bare of any soil. Larger evergreen and deciduous trees are offered balled-and-burlapped (B&B); these are dug from a growing field while dormant, and the mass of roots and attached soil (the "ball") are wrapped in burlap. An increasing number of trees and shrubs are grown and sold in plastic, cardboard, or metal containers. Bare root stock is only sold during times of the year when the plants are dormant—early winter to spring, depending on where you live. Plant them as soon after purchase as possible, before they break dormancy. Balled-and-burlapped and container-grown plants can be planted from spring to fall in cold-winter areas and from fall to spring where winters are mild.

When you select a tree or shrub at a nursery, examine it carefully. Avoid plants with damaged bark or branches. If the plant has leaves, check to see that they are healthy looking—

Avoid buying rootbound plants—roots growing on top or out of the bottom of a container are a tip-off that the roots are crowded.

not wilted or discolored—and that the soil in the container or rootball is moist. Soil in containers should be snug against the sides of the pot. Roots growing on top of or out of the bottom of a container are signs that the plant has been in the pot too long.

You can plant small trees and shrubs with little difficulty, but large balled-and-burlapped plants pose daunting transporting and planting challenges. Nurseries selling these large plants usually offer planting services or can recommend capable professionals.

Preparing to Plant

Digging is your first step in planting a tree or shrub. The hole must be large enough to accommodate the root ball easily. Depth is critical; the tree or shrub should be planted no deeper than it has been growing. This is easy to determine on container-grown plants. On balled-and-burlapped and bare-root plants, look for a change of color near the juncture of stem and roots. Don't disturb the soil at the very bottom of the hole; loose soil will settle after the tree or shrub has been planted, and the tree will sink. But use a rake or garden fork to loosen the soil on the sides of the hole and encourage root penetration out to the sides of the surrounding soil.

Place the soil you dig on a tarp nearby, and remove rocks and other debris. When you're planting trees and large shrubs you don't need to amend the soil. Research shows that they do best when planted in unamended sites. However, small shrubs and trees planted in the same beds as perennials will do fine in amended soil.

Poor drainage can doom a plant. To check the soil, fill the hole with water, as directed in Chapter 2, pages 35–36. Plant in another spot if standing water remains in the hole 24 hours after the second filling.

Make a berm around the planting hole to help hold water. The crown of the plant should be slightly higher than the surrounding moat so that it remains dry when you water.

Planting Container-Grown Trees & Shrubs

Container-grown trees and shrubs are planted the same way that you plant other container-grown plants. (See Chapter 4, page 68.) After digging the hole and thoroughly watering the plant (several hours before planting), remove it from the container, and untangle any circling roots. When you place it in the hole, make certain that the soil line on the trunk or stems lines up with the top of the hole. Fill the hole about halfway with the soil you removed, and water thoroughly. After the water is absorbed, finish filling the hole, and tamp the soil down firmly. As shown below, build a small berm of soil around the circumference of the planting hole. Water again before spreading 2 to 3 inches of bark chips, compost, or another organic mulch. Keep the mulch at least 6 inches away from the trunk.

Don't stake newly planted trees unless you live in a very windy area. In that case, drive two sturdy stakes on opposite sides of the planting hole and a foot or so outside its perimeter. Secure the trunk of the tree to the stakes with strong twine or wire threaded through a section of old garden hose to protect the trunk from abrasion. The fastenings should allow movement. Remove the stakes within one to two years so the tree can strengthen.

Eye-Catching Trees and Shrubs

The following are attractive in at least two seasons:

Deciduous Trees

Beech
Crape myrtle
Dogwood
(tree and shrub forms)
Hawthorne
'Heritage' river birch
Lacebark elm
Paper birch
Poplar
Viburnum
Redbud
Scarlet oak
Shagbark hickory
Serviceberry
Sour gum
Sourwood
Sycamore
Tree lilac
Yellowwood

Evergreen Trees

Bottlebrush
Eucalyptus
Holly
(tree and shrub forms)
Japanese black pine
Incense cedar
Lacebark pine
Loquat
Scotch pine
Southern magnolia
Madrone

Deciduous Shrubs

Blueberry
Chokeberry
Mock orange
Red-twig dogwood
Shrub roses

Evergreen Shrubs

California lilac
Camellia
Heather
Japanese pieris
Oregon grape
Rhododendron

Planting Bare-Root Trees & Shrubs

Plant bare-root trees or shrubs much as you do bare-root roses. (See Chapter 5, page 100.) Soak the roots for 12 to 24 hours in a weak solution of liquid fertilizer, and prune off any broken roots or stems. Place the tree or shrub in the hole, and spread out the roots to prevent circling. Fill the hole with soil, gently working it in around the roots. As you work, make certain that the plant is at the correct depth. Water and fill again as described in Chapter 5, page 100.

Planting Balled-and-Burlapped Trees & Shrubs

In some ways, a balled-and-burlapped plant can be thought of as growing in a large flexible container. Before planting, keep the rootball moist at all times. Always carry and move B&B plants by the rootball, not the stem.

Dig a wide, saucer-shaped planting hole that is a couple of inches shallower than the height of the rootball. Loosen the soil on the sides of the hole to encourage the roots to spread into the surrounding soil. Once the tree or shrub is placed in the hole, cut the twine and pull the burlap away, folding it down over the sides of the ball. Roots will grow through the burlap, which will eventually decompose. If the wrapping is plastic or another nonbiodegradable material, use a lever to pull it out from under the rootball.

Fold back the burlap on a B&B plant after lowering it into the planting hole. Completely remove nonbiodegradable materials such as plastic.

Giving a Good Start

Water newly planted trees and shrubs regularly, especially during the first year. Dry winters are particularly hard on evergreens. Trees usually don't need fertilizer in the first year. In the second and subsequent years, sprinkle a light dressing of a balanced granular fertilizer on the soil around them in early spring. Trees planted in a lawn usually get all the supplemental nutrients they need from fertilizers applied to the lawn.

New trees and shrubs don't need pruning other than trimming branches damaged in transport or planting. If you're plagued with bark-gnawing rabbits or mice, protect the trunk by wrapping it with tree wrap from the garden center, or with aluminum foil extended at least a foot above the height of the anticipated snow cover. A reflective tree wrap covering also protects young tree trunks from sunscald—damage induced in some areas of the country by exposure to intense summer sun or sun reflected off snow in winter.

Pruning Pointers

Pruning helps keep plants healthy, enhances their appearance, and helps control the extent and form of their growth. It can also be one of the most daunting tasks for beginners. Having invested considerable time and money in shrubs and trees, a novice is understandably reluctant to begin lopping off pieces of them. Fortunately, basic pruning is neither difficult nor demanding.

Pruning to maintain a plant's health is, for the most part, based on common sense. Removing dead, damaged, and diseased branches improves both health and appearance. So does thinning out plants that have grown too dense to admit light and air. And by doing some drastic pruning, you can reinvigorate plants that have simply grown old and tired.

Pruning for appearance is more subjective. Your idea of an attractively shaped shrub and your neighbor's idea may differ completely. Some people train, trim, and shear shrubs and trees into all sorts of shapes. Others try to maintain or enhance the shape nature provides. In either case, you'll need to prune to encourage compact growth or to direct a branch into an area.

The point of pruning is not simply to end up with less than you had. Good pruning actually encourages growth. A little elementary plant physiology will help you understand why. All plants produce growth hormones, or auxins, in the tips of growing shoots. These hormones stimulate growth at the tip and suppress it along the sides of the shoot. Removing the growing tip and its supply of hormones releases some of the buds along the shoot, called lateral buds, from dormancy, allowing them to grow into side shoots. (See page 270.) Thus, whether the plant is a rose, spirea,

Pruning Tools

Homeowners can take care of all their tree and shrub pruning needs with only a few tools. If you are on a tight budget, begin with a good pair of pruning shears and a small folding pruning saw. Add more tools as your plants grow over the years. Hedge shears or clippers are essential if you plant a hedge, and you'll need loppers to prune thick branches.

Bypass Shears

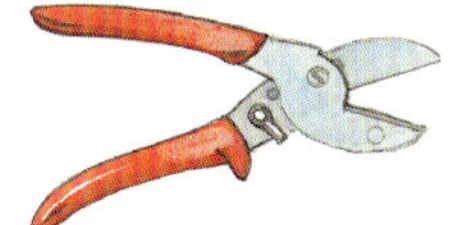

Anvil Shears

Pruning shears. For green twigs and branches up to about ½ inch thick. Bypass types are best; they have two curved blades that cut like scissors.

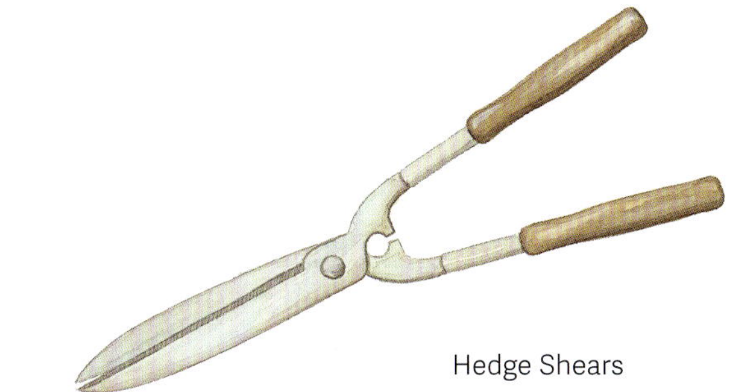

Hedge Shears

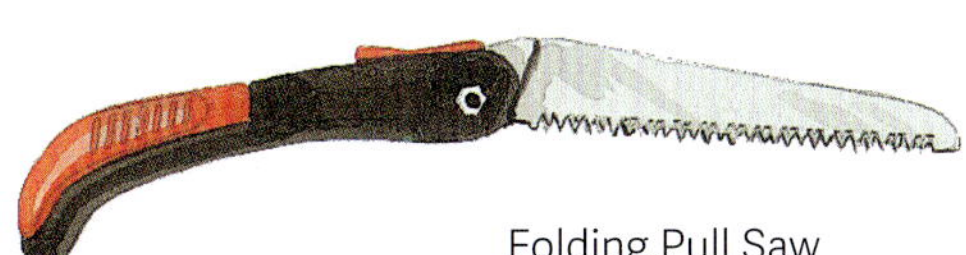

Folding Pull Saw

Electric Hedge Trimmer

Pruning saw. For branches up to 3 or 4 inches in diameter. Look for a folding saw with thin, hardened steel blades 8 to 12 inches long and long, thin teeth. Often advertised as "Japanese" saws, these are unsurpassed for efficiency and convenience.

Hedge shears. For trimming tender tip growth on hedges and shrubs. Essentially, these are heavy-duty scissors on long handles. If you have a lot of shearing and shaping to do, consider power hedge clippers.

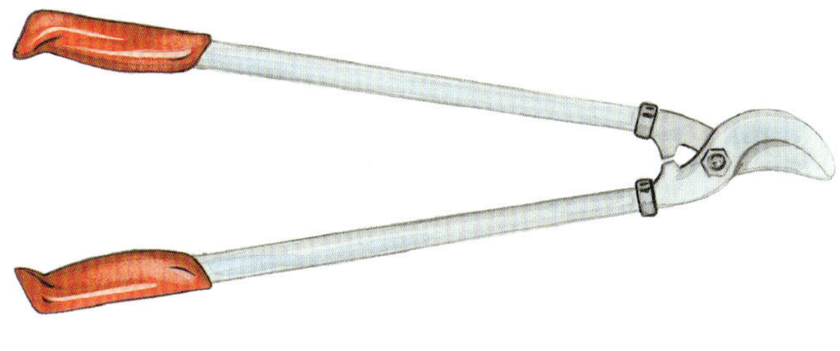

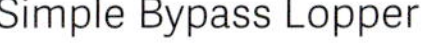

Simple Bypass Lopper

Ratcheted Anvil Lopper

Loppers. For heavier branches and those out of reach of pruning shears. Loppers are available with bypass blades or an anvil design, where one straight blade cuts against the soft metal surface of the other blade.

Pruning

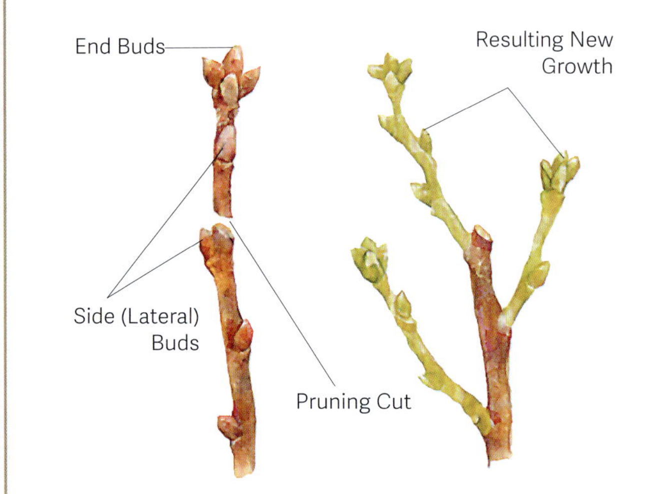

Pruning growing tips stimulates lateral buds to develop. When cutting stems with alternate buds, prune at a 45-deg. angle just above the bud you want to stimulate. If buds are opposite, cut across the stem in a straight line.

or yew, pruning off the growing tips of shoots and branches produces a bushier plant.

Cutting off more than just the growing tip is called heading back. Stems are usually headed back to a lateral (side) bud. Cutting whole stems back to the plant's crown, or severing lateral branches at the crotch where they arise, is called thinning. Thinning directs a plant's energy to producing vigorous new shoots.

Pruning Shrubs & Trees

Shrubs and trees come in a wide range of shapes and sizes. When you purchase a plant, ask how to prune it. If possible, watch an expert work on the same species. Fortunately, there are a few general pruning principles and practices.

When to Prune. Remove dead, damaged, or diseased growth as soon as you see it to minimize diseases and insects. Cut back to healthy wood. Although you can snip off a healthy stem or branch almost anytime, extensive pruning of healthy growth is best done at specific times of the year.

When flowers aren't a consideration, you have greater flexibility in pruning time. The structure of deciduous plants is easiest to see before they leaf out. Thus winter or early spring is a good time to prune them. Prune in the spring to encourage a bushy habit or to stimulate or direct growth. In cold-winter climates, be wary of pruning in the fall. Pruning always stimulates new growth; if it forms too late in the year to properly harden, it will be more susceptible to damage from cold, wind, and snow.

Light pruning. Many shrubs and trees thrive for years with a minimum of pruning. Even so, they can benefit from some of the following techniques:

- To force shrubs into bushier, more compact forms, pinch or cut off growing tips in the spring.
- Deadhead spent flowers to direct the energy that would otherwise be spent on forming seeds toward roots and shoots. Deadhead rhododendrons and azaleas as soon as possible after flowers fade because seed formation greatly reduces the number of flowers these plants produce the following year.
- Head back or thin out stems or branches that cross the center of a bush to reduce the incidence of diseases that breed in the humid conditions of dense growth. Similarly, remove stems that rub on neighboring growth; the damage they cause can open the tree to many diseases.
- Encourage branching into a particular area by finding a bud facing the direction you want a branch to grow and cutting just above it. Remember to cut at an angle close to a bud.
- New shoots that arise at the base of stems or from roots are called suckers. A few may be desirable; too many can produce a thicket. Cut them off flush with the stem base; pull up those sprouting from roots.

Heavy pruning. A few shrubs can be pruned heavily each year to produce robust new growth the following growing season. Spirea, red-twig dogwood, and shrub willows are often cut back almost to the ground. Other shrubs may be cut back to old wood or to just a few buds on new wood. Shrubs that die back to the ground in colder climates and renew themselves each spring, such as butterfly bush and caryopteris, should be cut close to the ground in late winter or early spring.

Tips for Pruning Flowering Shrubs

- Spring-flowering shrubs (forsythia, lilacs, etc.) usually bloom on growth formed the previous year, so prune them right after they bloom.
- Plants that flower later, such as potentilla and crape myrtle, bloom on the current season's growth, so prune them in late winter or early spring before growth begins.

Tips for Pruning Trees

A well-formed tree, planted and cared for correctly, should require little pruning when young and even less as it matures. This is particularly true of conifers, which may not need the attention of a pruning saw for years.

Pruning techniques are the same as for shrubs but size complicates matters—removing a 6-inch-diameter branch growing 30 feet above the ground can be both difficult and dangerous and should be done by a professional arborist. But you can do a great deal while standing firmly on the ground.

- Some trees, such as maples and birches, "bleed" if pruned when sap is rising in early spring; these are best pruned when dormant.
- Trees with a columnar shape such as oaks, pines, and spruces often have a dominant central trunk, called a leader. If a young conifer has two leaders, trim the second leader back to its base. Do the same with deciduous trees, or cut the second leader back by half to ensure that the tree develops the desired shape.
- Do not cut off, or "top," the central leader of a columnar tree. The sad results of such pruning can be seen wherever power companies have "pruned" trees away from their lines. Better to remove the tree and plant one that won't grow so tall.
- Open a tree to air and sun by thinning crowded branches and removing those that cross the center.
- Sometimes mature branches or trunks develop unattractive, slender, vertical shoots called watersprouts. Remove these by cutting flush with the parent branch.
- Don't use wound dressings; research shows they cause as many problems as they prevent. A healthy tree can protect itself from disease, particularly if you prune whole branches just beyond the collar.

Heavy pruning can bring new life to overgrown or tired shrubs. Some, such as mahonia, respond well if cut almost to the ground. But lilacs and cotoneaster respond when stems are headed back to several feet above the crown. Renew a rhododendron in stages—cut one-third of the stems back hard one year, another third the next year, and the remainder in the third year. Sometimes you can nurture selected suckers as replacement stems.

Heavy pruning can be risky. Most conifers, along with many broadleaved evergreens and deciduous shrubs, will not sprout from old leafless wood. They don't have latent buds below the foliage area; if you cut a branch past that area, it will die. If you're uncertain about a shrub's ability to rejuvenate, ask a local expert from the garden center before making any cuts.

Tree & Shrub Gallery

The following plant portraits introduce a selection of the most popular and useful species and cultivars from the vast range of trees and shrubs suitable for home landscapes. Cultural preferences vary within each genus and are mentioned only when particularly noteworthy. Check nursery tags for specific information on a particular plant, or consult with experienced gardeners and nursery staff to find plants that meet your needs and are proven performers in your area.

Trees

Ash *(Fraxinus species)*

These large, upright shade trees are familiar throughout much of North America. White, or American, ash (*F. americana*, Zone 3) and green ash (*F. pennsylvanica*, Zone 2) are two of the most commonly grown. Both are fast-growing deciduous trees that reach 50 feet or more in height, with distinctive compound leaves and bark that is divided by furrows into neat diamond shapes. Leaves of white ash turn yellow or purple in fall; green ash leaves turn yellow. White and green ashes are prone to insects and diseases, but any damage is often overcome by vigorous growth. However, homeowners should be vigilant.

Ash

Arizona ash (*F. velutina*, Zone 6) is a common deciduous street tree in the Southwest. Oregon ash (*F. latifolia*, Zone 6) is also deciduous and is used similarly in the Northwest.

Birch *(Betula species)*

Prized for their arresting bark and striking autumn foliage, these deciduous trees are frequently planted as eye-catching specimens or in groups as small groves. Fast-growing to 40 feet or so, often with multiple trunks, birches fit comfortably into most residential landscapes, where the leaves shimmer in the breeze and cast a dappled shade.

Birches suffer from a long list of insects and diseases, which is one of the reasons they're relatively short-lived trees. Before purchasing, it pays to research which birches do best in your area.

Paper Birch

European white birch (*B. pendula*, Zone 2) offers attractive white bark and drooping branchlets covered in fall with golden leaves, but is a poor choice because it is extremely prone to insects and diseases. Paper birch (*B. papyrifera*, Zone 2) also has lovely white bark, and is more insect resistant but less graceful than European white birch. Neither of these birches thrives in hot, humid weather. *B. nigra* 'Heritage' (Zone 4) is an exceptional tree that has good fall color and peeling pinkish or reddish bark. It tolerates heat and wet soil and is resistant to bronze birch borers, the bane of many white-barked birches. Whitespire birch (*B. platyphylla* var. *japonica* 'Whitespire', Zone 4) is an excellent single-trunked specimen with white

Pygmy Crab Apple

bark, yellow fall foliage, and resistance to the bronze birch borer. Sweet birch (*B. lenta*, Zone 3) has reddish-brown or black bark and exceptional fall color.

Crab apple *(Malus species)*
Spring wouldn't be nearly so uplifting without crab apples covered with appealing pink buds and then clouds of white, pink, or red flowers. They're not just one-season wonders, either. Summer foliage mixes rich greens with hints of red and purple. In late summer and fall, red and yellow foliage complements glossy fruit in shades of red, orange, and purple. The handsome branching patterns and long-lasting fruit of some crab apple cultivars extends their attraction through early winter.

When you choose a cultivar, you can select for the overall growth habit (weeping, upright, vase-shaped, or spreading), the color and fragrance of the flowers, and the size and character of the fruit (long-lasting on the tree, for example). The fruit can be as small as 3⁄8 inch in diameter or as large as 2 inches. They are a mixed blessing. Though attractive to the eye and useful for jams and jellies, they can become a lumpy mess on the ground. Resistance to pests and diseases is equally important. Some recently introduced hybrids, including Japanese flowering crabapple (*M. floribunda,* Zone 4) and tea crabapple (*M. hupehensis,* Zone 4), are resistant to scab, rust, and powdery mildew. Though these common diseases disfigure the leaves they seldom kill the tree.

There are crab apples for any size property. Sargent crab apple (*M. sargentii*, zone 5) grows only 6 to 10 feet tall and spreads half again as wide. It bears small fragrant white flowers and small fruit. Japanese crab apple and a wide range of hybrid crab apples (Zone 4) grow into handsome spreading trees between 20 and 30 feet tall and wide. Hybrid cultivars include 'Adams', with reddish pink flowers; 'Donald Wyman', with red buds, white flowers, and small fruits that cling to the tree until spring; and 'Prairiefire', which offers reddish-purple flowers, red-orange fall foliage, and eye-catching red twigs through the winter.

Crape myrtle *(Lagerstroemia indica)*
A small deciduous tree or shrub, crape myrtle produces large, eye-catching clusters of flowers from midsummer until early autumn. Grown with single or multiple trunks, planted individually or in small groves, crape myrtles are versatile landscape plants for properties of any size. The tree's flowers are rivaled by its colorful peeling bark. Leaves turn from yellow-bronze in spring to green in summer and to yellow, orange, or light red in fall.

Crape Myrtle

There are dozens of cultivars. They range in size from 3 to 25 feet and offer flowers colored white to pink to dark red. A series of cultivars with American Indian names ('Hopi' and 'Sioux') are mildew- and disease-resistant, as well as lovely. 'Natchez' is one of the most popular, with white flowers, striking bark, and orange-red fall foliage. All cultivars are hardy to Zone 7.

Dogwood *(Cornus species)*
Spring flowers, bright autumn foliage, eye-catching berries, handsome bark, attractive form, convenient size—dogwoods supply just about everything you could want in an ornamental tree. Flowering dogwood (*C. florida*, Zone 5) reaches 25

Pink Flowering Dogwood

feet or more. In early spring it produces cheerful white or pink flowers before the leaves appear. The "flowers" are actually bracts surrounding tiny true flowers. Dark green leaves turn red or maroon in fall, when they're joined by bright red berries. Kousa dogwoods (*C. kousa*, Zone 5) are Asian natives that resist insects and diseases now problematic for flowering dogwoods. About the same size as flowering dogwoods, their fruit and fall foliage are equally attractive. They bloom slightly later, after leaves have formed. Cornelian cherry dogwood (*C. mas*), a large shrub or small tree, is hardy to Zone 4. Its yellow flowers appear in very early spring. The bright red fruits attract birds and can be used for preserves. Fall foliage is colorful.

Holly *(Ilex species)*

Prized for the spiny, glossy dark green leaves and bright red berries that are familiar holiday decorations, hollies are more varied than you might imagine. Hollies can be trees or shrubs, deciduous as well as evergreen, with large or small, spiny or smooth-edged leaves and fruit of orange, yellow, or deep blue-black as well as red. The hollies mentioned here are often grown as trees. (See the Holly entry under shrubs, page 280, for discussion of smaller, more bushy hollies.)

American holly (*I. opaca*, Zone 5) grows 15 to 30 feet tall and is widely planted as a specimen tree in the East. It forms a pyramidal tree when young, but with age becomes more open, more irregular, and more picturesque. Evergreen leaves are dark green and spiny, the fruit a dull red.

Where summers are mild and not too humid, gardeners can grow the English holly (*I. aquifolium*). Most cultivars are confined to Zone 6 or warmer. Its spiny evergreen leaves and bright red berries make classic holiday sprigs and wreaths. It grows into a pyramidal tree 30 feet or more in height and bears small, white, fragrant flowers in late spring.

Gardeners with small properties should consider possum haw (*I. decidua*, Zone 5), a small deciduous tree with showy red, orange, or yellow berries and smooth-edged leaves that turn gold in fall.

Several other small holly trees make attractive specimens. Lusterleaf holly (*I. latifolia*, Zone 7) is a narrow upright tree with unusually long evergreen leaves—up to 8 inches—as well as fragrant yellow flowers in spring and clusters of large red berries in fall. Long-stalked holly (*I. pedunculosa*, Zone 5) bears its berries on stalks, like cherries. It grows 15 to 20 feet tall with graceful branches and leaves that are dark green in summer and yellow-green in winter. Yaupon holly (*I. vomitoria*, Zone 7) can be trained as a multi-trunked tree up to 20 feet tall with eye-catching twisty branches, narrow evergreen leaves, and abundant red berries.

To produce berries, female hollies need to be pollinated by a male holly. Your nursery can tell you which plants to pair

English Holly

up. Carried by bees, pollen from a single male can pollinate female plants several hundred yards away; before you buy, check to see if there's a suitable male plant within range of your property.

Magnolia *(Magnolia species)*

Magnolias, with their large, fragrant, almost succulent flowers and broad canopy of thick, leathery, dark green leaves, evoke the American South for many people. But magnolias also come in smaller sizes and thrive as far north as Zones 5 and even 4. Both evergreen and deciduous magnolias grow in the South, but magnolias hardy enough for northern winters are all deciduous.

Star magnolia (*M. stellata*, Zone 4 or 5) is a delicate little deciduous tree, one of the hardiest magnolias and the earliest to bloom. It's an excellent tree for small gardens. The slightly fragrant flowers are small by magnolia standards, but they float prettily among the leafless branches for several weeks and can appear as early as February in warm-winter areas. The dark green leaves are attractive all summer. Cultivars of *M.* 3 *loebneri* (Zone 4) produce similar flowers on larger, hardier, more widely adapted deciduous trees.

At the other end of the spectrum is southern magnolia (*M. grandiflora*, Zone 7), the grande dame of southern gardens, a majestic tree rising up to 80 feet with a broad canopy of graceful horizontal branches. Its evergreen leaves are as long as a foot, glossy, thick, and dark green with fuzzy brown undersides. Flowers appear in late spring, peak in early summer, and continue sporadically through the summer. They are very large, up to 10 inches or more wide, and deliciously fragrant. Cultivars provide the same beauty in smaller trees.

Saucer magnolia (*M.* 3 *soulangiana*, Zone 5) is a versatile plant, widely grown as a small, multi-trunked deciduous tree or shrub. It grows 20 to 30 feet tall, spreads as wide, and is used as a specimen or in groups. White, pink, or reddish purple flowers appear in early to midspring and sporadically thereafter. Leaves are 6 inches long and may turn yellow in fall.

Oyama magnolia (*M. sieboldii*, Zone 7) is another fine tree for small, warm-winter gardens, reaching 15 feet tall and wide, with 3-inch-wide, white, very fragrant flowers in late spring and early summer.

Saucer Magnolia

Maple *(Acer species)*

One of the most popular residential trees in North America, maples provide pretty little flowers in the spring, cooling shade in the summer, and spectacular foliage color in the fall. Large maples are grown for the shade and commanding presence they provide. Red maple (*A. rubrum*, Zone 3) grows quickly, reaching 40 to 80 feet high and 30 to 40 feet or more wide, depending on the cultivar. It produces red flowers early in spring and breathtaking fall foliage colors—reds, yellows, oranges, and pinks. Cultivars provide some opportunity to choose among fall colors. Sugar maple (*A. saccharum*, Zone 3) has equally brilliant fall colors but is less suitable than red maple for most landscape uses because of its size—up to 90 feet—as well as its susceptibility to problems caused by heat, drought, and a variety of insects and diseases. Silver maple (*A. saccharinum*, Zone 3) provides shade quickly and grows in almost any conditions. However, its limbs are weak and prone to breaking in storms. Also, its extensive system of shallow roots makes growing anything under or near it difficult, and it's attacked by numerous insects and diseases.

Japanese maples

Several of the smaller maples make fine shade trees more in keeping with the scale of ordinary city or suburban lots. Trident maple (*A. buergerianum*, Zone 4) reaches 25 to 30 feet tall and 20 feet wide. It has pretty flaking bark, red or yellow fall foliage, and less-competitive roots than most maples, making it easier to plant beneath. Amur maple (*A. tataricum* subspecies *ginnala*, Zone 3) is about the same size as trident maple but with multiple trunks, white spring flowers, and scarlet fall foliage.

Japanese maples (*A. palmatum*, Zone 5) are strikingly handsome small trees grown singly as specimens, or in large mixed borders. The foliage and form of the trees are equally compelling. Leaves are often deeply lobed, some to the point of laciness; leaf color ranges from green to red, bronze, or purple in summer, and most turn scarlet in fall. Branches are often twisted and strongly horizontal; some have particularly attractive bark. For striking bark, consider the paperbark maple (*A. griseum*, Zone 4), a slow-growing tree with curly, cinnamon-colored bark on its trunk and main limbs. Summer leaves are green; fall leaf color is variable, but can be striking.

Maples are often grown for their fall color, but you should be aware that this characteristic varies from region to region and from tree to tree; cultivars are likely to be more dependable. Consult with local arborists or nursery staff to learn which maples perform best in your area.

White Oak

Oak *(Quercus species)*

Oaks are rich in folklore and history. In the landscape, their trunks of majestic girth and canopies of impressive height and spread make them a sort of royalty. Because most oaks eventually become huge, ordinary urban and suburban properties have room for one or two at most.

Northern red oak (*Q. rubra*, Zone 4) is a widely grown shade tree that reaches as high as 90 feet with a round crown of up to 50 feet across. Fast growing, it may reach 20 feet or more in 20 years. Leaves can be up to 9 inches long and may turn bright red in fall. Pin oaks (*Q. palustris*, Zone 5) are also widely used, fast-growing shade trees. They mature to a tall (to 100 feet) narrow (40 feet or less) form, with lower limbs that droop attractively to the ground. Leaves are deeply cut and can turn copper-red in fall. Scarlet oak (*Q. coccinea*, Zone 5) is similar, but tolerates drier conditions and holds its bottom branches higher.

Midwesterners will be familiar with the native bur oak (*Q. macrocarpa*, Zone 3), a very hardy shade tree reaching 80 feet tall with an almost equal spread. It doesn't put on much of a show in autumn, but it does tolerate a wide range of poor growing conditions.

Gardeners in mild-winter climates can grow several evergreen oaks. Aged specimens of coast live oak (*Q. agrifolia*, Zone 9) are revered in California, where they reach 100 feet tall and wide with splendidly gnarled branches. Young live oaks grow quickly and are sometimes planted and pruned to form hedges. Holly oak (*Q. ilex*, Zone 7) is smaller but equally fast-growing and versatile. Southeastern native evergreen oaks include the southern live oak (*Q. virginiana*, Zone 7), a tree with a short thick trunk and a very large, spreading crown that can reach 60 feet tall by 100 feet wide. Laurel oaks (*Q. laurifolia*, Zone 7) are taller than wide and drop their leaves before spring.

Oaks aren't all behemoths. Sawtooth oak (*Q. acutissima*, Zone 5) reaches just 35 to 50 feet with an equal spread. Its long, deciduous leaves have serrated edges and turn from yellow-green in spring to dark green in summer and gold or brown in fall. Gambel oak (*Q. gambelii*, Zone 5) is even smaller—15 to 30 feet tall—and is grown as a single or multi-trunked specimen or *en masse* as a shrubby screen. Ideal as a specimen or screen in small yards is upright English oak (*Q. robur* 'Fastigiata', Zone 6), a cultivar of the venerable English oak that grows 50 feet high but only 15 feet wide.

Pine *(Pinus species)*

Pines are such familiar trees that many people refer to all coniferous evergreen trees as "pines." They are, of course, distinct

Austrian Pine

from other conifers, and are recognizable because their needles are gathered into clusters of two, three, or five. Many of the most popular species have long needles with the appealing look and feel of soft brushes. All pines bear cones and a few bear edible seeds (pine nuts). In the landscape, pines have a year-round presence as specimen or background plants. They range in size from dwarf plants only a few feet tall to stately 70- or 80-foot trees. Hedges and screens of pine are effective and attractive whether sheared or left natural. When young, many pines are upright, conical trees. With age, some develop a more open or irregular picturesque form. Some pines drop their bottom branches and, when large, can provide headroom for strollers and shade for a bench. Pine species also include weeping, narrowly upright, or spreading forms.

Eastern white pine (*P. strobus*, Zone 3) is a fast-growing tree with soft blue-green needles. Grown as a specimen, it can reach 80 feet tall—or it can be trained and sheared as a hedge or tall screen. Scotch pine (*P. sylvestris*, Zone 3), with its stiff needles and conical form, is familiar to many as a Christmas tree. Growing to 70 feet, older trees are handsome focal points with open, irregular branches and colorful peeling bark. Austrian pine (*P. nigra*, Zone 4) is one of the best pines for city conditions; it tolerates a wide range of of environments. Lacebark pine (*P. bungeana*, Zone 5) is a 50-foot, often multi-trunked tree prized for its colorful flaking bark. Mugo pine (*P. mugo*, Zone 3), a bushy tree with dense dark green foliage, ranges from a few feet to 15 feet tall. Its cultivars are popular and versatile landscape plants used as specimens or mass-planted.

Gardeners in the South and West can choose from many excellent native pines. Check with your local nursery or garden center to find which are good performers in your area. Of the southern pines, spruce pine (*P. glabra*) has a twisting trunk and irregular branches even as a young tree. Longleaf pine (*P. palustris*) has distinctive needles up to 18 inches long. Growing to 80 feet, longleaf pines make fine shade trees, as do loblolly pines (*P. taeda*). Most southern pines are hardy to Zone 7, some to Zone 6, so check labels or ask about hardiness when you buy.

In the west, the bristlecone pine (*P. aristata*) is noteworthy for its picturesque presence and its longevity—some specimens are believed to be 4,000 years old. Ponderosa pine (*P. ponderosa*) is a majestic shade tree growing to 60 feet with an open habit and handsome orange-tinted, furrowed bark. Western pines are frequently small trees, generally cold-hardy (to Zones 4 or 5) and tolerant of wind, heat, and drought, as befits their mountain and desert origins.

Shrubs

Boxwoods *(Buxus species)*

These evergreen shrubs are the quintessential plant for formal garden hedges. Their small, glossy leaves are packed densely on many branched twigs, making them ideal for shearing to precise shapes. Left on their own, boxwoods form tidy mounds. Various cultivars of littleleaf boxwood (*B. microphylla*, Zones 4 or 5) are widely available. Some grow faster than others; some are upright, others spread, and the leaves of some turn bronze in winter. Their mature size is about 3 to 4 feet tall and wide. In contrast, English boxwood (*B. sempervirens*, Zone 5) can grow much larger, to 20 feet tall and wide. Its cultivars are equally diverse, but all have the densely packed leaves that make them such good hedge plants.

Boxwoods grow slowly, so buy the largest plants you can afford. They thrive in full sun to partial shade but can be fussy about soil, water, heat, and pests—check with local nursery staff to find out which cultivars do best in your area.

Boxwood

Butterfly bush *(Buddleia species)*
Weeks-long displays of lovely fragrant, butterfly-attracting flowers earn these deciduous shrubs their place in the garden. Elongated clusters of tiny flowers form at the ends of arching branches from midsummer to fall. Flowers are pink, white, violet, lilac, blue, or purple. *B. davidii* (Zone 5) and its cultivars are widely available; other less-hardy species are available in the South. Plants can grow to 10 feet tall and wide, and there are compact or dwarf cultivars. Butterfly bush requires full sun. Cut the woody stems to 1-foot stubs in early spring; new shoots can reach 5 feet or taller over the growing season. In cold-winter climates top growth may die back over the winter, but the plant will regrow from the roots.

Butterfly Bush

Camellia *(Camellia species)*
Camellias are the glory of many home landscapes in the South, West, and coastal areas where the climate is mild enough to support them (Zone 8, sometimes 7). There are small camellias for patio containers, camellias that can be trained as espaliers, and camellias that form trees or bushes 15 feet tall and wide. All cultivars have attractive evergreen foliage and beautiful,

Camellia

sometimes spectacular flowers. The leaves are glossy, dark green, and leathery. Flowers can be single or double, from 3 to 9 inches across, in colors ranging from white to pink to red. Depending on cultivar and conditions, camellias begin blooming in fall, winter, or spring; they continue to flower for months. Cultivars of *C. japonica*, *C. sasanqua*, and *C. reticulata* are commonly available. *C. sasanqua* produces generally smaller plants and flowers than the others, and *C. reticulata* produces striking flowers on lanky plants. Camellias require partial shade.

Gardeners in colder climates may wish to search out oilseed camellia (*C. oleifera*) and the Ackerman hybrids developed from it. These are hardy to Zone 6 and may survive in protected spots in Zone 5.

Cotoneaster *(Cotoneaster species)*
These versatile plants include low-growing, spreading ground covers, upright shrubs with stiff branches, and tall plants with graceful arching limbs. Whether evergreen or deciduous, all bear spring flowers that are small, white or pink, and pretty if not spectacular. Colorful berries appear in fall and may last the winter.

Cotoneasters used for ground covers are discussed in Chapter 10, on page 255. Bigger shrubs used as specimens or in massed plantings include spreading cotoneaster (*C. divaricatus*, Zone 5), which forms a 10-foot-wide mound 5 or

Cotoneaster

6 feet tall. It has deciduous leaves that turn red in fall. Evergreen red clusterberry (*C. lacteus*, Zone 7) forms a dense mass of arching stems that are covered with large clusters of red berries for much of the winter. Willowleaf cotoneaster (C. salicifolius, Zone 6) has long narrow evergreen leaves that are green in summer, purple in winter. Cultivars include a low-growing ground cover as well as a shrub 10 feet tall and wide.

Cotoneasters grow in full sun or partial shade and tolerate a range of soils, heat, and drought. When stressed by hot weather or lack of water, they are susceptible to fire blight. Check with your local Cooperative Extension Service to learn whether fire blight-resistant cultivars are necessary in your area.

Dogwood *(Cornus stolonifera and C. alba)*
Several dogwoods are handsome and valuable landscaping shrubs. (Tree-form dogwoods are discussed on page 129.) Hardy to Zone 2, they have something to offer in every season. Siberian dogwood (*C. alba*), red-twig, and red-osier dogwood (*C. stolonifera*) are similar in many respects. All produce showy white or creamy flowers in spring and white or bluish white berries that stand out against the good-looking summer foliage. Leaves turn red or purple in fall. Colorful red stems brighten the winter landscape. Siberian dogwood forms a small, somewhat compact bush growing 6 to 8 feet tall, while red-twig dogwood grows 10 feet tall and wide. Cultivars offer variegated foliage, dwarf forms, and twigs colored yellow, coral, or maroon.

Shrub dogwoods grow in full sun to full shade. Cut oldest stems to the ground every two or three years to stimulate new, more colorful growth.

Siberian dogwood

Euonymus *(Euonymus species)*
Whether it's a low-growing, shrubby, or vining ground cover or a strikingly colorful fall accent, there's probably a place for at least one euonymus on your property. These tough plants grow in full sun or full shade. Burning bush (*E. alatus*, Zone 3) is prized for its blazing red fall foliage, but the

Euonymus

transition of the deciduous leaves from dark green to pale pink to red spreads out the enjoyment over months. Burning bush grows 6 to 10 feet high and wide, depending on the cultivar. The distinctive ridged twigs are interesting in winter and are the source of the plant's other common name, winged euonymus.

Winter creeper (*E. fortunei*, Zone 5) is less flamboyant. Evergreen leaves and varied growth habits make winter creepers good plants for adding structure to a planting. Vining forms make dense ground covers that can be invasive or climbers for walls or fences. Upright, bushy forms are effective in foundation or mass plantings and as informal hedges. Cultivars offer leaves that are variegated with white, cream, or gold edges or that change color in fall and winter. Inconspicuous flowers produce orange fruits that may last all winter.

Japanese euonymus (*E. japonicus*, Zone 7 or 8) is frequently used in warm-winter areas. It can be grown as an individual specimen, massed in groups, or as a hedge or screen. This species grows to 10 feet tall and 6 feet wide. Cultivars with variegated leaves edged in gold, cream, or white make striking accents, particularly since the colors don't fade in full sun or hot weather.

Holly *(Ilex species)*

In addition to handsome trees (see page 274), hollies include attractive shrubs for foundation plantings, mass plantings, hedges, or screens. Many can be used as formal, precisely sheared hedges; others look best in a more natural form. Evergreen hollies with spiny, shiny leaves and red berries are common. Chinese holly (*I. cornuta*, Zone 7) grows to 10 feet tall and wide. It thrives in the heat of the South and in the alkaline soils and hot, dry climate of the Southwest. Japanese holly (*I. crenata*, Zone 5 or 6) has small leaves and inconspicuous berries. The cultivars 'Compacta' and 'Helleri' make excellent natural hedges 4 to 6 feet tall. A number of hybrids developed by Mrs. Kathleen Meserve (*I.* 3 *meserveae*, Zone 4 or 5) are hardier plants, mostly with blue-green leaves and bright red berries. They include upright and mounded cultivars that grow 8 to 15 feet tall. Winterberry holly (*I. verticillata*, Zone 3) is a deciduous holly whose berry-covered stems are striking for months in the winter, or until appreciative birds harvest the fruit. Hollies require full sun to partial shade.

Hydrangea *(Hydrangea species)*

Gardeners have long valued hydrangeas for their large clusters of showy flowers. These deciduous plants grow as vines, shrubs, or small trees, with flat to spherical flower clusters up to a foot wide. Climbing hydrangea (*H. petiolaris*, Zone 5) is a vine reaching 60 feet or more in length. For several weeks in summer it bears flat flower clusters, 6 to 8 inches wide, that are white and slightly fragrant. The glossy dark-green foliage looks good through the summer and fall. The leaves drop to reveal pretty reddish- brown bark. This plant grows in full sun to full shade.

The familiar garden hydrangea (*H. macrophylla*, Zone 6) has large shiny leaves that make an attractive backdrop to the showy clusters of white, blue, pink, or red flowers. Flower color varies with the pH of your soil—acid soil produces blue flowers, neu-

Winterberry holly

Garden hydrangea

tral and alkaline soil make them pink or red. Flowers appear in summer and last until fall. The species reaches 4 to 8 feet tall and 6 to 10 feet wide, but much smaller cultivars are available. Garden hydrangeas prefer full sun to partial shade.

Gardeners in colder areas can grow *H. arborescens* 'Annabelle' or 'Grandiflora', which bloom on new growth and can be cut back to the ground each winter. Or they can grow PeeGee hydrangea (*H. paniculata* 'Grandiflora', Zone 3) whose 6- to 12-inch-wide flower clusters turn from white to pink to tan through the summer, fall, and into winter. Plants can reach 25 feet tall and wide, but are usually pruned to control the size.

Oakleaf hydrangea (*H. quercifolia*, Zone 5) is grown as much for its colorful oak-like leaves and shaggy red-brown bark as for the clusters of white flowers it produces in early summer. The dark green leaves turn red, orange, and purple in the fall. Oakleaf hydrangeas require partial sun or shade.

Juniper *(Juniperus species)*

Ubiquitous in the landscape, junipers come in a vast range of sizes and shapes suitable for just about every landscape purpose. The evergreen foliage is scaly or needlelike, varying from bright green to gray-green, blue-green, or even blue. Some cultivars turn purple or bronze in winter. The fleshy cones look like berries. For ground cover junipers (*J. horizontalis*, Zone 2), see Chapter 10, page 256. For foundation plantings, mass plantings, screens, and hedges, there are numerous shrubby forms, both spreading and upright. Most of these are cultivars of *J.* 3 *media* (Zone 4 or 5), shore juniper (*J. conferta*, Zone 6), savin juniper (*J. sabina*, Zone 3), eastern red cedar (*J. virginiana*, Zone 2), and Chinese juniper (*J. chinensis*, Zone 3). Use junipers with striking foliage, such as the bright-blue *J. squamata* 'Blue Star' as specimen plants. Junipers thrive in full sun.

Chinese juniper

Lilac *(Syringa species)*

Lilacs, with their large clusters of sweetly fragrant flowers, are a traditional staple of the spring landscape and a background plant the rest of the year. Many cultivars of the common lilac (*S. vulgaris*, Zone 4) are available, offering violet, blue, magenta, purple, pink, white, or, of course, lilac-colored flowers in midspring. Plants form thickets of upright stems reaching 20 feet tall and wide; stems are clad in dark green deciduous leaves. Common lilacs flower only after receiving several weeks of cold temperatures. Gardeners in warm-winter climates can grow Descanso hybrids, which have no chilling requirement.

'Miss Kim' lilac

Several lilac species are smaller, more compact plants that suit small properties and mixed borders better than the rangy common lilac. Dwarf lilac (*S. meyeri* 'Palibin', Zone 4) reaches 6 to 8 feet tall and wide and produces fragrant lavender flowers in midspring and sometimes again in fall. Miss Kim lilac (*S. patula* 'Miss Kim', Zone 4) is about the same size and blooms in early summer with pale lavender-blue flowers. The foliage turns purple in fall. Both of these small lilacs resist mildew, which often infests common lilac.

Japanese tree lilac (*S. reticulata*, Zone 3) grows to 30 feet tall and is frequently trained as a single or multi-trunked tree. Its foot-long clusters of fragrant white flowers are a handsome accent in the early summer garden. Deciduous foliage and attractive bark provide interest at other times.

Lilacs grow well in full or partial sun. Prune them after flowering, removing spent flowers to encourage formation of new buds.

Rhododendron and Azalea *(Rhododendron species)*
These shrubs are among the loveliest and best-loved garden plants. Prized above all for their splendid and distinctive clustered flowers, they also provide handsome evergreen or deciduous foliage on attractively formed plants. There are rhododendrons or azaleas suitable for almost every area of North America.

Deciduous azaleas produce flowers in a breathtaking range of colors—reds, pinks, yellows, lavenders, oranges, whites, numerous bicolors—and their fall foliage is often colorful, too. Many bloom in mid- to late spring, some bloom into early summer, and some are fragrant. Plant size varies among the numerous cultivars; many grow 4 to 6 feet tall and are either upright or spreading. Most are hardy to Zone 5 or 6. Northern gardeners should look for Northern Lights hybrids; these were developed at the University of Minnesota and are hardy to Zone 3.

Evergreen azaleas showcase trusses of bright spring flowers against rich green foliage that is attractive year-round. Plants can be low-growing spreaders or bushes, neat and rounded or upright. Flowers are seldom fragrant but can be very large, up to 5 inches across. Some evergreen azaleas are quite tender, surviving only in Zones 8 or 9, but others are hardy to Zone 6 or 7.

Azalea

Rhododendrons come in just about any size and flower color you could possibly want. Plants less than a foot tall nestle comfortably in a rock garden, while giant rhododendrons up to 20 feet tall and wide are a commanding presence in the largest of landscapes. A vast selection suitable for foundation plantings, screens, or specimen plants are 3 to 8 feet tall and wide. Most rhododendrons bloom in midspring and are evergreen. Leaves are green but vary in hue as well as in shape. Take these characteristics into consideration since they're on view far longer than the flowers. Many rhododendrons are hardy to Zone 5 or 6, but hardier cultivars are available.

Rhododendrons and azaleas grow easily in the Northeast, Northwest, Mid-Atlantic, and Southern regions. Elsewhere they can be rather fussy. In general, they grow best in light shade, in constantly moist but well-drained and acid soil with abundant organic matter. Hot summers, cold winter temperatures, and drying winds can damage leaves and sometimes kill plants, as can a range of insects and diseases. That said, the popularity of rhododendrons and azaleas is attested to by the number of gardeners who go to great lengths to grow them in less-than-ideal conditions.

Where soil is insufficiently acid or poorly drained, for example, gardeners grow rhododendrons and azaleas in deep raised beds filled with a rich mix of pH-adjusted, organically amended soil. Where winters are cold and windy, they construct protective shelters. If conditions are too problematic to alter in the garden, you can grow rhododendrons and azaleas in containers.

If you're a beginner in a region where rhododendrons and azaleas are not common, the best course of action is to consult with an experienced rhodendron or azalea gardener in your area, or ask the local garden club. They'll know which species, cultivars, and cultural practices have proven themselves in local conditions.

Spirea *(Spiraea species)*
Spring-blooming spireas, with long arching branches covered in tiny white flowers, are a long-time favorite. The most commonly planted spring-blooming spirea, *S.* 3 *vanhouttei* (Zone 4), grows 6 to 8 feet tall and wide and makes a formidable specimen or screen. During the summer, its deciduous leaves are a lovely, light blue-green color. *S. nipponica* 'Snowmound' (Zone 4) grows 2 to 4 feet tall and wide and has pure white flowers in late spring and early summer.

Gardeners with limited space and those who want a more dramatic plant can choose from a number of compact forms that offer flowers in summer and colorful leaves through the growing season. Japanese spirea (*S. japonica*, Zone 3) and the related S. × *bumalda cultivars* (Zone 3) grow up to 3 feet high and wide. The tidy, twiggy mounds are covered with clusters of tiny flowers in red, pink, or white for several weeks in summer; foliage is often attractive as well. 'Anthony Waterer' has rich pink-red flowers and pink-tinged green foliage. 'Goldflame' has deep pink flowers and golden leaves that are tinged in spring and fall with red and copper.

Spireas grow well in full or partial sun. They tolerate many soil types but do require good drainage.

Viburnum *(Viburnum species)*
Grown for their flowers, their foliage, and their berries, viburnums are excellent landscape and garden plants that can be evergreen or deciduous. All viburnums prefer full or partial sun.

Spirea

Korean spice viburnum (*V. carlesii*, Zone 4) produces rounded clusters of very fragrant flowers in midspring, preceded by pretty pink buds. Plants grow to 5 feet tall and wide. The dull green, deciduous foliage may turn red in fall. *Viburnum* 3 *burkwoodii* (Zone 5) grows to 12 feet tall and also has fragrant flowers in spring. Double-file viburnum (*V. plicatum* var. *tomentosum*, Zone 6) is a large shrub with tiers of branches and deciduous leaves that are green in sum-mer and red-purple in fall. Flat clusters of striking white flowers appear to float above the foliage in midspring. Bright red fruits follow, as do birds to feast on them.

European cranberry bush (*V. opulus*, Zone 3) features white flowers in May, red berries in fall and winter, and colorful fall foliage. This large species grows up to 12 to 15 feet tall and wide, but 'Compactum' is about half that size and 'Nanum' is tiny—just 2 feet tall and wide. Arrowwood viburnum (*V. dentatum*, Zone 3) stems were once harvested for arrow shafts. Today, gardeners are more likely to appreciate the patch of straight stems that can make an accent in an informal planting. Glossy, green deciduous leaves turn shades of red, purple, or orange in fall. Early summer's creamy white flowers produce blue berries that are much sought after by birds.

Evergreen viburnums include leatherleaf viburnum (*V. rhytidophyllum*, Zone 6), an upright shrub with shiny green leaves that drop in midwinter in colder areas. Large flat clusters of white flowers bloom in midspring, and the red berries darken to black. Laurustinus (*V. tinus*, Zone 7) is an erect shrub that can be pruned to form a hedge; its pink buds and clusters of slightly fragrant white flowers appear in late winter and early spring, followed by blue berries in summer. *V. davidii* (Zone 7) is a small shrub (3 feet tall and wide) with dark green leaves that show off scentless white flowers and pretty blue berries.

Viburnum × burkwoodii

APPENDIX

Seasonal Blooming Schedules

Spring tulips

The following blooming schedules provide a general guide to plants that bloom in each season. Remember that blooming times vary with location, microclimate in the garden, and yearly weather conditions. These lists focus primarily on outdoor plants in spring and summer. You'll find more houseplants in autumn and winter sections.

For each plant, you will find information in the following order: scientific name, common name, flower color, season of bloom, plant height, and type of plant. The categorization of plant types is rather broad. In particular, the term bulb is used for true bulbs and also bulblike structures such as corms, tubers, and tuberous roots. In the plant descriptions, "cold climates" generally refers to Zone 5 and colder zones; "tender" means killed by frost and therefore not hardy north of Zone 9. Page numbers following entries refer you to plant text profiles.

Geographical Note. These schedules are tailored loosely to gardens near 40 degrees north latitude. (That latitude is roughly a line running east to west from Philadelphia through Indianapolis, Denver, and Reno.) If you live south of that line, your plants will bloom at the beginning of the given range (or even a bit earlier in very warm climates). The farther north you live (or the higher your altitude), the later your plants will bloom. You may find that plants in your garden will bloom a bit earlier or later, even if you live near 40 degrees north latitude.

Spring

Early Spring Blooming

Abeliophyllum
A. distichum, Korean or white forsythia; white, fragrant flowers; late winter or early to midspring; 60 to 84 inches; shrub.

Adonis
A. amurensis, amur adonis; yellow; late winter to midspring; to 12 inches; perennial.

Anemone *pg. 78*
A. blanda, Grecian windflower; pink, blue, white; early to midspring; 6 to 8 inches; bulb.

Arabis
A. caucasica, wall rock cress; white; early spring; 6 to 12 inches; perennial. 'Flore Pleno' has double flowers; a single- flowered form is 'Snowcap.'

Aubrieta
A. deltoidea (A. × cultorum), purple rock cress; soft pink to deep purple, rarely white; early spring; 2 to 6 inches; perennial.

Aurinia *pg. 79*
Aurinia saxatilis (Alyssum saxatile), basket-of-gold; yellow; early spring; to 12 inches; perennial.

Chaenomeles
C. japonica, dwarf Japanese quince; orange to red; early to midspring; 36 inches; shrub. White cultivar available.
C. speciosa (C. lagenaria), Japanese quince; scarlet, red, pink, white; early to midspring; 48 to 72 inches; shrub.

Chionodoxa *pg. 214*
C. luciliae, glory-of-the-snow; blue with white center; late winter to early spring; 3 to 6 inches; bulb. Pink and white cultivars available.
C. sardensis, glory-of-the-snow; rich blue; 3 to 6 inches; late winter to early spring; bulb.

Clivia *pg. 215*
C. miniata, kaffir lily; orange-scarlet with yellow center; early spring (when grown outdoors in mild climates); 18 to 24 inches; tender bulb. Yellow cultivars are available.

Cornus
C. mas, Cornelian cherry; yellow; late winter to early spring; to 15 feet; shrub or small tree.

Crocus, *pg. 80, 176, 215*
C. vernus, common crocus; purple, white striped with purple; early spring; 3 to 4 inches; bulb.
***C.* Dutch hybrid crocuses**; purple, lilac, golden yellow, white, white striped with purple; early spring; 4 to 6 inches; bulb.

Daphne
D. mezereum, February daphne, mezereon; rosy purple to lilac-purple, fragrant; late winter to early spring; 18 to 36 inches; shrub. White cultivars available. ***D. odora***, winter daphne; rose to rosy purple, rarely white; late winter to midspring; 36 to 60 inches; shrub. Not hardy in cold climates.

Epimedium
E. × versicolor, Persian epimedium; pale yellow petals with rose center; early to midspring; to 12 inches; perennial ground cover.
E. × warleyense; pale orange with yellow center; early to midspring; 9 to 12 inches; perennial ground cover.

Erica
E. carnea, spring heath, winter heath; pink, white, red-violet; midwinter to early spring; to 12 inches; shrub.

Erythronium
E. californicum, fawn lily; creamy white; early spring; to 12 inches; bulb.
E. grandiflorum, avalanche lily; yellow; early spring; 12 to 24 inches; bulb.
E. montanum, alpine fawn lily; white with gold center; early spring; to 12 inches; bulb.
E. revolutum, coast fawn lily; cream flushed with lavender-pink; early spring; to 16 inches; bulb.
E. tuolumnense; buff yellow; early spring; to 12 inches; bulb.

Forsythia
F. × *intermedia*, border forsythia; yellow; early to midspring; 6 to 8 feet; shrub.
F. ovata, Korean forsythia; yellow; early to midspring; 60 inches; shrub.
F. suspensa, weeping forsythia; yellow; early to midspring; to 12 feet; shrub.

Fritillaria
F. meleagris, checkered lily, guinea-hen flower; white, pink checked with purple; early to midspring; 12 to 18 inches; bulb.
F. pudica, yellow fritillary; yellow, fragrant; early to midspring; to 9 inches; bulb.

Helleborus
H. orientalis, Lenten rose; greenish white to rose-purple; early to midspring; to 18 inches; perennial.

Ipheion
I. uniflorum, spring starflower; pale blue; early spring; to 8 inches; bulb. White and deeper blue cultivars available.

Iris *pg. 84–85, 188*
I. danfordiae; yellow; late winter to early spring; 4 to 6 inches; bulb.
I. reticulata; deep violet or blue; late winter to early spring; 6 to 12 inches; bulb. Pale blue cultivar available.
I. unguicularis, Algerian iris; lavender-blue; late winter to early spring; 12 to 24 inches; bulb. White and deeper violet cultivars available.

Lachenalia
L. aloides, cape cowslip; red and yellow; late winter to early spring; to 12 inches; tender bulb.

Leucojum
L. vernum, spring snowflake; white; early spring; 12 inches; bulb.

Lobularia
L. maritima, sweet alyssum; white, purple, pink; early spring to fall; 4 to 6 inches, sometimes to 12 inches; annual.

Lonicera
L. fragrantissima, winter honeysuckle; creamy white; fragrant; winter to early spring; 6 to 10 feet; shrub.

Magnolia
M. stellata, star magnolia; white, fragrant; early spring; to 15 feet; shrub. Pink cultivars available.

Mertensia
M. virginica, Virginia bluebells; lavender to blue; early to midspring; to 24 inches; perennial.

Muscari
M. armeniacum, grape hyacinth; deep blue-violet; early to midspring; to 12 inches; bulb.
M. azureum, grape hyacinth; azure blue; early to midspring; to 8 inches; bulb.
M. botryoides, common grape hyacinth; blue or white; early to midspring; to 12 inches.

Narcissus *pg. 86–87*
N. **cultivars**, daffodils and narcissus; shades of yellow, apricot, orange, cream, white, bicolors; early to midspring; 6 to 20 inches, depending on type; bulb.
N. cyclamineus; yellow; early spring; 6 inches; bulb.

Ornithogalum
O. nutans, star-of-Bethlehem; greenish white, fragrant; early to midspring; 8 to 12 inches; bulb.
O. umbellatum, star-of-Bethlehem; white; early to midspring; to 12 inches; bulb.

Pieris
P. floribunda, mountain andromeda; white; early to midspring; 36 to 48 inches; shrub.

Primula *pg. 89*
P. denticulata, drumstick primrose, Himalayan primrose; lilac, violet, white; early to midspring; to 10 inches; perennial.
P. polyanthus **hybrids**, primrose; red, rose, pink, blue, violet, yellow, white, with yellow eye; early spring; 6 to 8 inches; perennial.

Pulmonaria
P. angustifolia, blue lungwort; blue-violet; early to late spring; 6 to 12 inches; perennial.

Puschkinia
P. scilloides, striped squill; white to light blue with blue stripes; early to midspring; to 6 inches; bulb.
P. scilloides **var.** *libanotica*, blue puschkinia; light blue with darker blue stripes; early to midspring; 4 to 6 inches; bulb.

Rhododendron
R. calophytum, bigleaf rhododendron; white, pink, rose; early to midspring; to 36 feet; shrub. Not hardy in cold climates.
R. mucronulatum; rosy purple, pink; early to midspring; 72 inches; shrub.

Rosmarinus
R. officinalis, rosemary; light blue; early to midspring; to 72 inches in warm climates; shrub. Not hardy in cold climates. Pink, white, and darker blue cultivars available.

Salix
S. discolor, pussy willow; silvery catkins; early spring; 10 to 20 feet; shrub to small tree.

Scilla
S. siberica, Siberian squill; deep blue; late winter to midspring; 6 inches; bulb. White cultivar available.

Tulipa *pg. 89–91,189*
T. clusiana, lady tulip; rose red with white stripes; early to midspring; 8 inches; bulb. Red-and-yellow varieties available.
T. fosteriana, Fosteriana hybrid tulips; red, scarlet, orange, rose, white; early to midspring; 12 to 18 inches; bulb.
T. kaufmanniana, waterlily hybrid tulips; red, scarlet, salmon, rose, yellow, cream, bicolors; early to midspring; 6 to 10 inches; bulb.

'Ballerina' tulip

Veltheimia
V. bracteata, forest lily; pinkish purple; early spring; to 24 inches; tender bulb.

Vinca
V. minor, myrtle, periwinkle; light blue to pale violet; 4 to 8 inches; prostrate; early spring to summer; perennial ground cover. Darker and white varieties available.

Viola *pg. 91*
V. × wittrockiana, pansy; red, rose, pink, lavender, blue, purple, orange, yellow, white, bicolors; early spring until weather turns hot; 6 to 10 inches; annual.

Zephyranthes
Z. atamasco, atamasco lily; white; early spring; to 12 inches; tender bulb.

Midspring Blooming

Actaea
A. rubra, red baneberry; white; mid- to late spring (red berries in late summer to fall); 18 to 24 inches; perennial.

Alchemilla
A. mollis (A. vulgaris), lady's mantle; greenish yellow; midspring to early summer; 10 to 15 inches; perennial.

Allium
A. neapolitanum, daffodil garlic; white, fragrant; mid- to late spring; to 18 inches; bulb. Not hardy in cold climates.

Anemone *pg. 78, 172*
A. apennina, Apennine anemone; sky blue; midspring; 9 inches; perennial. Not hardy in cold climates.
A. coronaria, poppy anemone, florist's anemone; red, pink, blue-violet, white; midspring; 18 inches; bulb. Hardy only in warm climates.

Aquilegia
***A. flabellata* 'Nana Alba'**, Japanese fan columbine; white; mid- to late spring; 10 to 12 inches; perennial.

Arabis
***A.* 'Rosabella'**, wall rock cress; rose pink; mid- to late spring; 5 inches; perennial.

Armeria
A. maritima, thrift, sea pink; rosy pink; midspring to early summer; 6 inches; perennial.

Arctotheca
A. calendula, cape weed; yellow; midspring; to 12 inches; tender perennial.

Bergenia
B. cordifolia, heartleaf bergenia; light pink to rose; early to midspring; 12 to 18 inches; perennial.

Brunnera *pg. 79*
B. macrophylla (Anchusa myosotidiflora), Siberian bugloss; sky blue; midspring to early summer; 12 to 18 inches; perennial.

Caltha
C. palustris, marsh marigold; golden yellow; midspring; 12 to 24 inches; perennial. Needs wet soil.

Convallaria *pg. 186*
C. majalis, lily-of-the-valley; white, fragrant; mid- to late spring; 6 to 12 inches; bulb. Pink cultivar available.

Marsh marigold

Lily-of-the-valley

Dicentra *pg. 80–81*
D. cucullaria, Dutchman's breeches; white; midspring; 10 to 12 inches; perennial.
D. eximia, fringed bleeding heart; deep pink to red; midspring to midsummer, sporadically to early fall; 12 to 18 inches; perennial. White cultivars available.
D. spectabilis, bleeding heart; pink; midspring to early summer; 12 to 24 inches; perennial. White variety available.

Disporum
D. sessile, Japanese fairy bells; white; midspring; 18 to 24 inches; perennial.

Doronicum
D. orientale (D. cordatum, D. caucasicum), leopard's bane; yellow; midspring to late spring; 12 to 24 inches; perennial.

Draba
D. sibirica, Siberian draba; yellow; midspring; 2 inches; perennial.

Epimedium
E. grandiflorum, longspur epimedium; dusty rose with white spurs; mid- to late spring; 6 to 12 inches; perennial ground cover.
E. × rubrum, red epimedium; crimson with light pink center; midspring; to 12 inches; perennial ground cover.
E. × youngianum, snowy epimedium; white; mid- to late spring; 8 to 10 inches; perennial ground cover.

Erythronium
E. dens-canis, dog-tooth violet; rose to purple, rarely white; mid- to late spring; 6 inches; bulb.
***E.* 'Pagoda'**, hybrid trout lily; golden yellow; midspring; 10 to 12 inches; bulb. Pink and white hybrids also available.

Euphorbia
E. characias* subspecies *wulfenii; yellow-green; midspring; to 48 inches; perennial. ***E. myrsinites***, myrtle spurge; yellow-green; midspring; to 6 inches; perennial.
E. polychroma (E. epithymoides), cushion spurge; yellow; midspring; to 12 inches; perennial.

Fothergilla
F. gardenii, dwarf fothergilla; white; mid- to late spring; 36 inches; shrub. Nice autumn foliage.
F. major (F. monticola), large fothergilla; white; mid- to late spring; to 9 feet; shrub. Colorful autumn foliage.

Fritillaria
F. imperialis, crown imperial; orange-red, yellow; mid- to late spring; 36 inches; bulb.

Galium
G. odoratum (Asperula odorata), sweet woodruff; white; mid- to late spring; to 12 inches; perennial groundcover.

Geranium *pg. 82*
G. dalmaticum, Dalmatian cranesbill; pink; midspring to early summer; 6 inches; perennial.
G. himalayense, lilac cranesbill; violet-blue; mid- to late spring; 8 to 15 inches; perennial.

G. maculatum, spotted cranesbill; lilac-pink; midspring to early summer; 12 to 20 inches; perennial.

Geum
G. **'Borisii'**; scarlet-orange; mid- to late spring; 8 inches; perennial.
G. chiloense (G. quellyon) **'Mrs. Bradshaw'**; bright red; midspring to early summer; to 24 inches; perennial.
G. **'Georgenburg'**; yellow-orange; mid- to late spring; 8 inches; perennial.
G. reptans; yellow; midspring to early summer; 6 to 8 inches; perennial.

Hesperocallis
H. undulata, desert lily; white, fragrant; midspring; to 12 inches; tender bulb.
× Heucherella
× *H. tiarelloides*; pink; midspring to early summer; to 18 inches; perennial.

Hyacinthoides
H. hispanica (Endymion hispanicus, Scilla campanulata), Spanish bluebells; pastel pink, blue, white; midspring to early summer; to 18 inches; bulb.

Hyacinthus *pg. 83, 187–188*
H. orientalis **hybrids**, garden hyacinth; red, pink, purple, blue, yellow, white, fragrant; midspring; to 12 inches; bulb. Not hardy in very cold climates.

Iberis
I. saxatilis, rock candytuft; white; mid- to late spring; 6 inches; perennial.
I. sempervirens, perennial candytuft; white; mid- to late spring; to 12 inches; perennial.

Iris *pg. 84–85, 188*
I. cristata, crested iris; purple; midspring; 4 to 6 inches; perennial. White form available.
I. japonica, fringed iris; lilac; midspring; to 18 inches; tender perennial (not hardy north of Zone 8).
I. pumila, dwarf bearded iris; shades of violet, blue, yellow, pink, red, white; mid- to late spring; 4 to 8 inches; perennial.

Jasminum *pg. 219*
J. nudiflorum, winter jasmine; yellow, fragrant; to 10 feet; vine or shrub. Blooms in spring in cooler climates.

Lathyrus
L. latifolius, perennial pea; rose, pink, white; midspring to summer; to 10 feet; perennial vine.

Lilium *pg. 188*
L. longiflorum, Easter lily; white, fragrant; midspring to midsummer; tender bulb. Usually grows outside only in warm climates, though a hardy cultivar, 'Mount Everest', is also available.

Myosotis *pg. 85*
M. sylvatica, annual forget-me-not; blue; late spring to midsummer; 6 to 9 inches; annual or biennial, self-sows. Pink, and white cultivars available.

Narcissus *pg. 86-87*
N. **hybrids**, daffodils and narcissus; yellow, cream, white, bicolors; late varieties bloom in midspring; 6 to 20 inches; bulb.

Omphalodes
O. cappadocica, navelwort; blue with white center; midspring; 6 to 10 inches; perennial. Not hardy in cold climates.
O. verna, creeping forget-me-not; blue; midspring; to 8 inches; perennial. Not hardy in cold climates.

Paeonia *pg. 87*
P. suffruticosa, Japanese tree peony; rose-red; midspring to early summer; 48 to 84 inches; shrubby perennial. Cultivars come in white, yellow, pink, lavender, violet.
P. tenuifolia, fernleaf peony; red; midspring to early summer; to 24 inches; perennial.

Phlox *pg. 88–89*
P. divaricata, wild sweet William; lavender-blue, also a white form; early to midspring; to 18 inches; perennial.
P. stolonifera, creeping phlox; purple, blue, pink, white; mid- to late spring; 6 to 8 inches; perennial.

Phlox: *Moss pink 'Candy Stripe'*

P. subulata, moss pink; pink, rose, lilac, white; mid- to late spring; to 6 inches; perennial.

Pieris
P. japonica, Japanese andromeda; white; midspring; to 9 feet; shrub. Pink cultivars available.

Polemonium
P. caeruleum, Jacob's ladder; violet-blue, rarely white; midspring; 18 to 24 inches; perennial.
P. reptans, creeping polemonium; light blue; midspring; 8 to 12 inches; perennial.

Polygonatum
P. biflorum, small Solomon's seal; white; mid- to late spring; 24 to 36 inches; perennial.
P. odoratum, fragrant Solomon's seal; white, fragrant; mid- to late spring; to 42 inches; perennial.

Primula *pg. 89*
P. auricula, auricula primrose; yellow; many colors; mid- to late spring; 8 inches; perennial. Cultivars available in many colors.
P. × pruhoniciana, juliana hybrid primrose; red, rose, white; mid- to late spring; 5 inches; perennial.
P. veris, cowslip; orangy yellow, fragrant; mid- to late spring; 6 to 8 inches; perennial.

Pulmonaria
P. officinalis, common lungwort; pink, turning blue; mid- to late spring; 12 inches; perennial. White cultivars available.
P. saccharata, Bethlehem sage; reddish violet, blue, pink, white; mid- to late spring; 8 to 14 inches; perennial.

Pulsatilla
P. vulgaris **(formerly** ***Anemone pulsatilla)***, pasqueflower; lavender to purple, also red-and-white forms; early to midspring; 8 to 12 inches; perennial.

Ranunculus
R. asiaticus, Persian buttercup; red, pink, white, orange, yellow; mid- to late spring; 6 to 18 inches; bulb. Not hardy in cold climates.

Rhododendron
***R.* Kurume hybrid azaleas**; carmine, red, rose, salmon, orange-red, red-violet; mid- to late spring; 36 inches; shrub. Not hardy in cold climates.
***R.* 'PJM' hybrid rhododendron**; lavender-pink; midspring; to 48 inches; shrub.
R. yedoense, Yodogawa azalea; purple, pink; mid- to late spring; 60 inches; shrub.

Rosa
R. laevigata, Cherokee rose; white, fragrant; midspring; to 15 feet; climbing shrub. Grown in warm climates.

Saxifraga
S. stolonifera, strawberry geranium; white; midspring to summer; to 24 inches; perennial.
S.* × *urbium, London pride saxifrage; light pink; midspring; to 12 inches; perennial.

Shortia
S. galacifolia, oconee bells; white; midspring; 8 inches; perennial.

Smilacina
S. racemosa, false Solomon's seal; white; mid- to late spring; to 36 inches; perennial.

Trillium
T. grandiflorum, snow trillium; white; mid- to late spring; 12 to 15 inches; perennial.

Trollius
T.* × *cultorum, hybrid globeflower; orange, yellow; midspring to early summer; 24 to 36 inches; perennial. ***T. europaeus***, common globeflower; golden yellow; mid- to late spring; to 24 inches; perennial.

Tulipa *pg. 89–91, 189*
***T.* Darwin hybrid tulips**; red, rose, pink, yellow; midspring; 24 to 30 inches; bulb.
***T.* Double late hybrid tulips**; red, carmine, wine red, pink, yellow, white; mid- to late spring; 10 to 20 inches; bulb.
***T. gregii*, Gregii hybrid tulips**; red, rose, salmon, pink, bicolors; midspring; 8 to 14 inches; bulb.
***T.* Lily-flowered hybrid tulips**; ruby red, reddish purple, rose, pink, purple, yellow, white; mid- to late spring; 20 to 22 inches; bulb.
***T.* Triumph hybrid tulips**; red, deep red, scarlet, rose, pink, purple, yellow, white; midspring; 12 to 20 inches; bulb.

Viburnum
V.* × *burkwoodii, Burkwood viburnum; white, rarely pink, fragrant; midspring; to 8 feet; shrub.
V. carlesii, Korean spice viburnum; pinkish white, fragrant; midspring; 60 inches; shrub.
V. farreri (V. fragrans), fragrant viburnum; white, fragrant; midspring; 9 feet; shrub. Not hardy in cold climates.
V.* × *juddii, Judd viburnum; white, fragrant; midspring; 8 feet; shrub.

Viola *pg. 91*
***V. cornuta* cultivars**, viola, horned violet, tufted pansy; purple, yellow, apricot; midspring to summer, often rebloom in autumn; 5 to 8 inches; perennial. Grown as annual in very cold climates.

Viola: *Johnny-jump-up*

V. tricolor, Johnny-jump-up; purple, blue, yellow; midspring to summer in the North, winter in the South; 8 to 12 inches; perennial often grown as annual.

Late Spring Blooming

Acanthus
A. mollis, bear's breech; white, lilac, rose; late spring to early summer; 24 to 48 inches; perennial. Not hardy in cold climates.

Amberboa
A. moschata (Centaurea moschata), sweet sultan; red, pink, purple, yellow, white, fragrant; late spring to midsummer; 18 to 24 inches; annual.

Amsonia
A. tabernaemontana, blue star; bluish white; late spring; to 24 inches; perennial.

Anemone *pg. 78*
A. sylvestris, snowdrop windflower; white with light yellow center; late spring; to 18 inches; perennial.

Aquilegia *pg. 78*
***A.* Biedermeier strain**; mixed colors: red, pink, blue; late spring to early summer; to 18 inches; perennial.
A. caerulea, Rocky Mountain columbine; white petals with blue-violet spurs; late spring; to 24 inches; perennial.
A. canadensis, American columbine; red-and-yellow; late spring; 12 to 24 inches; perennial.
A. chrysantha; golden yellow; late spring to early summer; 24 to 30 inches; perennial. Hybrid 'Silver Queen' has white flowers.
***A.* Dragonfly hybrids**; mixed colors; late spring to early summer; 18 to 24 inches; perennial.
***A.* Langdon's Rainbow hybrids**; mixed bright colors; late spring to early summer; to 30 inches; perennial.
***A. longissima* 'Maxistar'**; yellow; late spring to early summer; 24 to 30 inches; perennial.

Astrantia
A. 'Margery Fish'; shades of pink and white; late spring to midsummer; 24 to 30 inches; perennial.

Baptisia
B. australis, blue false indigo; blue; late spring to early summer; 36 to 60 inches; perennial.

Campanula *pg. 139*
C. carpatica, Carpathian harebell; blue, white; late spring to midsummer; 6 to 12 inches; perennial.
C. garganica; purple; late spring to fall; to 6 inches; perennial.
C. medium, Canterbury bells; blue, pink, white; late spring to midsummer; 24 to 48 inches; biennial but treat as annual.
C. portenschlagiana, Dalmatian bellflower; deep purple; late spring to summer; 6 to 8 inches; perennial.

Catharanthus
C. roseus, Madagascar periwinkle; rose, pink, white; late spring to fall; 12 to 24 inches; tender perennial. Grown as annual in cold climates.

Centaurea
C. cyanus, bachelor's button, cornflower; blue, pink, white; late spring to midsummer; 12 to 24 inches; annual. Often reblooms if cut back after first bloom is over.

Cerastium
C. tomentosum, snow-in-summer; white; late spring to early summer; to 6 inches; perennial.

Chrysogonum
C. virginianum, golden star, green-and-gold; golden yellow; late spring to summer; 4 to 10 inches; perennial.

Clarkia
C. amoena, farewell-to-spring; red, pink, lavender, white, bicolors; late spring to late summer; 18 to 30 inches; annual.

Clematis
C. **'Duchess of Edinburgh'**; white, double; late spring to early summer and again in early autumn; to 9 feet; perennial vine.
C. montana; white; late spring to early summer; to 18 feet; perennial vine. Cultivar 'Tetra Rose' has deep pink flowers.
C. **'Nelly Moser'**; pink with deep rose stripe down center of each petal; late spring to early summer and again in early autumn; to 12 feet; perennial vine.
Other hybrid clematises bloom in shades of purple, pink, and white in late spring to early summer.

Cytisus
C. decumbens, prostrate broom; yellow; late spring and early summer; to 12 inches; shrub.
C. × praecox, Warminster broom; creamy yellow; late spring; to 60 inches; shrub. Gold, pink, and white cultivars available.

Daphne
***D. × burkwoodii* 'Somerset'**; white flushed with pink, fragrant; late spring to early summer; to 36 inches; shrub.

Dianthus *pg. 80*
D. × allwoodii, Allwood hybrids; red, rose, pink, white, bicolors, fragrant; late spring to summer; 4 to 12 inches; perennial.
D. barbatus, sweet William; red, pink, rosy purple, white, bicolors; late spring to early summer; 12 to 24 inches; biennial.
D. deltoides, maiden pink; red, rose, pink; late spring; 4 to 12 inches; perennial.
D. gratianopolitanus, cheddar pink; pink, fragrant; late spring to early summer; 6 to 8 inches; perennial.
D. plumarius, cottage pink, grass pink; light pink with red band around center; late spring to early summer; 9 to 18 inches; perennial. Cultivars available in several colors and bicolors.

Dodecatheon
D. meadia, common shooting star; rosy purple with white base, pink, or white; late spring; 12 to 24 inches; perennial.

Geranium
G. endressii; pink; late spring to midsummer; 18 to 24 inches; perennial.
G. **'Johnson's Blue'**, Johnson's blue cranesbill; blue-violet; late spring to early summer; to 24 inches; perennial.
G. macrorrhizum, bigroot cranesbill; pink; late spring to early summer; to 18 inches; perennial. White cultivar available.
G. sanguineum, bloody cranesbill, blood-red cranesbill; clear pink to violet; late spring to midsummer; 12 to 18 inches; perennial.

Hemerocallis
H. lilio-asphodelus (H. flava), lemon daylily; yellow, fragrant; late spring; to 36 inches; perennial.

Hesperis
H. matronalis, dame's rocket; purple, lilac-purple, mauve, white; late spring to midsummer; 24 to 36 in.; perennial.

Heuchera *pg. 83*
H. sanguinea, coral bells; deep red to pink; late spring to midsummer; 12 to 18 inches; perennial. White and coral pink cultivars available.

Incarvillea
I. delavayi, hardy gloxinia; deep pink with yellow throat; late spring to early summer; 12 to 18 inches; perennial.

Iris *pg. 84–85, 188*
I. **Bearded iris hybrids**; red, reddish brown, pink, rose, red-violet, purple, violet, blue, yellow, yellow-orange, bronze, peach, white, bicolors; late spring to early summer; 10 inches to 48 inches; perennial.
I. **Louisiana iris hybrids**; blue, red, yellow, white, veined and flushed with yellow; late spring to early summer; 36 to 48 inches.
I. **Pacific Coast irises**; pale purple, lavender, blue, white, pink, copper, with attractive veining and flushes of deeper blue or violet; late spring; to 24 inches or more; perennial. Most are difficult to grow in other parts of the country.
I. pseudacorus, yellow flag; yellow; late spring to midsummer; to 60 inches; perennial. Needs moist, marshy soil.
I. tectorum, roof iris; purple, white; late spring to early summer; 8 to 12 inches; perennial.

Lathyrus
L. odoratus, sweet pea; red, rose, pink, red-violet, violet, blue, yellow, white; late spring to early summer in temperate climates; 24 to 60 inches; annual vine.

Leucojum
L. aestivum, summer snowflake, giant snowflake; white; late spring to early summer; 12 to 18 inches; bulb.

Lilium
L. hansonii, Japanese turk's-cap lily; orange-yellow with red spots, fragrant; late spring to early summer; 48 to 60 inches; bulb.
L. pyrenaicum, yellow turk's cap lily; yellow; orange; late spring; 36 to 48 inches; bulb.

Linaria
L. genistifolia, toadflax; lemon yellow; late spring through midsummer; 30 inches; perennial.

Lonicera
L. caprifolium, Italian honeysuckle; creamy white, fragrant; late spring to early summer; to 20 feet; perennial vine.
L. flava, yellow honeysuckle; orange-yellow, fragrant; late spring to early summer; to 10 feet; perennial vine.
L. korolkowii; pale rose; late spring to early summer; 8 to 12 feet; shrub.
L. sempervirens, trumpet honeysuckle; scarlet-orange; late spring to late summer; to 12 feet; perennial vine. Yellow form available.

Lupinus
L. polyphyllus **cultivars**, perennial lupine; yellow, white, blue; late spring to early summer; 24 to 60 inches; perennial.
L. **Russell hybrids**; red, rose, pink, yellow, lavender, purple, blue, white, bicolors; late spring to early summer; 24 to 36 inches; perennial.

Lychnis
L. viscaria, German catch-fly; rosy red; late spring to midsummer; 12 to 18 inches; perennial. White cultivars available.

Lysimachia
L. punctata, yellow loosestrife; yellow; late spring to early summer; 24 to 36 inches; perennial.

Meconopsis
M. cambrica, Welsh poppy; bright yellow; late spring to early summer; to 24 inches; perennial. Orange variety available.

Myosotis
M. scorpioides, true forget-me-not; true blue to lavender-blue; late spring to midsummer; 12 to 18 inches; perennial.

Nemesia
N. strumosa; red, pink, blue, purple, yellow, white, bicolors; late spring to midsummer; 8 to 18 inches; annual.

Nigella
N. damascena, love-in-a-mist; blue, white; late spring to late summer; 12 to 15 inches; annual. Pink cultivars available.

Paeonia
P. lactiflora, Chinese peony; crimson, red, pink, white; late spring to early summer; 24 to 36 inches; perennial.
P. officinalis cultivars, common peony; red, rose-red, rose, pink, white; late spring to early summer; to 36 inches; perennial.

Papaver
P. nudicaule, Iceland poppy; red, orange, salmon, yellow, cream, white; late spring to early summer; 1 to 36 inches; perennial, often grown as an annual. (Blooms late winter to early spring in warm climates.)
P. orientale, Oriental poppy; red, orange, salmon, pink, with dark center; late spring to early summer; 12 to 48 inches; perennial.

Oriental poppy

Philadelphus
P. coronarius, common mock orange; creamy white, fragrant; late spring; to 10 feet; shrub.

Potentilla
P. × *tonguei*, staghorn cinquefoil; apricot-yellow; late spring to early summer; 8 to 12 inches; perennial.

Primula *pg. 89*
P. japonica, Japanese primrose; rose, purple, white; late spring to early summer; 12 to 24 inches; perennial.
P. sieboldii, Japanese star primrose; rose, magenta, lavender, periwinkle, white; late spring; to 12 inches; perennial.

Ranunculus
R. repens **'Pleniflorus' ('Flore Pleno')**; double creeping buttercup; yellow; late spring to early summer; 12 to 24 inches; perennial.

Rhododendron
R. carolinianum, Carolina rhododendron; rosy purple; late spring; 72 inches; shrub.
R. catawbiense **hybrids**, catawba rhododendron; red, pink, rose, lilac, purple, violet, white; late spring; 72 inches or more; shrub.
R. fortunei **hybrids**, fortune rhododendron; carmine, red, rosy lilac, pink, mauve, rose, fragrant; late spring; 12 feet; shrub. Not hardy in cold climates.
R. **Ghent hybrid azaleas**; carmine, scarlet, red-orange, pink, orange, yellow-orange, bronze, yellow, white; late spring; 6 to 10 feet; shrub.
R. **Indian hybrid azaleas**; red, rose, pink, salmon, white; late spring; 24 to 72 inches; shrub. Grown outdoors in warm climates; indoors in cold climates.

'Guy Yerkes' rhododendron

R. **Kaempferi hybrid azaleas**; red, red-violet, magenta, rose, pink; late spring; 6 to 10 feet; shrub. Not hardy in cold climates.
R. **Knap Hill-Exbury hybrid azaleas**; red, red-orange, rose-pink, pink, orange, apricot, orange-yellow, yellow, white; late spring; 84 inches; shrub.
R. **Mollis hybrid azaleas**; shades of red, rose, pink, ivory, white; late spring; 60 inches; shrub.
R. vaseyi, pinkshell azalea; light rose; late spring; 6 to 9 feet; shrub. Very hardy.
R. yunnanense, Yunnan rhododendron; lavender, pink, white; late spring; 10 feet; shrub. Not hardy in cold climates.

Saponaria
S. ocymoides, rock soapwort; pink, red, white; late spring to early summer; 6 to 12 inches; perennial.

Stylophorum
S. diphyllum, celandine poppy; yellow; late spring; to 18 inches; perennial.

Syringa
S. vulgaris, common lilac; purple, lilac, white, pink, fragrant; late spring; to 20 feet; shrub.

Thalictrum
T. aquilegiifolium, columbine meadowrue; deep purple; lavender, light pink, orange, white; late spring to early summer; 24 to 36 inches; perennial.

Thermopsis
T. villosa (T. caroliniana), Carolina thermopsis, false lupine; yellow; late spring to early summer; to 48 inches; perennial.

Tradescantia
T.* Andersoniana Group *(T. × andersoniana), common spiderwort hybrids; pink with rosy red center, blue, white, pink, purple; late spring to early summer; 24 to 30 inches; perennial.

Trollius
T. × cultorum, hybrid globeflower; yellow, orange; late spring to early summer; 24 to 36 inches; perennial.

Tulipa *pg. 89–91, 189*
***T.* Fringed hybrid tulips**; red, violet, yellow, white, with fringed petals; late spring; 18 to 24 inches; bulb.
***T.* Parrot hybrid tulips**; red, rose, pink, salmon, purple, yellow, white, often flamed or striped with contrasting color, and with fringed petals; late spring; 20 inches; bulb.
***T.* Single late hybrid tulips (cottage and old Darwin hybrids)**; shades of red, rose, pink, purple, violet, yellow, white; late spring; 18 to 30 inches; bulb.
***T. viridiflora* hybrid tulips**; rose, pink, yellow, white, with green stripes or markings; late spring; 16 to 22 inches; bulb.

Valeriana
V. officinalis, common valerian; pink, pale lavender, white; late spring to early summer; 24 to 48 inches; perennial.

Veronica
***V. austriaca* subspecies *teucrium* (*V. teucrium, V. latifolium*)**, germander speedwell, rock speedwell; deep blue, white; late spring to midsummer; 12 to 18 inches; perennial. 'Crater Lake Blue' is a popular cultivar.

Viola *pg. 91*
V. odorata, sweet violet; shades of purple, white veined with purple, fragrant; late spring; 6 to 8 inches; perennial.

Weigela
W. florida; rosy red, pink, white; late spring to early summer; 8 to 10 feet; shrub.

Wisteria
W. floribunda, Japanese wisteria; purple, white, fragrant; late spring to early summer; to 25 feet; perennial vine.
W. sinensis, Chinese wisteria; purple, mauve, white, fragrant; late spring to early summer; to 30 feet; perennial vine.

Zantedeschia *pg. 189*
Z. aethiopica, calla lily; white; late spring to early summer outdoors; 1 to 36 inches; tender bulb.

Spring-Blooming Houseplants

Abutilon *pg. 214*
***A. megapotamicum* 'Variegatum'**, trailing flowering maple; lemon yellow with red calyxes, variegated leaves; to 48 inches; late spring to midautumn; tender shrub.

Acacia
A. paradoxa (A. armata), kangaroo thorn; bright yellow; early to midspring; to 6 feet or more; tender shrub. Needs moderate light.

Bougainvillea
***B.* hybrids**, paper flower; brilliant red, crimson, magenta, rose, pink, salmon, orange, purple, white; blooms indoors in spring, outdoors in warm climates in spring and summer; to 15 feet or more; tender perennial vine. Needs greenhouse or very sunny window, warm and somewhat dry, to bloom indoors.

Clerodendrum
C. thomsoniae, bleeding heart vine, glory bower; red flowers with white sepals; spring and summer, may bloom again in fall; to 12 feet; tender vine. Especially nice when trained around a window.

Clivia *pg. 215*
C. miniata, kaffir lily; orange-scarlet with yellow interior; spring; 18 to 24 inches; tender bulb.

Episcia *pg. 81*
E. cupreata, flame violet; red; spring into summer; to 12 inches, often semitrailing.

Euphorbia
E. milii, crown of thorns; salmon pink, red, yellow; spring; to 36 inches; tender spiny shrub.

Fuchsia
***F.* hybrids**; shades and combinations of red, rose, pink, purple, white; spring and summer; to 24 inches; tender shrub. Grow in hanging baskets.

Gardenia *pg. 81*
G. augusta (G. jasminoides), common gardenia, Cape jasmine; creamy white, very fragrant; may bloom from late winter into summer, depending on conditions; 24 to 48 inches; shrub.

Hatiora *pg. 82*
H.* cultivars *(Rhipsalidopsis* cultivars*), Easter cactus; red, rose, pink, salmon, white; spring; 12 inches; tender perennial.

Hibiscus
H. rosa-sinensis, Chinese hibiscus, rose of China; red, pink, orange, yellow, white; can bloom in late winter through spring indoors; 36 to 48 inches; tender shrub.

Justicia
J. brandegeana, shrimp plant; bronze, pink, yellow-green; spring through summer; to 36 inches; tender shrub.

Lachenalia
L. aloides, cape cowslip; yellow, usually tinged with red; blooms in early spring if planted in late summer; to 12 inches; tender bulb.

Ledebouria
L. socialis; greenish white; spring; 6 inches; bulb. Blooms same season if planted in early spring.

Manettia
M. luteorubra (M. inflata), Brazilian firecracker, firecracker vine; red tipped with yellow; spring and/or fall; 6 to 12 feet; tender trailing vine.

Pelargonium *pg. 145*
P. × domesticum, Martha Washington geranium, regal geranium; red, rose, pink, white; spring and summer; 18 inches; tender perennial.
P. peltatum, ivy-leaved geranium; red, pink, reddish purple, white; 6 to 36 inches (trailing); spring and summer; tender perennial.

Summer

Early Summer Blooming

Achillea *pg. 136*
A. **'Coronation Gold'**; large yellow flower heads; early to midsummer; 24 to 36 inches; perennial.
A. filipendulina, fernleaf yarrow; yellow; early to midsummer; 36 to 48 inches; perennial. 'Gold Plate' is a 4-foot cultivar with especially large flowers.
A. **German Galaxy hybrids**; pale yellow, rose, amber, orange, pink, salmon, brick; all summer; 18 to 30 inches; perennial. 'Fanal' is a popular cultivar.
A. millefolium, common yarrow, milfoil; white, pink, red; all summer; 18 to 24 inches; perennial.
A. **'Moonshine'**; pale yellow; early summer to early fall; 18 to 24 inches; perennial.
A. ptarmica **'The Pearl'**; white; early summer to early fall; 36 to 48 inches; perennial.

Ageratum *pg. 136*
A. houstonianum, flossflower; blue, white; all summer; 6 to 18 inches; annual.

Alcea *pg. 137*
A. rosea (Althaea rosea) **cultivars**, hollyhock; pink, rose, red, maroon, violet, yellow, copper, cream; early summer to late summer; 24 to 72 inches; biennial but often self-sows.

Allium
A. giganteum, giant garlic; rosy purple; early summer; 36 to 48 inches; bulb.

Amorpha
A. fruticosa, false indigo; blue-violet; early summer; to 15 feet; shrub.

Anthemis
A. tinctoria, golden marguerite; golden yellow; all summer; to 36 inches; perennial. Pale yellow and darker cultivars available.

Anthericum
A. liliago, St. Bernard's lily; white; early to midsummer; to 36 inches; perennial.

Antirrhinum *pg. 137*
A. majus, snapdragon; crimson, scarlet, rose, pink, purple, orange, yellow, white, bicolors; early summer to midsummer; 7 to 24 inches; annual. Blooms in winter in mild climates.

Armeria
A. maritima, thrift, sea pink; rosy pink; midspring to early summer; 6 inches; perennial.

Aruncus
A. dioicus (A. sylvester), goatsbeard; white; early to mid- summer; 60 to 72 inches; perennial.

Astilbe *pg. 138*
A. × arendsii **cultivars**, astilbe, false spirea; white, pink, rose, red; early to midsummer; 24 to 36 inches; perennial.

Baptisia
B. australis, blue false indigo; blue; late spring to early summer; 36 to 60 inches; perennial.

Begonia *pg. 138, 186*
B. **Semperflorens-Cultorum hybrids**, wax begonia; red, scarlet, salmon, rose, pink, white; early summer to fall; to 12 inches; tender annual.

Bougainvillea
B. **hybrids**, paper flower; brilliant red, crimson, magenta, rose, pink, salmon, orange, purple, yellow, white; all summer; to 60 feet; tender perennial vine. Grown outdoors only in warm climates.

Brachycome
B. iberidifolia, Swan River daisy; blue, pink, white; early summer to fall; to 18 inches; annual.

Calendula
C. officinalis, pot marigold; orange, yellow, gold, cream; early summer to fall, winter in warm climates; 12 to 24 inches; annual.

Campanula *pg. 139*
C. carpatica, Carpathian harebell; blue, white; late spring to midsummer; 6 to 12 inches; perennial.
C. glomerata, clustered bellflower; violet, white; early to midsummer; 12 to 18 inches; perennial.
C. latifolia; blue-violet, white; early to midsummer; 24 to 48 inches; perennial.
C. persicifolia, peach-leaved bellflower, peach bells; blue, white, pink; early to mid- summer; 24 to 30 inches; perennial.

Centaurea
C. cyanus, bachelor's button; blue, pink, purple, white; early to late summer; 12 to 36 inches; annual.
C. dealbata, Persian cornflower; rose-pink to white; early to midsummer; 18 to 30 inches; perennial.
C. macrocephala, globe centaurea; yellow; early to midsummer; 24 to 48 inches; perennial.
C. montana, mountain bluet; blue; violet; early to late summer; 18 to 24 inches; perennial. May bloom again in fall.

Centranthus
C. ruber, red valerian, Jupiter's beard; rosy red, white; early summer into fall; to 36 inches; perennial.

Clematis
C. integrifolia **'Caerulea'**, blue solitary clematis; porcelain blue; early summer to mid- autumn; 30 inches; perennial.
C. recta **'Grandiflora'**, ground clematis; white, fragrant; early to late summer; 24 to 60 inches; perennial.

Cleome
C. hassleriana (C. spinosa), spider flower; rose, pink, light purple, white; early summer to fall; to 48 inches; annual.

Consolida
C. ambigua (Delphinium ajacis), annual or rocket larkspur; pink, lavender, purple, blue, white; early to late summer; 18 to 60 inches; annual.

Coreopsis *pg. 140*
C. auriculata **'Nana'**, mouse-eared coreopsis; orange-yellow; early to midsummer; 8 inches; perennial.
C. lanceolata, lance-leaved coreopsis; yellow; early to late summer; to 36 inches; perennial.

Cosmos
C. bipinnatus; rosy red, pink, white; early summer to fall; 36 to 72 inches; annual. Shorter cultivars available.

Centaurea: *Bachelor's button*

C. sulphureus, yellow cosmos; orange, yellow, red; early summer to fall; to 48 inches; annual.

'Sonata' cosmos

Dictamnus
D. albus, gas plant, fraxinella; white to pinkish; early summer; 24 to 36 inches; perennial. Red-violet cultivars available.

Digitalis
D. purpurea, foxglove; purple-spotted, white, pink, lavender; 24 to 48 inches; early to midsummer; biennial.

Eremurus
E. stenophyllus, foxtail lily, desert candle; orange-gold; early summer; 24 to 60 inches; perennial. Yellow, white, pink, and orange-red hybrids available.

Erigeron
***E.* hybrids**, fleabane; dark violet, violet-blue, lavender, rose, pink, white; early to late summer; 12 to 24 inches; perennial. May bloom all year in warm West Coast climates.

Erodium
E. reichardii (E. chamaedryoides), white veined with pink; early to midsummer; 4 inches; perennial. Not hardy in cold climates.

Eschscholzia
E. californica, California poppy; yellow-orange; early summer to fall; 6 to 18 inches; annual. Pink, cream, yellow, and red cultivars available.

Eustoma
E. grandiflorum (Lisi anthus russellianus) cultivars, prairie gentian; purple, pink, blue, white; all summer; 24 to 36 inches; biennial grown as annual.

Filipendula
F. rubra, queen-of-the-prairie; pink, magenta; early to midsummer; 48 to 84 inches; perennial.
F. ulmaria, queen-of-the-meadow; white; early to midsummer; 36 to 60 inches; perennial.
F. vulgaris (F. hexapetala) **'Flore Pleno'**, dropwort; white; early summer; 24 to 36 inches; perennial.

Gaillardia
G.* × *grandiflora, blanket flower; yellow flushed with red in center; all summer; 24 to 36 inches; perennial. Burgundy and all-yellow cultivars available.

Galega
G. officinalis, goat's rue; pink, lavender, white; all summer; 24 to 36 inches; perennial.

Geranium *pg. 82*
***G. cinereum* cultivars**; lilac to bright magenta; all summer; 6 inches; perennial.
G. ibericum, Iberian cranesbill; violet-blue; early to mid- summer; 10 to 20 inches; perennial.
G. psilostemon, Armenian cranesbill; magenta to rose, with dark centers; early summer; 24 to 48 inches; perennial.

Gypsophila
G. repens, creeping baby's breath; white, pink; early to midsummer; 6 to 8 inches; perennial.

Hemerocallis *pg. 143*
***H.* hybrids**, daylily; red, scarlet, orange, gold, yellow, apricot, cream, other warm shades; early to late summer; 12 to 36 inches; perennial.

Iberis *pg. 83*
I. umbellata, annual candytuft, globe candytuft; pink, lavender, purple, white; early summer to early fall; 8 to 15 inches; annual. Often self-sows.

Impatiens *pg. 143*
***I.* cultivars**; shades of red, rose, pink, orange, lavender, white, bicolors; early summer to fall; bedding impatiens, 6 to 12 inches, New Guinea impatiens, to 24 inches; tender perennial grown as an annual.

Inula
I. ensifolia, swordleaf inula; yellow; early to midsummer; to 12 inches; perennial.

Iris *pg. 84–85, 188*
I. ensata (I. kaempferi), Japanese iris; purple, blue-violet, red-violet, white; early to midsummer; 36 to 48 inches; perennial.
I. sibirica, Siberian iris; deep purple; early summer; 24 to 48 inches; perennial. Hybrids available in many colors.

Kniphofia
K. uvaria, red-hot poker; scarlet, red, orange, yellow; early summer to fall; 24 to 72 inches; perennial.

Lantana
L. camara, yellow sage; yellow, orange-yellow changing to red or white; early summer; to 48 inches; tender shrub, grown as an annual in all but the warmest climates. Dwarf cultivars and hybrids available in many shades of yellow, pink, orange, and white.

Lavandula
L. angustifolia (L. officinalis), lavender; lavender to purple; early to midsummer; 12 to 36 inches; perennial. Pink and white cultivars available.

Lavatera
L. trimestris, tree mallow; red, pink, white; early summer to fall; 24 to 48 inches; annual.

Leucanthemum
***L.* × *superbum (Chrysanthemum* × *superbum, C. maximum)* cultivars**, Shasta daisy; white with yellow center, single or double; early summer to early fall; 12 to 24 inches; perennial.

Lilium
L. canadense, meadow lily; yellow, yellow-orange, red, with dark spots; early summer; to 60 inches; bulb.
L. candidum, Madonna lily; white, fragrant; early to midsummer; 42 inches; bulb.
L. concolor, morning star lily; bright red; early summer; 36 to 48 inches; bulb.
L. martagon, turk's-cap lily; carmine-rose; early to midsummer; 48 to 72 inches; bulb. The variety album has white flowers.

Longiflorum lily

L. pumilum, coral lily; coral-red; early summer; 24 inches; bulb.
L. regale, regal lily; white brushed with rosy purple, yellow throat, fragrant; early to midsummer; 48 to 72 inches; bulb.

Linum
L. flavum, golden flax; gold; early summer; 12 to 24 inches; perennial.
***L. perenne* and cultivars**, blue flax, perennial flax; blue, white; all summer; 12 to 24 inches; perennial.

Lobelia
L. erinus, edging lobelia; blue, rosy red, white; early summer to fall; 4 to 8 inches; annual.

Lonicera
L. henryi, honeysuckle; red-violet; all summer; to 30 feet; perennial vine.

Lychnis
L. chalcedonica, Maltese cross; scarlet; early to midsummer; 18 to 36 inches; perennial.
L. coronaria, rose campion; magenta; early summer to fall; 18 to 36 inches; perennial.

Lysimachia
L. clethroides, gooseneck loosestrife; white; early to midsummer; 24 to 36 inches; perennial.

Malva
M. alcea, hollyhock mallow; lavender-pink; early to midsummer; 24 to 48 inches; perennial.

Melampodium
M. leucanthum (M. paludosum), melampodium, blackfoot daisy; yellow; early summer to fall; 12 to 18 inches; annual.

Mimulus
M. × hybridus, monkey flower; red, yellow, bicolors; early summer to fall; to 12 inches; tender perennial often grown as an annual.

Nicotiana
N. × sanderae, flowering tobacco; red, pink, lavender, white, green; early summer to fall; 24 to 60 inches; annual.

Oenothera
O. fruiticosa (O. tetragona), evening primrose, sundrops; bright yellow; early to midsummer; 18 to 24 inches; perennial.
O. macrocarpa (O. missouriensis), Missouri primrose, Ozark sundrops; yellow; early to midsummer; to 6 inches; perennial.
O. speciosa, showy primrose; pale pink; early summer; 6 to 18 inches; perennial.

Opuntia
O. compressa (O. humifusa), prickly pear cactus; yellow; early to midsummer; 6 to 12 inches; perennial.

Papaver *pg. 88*
P. rhoeas, Shirley poppy; red, rose, pink, salmon; early summer; 18 to 24 inches; annual.

Pelargonium *pg. 145*
***P.* cultivars**, zonal geranium, ivy geranium; shades of red, pink, white, orange, salmon; early summer to fall; to 36 inches; tender perennial.

Petunia *pg. 146*
P. × hybrida, petunia; all colors plus bicolors; early summer into fall; 12 to 24 inches; annual.

Petunia

'Roman Holiday' rose

Portulaca
P. grandiflora, rose moss; shades of red, pink, rose, orange, apricot, yellow, white; early summer to fall; 6 to 8 inches; annual.

Potentilla
P. fruticosa, shrubby cinquefoil; yellow; early to late summer; 24 to 48 inches; shrub. Cultivars available in white, red, pink, apricot.
P. nepalensis, Nepal cinquefoil; rose; early to late summer; 24 inches; shrub. Cultivars available in white, red, pink, apricot; perennial. Red cultivars available.

Rhododendron
R. arborescens, sweet azalea; white, fragrant; early summer; to 9 feet; shrub. Very hardy.
R. calendulaceum, flame azalea; yellow, orange, red-orange; early summer; 9 feet; shrub.
R. decorum, sweetshell azalea; white to pink, fragrant; early summer; 18 feet; shrub.
R. viscosum, swamp azalea; white, sometimes tinged pink, fragrant; early to midsummer; 9 feet or more; shrub. Very hardy.

Rosa *pg. 147–148*
***R.* Climbing roses**; bloom off and on all summer; shades of red, pink, yellow, white, some are fragrant; 10 feet; shrub.
***R.* Floribunda roses**; many shades of red, rose, pink, yellow, white, bicolors, many are fragrant; all summer; 24 to 48 inches; shrub.
***R.* Grandiflora roses**; shades of red, rose, pink, orange, yellow, white, some are fragrant; all summer; 60 to 72 inches; shrub.
***R.* Hybrid tea roses**; many shades of red, rose, pink, orange, yellow, white, bicolors, some are fragrant; all summer; 36 to 60 inches or more; shrub.
***R.* Miniature roses**; shades of red, rose, pink, orange, yellow, white, bicolors, some are fragrant; all summer; 12 to 24 inches; shrub.
***R.* Shrub roses**; some types bloom once in early summer, others bloom continuously all summer; shades of rose, pink, yellow, white, some are fragrant; 2 to 8 feet or more; shrub.

Scabiosa
***S. atropurpurea* and cultivars**, pincushion flower; red, rose, salmon, lavender, blue, white; early summer to early fall; 18 to 36 inches; annual.
S. caucasica, pincushion flower; lavender-blue; early summer; 18 to 24 inches; perennial. White cultivars available.

Sidalcea
***S. malviflora* cultivars**, checker-bloom, prairie mallow; pink, white, purplish; early to midsummer; 18 to 42 inches; perennial.

Stachys
S. byzantina, lamb's ears; grown for its silvery leaves; all summer (also small, rosy purple flowers in early to midsum-mer); to 18 inches; perennial.

Tagetes *pg. 148–149*
***T. erecta, T. patula, T. tenuifolia, T.* hybrids**, marigolds; yellow, gold, orange, rust, cream, bicolors; early summer into fall; 7 to 36 inches; annual.

Tanacetum
***T. coccineum (Chrysanthemum coccineum)* cultivars**, pyrethrum, painted daisy; red, pink, white, with yellow centers; early to midsummer; 24 to 30 inches; perennial.

Thunbergia
T. alata, black-eyed Susan vine; orange, yellow, white; early summer to fall; to 10 feet; annual.

Tradescantia
T. virginiana, spiderwort; pink, blue; early summer; 24 to 30 inches; perennial. Hybrids available in many colors. (See page 291.)

Tropaeolum
***T. majus* and cultivars**, nasturtium; yellow, orange, crimson, mahogany, pink, cream; all summer; 6 to 24 inches; annual. Some old-fashioned cultivars can trail up to 8 feet long.

Verbascum
***V.* cultivars**, mullein; white, yellow; early to midsummer; 36 to 60 inches; perennial.

Verbena
V. × hybrida (V. hortensis), garden verbena; red, pink, violet-blue, yellow, white, sometimes fragrant; early to late summer; to 12 inches; tender perennial usually grown as an annual.
V. peruviana; red; early to midsummer; 3 to 4 inches; tender perennial.
V. rigida, vervain; pinkish purple; early to midsummer; 12 to 24 inches; perennial.

Veronica *pg. 149*
V. incana, woolly speedwell; blue; early to midsummer; 12 to 18 inches; perennial.
***V. longifolia* cultivars**; blue, white, rose; early to late summer; 24 to 48 inches; perennial.
V. spicata, spike speedwell; violet-blue, white, pink; early to late summer; 15 to 24 inches; perennial.

Zinnia *pg. 149*
Z. angustifolia, narrow-leaved zinnia; orange, yellow, white; early summer to fall; to 12 inches; annual.
***Z. elegans* cultivars**, zinnia; all colors except blue; all summer; 8 inches to 36 inches; annual.

Achillea: *'Inca Gold' yarrow*

Midsummer Blooming

Abelia
A. × grandiflora, white, pink; midsummer to fall; 36 to 72 inches; shrub. Not hardy in cold climates.

Achillea *pg. 136*
A. tomentosa, woolly yarrow; pale yellow; midsummer to late summer; 10 inches; perennial.

Adenophora
A. confusa (A. farreri), ladybells; violet; midsummer to late summer; 36 inches; perennial.

Agapanthus
A. africanus, African lily, lily-of-the-Nile; blue, violet, white; midsummer; 18 to 42 inches; tender bulb.
***A. praecox* subspecies *orientalis* (*A. orientalis*)**; blue; midsummer; 24 to 36 inches; tender bulb.

Allium
A. carinatum* subspecies *pulchellum; pinkish purple; midsummer; 18 to 24 inches; bulb. White form available.
A. senescens; pink; midsummer; to 24 inches; hardy bulb.
A. stellatum, prairie onion; rosy pink; midsummer to autumn; to 18 inches; bulb.

Anaphalis
A. margaritacea, pearly everlasting; white; midsummer to late summer; 12 to 36 inches; perennial.

Arctotis
A.* hybrids, *A. venusta, African daisy; red, orange, pink, yellow, white; midsummer to fall; to 24 inches; annual.

Asclepias
A. tuberosa, butterfly weed; orange; midsummer to late summer; 18 to 24 inches; perennial. Yellow and red cultivars available.

Aster *pg. 173*
A. amellus, Italian aster; purple; midsummer to late summer; 18 inches; perennial.

Begonia *pg. 138, 186*
***B.* Tuberhybrida hybrids**, tuberous begonia; red, orange, pink, yellow, white; midsummer to fall; to 18 inches, many cascading; tender bulb.

Tuberous begonia

Belamcanda
B. chinensis, blackberry lily; orange, yellow; midsummer to late summer; 24 to 36 inches; perennial.

Buddleia
B. davidii, butterfly bush; lilac, mauve, rose-purple, white; midsummer to early fall; 4 to 10 feet; shrub.

Callistephus *pg. 139*
***C. chinensis* cultivars**, China aster; white, pink, rose, scarlet, blue, yellow; midsummer to frost; 9 to 36 inches; annual.

Campanula *pg. 139*
C. lactiflora, milky bellflower; blue, white; midsummer to early fall; 36 to 60 inches; perennial.

Campsis
C. radicans, trumpet vine; orange-red; midsummer to late summer; to 30 feet; perennial vine. A yellow form is available.

Celosia
C.* Cristata group *(C. cristata), crested cockscomb; yellow, orange, bright red, magenta; midsummer to frost; 10 to 24 inches; annual.
C.* Plumosa group *(C. plumosa), plumed celosia; deep red, gold, bronze, orange, apricot, yellow, cream; midsummer to frost; 12 to 30 inches; annual.

Centaurea
C. americana, basket flower; rose, pink, white; midsummer; 48 to 72 inches; annual.
***C. dealbata* 'Steenbergii'**, Persian centaurea; rosy red; midsummer to late summer; 24 inches; perennial.

Chelone
C. glabra, turtlehead; pinkish to white; midsummer to fall; 30 to 36 inches; perennial.

Cimicifuga
C. racemosa, black snakeroot, black cohosh; white; midsummer; 48 to 84 inches; perennial.

Clematis
C.* × *jackmanii, violet-purple; midsummer; to 12 feet; perennial vine.
C. viticella, Italian clematis; purple, violet, rose-purple; midsummer to fall; to 16 feet; perennial vine.

Coreopsis *pg. 140*
C. rosea, pink tickseed; rosy pink, midsummer to early fall; 24 inches; perennial.
C. verticillata, threadleaf coreopsis; bright yellow; midsummer to late summer; 24 to 36 inches; perennial.
***C. verticillata* 'Moonbeam'**, soft yellow; midsummer to early autumn; 18 to 24 inches; perennial.

Crocosmia
C.* × *crocosmiiflora (Tritonia crocosmiiflora), montbretia; orange-red; mid- to late summer; bulb. In cold climates grow like gladiolus. Yellow and red cultivars available.

'Fascination' dahlia

Dahlia *pg. 140–141*
***D.* hybrids**; shades of red, pink, orange, yellow, purple, white, bicolors; bloom from midsummer well into autumn; 12 to 72 inches; tender bulb.

Delphinium *pg. 141–142*
***D. elatum* hybrids**; purple, violet, blue, lavender, pink, white, bicolors; midsummer; to 72 inches; perennial.

Dianthus *pg. 80*
***D. caryophyllus* and cultivars**, carnation; pink, red, white, sometimes fragrant; midsummer to early fall; treat as annual.

Echinacea
E. purpurea, purple coneflower; rosy purple; midsummer to early fall; 24 to 48 inches; perennial. White cultivars available.

Echinops
E. ritro, small globe thistle; blue; midsummer to late summer; 36 to 48 inches; perennial.
***E.* 'Taplow Blue'**, globe thistle; steel blue; midsummer to early fall; 36 to 48 inches; perennial.

Erigeron
E. aurantiacus, double orange daisy; bright orange; mid-summer to late summer; to 10 inches; perennial.

Eryngium
E. alpinum, alpine sea holly; soft blue; midsummer; 30 inches; perennial.
E. amethystinum, amethyst sea holly; steel gray to amethyst; mid- to late summer; 24 to 30 inches; perennial.
E. giganteum, Miss Willmott's ghost; silvery gray, tinged with blue or violet; midsummer; 24 to 36 inches; perennial.

Euphorbia
E. corollata, flowering spurge; white; mid- to late summer; 12 to 36 inches; perennial.

Fuchsia
***F.* hybrids**; shades of red, rose, pink, purple, white, and bicolors; all summer; trailing or upright to 36 inches or more; tender shrub. Grown outdoors in warm climates; elsewhere as summer bedding or hanging basket plants.

Gentiana
G. asclepiadea, willow gentian; deep blue; midsummer to late summer; 24 inches; perennial.

Gladiolus
***G.* hybrids**; many shades of red, rose, pink, salmon, orange, yellow, lavender, purple, and white; bloom from midsummer until frost, depending on planting date and variety; 24 to 60 inches; tender bulb.
G. tristis; yellowish white, sometimes with purple streaks, fragrant at night; midsummer; 24 to 36 inches; tender bulb.

Gomphrena
G. species, globe amaranth; red, pink, purple, white, orange; midsummer to fall; 8 to 24 inches; annual.

Gypsophila
G. elegans, annual baby's breath; white; mid- to late summer; 10 to 18 inches; annual. Pink and rose cultivars available.
G. paniculata, baby's breath; white, pink; mid- to late summer; 18 to 48 inches; perennial. 'Bristol Fairy' is a double-flowered cultivar.

Helianthus
H. annuus, common sunflower; yellow with brownish center; midsummer to early fall; to 12 feet; annual.
H. decapetalus, river sunflower; yellow; midsummer to early fall; to 60 inches; perennial.

Heliopsis
H. helianthoides, false sunflower; yellow; midsummer to early fall; 36 to 60 inches; perennial. Cultivars include 'Gold Greenheart' (bright yellow) and 'Incomparabilis' (yellow).
H. scabra, orange sunflower; orange-yellow; midsummer to early fall; 36 to 60 inches; perennial.

Hemerocallis
H. fulva, tawny daylily; orange; midsummer; 36 to 48 inches; perennial.
Hybrid daylilies are in peak bloom in midsummer.

Hosta
H. fortunei; lavender; mid- to late summer; 18 to 30 inches; perennial. Cultivars include 'Albomarginata' (light green leaves edged in white), 'Albopicta' (light green leaves), and 'Honeybells' (grass-green leaves).
H. sieboldiana; lilac; midsummer; 24 to 48 inches; perennial. Cultivars include 'Elegans' (blue-green leaves) and 'Frances Williams' (deep green leaves edged in gold).
***H. undulata* 'Erromena'**; pale lavender; mid- to late summer; 30 to 42 inches; perennial. Bright green leaves.
H. ventricosa; purple; mid- to late summer; 36 inches; perennial. Has larger, showier flowers than most hostas.

Hydrangea
H. macrophylla, hortensia (mophead) and lacecap hydrangeas; pink, blue; midsummer; 36 to 72 inches, taller in warm climates; shrub. Not hardy in cold climates; this is the hydrangea sold by florists.
***H. paniculata* 'Grandiflora'**, PeeGee hydrangea; white, changing to pink or pale purple; midsummer; 8 to 25 feet; shrub.

Hemerocallis: *'Role Model' daylily*

H. quercifolia, oakleaf hydrangea; white; midsummer; to 72 inches; shrub.
H. serrata, tea-of-heaven; blue, white, pink; midsummer; 36 to 60 inches; shrub. Not hardy in cold climates.

Hypericum
H. kalmianum, St. John's wort; yellow; mid- to late summer; 24 to 36 inches; perennial.
H. prolificum, shrubby St. John's wort, bush broom; yellow; midsummer to early fall; 48 to 60 inches; shrub.
H. pseudohenryi (H. patulum var. henryi), St. John's wort; yellow; midsummer to early fall; to 60 inches; shrub.

Ipomoea
***I.* species and cultivars**, morning glory; shades of pink, purple, blue, red, white, bicolors; midsummer to fall; to 10 feet; annual.

Lamium
L. maculatum, spotted dead nettle; red-violet, white; midsummer; to 18 inches; perennial. Cultivars include 'Beacon Silver' (silvery leaves, pink flowers), 'Aureum' (yellowish leaves) and 'White Nancy' (silvery leaves, white flowers).

Liatris
L. punctata; rose-purple; mid- to late summer; 12 to 20 inches; perennial.
L. pycnostachya, Kansas gayfeather; rose-purple; mid- to late summer; 36 to 72 inches; perennial.
L. scariosa, tall gayfeather; bluish purple, white; mid- to late summer; 36 to 60 inches; perennial. Not hardy in very cold climates.
L. spicata, spike gayfeather; rosy purple, white; midsummer to early fall; 36 to 60 inches; perennial. Compact 'Kobold' is only 2 ft. tall.

Lilium *pg. 144*
L. auratum, gold-band lily; white banded with gold; midsummer; 42 to 60 inches; bulb.
L. canadense, meadow lily; red, orange-yellow, yellow, with red spots; early to midsummer; 60 inches; bulb.
L. chalcedonicum, scarlet turk's-cap lily; scarlet; midsummer; 36 to 48 inches; bulb.
L. pardalinum, leopard lily; orange to red-orange with purple spots; midsummer; 60 to 84 inches; bulb.
There are also many hybrid lilies flowering in midsummer. (See page 144 for more information.)

Limonium
L. latifolium, sea lavender, statice; lavender-blue, white; mid- to late summer; to 24 inches; perennial.
L. sinuatum, statice; violet, lavender, rose, yellow, white; midsummer to early fall; 18 to 30 inches; perennial usually grown as an annual. This is the brightly colored type grown for the florist trade.

Lobelia
L. cardinalis, cardinal flower; red; midsummer to early fall; 24 to 48 inches; perennial.

Lonicera
L. × heckrotti, goldflame honeysuckle; purplish pink outside, yellow inside; midsummer; to 20 feet; perennial vine (sometimes shrublike).

Macleaya
M. cordata, plume poppy; cream to white; mid- to late summer; to 84 inches; perennial.

Malva
M. moschata, musk mallow; pink, white; mid- to late summer; 24 to 36 inches; perennial.

Garden phlox

Monarda
M. didyma, bee balm, bergamot; scarlet; mid- to late summer; 24 to 36 inches; perennial. Cultivars include 'Gardenview Scarlet' (bright red) and 'Croftway Pink' (soft pink); white, rose, and purple cultivars also available.

Nymphaea
***N.* hybrids**; water lilies; red, rose, pink, purple, blue, orange, yellow, white; all summer. Both hardy and tropical water lilies bloom in summer. Many cultivars available.

Penstemon
P. barbatus, beard tongue; red; midsummer; 24 to 48 inches; perennial. Pink, purple, white, and salmon cultivars available.

Phlox *pg. 88–89, 146*
P. drummondii, annual phlox; red, rose, pink, lavender, purple, white; mid- to late summer; to 18 inches; annual.

P. paniculata, garden phlox; rose, pink, salmon, lavender, purple, white, fragrant; mid- to late summer (to early autumn, for some cvs.); 36 to 48 inches; perennial.

Physalis
P. alkekengi, Chinese lantern; orange (small whitish flowers in late spring), orange "lanterns" in summer; to 24 inches; perennial.

Physostegia
P. virginiana, false dragonhead; lavender, pink, white; midsummer to early fall; 24 to 48 inches; perennial.

Platycodon
P. grandiflorus, balloon flower; purple-blue, white, pink; mid- to late summer; 18 to 36 inches; perennial.

Rosa *pg. 147–148*
***R.* Bush roses**—floribundas, grandifloras, hybrid teas, miniatures, and many shrub roses—are still in bloom in midsummer.

Rudbeckia
***R. fulgida* 'Goldsturm'**, black-eyed Susan; golden yellow with dark center; midsummer to frost; 24 inches; perennial.

Salpiglossis
***S. sinuata* and cultivars**, painted tongue; red, maroon, yellow, orange, blue; 24 to 36 inches; annual.

Salvia *pg. 148*
S. farinacea, mealycup sage; blue, white; early summer to early fall; 18 to 36 inches; tender perennial. Cultivars include 'Blue Bedder' and 'Victoria'. Grown as annual except in warm climates.
S. praetensis, meadow clary; lavender-blue, rarely white; mid- to late summer; to 36 inches; perennial.
***S. splendens* cultivars**, scarlet sage; brilliant scarlet; midsummer to fall; 12 to 36 inches; tender perennial grown as an annual. Purple, salmon, and white cultivars available.
S.* × *sylvestris (S. superba), violet sage; purple, deep violet; mid- to late summer; 18 to 36 inches; perennial. Cultivars include 'East Friesland' (purple) and 'Mainacht' ('May Night', dark blue-violet).

Sanguisorba
S. obtusa, Japanese burnet; pink; mid- to late summer; 36 inches; perennial.

Saponaria
S. officinalis, bouncing bet, soapwort; white to pink; midsummer; 12 to 36 inches; perennial.

Sedum
S. spurium; pale pink; midsummer; to 6 inches; perennial. Dark pink to deep red cultivars available.

Senna
S. marilandica (Cassia marilandica), wild senna; yellow; midsummer; 36 to 60 inches; perennial.

Stachys
S. macrantha (S. grandiflora), big betony; violet, pink; midsummer; 18 to 24 inches; perennial. White cultivar available.

Stokesia
***S. laevis* cultivars**, Stokes' aster; blue, pink, white; midsummer to fall (early summer in warm climates); 12 to 18 inches; perennial.

Tanacetum
T. parthenium (Chyrsanthemum parthenium), feverfew; white with yellow center; midsummer; 24 to 42 inches; perennial.

Tithonia
T. rotundifolia, Mexican sunflower; orange, scarlet; midsummer to fall; to 60 inches; annual.

Torenia
T. fournieri, wishbone flower; purple, rosy pink, white, bicolored; midsummer to fall; to 12 inches; annual.

Yucca
Y. filamentosa, Adam's needle; creamy white; midsummer; 60 to 72 inches; perennial.

Late Summer Blooming

Aconitum *pg. 172*
A.* × *cammarum* 'Bicolor' *(A.* × *bicolor), bicolor monkshood; blue tinged with white; late summer; 36 to 48 inches; perennial.

A. carmichaelii, azure monkshood; violet-blue; late sum- mer to fall; 24 to 48 inches; perennial.
A. napellus, common monkshood; blue-violet to purple; late summer to fall; to 36 inches; perennial.

Buddleia
B. davidii, butterfly bush; lilac, mauve, rose-purple, white; midsummer to early fall; 4 to 10 feet; shrub.

Chelone
C. lyonii, pink turtlehead; deep rose; late summer to early fall; 30 to 36 inches; perennial.

Chrysanthemum *pg. 174–175*
C. × *grandiflorum (C.* × *morifolium, Dendranthema* × *grandiflorum)*, garden or hardy chrysanthemum; shades of red, orange, rust, bronze, yellow, pink, purple, white; 12 to 36 inches; perennial. Hybrid chrysanthemums begin blooming in late summer but reach their peak in early autumn.

Clematis
C. heracleifolia var. *davidiana*, blue tube clematis; deep blue, fragrant; late summer; 24 to 36 inches; shrub.
C. texensis, scarlet clematis; scarlet, rosy pink; late summer; 48 to 72 inches; perennial vine.

Clethra
C. alnifolia, sweet pepper bush, summersweet; white, fragrant; late summer to mid-autumn; 3 to 9 feet; shrub. Pink cultivars available.

Coreopsis *pg. 140*
C. rosea, pink tickseed; rosy pink, midsummer to early fall; 24 inches; perennial.

Eryngium
E. bourgatii, Mediterranean sea holly; steel blue; late summer; 18 inches; perennial.

Gentiana
G. septemfida, crested gentian; deep blue; late summer to early fall; 9 to 15 inches; perennial.
G. sino-ornata; violet-blue; late summer to early fall; 6 to 8 inches; perennial.

Helenium
H. autumnale, sneezeweed; yellow, orange, mahogany; late summer to early fall; 36 to 72 inches; perennial.

Hibiscus
H. moscheutos **hybrids**, hardy hibiscus, rose mallow; red, pink, white; late summer to early fall; 36 to 84 inches; perennial.
H. syriacus, rose-of-Sharon; red, pink, magenta, blue, white; late summer; 5 to 15 feet; shrub.

'Autumn Joy' sedum

Hosta
H. lancifolia; lavender; late summer to early fall; 24 inches; perennial.
H. undulata; lilac; late summer; 18 inches; perennial. A popular cultivar is 'Albomarginata', which has green-and-white variegated foliage.

Hyssopus
H. officinalis, hyssop; blue; late summer; 18 to 24 inches; perennial. White and pink forms available.

Lagerstroemia
L. indica, crape myrtle; red, pink, white, lavender; late summer; 5 to 25 feet; shrub. Some varieties bloom earlier in summer.

Ligularia
L. dentata, ragwort; orange, orange-yellow, gold; late summer; 36 to 48 inches; perennial.

Lilium *pg. 144*
L. formosanum; white, fragrant; late summer; 18 inches; bulb. The late-blooming form of this lily flowers in late summer.
L. henryi; orange with brown spots; late summer; 84 inches; bulb.
L. lancifolium (L. tigrinum), tiger lily; orange with purple spots; late summer to early fall; 48 to 60 inches; bulb. Yellow, cream, pink, and red cultivars available.
L. speciosum, Japanese lily; white or pinkish with red spots, fragrant; late summer; 36 to 60 inches; bulb. Rosy pink cultivar available.
Many hybrid lilies bloom in late summer.

Lobelia
L. siphilitica, blue lobelia, great lobelia; deep blue to blue-violet; late summer to early fall; 36 inches; perennial.

Polygonum
P. aubertii, silver lace vine; white, fragrant; late summer to early fall; to 25 feet or more; perennial vine.

Rudbeckia
R. hirta **hybrids**, black-eyed Susan, gloriosa daisy; yellow, red-brown, bronze, bicolors; late summer to early fall; 12 to 36 inches; annual or biennial.
R. laciniata **'Goldquelle'**, dwarf golden glow; yellow; late summer to fall; to 36 inches; perennial.

Salvia *pg. 148*
S. azurea **var.** *grandiflora*, azure sage; true blue; late summer to early fall; 48 to 60 inches; perennial.
S. patens, blue sage, gentian sage; blue; late summer; 18 to 30 inches; perennial, grown as an annual in cold climates.

Sanguisorba
S. canadensis, great burnet; creamy white; late summer to fall; 36 to 72 inches; perennial.

Sedum
***S. maximum* cultivars** ***(Hylotelephium* cultivars)**; pink; late summer to fall; 12 to 24 inches; perennial. Darker cultivars available.
***S.* 'Autumn Joy'** ***(Hylotelephium* 'Autumn Joy')**; rosy pink changing to salmony bronze; late summer to early fall; to 24 inches; perennial.

Thalictrum
***T. rochebrunianum* 'Lavender Mist'**, lavender mist meadowrue; lavender; late summer to early fall; 48 to 72 inches; perennial.

Zauschneria
Z. californica (Epilobium canum), California fuchsia; scarlet; late summer to early fall; 8 to 15 inches; perennial.

Summer-Blooming Houseplants

Achimenes
***A.* hybrids**, magic flower, monkey-faced pansy; red, rose, pink, lavender, purple, yellow, white; all summer; 10 to 30 inches, upright or trailing; tender perennial. Trailing forms are pretty in hanging baskets, indoors or outdoors.

Agapanthus
See listing on page 295. Can be grown indoors or outdoors.

Aphelandra
A. squarrosa, zebra plant; yellow, orange; summer; to 24 inches. Flower spikes last up to six weeks.

'Patriot Honeylove' lantana

Campanula
C. isophylla, Italian bellflower; violet-blue, white; summer; 18 to 24 inches; trailing tender perennial. Good indoor hanging basket plant.

Crossandra
C. infundibuliformis, firecracker flower; salmon-pink to orange; all summer; 12 to 24 inches; tender shrub.

Fuchsia
***F.* hybrids**; shades and combinations of red, rose, pink, purple, white; all summer; trailing or upright to 24 inches or more; tender shrub. Need bright light and cool temperatures indoors. Also grown outdoors; see page 296.

Gloriosa
***G. superba* 'Rothschildiana'** ***(G.* rothschildiana)**, glory lily, gloriosa lily; red and yellow; late summer; to 48 inches; tender bulb.

Hoya
H. carnosa, honey plant, wax plant; red, pink, white, fragrant; all summer; to 10 feet or more; tender perennial vine.
H. lanceolata* subspecies *bella (H. bella), miniature wax plant; white with pink center, fragrant; all summer into fall; 12 to 24 inches; tender shrub. Good in hanging baskets.

Ixora
I. coccinea, flame of the woods, jungle geranium; salmony red; summer into fall; to 48 inches; tender shrub.

Jasminum
J. officinale, common jasmine; white, fragrant; summer into fall; to 15 feet or more; vine or shrub. Not hardy in cold climates.

Kohleria
K. amabilis, tree gloxinia; rose spotted and banded with red-violet; summer into fall; 24 inches; tender perennial.
K. bogotensis, tree gloxinia; yellow with red spots; summer into fall; to 24 inches; tender perennial.
K. eriantha, tree gloxinia; orange-red with yellow spots; summer into fall; to 48 inches; tender perennial.
K. hirsuta, tree gloxinia; orange-red; summer into fall; to 36 inches; tender perennial.

Lantana
L. camara, yellow sage; yellow, orange-yellow changing to red or white; summer; to 48 inches; tender shrub. Dwarf cultivars and hybrids available in many shades of yellow, pink, orange, and white.
L. montevidensis, weeping lantana; rose-pink with yellow center, lavender, white, fragrant; summer; trailing, to 36 inches long; tender perennial.

Pachystachys
P. lutea, lollipop plant; yellow and white; all summer; to 18 inches; tender shrub.

Passiflora
P. × alatocaerulea, passionflower; purple and white; late summer to early fall; to 20 feet; tender perennial vine.

P. caerulea, blue passionflower; combination of white, purple, and blue in each flower; late summer to early fall; to 20 feet; perennial vine. Also grows outdoors in all but the coldest climates.
P. vitifolia, crimson passionflower; bright red; summer; to 20 feet; tender perennial vine.

Sinningia
S. speciosa **hybrids**, florists' gloxinia; red, violet, white, bicolors; summer; 12 inches; tuberous tender perennial.

Autumn

Outdoors Blooming

Abelia
A. chinensis, Chinese abelia; white, fragrant; summer to early autumn; 36 to 60 inches; shrub. Not reliably hardy north of Philadelphia but can survive with winter protection.

Aconitum *pg. 172*
A. carmichaelii, azure monkshood; violet-blue; late summer to autumn; to 48 inches; perennial.

Allium
A. tuberosum, garlic chives; white, fragrant; early autumn; 15 to 20 inches; perennial.

Anemone *pg. 78, 172*
A. × hybrida (A. japonica, A. huphensis var. *japonica)*, Japanese anemone; crimson, rose-red, rosy pink, pink, white; late summer to early autumn; 24 to 48 inches; perennial.

Arum
A. italicum, Italian arum; produces spikes of bright red berries in autumn; 12 to 18 inches; perennial.

Aster *pg. 173*
A. ericoides, heath aster; tiny white flower heads; early to late autumn; 36 inches; perennial.
A. × frikartii, lavender-blue, fragrant; late summer to early autumn; 24 to 36 inches; perennial. The best cultivar is 'Wonder of Staffa'.
A. novae-angliae, New England aster, Michaelmas daisy; red, rose, pink, lilac, purple; early to midautumn; 36 to 60 inches; perennial 'Purple Dome' is a 24-inch cultivar.
A. novi-belgii, Michaelmas daisy, New York aster; red, rose, pink, lilac, blue, purple, white; early autumn; 12 to 48 inches; perennial.

Boltonia *pg. 173-174*
B. asteroides; white, pink; early to midautumn; 36 to 48 inches; perennial.

Calluna
C. vulgaris, heather; red, rosy pink, white; early autumn; to 18 inches; shrub. Blooms from midsummer to midautumn, depending on location and variety.

Camellia
C. japonica **and hybrids**, camellia; red, rose, pink, white; late autumn and winter, late varieties bloom in spring; to 25 feet; shrub. Not hardy in cold climates.

Caryopteris
C. × clandonensis, bluebeard, blue spirea, bluish purple flower clusters; early to mid- autumn; 24 inches, taller cultivars available; shrub.
C. incana, blue spirea, blue mist; bluish purple flower clusters; early to midautumn; 24 to 60 inches; shrub. Not hardy in very cold climates.

Ceratostigma
C. plumbaginoides, plumbago, leadwort; deep gentian blue; late summer to early autumn; 6 to 10 inches; perennial. Not hardy in very cold climates.

Chrysanthemum *pg. 174–175*
C. × grandiflorum (C. × morifolium, Dendranthema × grandiflorum), garden or hardy chrysanthemums; red, rose, pink, salmon, orange, terra-cotta, rust, yellow, gold, bronze, lilac, purple, white; late summer to midautumn; 12 to 36 inches; perennial. See page 299 for more information.

Cimicifuga
C. simplex, Kamchatka snakeroot; white; early to mid- autumn; 36 to 48 inches; perennial.

Clematis
C. terniflora (C. paniculata), sweet autumn clematis; white, fragrant; early to midautumn; 20 to 30 feet; perennial vine.

Colchicum *pg. 176*
C. autumnale, autumn crocus, meadow saffron; rosy purple, lilac, white; early autumn; 4 to 6 inches; bulb.
C. bornmuelleri, autumn crocus; pale pink deepening as flowers age; early to late autumn; 6 inches; bulb.
C. speciosum, autumn crocus; raspberry red; early to mid-autumn; 5 inches; bulb.
C. **'Waterlily'**; rich rosy lavender, double; early to mid- autumn, 6 inches; bulb.

Crocus *pg. 176*
C. goulimyi, autumn crocus; pale to deep purple; early autumn; 4 inches; bulb.
C. kotschyanus, autumn crocus; pale lilac-blue; early to midautumn; 4 inches; bulb.
C. laevigatus, autumn crocus; rose-lilac to white, fragrant; late autumn to early winter; 3 inches; bulb.
C. medius, autumn crocus; deep lavender-purple; mid-autumn; 4 inches; bulb.
C. pulchellus, autumn crocus; lilac or lavender with faint blue stripes and yellow throat, fragrant; early to midautumn; 4 inches; bulb.
C. sativus, saffron crocus; white, lilac; midautumn; 4 inches; bulb.
C. speciosus, autumn crocus; blue-purple, lilac, white; early to midautumn; 4 inches; bulb.

Cyclamen
C. hederifolium (C. neapolitanum), hardy cyclamen; rosy pink; early autumn; to 6 inches; bulb. A white form is available.

Elaeagnus
E. pungens, thorny elaeagnus; white, fragrant; early to mid-autumn in cold climates, mid- to late autumn in warm climates; 10 to 15 feet; shrub.

Elsholtzia
E. stauntonii; pinkish lavender, fragrant; early to midautumn; 36 to 60 inches; shrub.

Eupatorium
E. coelestinum (Conoclinum coelestinum), hardy ageratum, mistflower; light blue to violet-blue; early autumn; 24 to 36 inches; perennial.
E. purpureum, Joe-Pye weed; pinkish purple; late summer to early autumn; to 84 inches; perennial.

Gentiana
G. andrewsii, bottle gentian; purplish blue; early to mid-autumn; 12 to 18 inches; perennial.

Helenium
H. hoopsei, orange sneezeweed; yellow to orange; late summer to midautumn; 24 to 36 inches; perennial.

Lespedeza
L. thunbergii, bush clover; rosy purple; late summer to mid- autumn; 36 to 72 inches; perennial.

Leucojum *pg. 177*
L. autmnale, autumn snowflake; white; early autumn; 6 inches; bulb.

Lilium
L. speciosum 'Uchida'; deep rosy crimson marked with white; early autumn; 36 to 48 inches; bulb.
L. lancifolium (L. tigrinum), tiger lily; orange with purple spots; reaches its peak in early autumn; 48 to 60 inches; bulb. Yellow, cream, pink, and red cultivars available.

Lycoris *pg. 177*
L. radiata, spider lily; pink to bright crimson; early autumn; 12 to 18 inches; bulb. Not hardy in cold climates.
L. squamigera, magic lily; lilac-pink, fragrant; late summer to early autumn; 24 to 36 inches; bulb. Not hardy in very cold climates.

Nerine
N. bowdenii, nerine lily; pink; early autumn; 12 to 18 inches; bulb. Grow outdoors in warm climates, indoors in a cool greenhouse in cold climates.

Nipponanthemum
N. nipponicum (Chrysanthemum nipponicum), Nippon chrysanthemum; white with yellow center; early autumn; 18 to 24 inches; perennial.

Osmanthus
O. × *fortunei*, hybrid sweet olive; white, fragrant; early autumn; 6 to 25 feet; shrub.

Oxalis
O. bowiei; rosy purple; early autumn; 8 to 10 inches; tender bulb. Grow like gladiolus.

Polianthes
P. tuberosa, tuberose; white, fragrant; late summer to autumn in warm climates; 24 to 42 inches; tender bulb. Grown indoors in cold climates.

Polygonum
P. aubertii, silver lace vine; white, fragrant; late summer to early autumn; to 25 feet or more; perennial vine.

Prunus
P. subhirtella 'Autumnalis'; white, semidouble; blooms in either spring or fall; 6 to 12 feet; shrub or small tree. Pink cultivar is available.

Salvia
S. azurea var. *grandiflora*, azure sage; true blue; late summer to early autumn; 48 to 60 inches; perennial.

Schizostylis
S. coccinea, crimson flag, kaffir lily; scarlet, pink; early to midautumn; to 24 inches; tender bulb. Grown outdoors in warm climates, indoors in cold climates.

Sedum
S. sieboldii (Hylotelephium sieboldii); pink; early to midautumn; to 12 inches; perennial. Hardy, but blooms best in areas where autumn weather is mild.

Sternbergia
S. lutea, winter daffodil, lily-of-the-field; rich golden yellow; midautumn; 8 to 12 inches; bulb.

Tricyrtis
T. hirta, toad lily; white spotted with purple outside, blackish inside; autumn; 24 to 36 inches; bulb.

Urginea
U. maritima, sea onion, sea squill; whitish; autumn; 18 to 60 inches; tender bulb. Not hardy in the North.

Vernonia
V. noveboracensis, ironweed; dark purple; late summer to early autumn; 36 to 84 inches; perennial. Best in the wild garden.

Yucca
Y. gloriosa, Spanish dagger; creamy white, sometimes tinged with red; early autumn; 30 to 72 inches; shrub. Not hardy in cold climates.

Autumn-Blooming Houseplants

Exacum
E. affine, Persian violet; lavender-blue, fragrant; autumn; to 14 inches; perennial. Hard to get to rebloom; treat as annual and discard after flowering.

Laelia
L. autumnalis; rosy purple with white or purple lip, fragrant; late autumn to early winter; 12 to 36 inches; tender perennial.
L. pumila; rosy purple with deep mauve lip; autumn; to 8 inches; tender perennial.

Ludisia
L. discolor (Haemaria discolor), gold-lace orchid, jewel orchid; white to pink, fragrant; autumn to early spring; 6 inches; tender perennial. Has beautiful dark green leaves veined with red and white.

Manettia
M. luteorubra (M. inflata), Brazilian firecracker, firecracker vine; red with yellow tips; spring and/or fall; 6 to 12 feet; tender perennial vine. Likes a warm room.

Myrtus
M. communis, Greek myrtle; white to pink; autumn; to 36 inches; shrub. Foliage is aromatic. Can be grown outdoors in warm climates.

Oxalis
O. **species**, shamrock plant; pink, rose, lilac, white; blooms off and on all year but most heavily in autumn; to 12 inches; bulb.

Paphiopedilum
P. insigne, lady slipper orchid; green sepals with brown spots and green veins, pale yellow petals with brown veins, yellow-green pouch; autumn to spring; to 10 inches; tender perennial.

Pentas
P. lanceolata **cultivars**, Egyptian star cluster; pink, lilac, purple, white; autumn and late winter; 12 to 24 inches; tender perennial.

Phalaenopsis
P. amabilis, moth orchid; white with white-and-yellow lip marked with red; autumn through winter; 12 to 36 inches; orchid; tender perennial. Hybrids also available, in a range of colors; some bloom in autumn and winter.

Rivina
R. humilis, rouge plant; small white flowers followed by sprays of red berries in fall; to 24 inches; tender perennial.

Ruellia
R. makoyana, trailing velvet plant, monkey plant; rose; autumn and winter; to 24 inches; tender perennial.

Schlumbergera *pg. 178–179*
***S. truncata* hybrids**, Thanksgiving cactus; red, rose, pink, orange, white; mid- to late autumn; branches to 36 inches long; tender perennial.

Veltheimia
V. bracteata, forest lily; pinkish purple; late autumn to late winter, if planted in late summer or fall; 24 inches; tender bulb.

Winter

Outdoors Blooming

Abeliophyllum
A. distichum, Korean or white forsythia; white, 60 to 84 inches; late winter to midspring; shrub.

Adonis
A. amurensis, amur adonis; yellow; late winter to midspring; to 12 inches; perennial.

Bulbocodium
B. vernum, spring meadow saffron; pinkish purple; late winter to very early spring; 3 inches; bulb.

Calendula
C. officinalis, pot marigold; yellow, orange, gold, cream; mid- to late winter in warm climates; to 24 inches; annual. Can also be grown as a houseplant in a cool room.

Camellia
***C. japonica* and hybrids**, camellia; white, pink, rose, red, crimson; late autumn to midwinter, late varieties bloom in early spring; to 25 feet; shrub. Not hardy in cold climates.

Chimonanthus
C. praecox, wintersweet; pale cream to yellow, fragrant; mid- to late winter; 8 to 15 feet; shrub. Not hardy in cold climates, but in a sheltered spot may survive as far north as New York City. Flowers are valued more for their fragrance than their looks.

Chionodoxa *pg. 214–215*
C. luciliae, glory-of-the-snow; blue with white center; late winter to early spring; 3 to 6 inches; bulb.
C. sardensis, glory-of-the-snow; blue; 3 to 6 inches; late winter to early spring; bulb.

Crocus *pg. 80, 176, 215*
C. angustifolius (C. susianus), cloth-of-gold; orange-yellow; late winter to early spring; 3 to 4 inches; bulb.
C. biflorus, Scotch crocus; white or lilac-blue, striped or flushed with purple; late winter to early spring; 3 to 4 inches; bulb.
***C. chrysanthus* hybrids**, snow crocus; shades of blue, purple, yellow, white; late winter to early spring; 4 inches; bulb.
C. imperati; buff or yellowish outside, purple inside; late winter; 3 to 6 inches; bulb.
C. tommasinianus, tommies; pale lavender; late winter to early spring; 3 to 4 inches; bulb. Cultivars available in purple and reddish purple.

Daphne
D. mezereum, February daphne, mezereon; lilac-purple to pinkish purple, fragrant; late winter to early spring; 18 to 36 inches; shrub. White cultivars available.
D. odora, winter daphne; rose to pinkish purple, fragrant; late winter to midspring; 36 to 60 inches; shrub. Not hardy in cold climates.

Eranthis *pg. 216–217*
E. hyemalis, winter aconite; golden yellow; late winter to early spring; 3 to 8 inches; bulb.

Erica
E. carnea, spring heath, winter heath; red-violet, rose, or white; midwinter to early spring; 12 inches; shrub.

Galanthus *pg. 217–218*
G. elwesii, giant snowdrop; white with green spots at tip of petals; late winter to early spring; 10 to 15 inches; bulb.
G. nivalis, snowdrop; white with green spots at tip of petals; late winter to early spring; 6 to 10 inches; bulb.

Hamamelis *pg. 218*
H. × intermedia, hybrid witch hazel; yellow to red, fragrant; mid- to late winter; to 20 feet; shrub. 'Arnold Promise' has clear yellow flowers; 'Diane' has coppery red flowers; 'Jelena' has coppery orange flowers.

Helleborus *pg. 218*
H. niger, Christmas rose; white flushed with green or pink; early winter to early spring; to 12 inches; perennial. Long-lasting in garden; cut flowers last up to three weeks.
H. foetidus, stinking hellebore, bear's-foot hellebore; green edged with maroon; late winter to early or midspring; 12 to 18 inches; perennial.

Iberis
I. sempervirens, perennial candytuft; white; blooms in late winter in warm climates; to 12 inches; perennial.

Iris *pg. 84–85, 188*
I. danfordiae, yellow; late winter to early spring; 4 to 6 inches; bulb.

Calendula: *Pot marigold*

***I.* Dutch iris hybrids**; blue, purple, yellow, white; bloom in winter in the deep South and along the West Coast if planted in fall (bloom in spring in Zones 6–8); 18 to 22 inches; bulb.
I. reticulata; violet-purple or blue, fragrant; late winter to early spring; 6 to 12 inches. A pale blue cultivar is available. Can also be forced indoors.
I. unguicularis, Algerian iris; lavender-blue; midwinter to early spring (rarely in late autumn); 12 to 24 inches; perennial. White and deeper violet cultivars available.

Jasminum *pg. 219*
J. nudiflorum, winter jasmine; yellow, fragrant; all winter in protected places, though flower buds may freeze in cooler climates; to 10 feet; vine or shrub.

Lonicera
L. fragrantissima, winter honeysuckle; creamy white, fragrant; winter to early spring; 6 to 10 feet; shrub.

Narcissus *pg. 86–87*
***N.* 'February Gold'**; yellow; late winter in the warm climates; to 12 inches; bulb.
***N.* 'February Silver'**; white with pale yellow cup; late winter in warm climates; to 12 inches; bulb.
***N.* 'Ziva'**; white, fragrant; outdoors in winter in warm climates; to 18 inches; tender bulb. Also forced indoors like other paperwhite narcissus cultivars.

Primula *pg. 221*
***P. polyanthus* hybrids**; primrose; red, rose, pink, yellow, blue, violet, white, with yellow center; winter in the South and California, spring in cooler climates; 6 to 8 inches; perennial, grown as a winter annual in warm climates.
P. vulgaris, common primrose, English primrose; yellow; late winter to spring; 6 inches; perennial.

Scilla *pg. 223*
S. mischtschenkoana (S. tubergeniana), Persian squill; blue-white with a darker stripe; late winter to early spring; 4 to 5 inches; bulb.

Viburnum
V. farreri (V. fragrans), fragrant viburnum; white, fragrant; blooms in winter in warm climates; 9 feet; shrub. Not hardy in cold climates.
Hardy annuals can also be grown for winter flowers in warm climates. (See sidebar on page 203.)

Winter-Blooming Houseplants

Abutilon *pg. 214*
***A.* hybrids**, flowering maple; shades of red, orange, yellow, pink; winter (or nearly year-round); to 36 inches or more; tender shrub. Needs a cool room. Cultivars available in many colors.

Anemone *pg. 78*
A. coronaria, poppy anemone, florist's anemone; red, pink, blue, violet, white with dark center; mid- to late winter when forced; 6 to 18 inches high; bulb.

Antirrhinum *pg. 137*
A. majus, snapdragon; red, crimson, scarlet, pink, purple, orange, yellow, white, bicolors; blooms in winter from seed sown in summer; 8 to 36 inches high; annual.

Ardisia
A. crenata, coralberry; white to pinkish flowers in spring, but grown mostly for red berries, which last all winter; 24 inches; tender shrub.

Begonia *pg. 138–139*
***B.* Semperflorens-Cultorum hybrids**, wax begonia; red, scarlet, salmon, rose, pink, white; blooms indoors in winter from seed sown in late summer or from cuttings taken in fall from outdoor plants; 6 to 12 inches high; tender annual. Try compact varieties such as the Cocktail Series.

Browallia
B. speciosa, sapphire flower; violet, blue, white; blooms in late winter from seed sown in midsummer; 24 inches; tender perennial.

Brunfelsia
B. pauciflora, yesterday, today, and tomorrow; purple with white centers; midwinter until summer; 24 to 36 inches; shrub.

Calceolaria
***C. Herbeohybrida* group hybrids**, pocketbook plant; maroon, yellow, orange, bronze, spotted with purple or bronze; late winter to early spring in bright, cool window; 12 to 24 inches; tender annual.

Callistephus
***C. chinensis* cultivars**, China aster; scarlet, rose, pink, blue, yellow, white; compact varieties such as 'Pot n' Patio' bloom indoors in winter from seed sown in summer; 6 to 10 inches; annual.

Camellia
***C. japonica* and hybrids**, camellia; pink, rose, red, white; late winter indoors; to 72 inches indoors; shrub. Needs a cool room.

Capsicum
C. annuum, ornamental pepper; red fruits in winter; 12 inches; tender perennial but treat as annual.

Carissa
C. macrocarpa (C. grandiflora), Natal plum; white, fragrant; winter indoors in cool room; to 72 inches or more; tender shrub. Can be grown outdoors in warm climates, where it may reach 15 feet.

Celosia
C. argentea plumosa* group *(C. plumosa), plumed celosia; orange, apricot, gold, bronze, deep red, yellow, cream; blooms indoors in winter from seed started in summer; 12 to 30 inches; tender perennial, usually grown as an annual.

Chrysanthemum
***Chrysanthemum* × *grandiflorum* (*C.* × *morifolium*, *Dendranthema* × *grandiflorum*)**, florist's or garden chrysanthemum; red, crimson, orange, yellow, bronze, apricot, pink, mauve, purple, white, cream; 12 to 24 inches; can be forced with some difficulty for winter bloom indoors; perennial.

Citrofortunella
× *C. microcarpa (Citrus mitis)*, calamondin orange; small white flowers in spring to summer, decorative orange fruits in winter; 2 to 15 feet; tender shrub.

Clarkia
C. unguiculata (C. elegans), satin flower, godetia; rose, purple, pink; 18 to 36 inches; blooms indoors in winter from seed sown in summer; annual.

Coffea
C. arabica, Arabian coffee plant; white, fragrant; blooms indoors in winter; 48 to 72 inches; tender shrub.

Convallaria
C. majalis, lily-of-the-valley; white, fragrant; 6 to 12 inches; mid- to late winter when forced indoors; bulb. Pink cultivar available.

Crocus *pg. 80, 176, 215*
C. Dutch hybrid crocuses; lavender, purple, gold, white, cream, bicolors; 4 to 6 inches high; mid- to late winter when forced indoors; bulb.

Cuphea
C. ignea (C. platycentra), cigar plant; red with white rim and black tips; winter; 8 to 10 inches; tender perennial. Can also be grown outdoors as a summer bedding plant.

Cyclamen *pg. 216*
C. persicum (C. indicum), florist's cyclamen; red, rose, pink, purple, white; 8 inches; all winter in a cool room; tender bulb.

Eranthemum
E. pulchellum, blue sage; blue; late winter to early spring; 24 to 48 inches; tender shrub.

Euphorbia *pg. 217*
E. fulgens, scarlet plume; scarlet, 24 to 48 inches; winter; tender shrub. White form available.
E. pulcherrima, poinsettia; red, pink, white; 24 to 36 inches; early to midwinter; tender shrub.

Exacum
E. affine, Persian violet; blue, fragrant; 8 to 10 inches; blooms in winter from seed started in summer; tender perennial, treat as annual.

Forsythia
***F.* species and cultivars**; yellow; branches cut from outdoor shrubs can be forced into bloom indoors in late winter.

Freesia *pg. 187*
***F.* hybrids**; rose, pink, lavender, purple, yellow, white, fragrant; can be forced for winter bloom; 12 inches; tender bulb.

Euphorbia: *Poinsettia*

Heliotropium
***H. arborescens* (*H. peruvianum*)**, heliotrope; deep violet, lavender-blue; fragrant; blooms in winter from seed sown in summer; 12 to 24 inches; tender perennial, treat as annual.

Hibiscus
H. rosa-sinensis, Chinese hibiscus, rose of China; various shades of red, pink, orange, yellow, white; can bloom in late winter through spring indoors; 36 to 48 inches; tender shrub.

Hippeastrum *pg. 187*
***H.* hybrids**, amaryllis; red, pink, orange, salmon, white, bicolors; early to midwinter when forced; 24 inches; tender bulb.

Hyacinthus
***H. orientalis* hybrids**, hyacinth; red, rose, pink, purple, violet, blue, yellow, white, fragrant; midwinter when forced; to 12 inches; bulb.

Impatiens *pg. 143*
***I.* hybrids**; red, rose, salmon, pink, orange, purple, white, bicolors; bloom in winter from seed sown in summer, 6 to 12 inches high; tender perennial, treat as annual. Try compact varieties such as the Accent Series or Super Elfin Series.

Jasminum *pg. 219*
J. polyanthum; rosy pink outside, white inside; fragrant; winter to early spring; to 10 feet; tender vine or shrub.
J. sambac, Arabian jasmine; white, fragrant; winter; to 72 inches or more; tender vine.

Kalanchoe *pg. 220*
K. blossfeldiana; red, orange; 12 inches; early winter to early spring; tender perennial. White, yellow, pink cultivars available.

Lachenalia
L. aloides, cape cowslip; red and yellow; to 12 inches; late winter to early spring; tender bulb.

Lantana
L. camara, yellow sage; orange-yellow changing to red or white; cultivars available in red, yellow, lilac blue, white; 12 to 48 inches; blooms in winter if seeds are sown in summer; tender perennial.

Mimulus
***M.* hybrids**, monkey flower; yellow, orange, rose, red, rosy purple; blooms in winter from seed sown in summer; to 24 inches; tender annual.

Muscari
M. armeniacum, grape hyacinth; deep blue-violet; can be forced indoors for winter bloom; 8 to 12 inches; bulb.

Narcissus *pg. 86–87, 188–189*
***N.* 'Grand Soleil d'Or'**; yellow, fragrant; 12 to 14 inches; early to late winter when forced; bulb.
***N.* hybrids**, daffodils and narcissus; yellow, cream, white, bicolors; mid- to late winter when forced; 12 to 18 inches; bulb.
N. papyraceus, paperwhite narcissus; white, fragrant; 18 inches; early to late winter when forced; bulb.

Ornithogalum
***O.* species**, star-of-Bethlehem; white, fragrant; blooms in winter indoors; 12 inches; bulb.

Osmanthus
O. fragrans, sweet olive; white, fragrant; early to late winter in bright light; 36 to 72 inches indoors; tender shrub.

Oxalis
O. triangularis, pink; blooms in winter indoors; to 10 inches; bulb. Also hardy outdoors in Zones 7–9.

Paphiopedilum *pg. 220*
P. insigne, lady slipper orchid; green sepals with brown spots and green veins, pale yellow petals with brown veins, yellow-green pouch; autumn to spring; to 10 inches; tender perennial.
P. villosum, slipper orchid; yellow-brown and white; winter; to 10 inches; tender perennial.
Some *Paphiopedilum* hybrids also bloom in winter with as little as two hours of sun a day.

Pelargonium *pg. 145*
P. × hortorum, zonal geranium; red, pink, salmon, magenta, white; blooms in winter from seed started in summer or cuttings taken from outdoor plants in early fall; 24 to 36 inches; tender perennial grown as annual.
***P.* species and cultivars**, scented geraniums; pink, white, with fragrant foliage; often bloom in winter; 6 to 20 inches; perennial. Cut back plants to keep them compact.

Pentas
***P. lanceolata* cultivars**, Egyptian star cluster; pink, lilac, purple, white; autumn and late winter; to 24 inches; tender perennial. Also grown as outdoor summer annual.

Pericallis
P. × hybrida (Senecio × hybridus), cineraria; red, rose, pink, purple, white; late winter; to 24 inches; tender perennial. Needs bright, cool window. Discard after blooming.

Phalaenopsis *pg. 221*
P. amabilis, moth orchid; white and yellow with red markings; all winter; 12 to 36 inches; tender perennial. Hybrids come in several colors; some of these are also winter bloomers.

Primula *pg. 221*
P. malacoides, fairy primrose; red, pink, mauve, lilac, white; 12 to 24 inches; winter to spring; tender perennial, grown as annual.
P. sinensis, Chinese primrose; red, pink, purple, white, with yellow eye; 12 inches; winter to spring; tender perennial, grown as annual.

Punica
***P. granatum* 'Nana'**, dwarf pomegranate; orange summer flowers followed by reddish fruit in winter; to 36 inches; tender shrub.

Rhododendron
***R.* hybrids**, azalea; red, rose, pink, white; late winter in a cool room; 6 to 48 inches; shrub. Difficult to get to rebloom indoors; discard after flowering.

Rosa *pg. 147–148*
***R.* hybrids**, miniature roses; red, pink, orange, yellow, white, bicolors; bloom indoors six to eight weeks after beginning to grow following a dormant period; 12 to 24 inches; shrub.

Saintpaulia *pg. 222*
***S.* hybrids**, African violet; purple, violet, pink, rose, white, lavender, bicolors; 6 inches; tender perennial. Bloom off and on all year.

Salix
S. discolor, pussy willow; silvery catkins in early spring; can be forced indoors in midwinter; 10 to 20 feet; shrub to small tree.

Salpiglossis
***S. sinuata* cultivars**, painted tongue, velvet flower; red, crimson, rose, pink, gold, blue; blooms in winter from seed sown in summer; 24 to 36 inches; tender annual.

Schlumbergera *pg. 222–223*
***S. × buckleyi (S. bridgesii)* hybrids**, Christmas cactus; red, rose, pink, salmon, white; to 36 inches; early to midwinter; tender perennial.

Solanum
***S. pseudocapsicum* 'Nanum'**, Christmas cherry, Jerusalem cherry; scarlet fruits; early to midwinter; 10 to 12 inches; tender biennial.

Streptocarpus *pg. 223*
***S.* hybrids**, Cape primrose; purple, violet, rose, pink, white; 6 to 10 inches; tender perennial.

Tagetes *pg. 148–149*
***T. patula* hybrids**, French marigolds; yellow, orange, cream, bicolors; bloom in winter from seed sown in summer; 6 to 10 inches; tender annual. Try dwarf varieties.

Thunbergia
T. alata, black-eyed Susan vine, clock vine; yellow, orange, or white, with black center; blooms in winter from seed sown in summer; 24 to 48 inches long; tender perennial.

Torenia
T. fournieri, wishbone flower; blue-violet, rosy pink, white; blooms in winter from seed sown in summer; 8 inches; tender annual. Cultivars available with a mix of white, pink, and blue-violet.

Tropaeolum
***T. majus* and cultivars**, nasturtium; mahogany, red, orange, yellow, pink, cream; blooms in winter from seed sown in summer or cuttings taken in early fall; 12 to 36 inches; tender annual.

Tulipa *pg. 89–91, 189*
***T.* hybrids**, tulips; red, scarlet salmon, pink, orange, yellow, purple white, bicolors; mid- to late winter when forced; 12 to 24 inches; bulb.

Veltheimia
V. bracteata, forest lily; pinkish purple; late autumn to late winter if planted in late summer or fall; to 24 inches; tender bulb.

Zantedeschia *pg. 189*
Z. aethiopica, calla lily; white; winter when forced; 12 to 36 inches; tender bulb.

Zantedeschia: Calla lily

Glossary

Amendments. Organic materials (such as peat moss and compost) and inorganic material (such as vermiculite) that improve soil structure, drainage, and nutrient-holding capacity.

Annual. A plant that completes its entire life cycle in one growing season.

Axil. The upper angle at which a leaf (or other plant part) joins a stem.

Biennial. A plant that completes its life cycle in two years. Most biennials form just leaves the first year—flowers and seeds the second year.

Bract. A modified leaf or leaflike structure that often embraces a flower bud and opens with the flower. Bracts occur at the base of the flower. Usually small and green, some bracts, such the red bracts of poinsettia, are mistaken for flower petals.

Bud. A small bump on a plant stem in which an embryonic flower, leaf, or stem is enclosed.

Bulb. A fleshy underground structure from which a flowering plant develops. The term bulb is often used loosely to refer to corms, rhizomes, and tubers, as well as true bulbs.

Clay. Soil consisting of extremely fine particles that pack tightly and leave minimal space for air that plant roots need. Clay soils are heavy but fertile and moisture retentive.

Compost. Decomposed organic materials, such as plant parts and kitchen scraps. The crumbly, black end-product holds and slowly releases nutrients and water to plant roots. Rich in beneficial microorganisms, it is ideal for amending and topdressing soil.

Corm. A fleshy underground structure containing a solid stem or base of a stem, from which a flowering plant grows. Gladiolus, crocus, and freesia grow from corms.

Cotyledon (pronounced cot-l-EED-n). The first leaf or pair of leaves a seedling sprouts. Also called seed leaves, they are usually round or oval.

Crown. The junction of roots and stem, usually at soil level.

Cultivar. Short for cultivated variety. A plant variety developed in cultivation rather than occurring in nature. Cultivar names are usually enclosed in single quotation marks.

Cutting. A plant part (usually a stem or leaf section) removed and planted to grow roots and become a new plant.

Damping-off. A fungal disease that attacks seedlings and causes them to collapse.

Day-neutral. Describes a plant that does not require a particular day length in order to bloom.

Deadheading. Removing flowers as they fade. This improves the appearance of the plant and redirects the plant's energy to the creation of new flowers rather than the formation of seeds.

Disbudding. Removing some flower buds to promote larger flowers from remaining buds.

Division. A propagation method that separates a plant into two or more similar pieces, each with at least one bud and some roots.

Dormant period. The time when a plant's growth naturally slows, often after flowering.

Forcing. Causing a plant to flower indoors ahead of its natural blooming time.

Genus (plural: genera). A closely related group of species sharing similar characteristics and probably evolved from the same ancestors. Genus names are italicized and begin with an initial capital letter. See *Species*.

Germination. The sprouting of a seed.

Habit. The characteristic shape or form a plant assumes as it grows.

Harden Off. To gradually acclimate a seedling started indoors to the harsher outdoor environment.

Hardy Annual. An annual that can tolerate frost and prefers cool temperatures.

Hardiness. A plant's ability to survive the climate in an area without protection from winter cold or summer heat, often described in relation to official Hardiness Zones .

Horticultural Charcoal. A clean by-product of burned wood. Applied to plant wounds, it decreases the chances of diseases starting there. Also used to keep water fresh.

Humus. Completely decomposed organic matter, the end-product of composting.

Leaf Cutting. The portion of a leaf that is stimulated to grow into a new plant.

Leggy. Describes a stem showing weak elongated growth, usually caused by insufficient light.

Loam. Soil containing varying amounts of clay, silt, and sand; fertile, moisture retentive but drains well, and ideal for gardening.

Microclimate. Local conditions of sun, shade, exposure, wind, drainage, and other factors at a particular site.

Mist. To spray a plant with water droplets. Misting cleans foliage and adds humidity to the plant's immediate environment.

Mulch. A layer of compost, bark chips, straw, leaves, gravel, or other material spread over planted areas.

Node. The point along a stem from which leaves or shoots emerge.

Nutrients. Nitrogen, phosphorus, potassium, calcium, magnesium, sulfur, iron, and other elements needed by growing plants. Nutrients are supplied by the minerals and organic matter in the soil and by fertilizers.

Offset. A new plant that forms vegetatively, often at the base of the parent plant. Many bulbs reproduce by means of offsets.

Perennial. A plant that normally lives for three or more growing seasons.

Perlite. Heat-expanded volcanic glass used to lighten potting mediums and create space for air particles.

pH. The measure of a soil's hydrogen content on a scale of 1 to 14, with 7 considered neutral. A pH above 7 is considered alkaline, and a pH below 7 is considered acidic. Soil pH affects availability of nutrients to plants.

Pinching. Removing the growing tips of branches or shoots to encourage lush, bushy growth.

Potbound. A plant with a root mass that has grown too large for its container. The overgrown roots take on the shape of the pot, grow in tangles, and may eventually strangle the plant.

Potting medium (potting mix). The material in which a plant is potted.

Propagate. To create more plants either from seeds or by vegetative methods.

Repot. Transplant from one container to another, to provide fresh potting mix or a larger container to accommodate the expanding root mass.

Rhizome. A horizontally creeping, often enlarged, stem that lies at or just under the soil surface. Both shoots and roots can form at nodes along the rhizome. See *Bulb*.

Rootball. A plant's combined mass of roots and soil.

Rooting Hormone. A liquid or powder that encourages cuttings to root.

Seedling. A tiny new plant that has grown from a seed.

Silt. Soil particles that are much finer than sand, though coarser than clay. Silt is fairly fertile, compacts easily, and feels slippery.

Species. A group of very similar plants that share many characteristics and can interbreed freely; the basic category of plant classification.

Stem Cutting. A propagation method that stimulates root growth from the cut end of a stem.

Sucker. A stem arising from the rootstalk of a woody plant.

Tender Perennial. A plant that is perennial in frost-free environments but dies when exposed to freezing temperatures.

Topdress. To cover the surface of soil with a thin layer of compost or fertilizer.

True Leaves. The second and subsequent leaves or sets of leaves that a plant produces. These have the distinctive shape of leaves of the mature plant.

Variegated. Irregularly pigmented foliage that is marked, striped, or blotched with a color or colors other than the basic green.

Variety. A variant of a species that is the result of natural mutation. See *Cultivar*.

Index

Page numbers in ***bold italics*** indicate photographs and illustrations

A

B

C

D

E

F

G

L

M

N

O

P

Q

R

S

T

U

V

W

X

Y

Z

Photo Credits

All photographs by Neil Soderstrom unless otherwise noted.

Page 1: *Derek Fell* **page 2:** *Mark Bolton/Garden Picture Library* **page 4:** *left David Cavagnaro* **page 5:** *left John Glover right Jim Steinberg/Photo Researchers* **pages 8–9:** *left Jerry Pavia center Eric Crichton/Garden Picture Library top right John Glover bottom right Derek Fell* **pages 12–13:** *John Glover* **page 15:** *top Charles Mann* **page 16:** *bottom left Charles Mann* **page 19:** *Charles Mann* **page 20:** *top Karen Bussolini/Positive Images bottom left and right John Glover* **page 21:** *bottom left Mel Watson/Garden Picture Library bottom right John Glover* **page 22:** *top right John Glover bottom Jerry Pavia* **page 23:** *John Glover* **page 24:** *left John Glover right Jerry Pavia* **page 25:** *top left and right John Glover bottom David Cavagnaro* **page 26:** *top Derek Fell bottom Michael S. Thompson* **page 28:** *Derek Fell* **page 31:** *left Michael S. Thompson right Jerry Pavia* **page 32:** *Derek Fell* **page 33:** *Janet Loughrey* **page 35:** *left Netafilm Irrigation* **page 36:** *left Roger Foley* **page 41:** *top row Alan and Linda Detrick bottom Jane Grushow/Grant Heilman* **page 44:** *Michael S. Thompson* **page 46:** *top left Derek Fell* **page 50:** *right Christie Carter/Grant Heilman* **page 51:** *Michael Thompson* **page 52:** *bottom David Cavagnaro* **page 53:** *top left (both) Arthur Smith top right Grant Heilman/Grant Heilman inset: Dwight Kuhn center left Alan & Linda Detrick center right Gardens Alive bottom left Nigel Caitlin/Photo Researchers bottom right Runk/Schoenberger/Grant Heilman* **page 55:** *Gardens Alive* **page 56:** *top left Runk/Schoenberger/Grant Heilman top center Dwight Kuhn top right Alan and Linda Detrick bottom left David M. Schleser/Nature's Images bottom right Alan & Linda Detrick* **page 58:** *top left (both) Alan & Linda Detrick top right Holt Studios/Photo Researchers bottom left Kathy Merrifield/Photo Researchers bottom right Alan & Linda Detrick* **page 58:** *top left Derek Fell top right and bottom left Alan and Linda Detrick bottom right Nigel Caitlin/Photo Researchers* **page 59:** *all Alan & Linda Detrick* **page 60:** *Grant Heilman* **page 61:** *Alan and Linda Detrick* **page 62:** *Jane Grushow/Grant Heilman* **page 63:** *top left Jerry Pavia top right Alan and Linda Detrick middle left Charles Mann middle right Jerry Harper bottom left Alan and Linda Detrick bottom right John Glover* **page 64:** *Jerry Pavia* **page 67:** *top Garden Picture Library* **page 68:** *top Michael Thompson* **pages 70–71:** *Derek Fell* **page 72:** *Mark Bolton/Garden Picture Library* **page 74:** *Michael S. Thompson* **page 75:** *John Glover* **page 78:** *left Mark Bolton/Garden Picture Library right David Cavagnaro* **page 79:** *left John Glover middle Charles Mann right David Cavagnaro* **page 80:** *top David Cavagnaro bottom left Derek Fell bottom right Steven Wooster/Garden Picture Library* **page 81:** *top left David Cavagnaro bottom left Lee Lockwood/Positive Images right Judy White* **page 82:** *top David Cavagnaro bottom Friedrich Strauss/Garden Picture Library* **page 83:** *top David Cavagnaro bottom left John Glover bottom right Jerry Pavia* **page 84:** *top left Jerry Pavia top middle David Cavagnaro top right Michael S. Thompson* **page 85:** *both Derek Fell* **pages 86–87:** *left Michael S. Thompson right Michael Howes/Garden Picture Library far right (left) John Glover (right) David Askham/Garden Picture Library* **page 88:** *top left Geoff Bryant/Positive Images middle David Askham/Garden Picture Library right David Cavagnaro* **page 89:** *left Howard Rice/Garden Picture Library right Michael S. Thompson* **page 90:** *top right Michael S. Thompson middle left David Cavagnaro* **page 91:** *top Howard Rice/Garden Picture Library* **page 96:** *top John Glover* **page 98:** *both David Cavagnaro* **page 100:** *left Derek Fell* **page 101:** *top David Cavagnaro* **page 103:** *right David Cavagnaro* **page 104:** *left Derek Fell* **page 105:** *all right David Van Zanten* **page 106:** *Garden Picture Library* **page 108:** *Derek Fell* **page 109:** *both Garden Picture Library* **page 112:** *top and bottom right Derek Fell bottom left Michael S. Thompson* **page 113:** *top left Michael S. Thompson bottom left John Glover right Derek Fell* **page 114:** *left John Glover* **page 115:** *top Derek Fell bottom David Van Zanten* **page 118:** *left Juliette Wade/Garden Picture Library right Michael S. Thompson* **page 119:** *top Michael S. Thompson bottom Derek Fell* **page 120:** *J.S. Sira/Garden Picture Library* **page 121:** *top Charles Mann bottom Jerry Pavia* **page 122:** *Jerry Pavia* **page 124:** *Derek Fell* **page 125:** *left Derek Fell right David Cavagnaro* **page 126:** *all Neil Soderstrom* **page 127:** *center David Cavagnaro* **page 128:** *bottom right Jerry Howard/Positive Images* **page 132:** *top Patricia Bruno/Positive Images bottom David Cavagnaro* **page 134:** *top Derek Fell* **page 135:** *all David Van Zanten* **page 136:** *left John Glover* **page 137:** *left Derek Fell center Ben Phillips/Positive Images both top right Rick Mastelli* **page 138:** *bottom left John Glover* **page 139:** *top David Van Zanten bottom Charles Mann* **page 140:** *left Charles Mann right Derek Fell* **page 141:** *top left John Glover bottom right Charles Mann* **page 142:** *top Derek Fell bottom David Cavagnaro* **page 143:** *center right David Cavagnaro bottom Michael S. Thompson* **page 144:** *top John Glover* **page 145:** *top John Glover bottom Derek Fell* **page 146:** *bottom David Cavagnaro* **page 147:** *top right David Cavagnaro* **page 148:** *both right John Glover top left David Cavagnaro center John Glover* **page 149:** *David Cavagnaro* **page 152:** *both left David Cavagnaro* **page 158:** *top David Van Zanten bottom right Michael S. Thompson* **page 159:** *top left David Van Zanten bottom David Van Zanten* **page 160:** *Derek Fell* **page 162:** *both David Cavagnaro* **page 163:** *John Glover* **page 165:** *top left John Glover bottom right Christel Rosenfeld/Garden Picture Library* **pages 166–-167:** *left Image Bank center and right David Van Zanten* **pages 168–169:** *top center David Van Zanten bottom center Crandall & Crandall right Walter Chandoha* **page 170:** *both David Van Zanten* **page 172:** *left Howard Rice/Garden Picture Library right John Glover* **page 173:** *left Jerry Pavia center Eric Crichton/Garden Picture Library right Michael S. Thompson* **page 174:** *top left Jerry Pavia top right and bottom left J.S. Sira/Garden Picture Library bottom right John Glover* **page 175:** *top left and right Michael S. Thompson bottom left Derek Fell bottom right Brian Carter/Garden Picture Library* **page 176:** *both John Glover* **page 177:** *left John Glover right Derek Fell* **page 178:** *left Derek Fell right David Van Zanten* **page 179:** *top John Glover* **page 180:** *Derek Fell* **page 181:** *left Derek Fell* **page 184:** *top Walter Chandoha bottom Derek Fell* **page 185:** *top right Michael S. Thompson bottom left John Glover* **page 186:** *top left Photos Horticultural top center courtesy of International Netherland Bulb Co. top right John Glover bottom David Cavagnaro* **page 187:** *left David Van Zanten center Walter Chandoha right Meyer/LeScanff/Garden Picture Library* **page 188:** *left and center courtesy of International Netherland Bulb Co. right Walter Chandoha* **page 189:** *center courtesy of International Netherland Bulb Co. right David Van Zanten* **page 190:** *both David Van Zanten* **page 191:** *top John Glover bottom David Van Zanten* **page 192:** *left Michael S. Thompson right Derek Fell* **page 193:** *both right Walter Chandoha* **page 194:** *left Walter Chandoha top right Michael S. Thompson bottom right David Cavagnaro* **page 195:** *left Photos Horticultural right Walter Chandoha* **page 196:** *right David Cavagnaro* **page 197:** *left Walter Chandoha* **page 198:** *Walter Chandoha* **page 199:** *top left Michael S. Thompson bottom left Walter Chandoha right Derek Fell* **page 200:** *Photos Horticultural* **page 202:** *Eric Heyer/Grant Heilman* **pages 204–205:** *far right Howard Rice/Garden Picture Library* **page 206:** *bottom John Glover* **page 207:** *top Howard Rice/Garden Picture Library bottom Derek Fell* **page 208:** *top left David Van Zanten top right PW Flowers/Garden Picture Library* **210:** *top Walter Chandoha middle left Patricia Bruno/Positive Images bottom right Jerry Howard/Positive Images* **page 211:** *top Meyer/LeScanff/Garden Picture Library* **page 213:** *Photos Horticultural* **page 214:** *Friedrich Strauss/Garden Picture Library* **page 215:** *left John Glover center David Van Zanten right Howard Rice/Garden Picture Library* **page 216:** *both Walter Chandoha* **page 217:** *right John Glover* **page 218:** *top left JS Sira/Garden Picture Library top right Howard Rice/Garden Picture Library bottom Lefever/Grushow/Grant Heilman* **page 219:** *left Walter Chandoha right Michael S. Thompson* **page 220:** *both David Van Zanten* **page 221:** *top David Van Zanten* **page 222:** *top left and bottom David Van Zanten* **page 223:** *top David Van Zanten bottom John Glover* **page 224:** *David Van Zanten* **page 225:** *left Jerry Howard/Positive Images* **page 226:** *left David Van Zanten right Charley's Greenhouse & Garden Supplies* **page 227:** *left David Van Zanten* **page 229:** *bottom Stephen E. Munz* **page 232:** *left Derek Fell right David Van Zanten* **page 233:** *all David Van Zanten* **pages 234–235:** *John Glover* **page 236:** *Larry Lefever/Grant Heilman* **page 237:** *Ron Evans* **page 238:** *Michael S. Thompson* **page 239:** *top Lynn Brotchie/Garden Picture Library bottom left Andrew Lawson bottom right Karen Bussolini/Positive Images* **page 240:** *Derek Fell* **page 241:** *left Charles Mann right David Cavagnaro* **page 242:** *all but bottom right David Cavagnaro bottom right Susan Roth* **page 243:** *all but bottom right David Cavagnaro bottom right Geoff Bryant/Photo Researchers* **page 244:** *top left David Cavagnaro top right Derek Fell middle left Lefever/Grushow/Grant Heilman bottom left David Cavagnaro bottom right Derek Fell* **page 245:** *top and bottom left Derek Fell top right David Cavagnaro bottom right Amla Sanghvi* **page 246:** *all but top right David Cavagnaro top right Derek Fell* **page 247:** *top left David Cavagnaro bottom left John Kaprielian top right Judy White bottom right Derek Fell* **page 248:** *Brigitte Thomas/Garden Picture Library* **page 249:** *Christie Carter/Grant Heilman* **page 250:** *Barry Runk/Grant Heilman* **page 251:** *top left and bottom Derek Fell top right Grant Heilman* **page 252:** *both Michael S. Thompson* **page 253:** *top Mel Watson/Garden Picture Library bottom left Derek Fell bottom right Neil Soderstrom* **page 254:** *top left and right Derek Fell bottom left Sunniva Harte/Garden Picture Library bottom right Derek Fell* **page 255:** *top left Richard Shiell/Dembinsky Photo Association top right Alan and Linda Detrick bottom left Howard Rice/Garden Picture Library bottom right Derek Fell* **page 256:** *top and bottom left Derek Fell top right Lefever/Grushow/Grant Heilman bottom right Jane Grushow/Grant Heilman* **page 257:** *top left Michael S. Thompson top right Susan Roth bottom Alan and Linda Detrick* **page 258:** *top left Lefever/Grushow/Grant Heilman top and bottom right Susan Roth bottom left Jane Grushow/Grant Heilman* **page 259:** *top left John Shaw top right Derek Fell bottom left and right Judy White* **page 260:** *Lefever/Grushow/Grant Heilman* **page 261:** *Judy White* **page 262:** *left Derek Fell* **page 263:** *Allan Mandell* **page 264:** *top Derek Fell bottom Rick Mastelli* **page 265:** *top Jerry Harpur bottom Jane Grushow/Grant Heilman* **page 266:** *left Jerry Pavia* **page 268:** *Derek Fell* **page 272:** *left Derek Fell both right David Cavagnaro* **page 273:** *top left Jim Steinberg/Photo Researchers top right Derek Fell bottom Susan Roth* **page 274:** *Michael S. Thompson* **page 275:** *left Alan and Linda Detrick right Jane Grushow/Grant Heilman* **page 276:** *Michael Dirr* **page 277:** *Derek Fell* **page 278:** *top left David Cavagnaro bottom left Alan and Linda Detrick top right Derek Fell inset David Cavagnaro* **page 279:** *top left Richard Shiell/Dembinsky Photo Association top right and bottom Derek Fell* **page 280:** *left Pam Spaulding/Positive Images* **page 281:** *left Jane Grushow/Grant Heilman right Charles Mann* **page 282:** *Alan and Linda Detrick* **page 283:** *left David Cavagnaro right Geoff Bryant/Photo Researchers* **page 284:** *Jerry Pavia* **page 287:** *David Cavagnaro* **page 295:** *left John Glover* **page 298:** *David Cavagnaro*